GOD, REVELATION AND AUTHORITY

Volume II
GOD WHO SPEAKS AND SHOWS

Fifteen Theses, Part One

GOD, REVELATION AND AUTHORITY

VOLUME II

GOD WHO SPEAKS AND SHOWS

Fifteen Theses, Part One

CARL F. H. HENRY

CROSSWAY BOOKS • WHEATON, ILLINOIS
A DIVISION OF GOOD NEWS PUBLISHERS

God, Revelation and Authority Volume II: God Who Speaks and Shows Fifteen Theses, Part One
Copyright © originally copyrighted and published in 1976. This edition copyright © 1999 by Carl F. H. Henry.

This edition published by Crossway Books
        A division of Good News Publishers
        1300 Crescent Street
        Wheaton, Illinois 60187

Published in association with the *Carl F. H. Henry Institute for Evangelical Engagement,* The Southern Baptist Theological Seminary, Louisville, Kentucky. For more information concerning the *Henry Institute,* contact Southern Baptist Theological Seminary, 2825 Lexington Road, Louisville, KY 40280; or call toll free, 1-800-626-5525.

The publisher gratefully acknowledges the support of Southern Baptist Theological Seminary and Dr. R. Albert Mohler, Jr., President, in helping to underwrite the publication of this new edition of *God, Revelation and Authority.*

Hardcover design by: Cindy Kiple
Paperback cover design by: D² DesignWorks
First Crossway printing, 1999
Printed in the United States of America
ISBN 1-58134-080-X (Set of 6 volumes : hc)
ISBN 1-58134-056-7 (Set of 6 volumes : pbk)

Bible quotations from *Revised Standard Version,* copyright © 1946, 1952, 1971, 1973 by the Division of Christian Education of the National Council of the Churches of Christ in the U.S.A. Used by permission.

Bible quotations marked KJV are from the *Authorized* or *King James Version.*

Library of Congress Cataloging-in-Publication Data
Henry, Carl Ferdinand Howard, 1913–
  God, revelation, and authority / Carl F.H. Henry.
    p.   cm.
  Originally published: Waco, Tex. : Word Books, c1976–c1983.
  Includes bibliographical references and index.
  Contents: v. 1. God who speaks and shows, preliminary considerations — v. 2-4.
God who speaks and shows, fifteen theses — v. 5-6. God who stands and stays.
    ISBN 1-58134-081-8 (v. 1 : hc) ISBN 1-58134-041-9 (v. 1 : pbk)
    ISBN 1-58134-082-6 (v. 2 : hc) ISBN 1-58134-042-7 (v. 2 : pbk)
    ISBN 1-58134-083-4 (v. 3 : hc) ISBN 1-58134-043-5 (v. 3 : pbk)
    ISBN 1-58134-084-2 (v. 4 : hc) ISBN 1-58134-044-3 (v. 4 : pbk)
    ISBN 1-58134-085-0 (v. 5 : hc) ISBN 1-58134-045-1 (v. 5 : pbk)
    ISBN 1-58134-086-9 (v. 6 : hc) ISBN 1-58134-046-X (v. 6 : pbk).
    1. Evangelicalism. I. Title.
BR1640.A25H45   1999
230'.044—dc21   98-51637

15 14 13 12 11 10 09 08 07 06 05 04 03 02 01 00 99
15 14 13 12 11 10 9 8 7 6 5 4 3 2 1

Contents

Introduction

Divine Revelation: Fifteen Theses

NOWHERE DOES THE CRISIS of modern theology find a more critical center than in the controversy over the reality and nature of divine disclosure. The time has therefore come for a comprehensive overview of revelation in biblical terms, in terms of the living God who speaks and shows, the God who gains and merits his own audibility and visibility. God is not the Great Perhaps, a clueless shadow character in a Scotland Yard mystery. Far less is he a nameless spirit awaiting post-mortem examination in some theological morgue. He is a very particular and specific divinity, known from the beginning solely on the basis of his works and self-declaration as the one living God. Only theorists who ignore divine self-disclosure are prone to identify God as the nondescript John Doe of religious philosophy.

God heralds his unchanging truth to man once for all and ongoingly; man meanwhile asserts a multiplicity of contrary things about God and his Word. Few concepts have in fact encountered and endured such radical revision throughout the long history of ideas as has the concept of divine revelation. Especially within the last two centuries divine revelation has been stretched into everything, stripped into nothing, or modeled into innumerable compromises of such outrageous extremes. Hegel mistook man and the world to be veritable parts of God, that is, the visible evolution of deity; whatever man thinks and does was assertedly what the Absolute thinks and does. This exaggeration brought inevitable repercussions. Naturalists overreacted by emptying the idea of revelation of its former supernatural associations and deflated it into a vulgar commonplace. Any report of scandal, the gossiping of a secret, tattling by a stool pigeon, even a private hunch about a winning horse in the fifth at Belmont was called a "revelation." In the recent past, the "Watergate revelations" stunned many Americans. Twentieth-century neo-Protestant theologians have meanwhile expanded and contracted the term *revelation* like an accordian played at whim for their own private enjoyment.

Fifteen theses summarize what can be said for divine revelation in terms of the living God who shows himself and speaks for himself. They supply a framework for Volumes II and III of *God, Revelation and Authority.*

1. *Revelation is a divinely initiated activity, God's free communication by which he alone turns his personal privacy into a deliberate disclosure of his reality.*

All merely human affirmations about God curl into a question mark. We cannot spy out the secrets of God by obtrusive curiosity. Not even theologians of a technological era, not even Americans with their skill in probing the surface of the moon, have any special radar for penetrating the mysteries of God's being and ways. Apart from God's initiative, God's act, God's revelation, no confident basis exists for God-talk. "The things of God none knoweth, save the Spirit of God" (1 Cor. 2:11b, ASV). If we are authorized to say anything at all about the living God, it is only because of God's initiative and revelation. God's disclosure alone can transform our wavering questions concerning ultimate reality into confident exclamations!

Human beings know only what God has chosen to reveal concerning the spiritual world. "Things which eye saw not, and ear heard not, and which entered not into the heart of man . . . unto us God revealed them through the Spirit" (1 Cor. 2:9–10, ASV). Revelation is always God's communication; in John the Baptist's words, "a man can receive nothing, except it have been given him from heaven" (John 3:27, ASV).

2. *Divine revelation is given for human benefit, offering us privileged communion with our Creator in the kingdom of God.*

That divine revelation is addressed to man and is "for man's benefit" is wholly a matter of God's will and grace, for God alone determines the *why* of his disclosure. God might have given revelation a quite different direction and content: his revelation might have been addressed to another planet and confined to another species, or even *against* fallen mankind. But it is of man made in his image that God has been specially mindful in his self-revelation (Heb. 2:6).

The revelation of flame and sword in Paradise Lost might have exhausted his disclosure, or he could have bared his final wrath on crucifixion weekend. Yet divine revelation offers fallen man a place in God's kingdom: "Wherefore (as the Holy Ghost saith, To day if ye will hear his voice, harden not your hearts . . .)" (Heb. 3:7–8, KJV). God's revelation has not only been specially addressed and given to man once for all in the past, but it also embraces man *today* and includes an imperative *here* and *now* in the present. The Word of God remains no less critically decisive for man's destiny today than at the beginnings of human history.

3. *Divine revelation does not completely erase God's transcendent mystery, inasmuch as God the Revealer transcends his own revelation.*

The revelation given to man is not exhaustive of God. The God of revelation transcends his creation, transcends his activity, transcends his own disclosure. We do not "see everything from God's point of view." Even the chosen apostles concede that their knowledge on the basis of divine revelation is but "in part" and not yet "face to face" (1 Cor. 13:12).

Nor did the biblical prophets and apostles bear revelation on their persons as a possession inherent or immanent in themselves. Christianity makes no room for pantheistic notions that human reason is the divine Mind in extenso, and that man and the world externalize God's being and activity. In striking contrast to the Greek notion of prophecy, the Bible disavows any divine spark in man, any potentiality in man for divinization that qualifies him permanently to be a means of divine revelation.

4. *The very fact of disclosure by the one living God assures the comprehensive unity of divine revelation.*

The polytheistic religions played off one deity against another. On the presupposition of many competitive gods there can be no unified divine revelation. The sense of the Hebrew Shema ("the Lord our God is one God") may well be that Yahweh cannot be split up into such multiple divinities. From the very outset the self-revealing God of Scripture stands out as Creator and Lord of all. God who makes himself known in revelation is the one sovereign God. Elijah knew that the issue at Carmel was God *or* Baal, not God *and* Baal. The Bible relates the whole of history to the one God. In his letter to the Romans the apostle Paul underscores this very point: "Do you suppose God is the God of the Jews alone? . . . Certainly, of Gentiles also, if it be true that God is one" (Rom. 3:29–30, NEB). Only the fact that the one sovereign God, the Creator and Lord of all, stands at the center of divine disclosure, guarantees a unified divine revelation. While this revelation awaits completion in the future, the knowledge "in part" given prophets and apostles is nonetheless trustworthy and coherent however incomplete it may be. Divine revelation is reliable and consistent, or it would not be revelation. The capstone revelation of the end-time will confirm all past and present disclosure of God. The fact of revelation by the one sovereign God assures the comprehensive unity of God's disclosure.

5. *Not only the occurrence of divine revelation, but also its very nature, content, and variety are exclusively God's determination.*

God determines not only the *if* and *why* of divine disclosure, but also the *when, where, what, how* and *who.* If there is to be a general revelation—a revelation universally given in nature, in history, and in the reason and conscience of every man—then that is God's decision. If there is to be a special or particular revelation, that, too, is God's decision and his alone. Only because God so wills it is there a cosmic-anthropological revelation. It is solely because of divine determination, Paul reminds us, that "that which may be known of God is manifest . . . for God hath shewed it. . . . For the invisible things of him from the creation of the world are clearly seen, being understood by the things that are made, even his eternal power and Godhead" (Rom. 1:19–20, KJV). It is solely by God's own determination that he reveals himself universally in the history of the nations and in the ordinary course of human events. He is nowhere without a witness (Acts 14:17) and is everywhere active either in grace or in judgment. The living God "created every race of men of one stock, to inhabit the whole earth's surface. He fixed the epochs of their history and the limits of their territory," as the apostle Paul reminds the Athenians (Acts 17:26, NEB). And likewise only by his determination the Logos of God "lights every man" (John 1:9) as John declares.

Only because God so wills is there a special revelation that centers in the redemptive acts of Hebrew history from the exodus to the resurrection of Jesus of Nazareth, and in the communication of the meaning of these saving acts in both the prophetic and the apostolic word. Only because God so wills is the truth of God given in the special form of inspired writings; only because God so wills is his special revelation crowned by the incarnation of the Logos in Jesus of Nazareth. God has chosen to reveal himself in different times and in different modes: "God, who at sundry times and in divers manners spake in time past unto the fathers by the prophets, hath in these last days spoken unto us by his Son" (Heb. 1:1, KJV). In an amazing variety of ways—in every way except in his final eschatological revelation (and for the sake of those who still reject him we may be glad that this end-time revelation has not yet been given) —God has made himself known. In both general and special revelation— in nature and in history, in the mind and conscience of man, in written Scriptures, and in Jesus of Nazareth—he has disclosed himself.

6. God's revelation is uniquely personal both in content and form.

God discloses his very own name as a controlling feature of his revelation. Centuries before the Greek philosophers tried to storm the invisible world by their conjectures about ultimate reality, the Hebrew prophets phrased the crucial question: "What is God's name?" From the outset they knew the Ultimate to be not an "it," not some impersonal principle, but the God who makes himself known in person. From the revelation associated with God's name they learned both his character and his purposes. Yahweh is the self-disclosing God who *is,* and who *pledges his personal presence.* Yahweh expressly prohibits graven visual images in order to make himself known in audible communication, that is, in his Word. Nonetheless, in his own time and way he provides even a visible enfleshed manifestation of himself. In both content and form, God's revelation is uniquely personal.

7. *God reveals himself not only universally in the history of the cosmos and of the nations, but also redemptively within this external history in unique saving acts.*

God reveals himself particularly in his election-love of the Hebrews that reaches from the exodus through the founding of the Hebrew nation, and supremely in the gift of his promised Son and in the founding of the church of Christ. The Apostles' Creed is mainly a recital of the divine salvation acts in Hebrew-Christian history, acts set in the context of God's special promise and fulfillment. The incarnation, crucifixion and resurrection of Jesus Christ comprise the critical center of salvation history. In the resurrection of the crucified Jesus from the dead, God dramatically publishes the future direction and goal of both church history and world history, publicly identifies the risen Redeemer and future Judge of the human race, and tilts the balance of prophetic religion to begin "the last days," or the aeon before the end. In his Mars Hill address, Paul forewarned both the Greek philosophers and the people generally that the living God "has fixed the day on which he will have the world judged, and justly judged, by a man of his choosing; of this he has given assurance to all by raising him [Jesus] from the dead" (Acts 17:31, NEB). This already risen Redeemer and Judge of all assures the coming judgment of individuals and of the nations.

8. *The climax of God's special revelation is Jesus of Nazareth, the personal incarnation of God in the flesh; in Jesus Christ the source and content of revelation converge and coincide.*

Jesus Christ is not only the proclaimer of a divinely given Word, but also, on the basis of his inherent divine authority, himself stipulates and determines the Word of God. The prophetic formula "the Word of the Lord came unto me" is replaced on Jesus' lips by "But I say unto you." Jesus of Nazareth is not simply the bearer of an inner divine authority, but is himself the Word enfleshed, the Word become flesh (John 1:14). He is the visible expression of the invisible God (Col. 1:15) to whom the same honor is due as to the Father (John 5:23). In Jesus of Nazareth the divine source of revelation and the divine content of that revelation converge and coincide.

9. *The mediating agent in all divine revelation is the Eternal Logos—preexistent, incarnate, and now glorified.*

Just as he is the divine Agent in creation, redemption and judgment, so also the Logos who became incarnate in Jesus Christ is the divine Agent in revelation. God who creates, redeems and judges by his Word (cf. Gen. 1; John 1; 5) also reveals himself by that selfsame living Word. Over against mystical theories that consider the Divine to be beyond truth-and-falsehood or beyond good-and-evil, Christianity has always recognized the Logos as central to the Godhead. While the term *Logos* is borrowed from the Greek language, its New Testament sense is not derived from secular sources. The Logos-concept was no late and extraneous addition to the Fourth Gospel as a kind of foreword to commend that New Testament work to Greek readers. Early Christians were doubtless aware of pagan logos-theories. But the Prologue is so preoccupied with its own exposition of the Logos that we could not from its affirmations establish their existence and identity. The Logos-idea is integral to the Book of Signs itself in which the themes of the Prologue are restated at the completion of the signs and before the Passion-narrative. Moreover, John's Gospel is not the only one that presents Jesus of Nazareth as the Logos of God (cf. Luke 1:2). Elsewhere in the New Testament, although the Logos-terminology is not specifically used, Jesus Christ clearly fulfills the Logos-function. The overall New Testament concept of the Word, the Logos, is illuminated by Old Testament backgrounds, rather than by contemporary Greco-Roman philosophy from which its New Testament meaning must be sharply distinguished. This emphasis that the eternal Logos is mediator of all divine revelation guards against two prevalent errors, namely, that of reducing all revelation to the revelation found in Jesus of Nazareth; and that of isolating general revelation by treating revelation outside Jesus of Nazareth as something independent of the Logos who became incarnate.

10. *God's revelation is rational communication conveyed in intelligible ideas and meaningful words, that is, in conceptual-verbal form.*

The motif of a speaking God is found in the great world religions only in Judaism, Christianity and Islam. And the thesis that God speaks his mind intelligibly is a fundamental emphasis especially of Judeo-Christian religion. The loss of revelation as a mental concept has had devastating consequences in modern theology. To deny the rational intelligibility of divine revelation is to forego the connection between authentic faith in God and any necessary adherence to particular beliefs. When Karl Barth rejected the objective, rational-verbal character of revelation, Rudolf Bultmann and the existentialists swiftly eroded Barth's weaker alternative of a supposedly paradoxical supernatural Word. In the Bible "the word of the Lord" is an intelligible divine Word, not simply a human interpretation of the deeds of God or an existential inner response to a spiritual confrontation; in his redemptive disclosure, God often speaks *before* he acts. In the case of the exodus, for example, Yahweh's explicit declaration of his purpose precedes the saving act itself. The Old Testament prophets were spokesmen of a mediated Word of God. In proclaiming "thus saith the Lord" they do not exhort their hearers to enter into or seek the same special experience of revelation that they have had. Rather the prophets declare themselves to be divinely chosen to bear to others God's specially given message. Even Jesus of Nazareth, the climax of God's personal manifestation, in his own teaching and practice endorses the view that revelation takes conceptual-verbal form. Not only does Jesus identify his very "words" as revelation (John 14:10) but he also identifies the Word of God in terms of what "stands written" (Matt. 4:4, literal).

11. *The Bible is the reservoir and conduit of divine truth.*

The Scriptures are the authoritative written record and interpretation of God's revelatory deeds, and the ongoing source of reliable objective knowledge concerning God's nature and ways. Jesus of Nazareth stressed the importance of hearing the Old Testament revelation in order to understand the Messiah's life and work. "Search the scriptures . . . they are they which testify of me" (John 5:39, KJV); "Had ye believed Moses, ye would have believed me: for he wrote of me. But if ye believe not his writings, how shall ye believe my words?" (John 5:46–47, KJV); "If they hear not Moses and the prophets, neither will they be persuaded, though one rose from the dead" (Luke 16:31, KJV). The Scriptures offer a comprehensive and authoritative overview of God's revelatory disclosure and publish his purpose in the past, present and future. We are not now living in the dispensation of innocence, or in the Old Testament dispensation, nor are we contemporaries of Jesus of Nazareth or of the apostles. Nonetheless the Scriptures lay before us objectively the whole panorama of God's disclosure, and through many hundreds of translations bring this comprehensive revelation of God within the hearing and reading of men and women in all places and times.

12. *The Holy Spirit superintends the communication of divine revelation, first, by inspiring the prophetic-apostolic writings, and second, by illuminating and interpreting the scripturally given Word of God.*

The Holy Spirit is the communicator of the revealed truth of God, a role that includes both the inspiration of the writers of Scripture and the illumination of the readers and hearers of that Scripture.

In his work of inspiration, the Holy Spirit superintended the divinely chosen prophetic-apostolic recipients of the Word of God in their communication of the divine message to others. Moreover, the Spirit actively illuminates to successive generations the written revelation once for all given in its inspired, verbally articulated form. We distinguish, therefore, the Spirit-inspired communication to others of the revelation originally mediated to prophets and apostles by the Logos, from the Spirit's present function as authoritative interpreter in the believer's comprehension of the scripturally given revelation. The Spirit's role is indispensable both in inspiring the prophetic-apostolic scriptures, and in illuminating and interpreting the divinely given writings.

We must claim neither too much nor too little for the manuscripts we possess nor for the contemporary contributions to understanding them. The specially inspired prophetic-apostolic proclamation is the basis of the church's distinction between canonical and noncanonical writings and constitutes a standard for verifying Christian truth-claims as authentic and authoritative. Critical scholarship often tends to minimize the original inspiration of the sacred writings, and to exaggerate the illumination of the sacred writings by the critics; sometimes an impression is given that contemporary scholars are divinely inspired whereas the biblical witnesses at best are credited with only a high degree of insight, compounded at times with extensive fallibility. As a result both the legitimate basis of the canon and the reliability of the revelation are clouded. Ministerial students are indoctrinated in the decisive importance of such alleged sources as J, E, D, P, Q and Ur-Marcus, postulated sources for which the critics have adduced neither actual original sources nor extant fallible copies. At the same time these critics demean the only writings the church has received as a sacred trust. While the role of the biblical critic may or may not be significant for understanding the Scriptures, the Holy Spirit's role is indispensable.

In its original form the prophetic and apostolic witness, oral and written, had the special quality of inerrancy. Inerrancy pertains only to the oral or written proclamation of the originally inspired prophets and apostles. Not only was their communication of the Word of God efficacious in teaching the truth of revelation, but their transmission of that Word was error-free. Inerrancy does not extend to copies, translations or versions, however. Yet copies may be said to be infallible in that these extant derivatives of the autographs do not corrupt the original content but convey the truth of revelation in reliable verbal form, and infallibly lead the penitent reader to salvation. Jesus of Nazareth regarded the Old Testament copies of his day so approximate to and identical with the prophetic writings that he rebuked religious leaders with the warning, "Ye do err, not knowing the scriptures" (Matt. 22:29, KJV), and appealed to the Word of God as authoritative in its objective written form of the then-existing scrolls. The factor of human error in copying and translating the autographs justifies the critical search and demand for the best available texts. Translations and paraphrases may be said to be infallible only to the extent that they faithfully represent the copies available to us. The quality of paraphrases varies extensively, and their range of fallibility may at times corrupt the text, a danger from which even translations are not wholly free. If error had permeated the original prophetic-apostolic verbalization of the revelation, no essential connection would exist between the recovery of any preferred text and the authentic meaning of God's revelation.

In his supervision of the communication of revelation, the Holy Spirit conveys no new truth, whether in the activity of inspiration whereby he superintends the inerrant apostolic-prophetic transmission of the revelation of the Logos, or in the activity of illumination whereby the readers and hearers of the scriptural Word grasp the content of revelation. The Spirit superintends an already given revelation in its address to others by prophets and apostles, and subsequently illumines men in their subjective reception of that objective address. The Spirit's work of inspiration is therefore distinct from that of illumination; not even prophets and apostles always understood the full cognitive implication of the revelation they conveyed, even while the divine message was verbally given. Yet unless priority is given to the objectively inspired content of Scripture, Spirit-illumination readily gives way to private fantasy and mysticism. The Spirit illumines persons by reiterating the truth of the scriptural revelation and bearing witness to Jesus Christ. Spirit-illumination centers in the interpretation of the literal grammatical sense of Spirit-breathed Scripture. This Scripture the Holy Spirit is alone free to interpret authoritatively in the context of the progressive disclosure of the mind and purpose of God mediated by the Logos of God.

The church is neither the locus of divine revelation, nor the source of divine inspiration, nor a seat of infallibility. Rather, the church has the task of transmitting, translating, and expounding the prophetic-apostolic Scriptures.

In summary, inerrancy is a quality of the prophetic-apostolic originals or autographs. While inerrancy does not pertain to the copies, the errant copies do not corrupt prophetic-apostolic inspiration, and retain the quality of infallibility in leading men to the truth of God and to salvation. The Holy Spirit who inspired the prophetic-apostolic writers and writings authoritatively illumines mankind to comprehend the written revelation.

13. *As bestower of spiritual life the Holy Spirit enables individuals to appropriate God's revelation savingly, and thereby attests the redemptive power of the revealed truth of God in the personal experience of reborn sinners.*

The intention of God in redemption is not simply to engrave his revelation on stone, as in the case of the Decalogue, or merely to inscribe it in Scripture. Scripture itself is given so that the Holy Spirit may etch God's Word upon the hearts of his followers in ongoing sanctification that anticipates the believer's final, unerring conformity to the image of Jesus Christ, God's incarnate Word. The apostle Paul declares that "God, who commanded the light to shine out of darkness, hath shined in our hearts, to give the light of the knowledge of the glory of God in the face of Jesus Christ" (2 Cor. 4:6, KJV). The New Testament carries privileges beyond those of the old covenant; the risen Christ indwells believers by the Spirit so they may approximate the holy standard of the written code (Exod. 24) which he has met for them. Jesus of Nazareth, who became what he was not, God's enfleshed Son, enables fallen human beings to become what they are not, namely, obedient moral children of God (John 1:12). God proposes to etch his law upon the hearts of men, and the Holy Spirit is the personal divine power who by regeneration and sanctification conforms believers to the image of Christ.

14. *The church approximates the kingdom of God in miniature; as such she is to mirror to each successive generation the power and joy of the appropriated realities of divine revelation.*

Having enfleshed himself in the incarnate Christ, God seeks now to embody his revealed purpose in history in a corporate social organism over which Christ reigns as living Head. The church is to publish openly to the world the special divine revelation of which she was initially the beneficiary. To a rebellious race, in which she recognizes her own immediate and renegade past, the church witnesses of her own grateful reception and appropriation of the given revelation of God. This *given* is not now proclaimed simply as from a remote and distant past, however; since the completion of the New Testament writings, its vitalities have been freshly available to every generation of believers. In principle, therefore, men stand always but one generation removed from apostolic eyewitnesses and informed by them. As a new society that functions by the ideals and dynamics of a freshly appropriated way of life, the church brings the hesitant world around her under the purging fire of the age to come, and bears expectant witness to the coming King.

15. *The self-manifesting God will unveil his glory in a crowning revelation of power and judgment; in this disclosure at the consummation of the ages, God will vindicate righteousness and justice, finally subdue and subordinate evil, and bring into being a new heaven and earth.*

We must reckon not only with the speaking God. We have also to reckon with the God who will one day deliberately and forever withdraw his offer of pardon to the impenitent. The periodic silences that mark God's special saving revelation are anticipatory reminders of his final redemptive silence toward the wicked. The silence of prophecy in the interbiblical period, the silence of Jesus before Pilate, and God's other silences as well, sound unmistakable warnings of his coming final salvific silence toward the lost. God's progressive disclosure will climax in the final eschatological judgment of the unrepentant, and in a full and glorious sharing of himself with believers. Although God has already revealed himself, both universally and particularly, in an amazing variety of ways, his consummatory disclosure still lies before us. Grateful we may be, for the sake of those still unsheltered from the coming storm, that the God of the end-time has not yet spoken his final Word.

THESIS ONE:
Revelation is a divinely initiated activity,
God's free communication by which he alone turns his
personal privacy into a deliberate disclosure of his reality.

1.
The Awesome Disclosure
of God

DIVINE REVELATION PALPITATES with human surprise. Like a fiery bolt of lightning that unexpectedly zooms toward us and scores a direct hit, like an earthquake that suddenly shakes and engulfs us, it somersaults our private thoughts to abrupt awareness of ultimate destiny. By the unannounced intrusion of its omnipotent actuality, divine revelation lifts the present into the eternal and unmasks our pretensions of human omnicompetence. As if an invisible Concorde had burst the sound barrier overhead, it drives us to ponder whether the Other World has finally pinned us to the ground for a life-and-death response. Confronting us with a sense of cosmic arrest, it makes us ask whether the end of our world is at hand and propels us unasked before the Judge and Lord of the universe. Like some piercing air-raid siren it sends us scurrying from life's preoccupations and warns us that no escape remains if we neglect the only sure sanctuary. Even once-for-all revelation that has occurred in another time and place fills us with awe and wonder through its on-going significance and bears the character almost of a fresh miracle.

Because of revelation's engulfing impact, Karl Barth in *Evangelical Theology: An Introduction*[1] spoke of wonder as the primary trait of theological existence. Revelation is God's unmasking of himself, his voluntary act of disclosure. It comes from eternity, from beyond an absolute boundary that separates man from God. In *Revelation and Reason*, Emil Brunner wrote of divine revelation as "incursion from another dimension."

Calling attention to the new and unexpected, the introductory Greek interjection *ide—See! Behold!*—stands out of sentence construction to

---

1. Full bibliographical information on all sources cited in the text is given in the Bibliography at the end of this volume.

rivet biblical attention upon God's awesome intervention: "Look, the Lamb of God who takes away the sin of the world!" (John 1:29, NIV); "Look, the Lamb of God!" (John 1:36, NIV). The demonstrative particle *idou* is used by the evangelists not simply for vivacity of style but also to fix attention on the unexpected and even apparently impossible: "Behold, the angel of the Lord appeared" (Matt. 1:20, 2:13, KJV); "Behold, the heavens were opened and . . ." (Matt. 3:16, RSV); "Behold, angels came and began to minister to him" (Matt. 4:11, NAS); "Behold, Moses and Elijah appeared to them, talking with Him" (Matt. 17:3, NAS); "Behold, the curtain of the temple was torn in two, from top to bottom; and the earth shook; and the rocks were split; and the tombs also were opened" (Matt. 27: 51–52, RSV). "Lo, a voice from heaven, saying, 'This is my beloved Son, with whom I am well pleased' " (Matt. 3:17, RSV) is therefore paradigmatic; transcendent divine revelation is an awe-filled actuality that overtakes mankind through God's personal initiative.

"The idea of God *making Himself known*," writes H. D. McDonald, "is not so much *a* biblical idea, as it is *the* biblical idea" ("Revelation," p. 843a). In Barth's words, the God of the Bible is "the God to whom there is no way and bridge, of whom we could not say or have to say one single word, had He not of His own initiative met us as Deus revelatus" (*Church Dogmatics*, I/1, p. 368).

Had God insisted on remaining incommunicado we would know nothing whatever about him. Instead of his word to Moses, "No man can see Me and live" (Exod. 33:20, NAS), God might have determined instead that "no man shall know me and live." God cannot be known unless he wills to be known and to make himself known. Under no circumstances whatever can God's secrets be wrested from him by intrusive human curiosity. Were this not the case, then, as H. R. Mackintosh observes, "we should be committed to the incredible position that man can know God without His willing to be known" (*The Christian Apprehension of God*, p. 70). Apart from divine initiative man could not perceive even God's existence, let alone his perfections and purposes; God's very reality would remain wholly problematical had he not chosen to disclose himself. Zophar rightly asked Job: "Canst thou by searching find out God?" (Job 11:7, KJV; cf. Berkeley Version, "Can you fathom God's secrets?"), even as the apostle Paul reminded the Christians at Corinth: "The world did not know God through wisdom" (1 Cor. 1:21a, RSV). Apart from God's self-unveiling any affirmations about the Divine would be nothing more than speculation. Only *Deus revelatus* can banish *Deus dubitandus*. Not even modern theologians armed with sophisticated technological gadgetry could spy upon a reticent deity and program data about him. Barth spoke of "the impassable frontier, the unbridgeable gulf" and emphasized that "we could not utter one wretched syllable about the nature of the Word of God, if the Word of God had not been spoken to us as God's Word" (ibid., p. 187). The only confident basis for God-talk is God's revelation of himself. The self-revelation that God communicates provides what human ingenuity cannot achieve, namely, authentic information about the ultimate Who's Who.

The inaccessibility or accessibility of the Divine is, moreover, far more than simply a matter of God's decree. The very nature of divine reality and truth are such that, apart from divine initiative and disclosure, they remain intrinsically hidden. The God of the Bible is wholly determinative in respect to revelation. He is free either to reveal himself or not to reveal himself; he is sovereign in his self-disclosure. In addressing the Corinthians Paul reminds them that "no one knows the thoughts of God except the Spirit of God" and that the divine Spirit is instrumental in the communication of God's revelation (1 Cor. 2:10, 11, NIV). The Epistle to the Hebrews speaks of specific "times" of God's progressive revelation (Heb. 1:1-3). In his letter to the Colossians Paul emphasizes that the deep content of God's special disclosure remained *hidden* at various stages until the chosen moment of God's active revelation (Col. 2:2-3). According to Francis W. Beare, Paul's thought in this passage is that divine revelation gives us "access to unlimited stores of truth, which are by their nature 'secret,' not the public property of the human race, but belonging to 'the deep things of God'" (*The Interpreter's Bible*, 11:186). Christ's confident declaration to his disciples that the Holy Spirit would lead them into all truth (John 14:26) mirrors his conviction that God himself stands at the center of divine revelation and voluntarily steps out of the otherwise hidden supernatural in order to confront man with the erstwhile unknown and impenetrable.

Be they gods of secular philosophy or gods of the history of religion, the false gods can in principle be completely known for what they are simply through human inquiry and ingenuity. Given enough time and effort, any person can explore, expound and expose the nature of these "divinities." Their inscrutability is merely a matter of human ignorance. To banish the mist that clouds them one need only learn certain religious techniques or procedures set forth by certain "spiritual masters." Whoever appropriates certain "unveiling mechanisms" may pursue and interrogate the divine Mystery. But to speak of God and attribute specific characteristics to him apart from a basis in divine revelation is to play the gardener who, after spraying water into the sky from a hose, then welcomes the "rainfall" as "heaven-sent."

In primitive religion man is often said to ascend to the divine or to "revelation" through fetishes or sacred trees and other objects, or through medicine men and sacred chieftains or oracles. This approach assumes that man can comprehend the unseen world by human initiative. The supernatural is thought, without divine activity and self-manifestation, to be always accessible to man if he but perseveres in special rituals and ceremonies. In no way, however, is biblical revelation something "arrived at" in a divinatory way.

Like primitive religion the later mystery cults likewise assumed that no intrinsic gulf exists between God and man and that initiation into

these religions depends upon certain secret practices. But "in place of
the jealously secretive gods of the pagans," remarks Donald M.
MacKay of the University of Keele, England, Judeo-Christian religion knows the
self-revealed God "who is himself the giver of all that is true, and who
rejoices when any of his truth is brought to the light and obeyed in
humility" (International Conference on Human Engineering and the
Future of Man, Wheaton, Illinois, July 21, 1975). Mysticism comprehends
no revelation in the scriptural sense for here, as Albrecht Oepke notes,
"God does not actively move from Himself"; in Egypto-Hellenic religious
philosophy "the object of revelation is the ground of the world which is
only factually and not intrinsically hidden" ("Apokaluptō," 2:570).

Greek philosophy, similarly neglecting the reality of transcendent revelation, blends individual and cosmic reason. The Greeks seek to master
the universe by human reasoning. Extending the human ego cosmically
they then regard cosmic reason as immanent in nature and man. But
the Bible does not discuss the living God as an ontological inference
either from the physical world or from human psychology. The true God
is the hidden God (Isa. 45:15) who reveals himself only when he wills to
do so. "On the Greek view, man unveils God; on the biblical, God reveals
Himself to man. On the one side we have proofs of God and the praise of
man, on the other the praise of God" in view of his self-disclosure (ibid.,
p. 574). "In the strict sense revelation is always and everywhere the act
of God. No one has a right to it simply because he is a man. Even the
Israelite has no right to it because he is an Israelite" (ibid.).

Barth rightly notes "the extraordinary direction of vision" characteristic of the biblical witnesses to revelation. From a street window as it
were, we observe a million people crowding outside when suddenly we
notice more and more stopping, shading their eyes, and looking straight
up toward some compelling reality that is blocked out to others by the
roof above. The Bible's cloud of witnesses—heads high, eyes open, ears
attentive to God who commands attention and speaks his Word—pleads
with us not to pass heedlessly by. What the prophets and apostles say
about God these witnesses say on the basis of God's revelatory act, of
what God himself has made known.

The New Testament uses the Greek word mustērion—the root meaning
is "closed" or "hidden"—to signify what God himself has now made
plain by divine communication. As Scripture itself puts it, " 'Things beyond our seeing, things beyond our hearing, things beyond our imagining,
all prepared by God for those who love him,' these it is that God has
revealed to us through the Spirit" (1 Cor. 2:9–10, NEB; cf. Isa. 64:4).
Revelation occurs on God's R-Day as an act of transcendent disclosure.
It pulses with the surprise of foreign invasion, and opens before us like
the suddenly parted Red Sea waters. It stirs us like the angelic hosts
who appeared unscheduled to proclaim Messiah's birth, or overawes us
like the rushing mighty wind of Pentecost. The essence of revelation is

that God steps out of his hiddenness to disclose what would otherwise remain secret and unknown.

The word *reveal* and its cognates occur more than a score of times in the Old Testament and even more frequently in the New Testament. The specific Old Testament term meaning "to reveal" is the Hebrew verb *galah* and carries the idea of nakedness or the removal of barriers to perception. Its New Testament equivalent is the Greek verb *apokaluptō* and means "to uncover." Both terms, therefore, bear the sense of unveiling, disclosing, or making plain what was concealed.

Galah occurs some twenty-three times in connection with God's self-manifestation or communication of his message (cf. Num. 24:4; 1 Sam. 3:21; 2 Sam. 7:27; Dan. 2:47). Their divinely gifted knowledge of this revelation of God in his Word is the distinguishing mark of the Old Testament prophets: "The Lord [Yahweh] does nothing, without revealing his secret to his servants the prophets" (Amos 3:7, RSV). B. B. Warfield remarks: "It is undoubtedly the fundamental contention of the prophets that the revelations given through them are not their own but wholly God's" (*The Inspiration and Authority of the Bible*, pp. 89 f.). As Isaiah avers: "The Lord of hosts has revealed himself in my ears" (22:14, RSV).

Of God's unveiling of what was hidden the New Testament uses, synonymously with *apokaluptō*, the verb *phaneroō* meaning "to manifest," "to show one's self." When one considers how relatively seldom this word was used outside of and before New Testament Greek, it occurs with striking frequency in Scripture. (The Hebrew parallel is *anan*, used of Yahweh's manifestation to Israel in the cloud of his presence in the wilderness years; cf. Exod. 40:38.) The apostle Paul uses *phaneroō* synonymously with *apokaluptō* when he writes of God's universal and ongoing revelation in the creation (Rom. 1:17–21); when he speaks of the climactic revelation of God in Christ and the good news that believing Gentiles are no less heirs of salvation than are believing Jews (Eph. 3:5); and when he declares that the crucified and risen Messiah dwells personally in the hearts of his followers who look for the coming glory (Col. 1:26). The apostle John uses *phaneroō* much more frequently than *apokaluptō* and, like Paul, sometimes uses it synonymously with *gnōridzō* (compare John 17:6 and 26). Jesus of Nazareth manifests both the name of God (17:6) and the works of God (3:21, 9:3; cf. 1 John 3:5, 8). Paul uses the closely related noun *manifestation* when depicting Jesus as God "manifested in the flesh" (1 Tim. 3:16; cf. 1 John 1:2; 1 Pet. 1:20). Concerning both Jesus' earthly manifestations as a divine miracle and also anticipatively of his future eschatological appearance, the church fathers commonly use *phainomai*.

Revelation in the Bible refers first and foremost to what God himself unveils and that which would otherwise remain concealed. The concept of a "secret," a "mystery" (Hebrew, *sod*; Aramaic, *raz*) signified that hidden purpose of God concerning the last days (cf. Dan. 2:28, 47) which the New Testament gospel discloses (cf. Rom. 16:25; Eph. 3:6). Both the Old and New Testaments emphasize that God is universally and ongoingly revealed in his creation (Ps. 19; Rom. 1:17 ff.). His special redemptive revelation, however, is given once-for-all time. It is given not universally but in a disclosure addressed to the chosen Hebrew prophets and the New Testament apostles who witness to the incomparable news that God in redemptive grace comes by way of fulfilled prophecy in Christ Jesus. The verb *apokaluptō* occurs in Peter's confession of the deity of Jesus Christ: "Blessed are you, Simon Bar-Jona! For flesh and blood has not revealed this to you, but my Father who is in heaven" (Matt. 16:17, RSV). Its derivative noun *apokalupsis* occurs eighteen times in the New Testament, and it is to such "revelation" that Paul unqualifiedly ascribes the gospel message he proclaimed: "I did not receive it from man, nor was I taught it, but it came through a revelation of Jesus Christ" (Gal. 1:12, cf. 2:2, RSV).

The content of church proclamation is therefore not just anything and everything. The church's message to the world is not about the energy crisis, pollution, white or black power, détente, the Israeli-Arab conflict, ad infinitum. It is the very specific Word of God. The church is called to proclaim what God says and does. Unless it verbally articulates and communicates the revelation of God, the church has no distinctive right to be heard, to survive, or even to exist.

Nor is the Christian minister anything and everything—a fund-raiser, marriage-counselor, pulpit orator, public relations specialist, ad infinitum. He is primarily the proclaimer of God's revealed Word. Unless he declares the revelation of God he has no unique vocational claim and standing.

Such concerns as war and peace, environmental pollution, discrimination, and so on, are far from unimportant. They are indeed crucial, as are also the minister's role in marriage counseling and community affairs. But these matters are nonetheless footnotes on the main text, namely, that God has spoken and that what God says is what bears determinatively on all existence and life. The unmistakable priority of God's people, the church in the world, is to proclaim God's revealed Word. Divorced from this calling, the church and Christians are undurable and unendurable phenomena. By stifling divine revelation, they are, in fact, an affront to God. Devoid of motivation for implementing Christ's cause, they become both delinquents and delinquent in neighbor and world relations.

Why does the modern world so comfortably chain its passions to power, lucre and sex, instead of harnessing itself to God in his revelation? The answer lies not in any intrinsic weakness of Christianity, not in any peculiar contemporary antipathy for the gospel, and not even in the theological, evangelistic and social failures of the past generation of believers. The fault lies rather in timid preaching of God's revelation by professional pulpiteers, in presumptuous tampering with God's revelation by contemporary critics, and in subtle evasions of God's revelation not only in ecclesiastical bureaucracies and in seminary classrooms but also in the lives of many who are church-identified. The Word of the Lord is not being sounded in the land as it ought, and without the vision of God and his holy will people are miring daily into deeper carnality and spiritual obtuseness (Scripture calls it "blindness").

Whatever else may be said about early Christianity this basic fact remains: the church rejoiced in God's revealed truth, including the prophetic fulfillment to which John the Baptist bore witness (John 5:33); the truth that came by Christ Jesus (John 1:17); the truth of divine revelation of which the church is "the pillar and bulwark" (1 Tim. 3:15, RSV); the truth which is God's Word (John 17:17); the truth which is inviolable (Titus 1:1-2).

Nowhere is the repudiation of Christian belief in recent modern learning more insistent than in the rejection in philosophical and theological treatises of the very idea of transcendent divine revelation. Both outside and inside Christian circles the reality of supernatural revelation has been openly questioned and even ridiculed as human fiction. Kai Nielsen, for example, asks: "Who has seen or in any way apprehended Sedena, Yahweh, Zeus, Wotan or Fricka? We have no good evidence for their existence. . . . To believe . . . is just a bold superstition . . . like believing that there is a Santa Claus or that there are fairies" ("Religion and Commitment," p. 29). Not only is Yahweh the living God of the Bible here correlated with the religious myths, but supernatural reality is dismissed with no examination whatever of intelligible supports on the assumption that "no good evidence" exists. Van Austin Harvey likewise assimilates Judeo-Christian revelation to mythical views. After evaluating the case for Christianity through contemporary representations rather than on its intrinsic biblical merits, he concludes that the essential content of religious faith "can as well be mediated through a historically false . . . myth" as through a true narrative or through history (*The Historian and the Believer*, pp. 280 f.).

Philosophy of religion characteristically singles out the idea of God as its dominant and most important theoretical concept. But for more than a century it has frequently wrestled the case for or against theism on nonrevelational considerations and has become virtually synonymous with conjectural theology. Sketching the problems of belief in relation to the world, man, experience, or whatever else, it has usually ignored the biggest of all concerns, namely, whether God himself has addressed revelation to man and how, if he has not, the case for theistic personalism can be persuasively made in the absence of divine self-disclosure. Once this concern is abandoned or left in mid-air, secular theology is free to follow its own preferred course. The God of the Bible, if not completely forsaken, is swiftly reduced to a shadow-self, a tamed divinity in whose presence even the most wicked sinner and intellectual vagrant can feel comfortably at home. The rationalistic theologian or religious philosopher who ferrets "God" out of hiding and rescues this invisible Rip van Winkle from cosmic obscurity—or who "speaks well" of God, even if he is not quite sure of whom or of what he is speaking—can then congratulate himself that he is traversing the highway of modern-day faith rather than detouring along the ancient road of rebellion. Those who begin with an abstract notion called *deity*, and proceed to refine its content by reference to nature or to religious experience, have in their projection and production of divinities already far surpassed any heretofore known pantheon of gods. For all their confident appeal to "natural theology," the prestigious Gifford Lectures in Great Britain spooned up the general idea of God in a smorgasbord display of creative possibilities that provided a divinity for virtually every academic taste. Discussion of God that has no basis in divine disclosure is an oral drug that preserves the patient's energies during a coma of intellectual inconclusiveness but does little to guarantee meaningful survival for the truth of God. Critics of such theological enterprise have rightly complained of "a logic afflicted with lacunae, a causality suffering from hiatuses."

To evade the centrality of divine self-revelation spells invariable and inevitable defeat for philosophical theology. Erecting the case for theism apart from divine disclosure is like venturing to hatch a live chicken from an empty eggshell, a highly imaginative but futile project. God-talk based simply on sentiments about nature, or on human feelings and desires, launches an explorer missile that probes an absent and unknown God whose living word of revelation is deafened to silence by the verbalizing of self-appointed cosmonauts patroling the frontiers of the invisible world. While Albrecht Ritschl may not have made the best use of his emphasis, he was nonetheless right, over against the speculative rationalism of Hegel and the feeling-theology of Schleiermacher, when he insisted that it is impossible to teach anything about God except in the context of a real divine revelation (*Theologie und Metaphysik*, p. 34). Over against natural theology and mysticism he was equally right by insisting that "we can only know God in the measure that He puts Himself sovereignly within reach of our knowledge" (cited by H. R. Mackintosh, *The Problem of Religious Knowledge*, p. 147). However well-intentioned it may be, progressive slimming down of the God-concept finally leaves the case for theism a terminally ill skeleton. God is welcomed as simply a flexible metaphysical construct, as the guarantor of a crumbling social morality, or as the protector of venerable cultural institutions. When the God-idea is forced to walk on man-made stilts, the exalted stand-ins for the biblical self-revealing God of creation, redemption and judgment soon totter and tumble. Commanding at best only a temporary intellectual salute, they breed a generation of young intellectuals who are amused and amazed that scholars once took seriously these magnificent robots of religious imagination.

In view of God's self-disclosure, theology is not, in fact, limited to gleaning the truth about him from psychological inquiries into man's pious consciousness or from inferences from history or reflections on nature, or from conjectural postulations about the infinite and absolute. The Bible beats no drum whatever for "how I found God" explorers. As John Hick notes, "God was not" for the biblical writers "an inferred entity; he was an experienced reality" ("A Critique of the 'Second Argument,' " p. 344). This reality—it should be quickly added—was given in God's own self-manifestation. When divine revelation is the decisive category, it places every merely psychological, historical and speculative view on the defensive. Theology has access to God on the basis of his own normative disclosure. The God of revelation consequently calls a halt to self-oriented religious probings that simply correlate theological inquiry with man's own views, with his own culture and its reigning beliefs, with his insatiable need of an absolute, with his piety and aspirations, and so on.

To reject the self-revealedness of God soon leads to regarding heathenism or paganism as welcome steps on the evolutionary ladder. This process, in turn, soon elevates developmental relativity into a despotic absolute. Beclouding the God of revelation means that sooner or later every present norm will be condemned to the past. Even scriptural theism will become subject to alteration or displacement and its stern condemnation of false gods will be ignored. It will become easy to wink when others speak of "heresy." Absolute truth about religious reality will be considered ugly dogmatism, while the absolute affirmation that no religious assertions are final will be simultaneously dignified as tolerant and scholarly. K. H. Miskotte makes the point well: "He who is of the opinion that 'heathenism' is only a religious-historical concept will necessarily find that there are many chapters in the Old Testament which he cannot accept as relevant, as a message, much less as a proclamation of God" (When the Gods Are Silent, p. 134). This judgment, moreover, is scarcely confined to the Old Testament. If theological considerations are a matter of cultural fashion, then all norms go by the board. It is no accident that once Barth rediscovered the fact of special divine revelation he was constrained to deplore and to dismiss Protestant modernism as "heresy," as a falsification of the transcendently disclosed God.

Today in major branches of Christendom and in various of its denominations, those who speak blithely of "theological pluralism"—as if such diversity necessarily constitutes the patriotic basis of cooperative Christianity—blur the fact that the strength of revealed religion lies not in its inclusion of both Yahweh and Baal, but in its clear distinction and choice between Yahweh or Baal. As if by way of merciful preeschatological warning, Elijah's destruction of the priests of Baal followed their open demonstration of serving false gods. To be loyal to "no other God" but the God of revelation means that theological vacillation must be seen for what it is, namely, spiritual rebellion.

Only one prosecutor has ever told a jury in advance that some of his best informed jurors would not believe his word (Isa. 53:1); that many of those specially advised of his plans would disown their knowledge of him (Deut. 28:68; Jer. 5:21; cf. John 1:11); that one of the twelve most trusted witnesses possessing inside information would defect to the opposition (Ps. 41:9; 55:12; Zech. 11:12; cf. Matt. 26:15, 21–24; John 13:21); that many of the professional leaders supposedly most competent to give a verdict would stand against him and declare him deserving of death (John 5:18, 12:40) and welcome an interloper in his place (John 4:44); that he would be crucified with brazen criminals (Ps. 22:16–18; Isa. 53); that even among those committed to his cause after his resurrection from the dead there would be a serious "falling away" (2 Thess. 2:3; cf. 2 Pet. 2).

Yet what was told the people of God in prophetic revelation was addressed to them from the standpoint of sovereign confidence in the triumph of God's truth and cause. That multitudes of human beings would respond in a way contrary to what might rationally be expected— that is, the rejection of the Creator's universal self-revelation in nature and conscience (Rom. 1:17–20), the repudiation of scriptural revelation as a controlling principle even by those to whom God's Word was given in written form (Rom. 2:17–24), and the disavowal of the divinely promised Messiah by those who had the prophetic promises (Matt. 13:13; Luke 8:10; Mark 8:18; etc.)—was openly published not only in confirmation of the fierce sinfulness of man, but also in order to reinforce the family of faith against despair and doubt. Jesus warned that some religious leaders would think that they do God a service by persecuting and even killing disciples (John 16:2) who bear the world's best news, the gospel of divine redemption. Such revelational anticipations were vouchsafed to alert the faithful against being overtaken by satanic surprise, and to strengthen their otherwise vulnerable faith by assurances that the self-revealing God foreknows this evil turn of things, will put a limit on its possibilities, and will bring his cause to triumph.

God's ineradicable divine disclosure in nature and history and conscience (Acts 14:17; Rom. 1:19–22; 2:14–16) promises the sure victory of his revelational purpose. The triumphant resurrection of the crucified Jesus (John 20; 1 Cor. 15:1–5) and his inauguration of a new humanity and the new age (Eph. 2:1–22) have established the regenerate church mandated to proclaim him as the only way of rescue and hope in a morally rebellious and doomed world (Col. 1:17–27). Despite preinformation (Matt. 12:40; 16:21; 17:23; 20:19; 26:61; 27:63), some of Jesus' own disciples questioned the news of his resurrection from the dead, not simply because of unbelief but also because "it seemed too good to be true" (Luke 24:41, NEB).

The early Christians insisted that no rational basis exists for unbelief in Christ as God's supreme manifestation. As Saul of Tarsus, that towering Jewish leader, put it: "the Jews are entrusted with the oracles of

God" (Rom. 3:3, RSV). Invoking Old Testament warnings (cf. Ps. 69:22–28; Isa. 6:9; etc.) the New Testament frequently affirms that judicial blindness came upon Jewry because of unbelief. Even as the prophets had foretold (Isa. 42:6; cf. Luke 2:32 where "a light to the nations" is applied to Jesus, and Acts 13:47 where it is applied to the church), God dramatically addressed his redemptive revelation to the Gentile world (contrast Matt. 10:5 with Rom. 2:9–10), without, however, finally sealing off the Jews (Rom. 11:8–10). This disbelief in God's Word appears throughout the New Testament—refusal to honor the inspired prophets, refusal from which grows Hebrew rejection of Jesus Christ as the promised Messiah. Jesus put the problem succinctly: "You diligently study the Scriptures because you think that by them you possess eternal life. These are the Scriptures that testify about me, yet you refuse to come to me to have life. . . . But do not think I will accuse you before the Father. Your accuser is Moses, on whom your hopes are set. If you believed Moses, you would believe me, for he wrote about me. But since you do not believe what he wrote, how are you going to believe what I say?" (John 5:39–41, 45–47, NIV).

The wonder and astonishment elicited by the revelation of God permeate both Old and New Testaments, and the recurring themes of God's remarkable love and terrible judgment and his rule and direction of his people evoke the awe of the faithful. Georg Bertram remarks that the Old Testament concept of revelation which the Septuagint prominently associated with the concept of wonder was secularized and weakened by Hellenistic Judaism ("Thauma," 3:37). But the truth of revelation can be evaded even where wonder is present. Astonishment in itself is no adequate response to the revelation of God and at most is only preliminary to a faith that pleases him. Those who heard Jesus' inaugural sermon at Nazareth were indeed astonished at his proclamation of grace, but they nonetheless opposed him (Luke 4:22). It happened frequently that those who were astonished resisted him. In Acts 13:41 the apostle Paul cites Habbakuk 1:5 to warn those who though they marvel yet perish through unbelief. The force of Jesus' "Marvel not!" in John 5:28 (cf. 3:7) is that God's revealed truth requires far more than amazement; it demands commitment and appropriation. Nicodemus was told not to marvel at the imperative of the new birth. Similarly the Jews were told not to marvel that sinful man can pass here and now from death to eternal life, but were exhorted rather to live by faith. The essential purpose of divine disclosure is not simply to beget wonder but rather to communicate truth. Astonishment may preface not only obedience to God but also prostration before the demonic beast (cf. Rev. 17:6–7, where the seer is forbidden to fear what he beholds; note also 1 John 3:13; 1 Pet. 4:12). Those who respond only by astonishment may, in fact, easily miss the truth of revelation and fall prey to antichrist.

Pagans frequently invested the terrifying unusual with a sign-significance and used the Greek term *teras* to designate fearsome natural phenomena. Such wonders are often mentioned in Greek mythology where what is outside the ordinary and what is sinister or ominous are integrated into a polytheistic cultic scheme.

But in Scripture the author and instigator of the genuinely miraculous is the living God whose divine purpose governs everything that happens. His wonderful acts do not simply portend what is future but rather display his historical power in the present that bears decisively upon that future. Moreover wonder and God's work of revelation are explicitly related; what the Bible emphasizes is mediation of the revealed knowledge of God's will.

In the Septuagint, references to "signs and wonders" almost always recall Yahweh's deliverance of Israel from Egypt. In the New Testament the prophetic references are juxtaposed with signs that fulfill and enlarge their meaning (cf. Acts 2:19 and Joel 2:20). The word *sēmeion* (sign) occurs at least seventy-three times in the New Testament—twenty-four times in John, twenty-three in Luke, ten in Matthew, seven in Mark, eight in Paul's letters and once in Hebrews. While this term may but need not betoken a miracle, it often designates some notable feature that confirms the truth of the message—for example, the manger in which the shepherds would find the Christ-child, or the kiss by which Judas identifies Jesus. The term always means more than simply a wonder, although wonder does indeed pervade many of the Synoptic miracle-reports (e.g., Matt. 21:20; Mark 5:20; 7:37; Luke 9:43, 11:14). According to Karl Heinrich Rengstorf *teras* never appears alone in the New Testament but always in conjunction with *sēmeion* ("Teras," 8:124). The sign-significance of the miracles of Jesus gains dramatic significance for the outside world, and the sign of the Son of Man coming in his future glory in Matthew's Gospel (24:30–31) in its full meaning signals the end of the present course of world history. What is centrally at stake in the Gospel's interest in signs is Jesus' relation to the Father, that is, the issue of his essential sonship and immediacy to God—in brief, his claim to divinity. Jesus himself performs the signs in a climactic sense; the signs exhibit him as the Christ, as the one who is at the same time both the revealer and the revealed, the one in relation to whom the fate of all mankind will be decided. In the Book of Acts the signs performed by the apostles in Jesus' name point to the crucified and risen Lord and beyond him to God the Father who sent him and works through him.

Yet, as Rengstorf emphasizes, faith lives not by miracles but "by the Word to which the miracle is ordered and subordinated as *sēmeion*" ("Sēmeion," 7:240). The signs are not decisive for establishing faith even in Jesus as Messiah, nor do they supply the content of faith. Faith is in God and not in signs, and rests ultimately upon God's Word (John 4:48; 20:29). No new sign is needed for the post-Easter community for it has the sufficient word of inspired and accredited witnesses.

Pseudomessiahs also have their "signs and wonders" and on such a scale that "even God's chosen, if such a thing were possible" (Matt. 24:24, NEB) may be misled; in other words, some works of the Messiah may be counterfeited. The apostle Paul speaks of signs and wonders and powers when he writes of antichrist who acts under Satan's sway (2 Thess. 2:9; cf. Mark 13:22). And John writes that the beast from the pit, the pseudoforerunner of the pseudo-Christ, will do great signs (Rev. 13:13). Ancient pagan priests were known to produce artificially "fire from heaven" and by ventriloquism to give speech to idols; the passage in Revelation concerning antichrist seems to speak not merely of deception, however, but to ascribe supernatural powers.

The spiritual quality of signs depends finally on the moral nature of the one who works them and on the way in which power is deployed. While false workers of signs lead humans astray and into idolatry (Rev. 13:13–15) Jesus Christ leads into the presence of the Father (John 14:6). The works of Jesus are authentic signs because they manifest Yahweh the self-revealing God; they are works which the Father of promise accomplishes in and through him as the divinely sent Son (John 5:36, 38; 17:14).

THESIS TWO:
Divine revelation is given for human benefit,
offering us privileged communion with our Creator
in the kingdom of God.

2.
A Place in God's Kingdom

GOD WHO REVEALS HIMSELF in sovereign freedom does so first and foremost for his own glory. While divine revelation is indeed ordained for human benefit, it primarily unveils God's glory through the disclosure of himself and his numerous purposes and objectives. Herman Bavinck and Valentine Hepp wrote in former years of God's revelation of himself to himself before the creation of the universe within the eternal trinity and then later through his created works. Moreover, it is the glory of God that the created universe is said first and foremost to declare (Ps. 19:1).

While the spiritual host of the created heavenly world stand in some kind of revelatory relationship to God, the Creator nowhere addressed salvific revelation to any of the rebellious and fallen angels. But God conveyed redemptive revelation specially for man's sake, although he need not have done so. The human species is on the receiving end of a divine initiative wherein God makes known his sovereign grace. The thrust of the biblical creation account is that, however remarkable may be man's knowledge of the whence and wherefore of light and planets and birds and beasts, his special distinction lies in a unique personal relationship with the Creator-Redeemer God and in a privileged place in his will and ways.

God might have given his revelation a wholly different turn, disclosing himself instead to some other species of life created to populate other planets, or manifesting himself only to angelic intelligences in the spirit world. But God's decree to create the universe already anticipated divine disclosure correlated with human understanding and speech and communication. It is man that God created as capstone of his creation and human nature that he destined for special participation in his plan.

Divine displeasure over man's fall into moral disobedience might have

30

prompted God to completely redirect his revelation against mankind. His wrath unmitigated by any prospect of mercy or promise of human redemption, God might have climaxed and ended his disclosure in Paradise Lost. Scripture testifies that persistent wickedness despite God's redemptive promise (Gen. 3:15) provoked Yahweh even to repent of having made man (Gen. 6:7). Yet it is to fallen man, not to other created intelligences, not even to fallen angels, that God proffers redemption. In the words of Scripture, "angels long to see into" the "salvation . . . which the prophets pondered" and which the apostles "openly announced" to the world of fallen mankind. It was "for your sake," writes Peter (1 Pet. 1:10–12, 20), that Christ was manifested.

Further, God's revelation for man's benefit need not have continued until the present hour. His final wrath and future judgment, even if withheld from shrouding the very dawn of human history, might have been unleashed the weekend of Jesus Christ's crucifixion and resurrection, or might equally well have overtaken us all last night. That God's revelation was ventured for human benefit, and even now proffers fallen men and women a possibility of forgiveness and fellowship through redemptive reconciliation, is not a matter either of human deserving or of divine obligation.

If the living God should address mankind in any fleet moment at any point in space with but a simple sentence, with even one single *Thus saith the Lord!* what intelligent person would not stop, look and listen? Yet in his revelation God has published news incomparably important to every generation, past and present, of momentous value to each of us who lives in this present opportunity for decision. God's disclosure for us involves not simply a definitive word about the past and a remarkable declaration about the climactic future but has superscribed a decisive *now*. Its dateline includes *today* (this very day); God's disclosure is not exhausted by the revelation given *once upon a time* and *then and there*. God has your and my personal benefit in view as present-moment objects of his address. The plea "Today if ye shall hear his voice, harden not your hearts" (Heb. 4:7, ASV; cf. Ps. 95:7–8) carries no less urgency than the banner headlines of this morning's *New York Times* or of some television documentary on momentous world events. God's revelation is the headline above all headlines, directed to us from the world beyond all worlds, from God himself.

God's purpose in revelation is that we may know him personally as he is, may avail ourselves of his gracious forgiveness and offer of new life, may escape catastrophic judgment for our sins, and venture personal fellowship with him. "I . . . will be your God, and ye shall be my people" (Lev. 26:12, KJV), he declares. His revelation is not some impersonal mass media commercial or routine news report of the "state of the invisible world"; it is, rather, a personal call and command to each individual. God discloses priceless good news. Because of it human beings everywhere at this very moment have the prospect of peace and hope, of purity and happiness. Not forever to be sure, but for the moment redemptive rescue remains an immediate possibility for every race and for every land, for Jew and Arab, Chinese and Russian, and Latin and North American.

The kingdom is God's and his alone; only he has the sovereignty, authority, wisdom and freedom to rule as absolute Creator of all. Where God is present in person and in power, in righteousness and truth and love, there is the kingdom: it is wherever God holds sway. By the acknowledgment "Thine is the kingdom" that Jesus builds into the Lord's Prayer (Matt. 6:13, KJV) he reminds the disciples that the privilege of sharing in the kingdom comes only because of God's initiative and grace. Finite and fallen man has no inherent claim upon that kingdom. "Your Father has chosen to give you the kingdom" (Luke 12:32, NEB) said Jesus. James the Lord's brother makes the same point in question form: "Hath not God chosen the . . . heirs of the kingdom . . . ?" (James 2:5, KJV).

The creation account, as we have noted, reflects God's special interest in the human species from the very outset. Later on we shall emphasize that the universe itself was fashioned on redemption lines: Jesus Christ is the Lamb "slain from the foundation of the world" (Rev. 13:8, ASV). Human beings are intended to be God's partners in the special task of subordinating the created world to the Creator's moral and spiritual purposes, and it is within this great goal that the created world exists providentially for men. The *unto you*s of the creation account ("Every herb . . . and every tree . . . to you it shall be for food," Gen. 1:29, ASV), gather widening scope through the revelation and mercy of God until the Scripture phrases "for us," "for you," "for me" echo like rain-promising waves of thunder through the aridity of sinful man's misfortunes. Instead of forsaking the sin-deceived universe God chose and willed to be its Savior and Lord, to establish his divine rule within as well as over it, and to achieve through it his divine intention and goal. The kingdom of God is the kingdom of Heaven in which God's creation will either share or to which it will be subordinated in justice.

"I will take you to me for a people," declares God's merciful redemptive covenant with the Hebrews, "and I will be to you a God: and ye shall know that I am the Lord your God, which bringeth you out from under the burdens of the Egyptians. And I will bring you in unto the land, concerning the which I did swear to give it to Abraham, to Isaac, and to Jacob; and I will give it you for an heritage: I am the Lord" (Exod. 6:7–8, KJV). He furthermore prophetically pledges his gift of messianic salvation to the people of his redemptive love: "For unto us a child is born, unto us a son is given: and the government shall be upon his shoulder: and his name shall be called Wonderful, Counselor, The mighty God, The everlasting Father, The Prince of Peace" (Isa. 9:6, KJV). God anticipates a day when his purposes will be inscribed on the very hearts of his people: "For this is the covenant that I will make with the house of Israel after those days, saith the Lord; I will put my laws into their mind, and write them in their hearts: and I will be to them a God, and they shall be to me a people: And they shall not teach every man his neighbour, and every man his brother, saying, Know the Lord: for all shall know me, from the least to the greatest" (Heb. 8:10–11, KJV; cf. Jer. 31:34). *The Living Bible* paraphrase puts it: "No one then will need to speak to his friend or neighbor or brother, saying 'You, too, should know the Lord,' because everyone, great and small, will know me already."

Unto you, unto us! The great fulfillment of the prophetic promises rings out at the beginning of the Gospels: "unto you is born this day . . . a Saviour, which is Christ the Lord" (Luke 2:11, KJV). Likewise the apostolic message of redemption resounds at Pentecost: "For the promise is unto you, and to your children, and to all that are afar off, even as many as the Lord our God shall call" (Acts 2:39, KJV). It is *for you* the Lord's body was given and his blood shed (Luke 22:19–20); "this is my body," said Jesus, "which is broken for you" (1 Cor. 11:24, KJV). He the Holy One who died "for all" (2 Cor. 5:14, KJV) is made "to be sin for us" (2 Cor. 5:21, KJV). He sacrificed himself "for our sins" (Gal. 1:4, KJV). The Son of God "loved me, and gave himself for me" (Gal. 2:20, KJV). He was "made a curse for us" (Gal. 3:13, KJV). Christ "suffered for us" (1 Pet. 2:21, KJV); Christ "laid down his life for us" (1 John 3:16, KJV); Christ "loved you and gave himself up on your behalf" (Eph. 5:2, NEB); in "tasting death he [stood] for us all" (Heb. 2:9, NEB). For the life of the world Jesus gave his own flesh (John 6:51), for the ungodly Christ died (Rom. 5:6), for us "while we were yet sinners" (Rom. 5:8, KJV); "Christ died for our sins" (1 Cor. 15:3, KJV); Christ Jesus "gave himself a ransom for all" (1 Tim. 2:6, KJV).

Even now this Christ who died and was raised "pleads our cause" (Rom. 8:34, NEB); for us the forerunner exercises his priestly ministry in heaven (Heb. 6:20). "He died for us so that . . . we might live in company with him" (1 Thess. 5:10, NEB); Christ has entered the heavenly sanctuary "to appear now before God on our behalf" (Heb. 9:24, NEB); he makes ongoing intercession for us (Heb. 7:25). How better can we summarize what God's initiative provides *for us* than to say with James, the Lord's brother: "Every good and perfect gift is from above, coming down from the Father" (James 1:17, NIV)? As John expressed it: "Behold, what manner of love the Father hath bestowed upon us, that we should be called the sons of God" (1 John 3:1, KJV). The force of the "what manner of" (*potapēn*) is not only "what great" love but also "from what country" (that is, from the heavenly realm: as John declares elsewhere, love is "of God," 1 John 4:7, KJV).

We are offered, as we said, a place in God's kingdom. God liberates us for faith in him. The Old Testament depicts Yahweh as the only King, the absolute sovereign. At the rise of the Hebrew monarchy, the institution of a human king was declared almost an offense to Yahweh; at best a human king could but be his representative (1 Sam. 8:7; 10:19; 12:19). "The Lord shall reign for ever and ever," sang the Hebrews (Exod. 15:18, KJV) after the Red Sea deliverance. Yahweh is "King over all the earth" (Ps. 47:2, KJV), "King of all the earth" (Ps. 47:7, KJV), King of "the people" (Ps. 47:9, KJV; cf. Jer. 10:7) as well as King of heaven (Dan. 4:34). God's distinctive title is the King, the Lord of Hosts, in Isaiah (6:3), Jeremiah (46:18; 48:15; 51:57) and Zechariah (14:16).

That the people of God yearn for God's kingdom-rule to prevail ever more fully and absolutely is a mark of Yahweh's redemptive work in the life of sinful mankind. The ancient Hebrews looked for the kingdom. As the biblical writers portray it, the great tragedy of Jewry is that while it was "born to the kingdom" it failed to receive the promised Messiah (Matt. 8:12). There was indeed a remnant, including Simeon who looked for the restoration of Israel (Luke 2:25), and Joseph of Arimathea who eagerly "waited for the kingdom of God" (Mark 15:43; Luke 23:51, KJV). But religious leaders "shut the door of the kingdom . . . in men's faces"; refusing to enter themselves, they sought also to prevent others from entering (Matt. 23:13, NEB) so that the faithless heirs were deprived of the kingdom's benefits (Matt. 21:43). This tragedy is not Jewry's exclusively, nor for that matter did all Jews refuse to believe (the disciples were Jews, as were the apostle Paul and a multitude of believers contemporary with Jesus and the apostles; even today the number of "fulfilled Jews" continues to multiply and they will be among the "many" who come from east and west to feast with Abraham, Isaac and Jacob in the kingdom of Heaven—Matt. 8:11). A vast multitude of Gentiles for whom the door to the kingdom swung open have also forfeited the opportunity to enter. Many heard the word of the kingdom and turned away (Matt. 13:19). Some halted "not far from the kingdom of God" (Mark 12:34, KJV).

The kingdom-theme as it relates to the person of Jesus Christ must be correlated with the Old Testament prophecies and the dawning of the age of fulfillment. It was the dawning of the promised kingdom that John the Baptist proclaimed when he identified Jesus as Messiah and declared "the good news of the kingdom of God" (Luke 4:43, NEB). The New Testament gathers into one the Old Testament references to the Savior-King coming at the end of the age, and those to the promised Son of Man or Messiah of the House of David, just as in the Old Testament the kingship of God moves to a universal world-historical significance from a particularistic Israelitish emphasis, so now Messiah's kingdom reaches beyond a climactic significance for only the Hebrews to one of worldwide scope.

From place to place Jesus proclaimed "the glad tidings of the kingdom" (Luke 8:1, KJV) and concerning that kingdom spoke to the gathering multitudes (Luke 9:11). His beatitudes not only point to the kingdom of God but emphasize its blessedness: "Blessed are ye if. . . ." Herein is life's incomparable joy, to submit to Christ Jesus' livening touch the vacuous simplest pursuits of life. "Theirs is the kingdom of heaven," said Jesus (Matt. 5:3, 10, RSV); "Yours is the kingdom of God" (Luke 6:20, RSV). To have even the least place in God's kingdom might seem good reason for gratitude, but in exalting those who will be "called great in the kingdom of heaven," Jesus disparages those whose entrance is but marginal (Matt. 5:19; 18:1–3). Those who do the Father's will are assured entrance (Matt. 7:21). The "righteous will shine as brightly as the sun in the kingdom" (Matt. 13:43, NEB) and "Happy the man who shall sit at the feast in the kingdom of God" (Luke 14:15, NEB).

The promised kingdom drew near (Matt. 11:12; Mark 1:15; Luke 10:9–11; 17:20; cf. 16:16) with the coming of Jesus in whom the Father had vested the kingdom (Luke 22:29). However much they misunderstood Messiah's role, the Palm Sunday throngs hailed the coming kingdom (Mark 11:10). Manifesting "the powers of the world to come" (Heb. 6:5, KJV), Jesus' presence and actions among men meant the presence here on earth of the kingdom. In him God's very being and activity and speech were revealed in the flesh. Jesus mirrors the new man who inherits God's kingdom. Here on Planet Earth, in the context of all historical sovereignties and even in face of Satan's bold hostility, God has indissolubly, irrevocably and invincibly entrenched the unshakable kingdom (Heb. 12:28) of holy love. By his victory over sin and sickness and his decisive resurrection triumph over Satan and death (Matt. 12:28; Luke 9:2; 11:20), the crucified Jesus identified the kingdom with his own person. The fact that the kingdom has come first in him to whom we owe absolute loyalty—our souls and bodies—will keep us from confusing the kingdom of God with human ideologies and will force us to keep central the issues of sin and redemption.

For forty days before his ascension, the risen Jesus taught his disciples "things pertaining to the kingdom of God" (Acts 1:3, KJV), news that the early Christians eagerly shared. The apostle Paul spoke "boldly and freely about the kingdom of God" (Acts 19:8, NEB) not only in the synagogue in Ephesus but also in Rome (Acts 28:23) where a number of Jewish Christians worked with him "for the kingdom of God" (Col. 4:11, NEB). When the Samaritans heard Philip the African proclaim the kingdom (Acts 8:12) its message penetrated beyond Jewry. Through the present rule of the risen Lord, the early Christians knew the kingdom of God to be more than merely a future expectation: "The kingdom of God [is] . . . righteousness and peace and joy in the Holy Spirit" (Rom. 14:17, RSV); it is "power" (1 Cor. 4:20, RSV). As Paul expressed it to the Colossians: God "rescued us from the domain of darkness and brought us away into the kingdom of his dear Son, in whom our release is secured and our sins forgiven" (Col. 1:13, NEB). Christ guards his own from evil and brings them safely into his heavenly kingdom (2 Tim. 4:18). The Christian goal now became "to live lives worthy of the God who calls you into his kingdom and glory" (1 Thess. 2:12, NEB), and under persecution to show oneself "worthy of the kingdom of God" (2 Thess. 1:5, NEB).

We are already in the kingdom; we share in eternal life, live on speaking terms with the Lord in whom we have our new life and who indwells us. We are quickened by the power of the Holy Spirit to do his will and enlisted in the historical expansion of the kingdom from heaven to earth. The rule of the King is therefore far more than just a hope of redeemed individuals. We must not ignore the present claims that the rule of God makes upon government and society, nor must we minimize the fact that God is everywhere present and active either in grace or in judgment, even if in modern times the worldwide mission of the church has often become confused with a social and political idealism that reduces the kingdom of God to extending democracy or free enterprise or socialism or brotherhood among unregenerate humanity and substitutes a present activist-promoted millennium for one inaugurated by the Messiah.

That supernatural revelation is for man's benefit contradicts the Marxist notion that faith in God is an opiate competing with man's deepest needs and concerns. It also disputes humanists who claim that belief in a transcendent God weakens man's indignation over injustice. It deflates radical secularists who claim that self-fulfillment and creative individuality are achieved through deliberately rejecting transcendent truth, divine commandments, and supernatural reality. All such atheistic emphases truncate human selfhood in theory and in practice. Their uncritical denial of the God of revelation perpetuates human alienation from life's fundamental relationships to God that are integral to authentic human existence, and provide no stable basis whatever for norms of truth and morality. God's revelation gives the lie to all these falsehoods; God calls these mythmongers to repentance and unveils a kingdom that cannot fade away. The Creator's self-revelation enforces the absolute distinction between righteousness and unrighteousness, unyieldingly demands truth and goodness in all human affairs, and supplies ultimate sanctions for man's ethical behavior. Where God is heard and obeyed in his revelation, the stunted self is restored to those larger moral and spiritual relationships for which man is divinely intended by creation, and enterprising revisionists are hindered from conforming ethical ideals to their own preferences.

Though "not of this world" (John 18:36, KJV) the kingdom of God exists not on some invisible and inaccessible planet; in significant respects it is already a historical reality even here on earth where the risen Lord is sovereign in a kingdom that exists alongside other kingdoms and interpenetrates and confronts them as an invincible reality. In this world, where every historical institution and activity must fall under the judgment of God, and where the church even at her best is but an approximation of the kingdom of God, only the grace of Christ can avail for any of us. For all that, the kingdom is nonetheless not without historical presence and power.

The kingdom of God is to be proclaimed worldwide by its earthly ambassadors before the closing determination of history and acclaimed by its heavenly hosts at the coming of Christ in power and glory (Matt. 24:14). At the institution of the Lord's Supper Jesus spoke of the coming fellowship with his disciples "in the kingdom of my Father" (Matt. 26: 29, NEB; Mark 14:25; Luke 22:16–18). He briefed his disciples on signs of the end-time that would foreshadow the approaching climax of God's kingdom (Matt. 24:30–34; Luke 21:31). Speaking of the glory of Christ in the future kingdom, the Book of Revelation anticipates the heavenly shout: "The sovereignty of the world has passed to our Lord and his Christ, and he shall reign for ever and ever" (Rev. 11:15, NEB), and again, "Now is come salvation, and strength, and the kingdom of our God, and the power of his Christ" (Rev. 12:10, KJV). Christ wields the sceptre of an eternal kingdom (Heb. 1:8). That kingdom of Christ is in no way secondary to or different from God's kingdom; from the very first it is simply "the kingdom of Christ and of God" (Eph. 5:5, KJV). Christ will reign until God has put all enemies, including death itself by the resurrection of all mankind, under his feet (1 Cor. 15:25–26). When Christ has conquered every alien domination, authority and power, he will deliver up the kingdom to the Father (1 Cor. 15:24).

All this signals the incomparable imperative that overarches human existence: "Seek ye first the kingdom of God, and his righteousness," for then all else will be added (Matt. 6:33, KJV; Luke 12:31). The kingdom of heaven, said Jesus, is like a treasure, like the finest of pearls, for the sake of which a discerning human joyfully forfeits everything else (Matt. 13:44–45). No one will regret in the slightest having prized the kingdom even above home and family (Luke 18:29–30). God proffers us a place in the kingdom above all other kingdoms as privileged participants. The rule of God—with its astonishing implications for the course of the world and the destiny of mankind—reaches to us as special objects of divine love and grace, inviting us no longer to resist God's sovereignty but rather to glory in it. We move daily nearer that day when human law will no longer dangle on the whim of tyrants or the will of a fickle majority or the compromises of political puppets, that day when the command of God and the righteousness of Christ will prevail in every sphere of life. Although now only partly disclosed, Jesus in his rule is himself the kingdom of God until at "the end of the days" he will reign as King of the world and of all worlds.

3.
Not by Good Tidings Alone

PRECISELY BECAUSE divine revelation is for man's benefit we dare not obscure its informational content nor mistake God's disclosure as automatically saving. Supplying sinful mankind with a lucid divine assessment of its woeful predicament, God's revelation informs us as well of God's gracious provision and indispensable condition for reversing that condition.

Simply hearing God's revealed good news, his dramatic offer of redemption, does not redeem us automatically. In William Temple's words, "No greater gift can be offered to men; yet many refuse it" (*Readings in John's Gospel*, p. 50). We are not redeemed by "good tidings" alone.

God's revealed truth of saving grace may be repressed by impenitent rebellion or received with alacrity by repentant trust. His gracious invitation to life fit for eternity must be personally accepted; without personal appropriation God's promise of rescue in and of itself saves no one. Neglect and unbelief must be confronted as fatal possibilities and personal faith recognized as absolutely indispensable to reconciliation.

To spurn God's mercy is a double indignity. Scripture testifies that the renegade human species even before it confronts the good news of redemptive rescue universally suppresses God's revelation given in conscience and in the external world (Rom. 1:19–23; 2:14–16). Of the ancient Gentile world Paul writes: "they are without excuse"; their rejection and neglect of God's openly published disclosure is divinely blameworthy: "What can be known about God is plain to them, because God has shown it to them" (Rom. 1:19, 20, RSV). Rejection of the promised Redeemer reveals yet another tragic indignity; as John puts it: "He came unto his own, and his own received him not" (John 1:11, KJV).

After stressing that the mediation of God's only Son stems from divine love for the world, John, the apostle of love, immediately emphasizes also that unbelief brings inescapable judgment or condemnation (John 3:16–18). The fact that these words occur during Jesus' conversation with the Hebrew rabbi Nicodemus makes them all the more awesome. Not only Jews, however, but also Gentiles are in view in this forewarning. "He that believeth not," writes John, "is condemned already, because he hath not believed in the name of the only begotten Son of God" (3:18, KJV). The unbeliever "is condemned already," remarked Cyril of Alexandria, "because his refusal of the offered way of salvation is a kind of advance vote against himself as deserving judgment" (cited by M. F. Wiles, *The Spiritual Gospel*, p. 80). Yet it is not simply the unbeliever who judges himself; divine judgment will at the last day forever seal the unbeliever's present self-determined end. John goes on to emphasize, moreover, that "he who does not obey the Son shall not see life, but the wrath of God rests upon him" (3:36, RSV). In other words, some effects of the final future judgment already now shadow the life of the unbeliever. The concept of divine wrath is, to be sure, offensive to many moderns, as are other divine truths; some find even the reality of God repugnant. But to delete the concept of divine wrath violates both the teaching of Scripture and the moral nature of the self-revealing God. As Leon Morris comments, "If a man continues in unbelief and disobedience he can look for nothing other than the persisting wrath of God" (*The Gospel According to John*, p. 250). The unbeliever's confidence in his own ingenuity and works condemns him. His refusal to appropriate divinely proffered salvation reveals his true character and motives. The absence of faith, as C. K. Barrett remarks, is the subjective side of condemnation (*The Gospel According to John*, p. 181). Jesus spoke of the consequences of unbelief in stark and awesome words: "There will be wailing and grinding of teeth . . . when you see Abraham, Isaac, and Jacob, and all the prophets, in the kingdom of God, and you yourselves thrown out" (Luke 13:28, NEB).

In expounding the implications of faith and unbelief, the New Testament focuses not simply on the eschatological end-time, but also on the present in which God's eschatological action is already anticipatively underway. The end-time realities of resurrection, judgment and eternal life are in some respects already dramatically present in expectation of a coming universal human destiny (John 3:18; 5:24–29; 6:54; 12:31). Jesus himself drives home the point: "Anyone who gives heed to what I say and puts his trust in him who sent me has hold of eternal life, and does not come up for judgement, but has already passed from death to life. In truth, in very truth I tell you, a time is coming, indeed it is already here, when the dead shall hear the voice of the Son of God, and all who hear shall come to life" (John 5:24–25, NEB). Believing sons of God, the apostle Paul emphasizes, already have an "earnest" or sample of their coming inheritance (Eph. 1:14, KJV). In the Gospels Jesus promised to be ongoingly present with the people of God before his final return in judgment (John 14:3, 18–20); in the Book of Acts and the Epistles he attests his personal invisible presence among believers from the Day of Pentecost and confirms the reality of a continuing living relationship between himself and the church. As sharers of a life that anticipates the eternal order, the children of God already now participate in eternal life. At the raising of Lazarus, Martha's thoughts are turned from the future resurrection to resurrection and life as somehow already present realities for those made alive by Christ (John 11:25–27). As W. H. Cadman notes, this "two-sided eschatology is not peculiar to St. John in the New Testament" but pervades also the Pauline writings; Paul's assurance that "there is . . . no condemnation to them that are in Christ Jesus" (Rom. 8:1, ASV) means that "for them the eschatological judgment is over" (*The Open Heaven*, p. 46).

That Jesus Christ who died for doomed sinners does not automatically bring salvation apart from personal decision and faith is incontrovertibly clear. The evangelist of love puts the fact both positively and negatively in order to reinforce the awesome truth: "he that believeth" has eternal life (John 1:12; 3:16; 20:31); "he that believeth not" is condemned even now while persisting in unbelief (3:18, KJV). The apostle Paul likewise leaves no doubt that mankind makes one of only two possible responses to the crucified Christ: "to those who are perishing" he is foolishness, but "to us who are being saved" he is the power of God (1 Cor. 1:18, RSV).

G. C. Berkouwer is biblically justified in rejecting Barth's notion that all human beings already share universally in the salvation brought by Jesus Christ and therefore need only to be informed of the fact. The New Testament links the *already*, not with salvation, but with the condemnation of unbelievers (John 3:18). While Messiah's substitutionary redemptive provision is indeed complete, it prevails only for those who appropriate it. Berkouwer emphasizes that Barth detracts from "the seriousness of the human decision which, according to the overwhelming testimony of Scripture, is associated with the kerugma that goes out to the world" (*The Triumph of Grace in the Theology of Karl Barth*, p. 290). This defect in Barth's theology follows from his notions that all humanity is elected in Jesus as the God-man, and that sin and unbelief are ontologically impossible. The result, at least implicitly, is universal redemption, however much Barth may resist that outcome. In his majestic vision of the totality of God's triumph, and in deference to the irresistible power of grace, Barth ignores the conditional elements of the biblical revelation. He turns the sure triumph of divine grace into an implicit universalism of redemption that obscures the context of faith and obscures the indispensability of personal decision in this life for the inheritance of salvation. For Barth, unbelief in no way nullifies God's decision. God's liberating work is done, and therefore no one can undo that work. Since salvation is an accomplished fact, human beings need only to "know" that all is well.

Emil Brunner protests this view. If Barth is correct, he says, then we can no longer speak as does the Bible of lost mankind, and we remove all possibility of final judgment and damnation. In this notion that "all, believers and unbelievers, are saved from the wrath of God and participate in redemption through Jesus Christ," writes Brunner, "Barth is in absolute opposition, not only to the whole ecclesiastical tradition, but— and this alone is the final objection to it—to the clear teaching of the New Testament" (*The Christian Doctrine of God*, pp. 348 f.). For Barth the "turning-point" from "being-lost" to "being-saved" does not exist, says Brunner, "since it is no longer possible to be lost" (p. 351). But the biblical gospel is rather "the summons to decision" (p. 353). In short, the New Testament invariably associates "no condemnation" with the requisite of personal faith.

Speak as he may of the "fatal danger" of unbelief, notes Berkouwer, Barth renders human decision insignificant in contrast to God's decision. "Barth calls unbelief 'fatally dangerous' but this now and then repeated expression is flanked by extensive reflections on the ontological impossibility of unbelief. . . . The decisive grace of God . . . is *so* decisive that the *inevitability* of faith *lies involved* in it" (*The Triumph of Grace*, pp. 269 f.). Berkouwer is surely right in maintaining that "the Bible speaks in a different manner about the 'dynamic' of unbelief." It leaves no room for thinking that "the human decision has already been taken, is given and is involved *in* the encounter with revelation" (p. 270). "The Bible constantly calls to faith and warns in the most serious terms against unbelief" (p. 268). "We hear about the proclaimed word which was heard but which was *not profitable*, because it was not accompanied by faith. . . . There was no *profit*, no *benefit*. . . . The New Testament speaks of belief and unbelief as a choice, a serious . . . a *decisive* choice" (p. 270).

In his parables (Luke 14:12–24) Jesus emphasized that while the poor and the lame and the blind respond with alacrity, the self-righteous and self-sufficient spurn Messiah's invitation. It was to Nicodemus, a rabbi and member of the Sanhedrin, that he emphasized the universal and absolute indispensability of the new birth. Throughout the Christian ages to people of all classes, races and nations his words have underscored the need for personal decision and trust: "Except a man be born again, he cannot see the kingdom of God" (John 3:3, KJV). Unrepentant sinners "will not inherit the kingdom of God" (1 Cor. 6:9–10, RSV; cf. Gal. 5:21; Eph. 5:5). Christ's exhortation to "Repent: for the kingdom of heaven is at hand" (Matt. 4:17, KJV) has no less urgency today than when he first uttered those words.

That God weighs the actions of men (1 Sam. 2:3) and judges them truly (Rom. 2:2) is a sobering biblical theme. Even if Scripture focuses mainly on God's love and on the proclamation of good news, it is filled with warnings about neglect and indifference to that love and forthrightly declares the terrors of divine punishment if sinners do not turn to God. It was not lack of compassion that prompted Jesus to speak more explicitly of the woes of hell (Matt. 5:22, 29; 10:28; 18:9; 23:15, 33, etc.)

than of the bliss of heaven; full appreciation of one requires clear knowledge of the other. Physical death brings to an end all delayed opportunity for repentance and redemption (Heb. 9:27) and involves an immediate separation of the righteous from the wicked (Luke 16:19–31; Acts 7:59; Phil. 1:23). Final judgment is given into the hands of God's Son Jesus Christ, who not only came for our salvation and died for our sins (John 3:16–19; 5:22, 27; 9:39), but who also, in human flesh, offered for our redemption a pure life and sacrificial death (Rom. 5:9–11; 1 Cor. 15: 1–4).

God invites personal appropriation of revelational information that he has given as a prior knowledge and personal commitment to himself and his purposes; instead of recognizing that fact, recent dialectical and existential religious theory erroneously views revelation as a bestowal of self-giving divine love. To be sure, revelation and salvation are complementary. But, as Bernard Ramm observes, Catholic and Protestant dogmatics have historically emphasized, in conformity with Scripture, that the two themes are to be distinguished and are not organically equated or joined (*Types of Apologetic Systems*, pp. 66–67). The modern anti-intellectual theory of revelation maintains that personal awareness of revelation is itself redemptive. God is said to communicate himself, not truths about himself, and personal human response which supposedly consummates God's initiative and constitutes it revelation is held to be salvific inasmuch as it involves the restoration of a broken relationship. This misunderstanding has no basis in the Bible.

The main motif of Judeo-Christian religion is not revelation in and of itself but reconciliation. As Carl E. Braaten notes, "neither the Bible, nor the Reformation, nor the broad stream of Catholic tradition" exalted the concept of revelation to theology's dominant concern in a manner that implies "that man's essential predicament is his lack of knowledge." They insisted rather that "man's *guilt* is the problem" and "not revelation but *reconciliation* . . . the theological centrum" (*History and Hermeneutics*, p. 16). In contrast to historic Christian theology, modern philosophy has so isolated and elevated to priority the problem of religious knowledge that it substitutes the problem of ignorance for the problem of guilt. We would therefore insist, with Braaten, that "no doubt theology will have to take seriously the modern question of religious *knowledge*, but it should not assume that because this is *the* twentieth century question, it is necessarily the profoundest one, nor the one that correlates best with the heart of the biblical message" (ibid.).

Over against rationalistic philosophy, preoccupied with knowledge of God as a theoretical problem but disinterested in reconciliation between a holy God and sinful man, fresh emphasis was no doubt needed on the special orientation of God's revelation to human redemption. As Edward John Carnell pointed out, secular philosophy "has never been able to formulate an approach to God which appeals to the man on the street, for the God of the philosophers is postulated to account for about everything except unrest and guilt in his heart" (*The Philosophy of the Christian Religion*, p. 275). In view of the centrality the Bible gives to God's love for mankind, Reformed theologians called it a "document of God's grace," for the purpose of God's special revelation is to redeem otherwise doomed sinners. Insofar as he has only this special divine disclosure in view, Clark Pinnock is right in saying that revelation is "soteric in its intent" and defines revelation as "a gracious divine activity, a free and voluntary gift which has as its end the salvation of sinners" (*Biblical Revelation*, pp. 19, 20).

But Braaten sees in the recent enlargement of revelation into redemption a reflection of the modern speculative tendency to replace the problem of guilt by the problem of ignorance. To define revelation as intrinsically redemptive is to eclipse one extreme view by still another.

Barth espoused the organic union of revelation and salvation by contending that unless it is saving, revelation is not revelation. For Barth God's revelation is inherently redemptive; in other words, he equates revelation and reconciliation (*Church Dogmatics*, I/1, p. 468). Consequently no one can hold God's revelation in unbelief, no one enlightened by revelation can be lost; the world of unbelief must be viewed, therefore, as totally devoid of the light of revelation. "Revelation consists for the recipients of it in the fact that they . . . are sons of God" (I/1, p. 524). Hearing God's Word here involves merely a belated awareness that one is already redeemed, and not the news that salvation is conditionally suspended upon personal decision and trust as the occasion on which God's wrath and judgment are met and canceled through Jesus Christ's mediatorial life and work.

Paul Tillich similarly affirms, erroneously, that "the history of revelation and the history of salvation are the same history" (*Systematic Theology*, 1:144). Thomas F. Torrance likewise perpetuates the fallacy that revelation is salvific. We cannot know theological truth, he writes, "without being drawn into its redeeming and reconciling activity, without being renewed and re-ordered in accord with its saving will. . . . We cannot truly know God without being reconciled and renewed in Jesus Christ" (*Theological Science*, p. 41). Jesus Christ "does not communicate truths apart from [communicating] Himself" (p. 147). Here revelation is expanded into the experience of salvation.

But knowledge of the truth of God is by no means synonymous with personal salvation. Gordon H. Clark reminds us that according to the Epistle of James, "the demons believe" that there is one God (James 2:19, RSV)—a truth (monotheism) that they could not possess apart from revelation, and yet truth about God that they surely hold apart from redeeming grace; indeed, they tremble also in expectation of future torment which they know to be in prospect. If believing in demons is for some skeptics even more incredible than demons believing any theological truth, then let it be said that on the testimony of the Scriptures unredeemed (or unbelieving) human beings also know some truths about

God that are divinely revealed. When Barth says that we can know the revealed truth of God only when we obey it (*Church Dogmatics*, I/1, p. 311) and that if we are disobedient the truth of revelation "teaches us nothing" and "does not as dogma exist for us," he forfeits both biblical fidelity and a rational view of religious knowledge.

The Bible teaches as a truth of revelation that unrepentant sinners have enough knowledge of God to render them culpable, and it adduces numerous specific examples of that fact. One illustration is Cain who, despite his disobedience, knew that the sacrifices he offered were unacceptable to God and that capital punishment was a divinely approved penalty for his murder of Abel (Gen. 4:3–15). Another is Daniel, who warned Belshazzar about his disregard of knowledge of the Most High (Dan. 5:22). Jesus during his earthly ministry frequently condemned the Pharisees for defying scriptural revelation (John 5:45–46). The future judgment will doubtless surface innumerable examples of ignored revelation in our own time.

The biblical testimony of the self-revealed God provides no encouragement, however, for invariably associating revelation and redemption with no reference to judgment as a possible consequence of man's confrontation by the revelation of God. That God reveals himself for human benefit does not mean that all mankind benefits savingly from that revelation. That God in revelation offers reconciliation to all who personally receive his gracious offer in obedient trust does not mean that one shares God's grace by simply hearing of the revelation of the prospect of redemption. The nature of divine revelation is speculatively altered when revelation is redefined to mean God's saving action in behalf of mankind and no more. God's revelation does not bring to salvation all who comprehend it. Without personal appropriation God's revelation brings salvation to no one. The immediate correlate of divine revelation is not salvation but knowledge; the consequence of that knowledge is either salvation or judgment. The human response to God's disclosure is either acceptance or rejection, faith or unbelief.

Yet the entrance of God's light looks far beyond mere conveyance of astonishing information to redemptive enlistment of the whole person. To be sure, the Bible does not empty the reality of spiritual life simply into a relationship of trust, but insists also on the indispensability of spiritual knowledge that correlates life with light and with obedience. But the Bible resounds as well with a divinely initiated plea for and requirement of personal reconciliation. John's Gospel was written not simply to convey reliable information about Jesus of Nazareth and God's proffer of redemption. Amid the human predicament, enabling readers to know "that Jesus is the Christ, the Son of God," it was written also that "believing ye might have life in his name" (20:31, ASV; cf. 5:25; 11:25; 14:6). By addressing the human mind and confronting the human will, God's revelation requires a decision that encompasses the whole self. It calls us to inner repentance, to a reversal of life-style, to redemptive renewal and to obedient fellowship. The truth of God, as the New Testament indicates, is not simply to be known, but is also to be done (John 3:19). No one is ever saved from catastrophe by news alone. If we "clinch God's choice and calling" of us, as Peter says, we have by God's grace "full and free admission into the eternal kingdom of our Lord and Saviour Jesus Christ" (2 Pet. 1:10–11, NEB). Salvation is conditioned upon personally accepting and appropriating the truth of revelation.

The comprehension of revelation must therefore not be confused with the appropriation of salvation. While salvation forms the main theme of the special revelation of God, salvation is not the one and only theme of divine revelation. Knowledge of God's revelation invites punishment for rejecting its light and opportunity as surely as it points the way to redemptive rescue on condition of repentance and obedience. The Psalmist writes: "My people did not listen to my voice; Israel would have none of me. So I gave them over to their stubborn hearts, to follow their own counsels" (Ps. 81:11, RSV). The weight of the biblical witness is that man stands condemned not simply for ignorance of the true and living God, but especially because of his revolt against the light of revelation. The writer of Hebrews warns: "If the word spoken through angels had such force that any transgression or disobedience met with due retribution, what escape can there be for us if we ignore a deliverance so great?" (Heb. 2:2–3, NEB). In other words, what hope is there if we ignore the revelation given in Jesus Christ himself who crowns the earlier revelation of God? Salvation divinely disclosed can be forfeited precisely because unbelief can resist and neglect revelation that carries the offer of redemption. To emphasize the gravity of neglect, and the inevitability of judgment for such heightened culpability, the Epistle to the Hebrews rivets attention on the deliverance "announced through the lips of the Lord himself" (2:4, NEB), confirmed by the apostles and authenticated by miraculous signs. Those to whom the glorious news of deliverance comes can by choice or default spurn the very salvation accomplished by Jesus Christ himself. If, on the other hand, revelation were salvific, then the very possibility of such rejection of God's disclosure and of consequent punishment for human culpability would be precluded.

God's revelation is given for human benefit. But even in the twentieth century multitudes of human beings can and do know and hold down the truth of God in unbelief and rebellion. The witness of the Bible is that our sinful race swaggers in revolt against the light of revelation, turns aside from God's Word and is therefore doomed to divine judgment. For all that, God still proffers a gracious last-days message of rescue, offering man as the alternative to endless doom a place of fellowship in the kingdom of God. One of the most sobering doctrines of Scripture is that even as life on earth can carry expectations of a blessed destiny through the present possession of eternal life, so too it can contain anticipations of eternal judgment: the time comes when God gives the inordinately wicked up to a reprobate mind (Rom. 1:28). Equally sobering, and more gratifying, is the fact that the day of grace and opportunity for decision remains with us for yet another day. Both heartening and ominous is the message of John's Gospel that the Light *is shining* (ongoingly) in the darkness, and not even the direst darkness has been able to *extinguish it* (John 1:5).

THESIS THREE:
Divine revelation does not completely erase
God's transcendent mystery, inasmuch as God the Revealer
transcends his own revelation.

4.
The Hidden and
Revealed God

WHAT GOD WITHHOLDS about himself and his ways is beyond our knowing. "His understanding is inscrutable" (Isa. 40:28, NAS); no one can presume to comprehend his ways unaided (Isa. 40:13). "The secret things belong unto Jehovah our God; but the things that are revealed belong unto us and to our children for ever" (Deut. 29:29, ASV). Our knowledge of God's nature and purposes is limited by his disclosure; not a morsel of information can be confidently asserted about God and his will beyond what he has chosen to reveal.

Judeo-Christian religion insists that God's revelation does not totally exhaust his being and activity; even in his revelation he is the free sovereign God. Yahweh's voluntary self-disclosure does not wholly cancel his incomprehensibility nor eliminate all mystery. Scripture does not deplete all possible revelation; even on the basis of biblical revelation our knowledge of God is an incomplete knowledge. There is more to God's perfections and plans than we now know. Not until God's final eschatological disclosure to the redeemed in glory shall we "know even as [we] are known" (1 Cor. 13:12, KJV). Not until God's final unveiling at the end of the age will we see "face to face" (1 Cor. 13:12, KJV; cf. 1 John 3:2). "Many things are very obscure to us at present," John Calvin remarks, "and will continue to be so" until the life to come (*Institutes of the Christian Religion*, III, 2, 3). Hence even the apostle Paul writes: "My knowledge now is partial; then it will be whole, like God's knowledge of me" (1 Cor. 13:12, NEB).

The God of the Bible differs notably therefore from the pantheistic Absolute projected by speculative idealism. Pantheism considers the universe—man and nature—to be an exhaustive manifestation of the divine; it considers the space-time world the externalized Absolute.

47

Destruction of the universe would therefore mean the death of God. But the living God of revelation attested in the Bible is not imprisoned either by his majesty or by his revelation. While God is revealed in his creation, he nonetheless ontologically transcends the universe as its Creator, and transcends man epistemologically as well. His disclosure in its entirety is a free and voluntary manifestation suspended upon his transcendent will.

This fact of God's control of his revelation points up a decisive difference between biblical prophecy and so-called Greek prophecy. Both the Greek view and the Hebrew view stress the necessity for a prophet's unconditional dependence on the Divine. But the Hebrew-Christian view excludes any and every possibility of human divinization. Although the biblical prophet is distinguished from those he addresses as one to whom and through whom revelation comes, he is never permanently qualified as a personal center of revelation. In the Bible the divinely chosen prophets are never assimilated to revelation in a manner that destroys the objective reality of the Divine in distinction from the human. Revelation in the Bible is the unveiling of what was hidden and inaccessible but is now made manifest by God's initiative and act. As Walther Eichrodt remarks, in biblical prophecy "even the man of God can only have a share in miraculous powers and superhuman knowledge because of the entry into himself of the wondrous living materia over which Yahweh alone has ultimate control" (*Theology of the Old Testament*, 1:319).

No a priori reasons can be adduced for "expecting" a divine revelation. When the Baptist theologian A. H. Strong cited "reasons a priori for expecting a revelation from God" (*Systematic Theology*, 1:111), and concluded that while the facts do not justify "that larger degree of expectation which we call assurance" they do "warrant that degree of expectation which we call hope" (1:113), he read the human situation too much in the light of historical actualities. Strong shifts the human expectation of divine revelation to subjective considerations when he finds in the circumstance that man's intellectual and moral nature would otherwise not be preserved from deterioration an a priori basis for expecting a divine disclosure. H. C. Thiessen similarly makes divine revelation likely in advance: "Man being what he is and God being what He is, we may possibly expect a revelation from God and also an embodiment of such parts of that revelation as are needed to supply a reliable and infallible source of theological truth" (*Lectures in Systematic Theology*, p. 81). But on what other basis than previous divine revelation can we justify confident knowledge about "God being what He is"? Thiessen grants that "this argument does not take us beyond the point of possibility, or, at the most, of probability. . . . But even so, the argument has some value as inspiring hope that God will provide for the profoundest needs of man" (pp. 81 f.). But the argument supports neither probability nor possibility, unless on the basis of revelation we are already privileged to make certain affirmations about God. Certainly no information about him can be provided independently of his self-revelation.

Such prospects of a revelational inheritance always presuppose considerable advance knowledge of the divine benefactor. From whence, in the absence of revelation itself, are we to derive private information about God's predilections? Surely human ingenuity supplies no creaturely capacity for charting God's intentions, let alone ghost-writing his speeches or sending an advance guard to supervise his activities. However insightfully modern he or she may be, no theologian carries a reliable divinity compass among his or her possessions or is expert at prognosticating divine revelation. God is himself the Ultimate Benefactor of revelation. (Cf. Job 41:11, "Who has given a gift to him?"—that God needs to repay.) Divine revelation creates an unprecedented situation in human affairs. It does not operate on flight schedules charted by travel agents who traffic in domestic routines; rather, God's disclosure overtakes its unsuspecting recipients unannounced like some low-swooping jet that on its way to the landing strip roars over a startled motorist below. Revelation is God's free disclosure in deed and word and time, a voluntary divine determination.

In other relationships of life, man stands superior to the object of his study and is largely free to determine the time and circumstances of his inquiry. In the space-time world he is nature's capstone; among the creatures of earth he reigns supreme. In respect to God, however, man is always fully dependent upon God's purposes and subject to the reality of God's revelation.

If we take seriously the prima facie data of biblical prophets who set forth their own deep self-understanding of divine disclosure, there can be no doubt that these spokesmen deny that the message they convey is of their own making. We are left with a choice between dismissing them as self-deceived psychotics who were victims of auditory or visual hallucinations, or men for whom transcendent divine revelation was a striking reality. Any attempt to reduce the content of their message to a studied exposition of their own religious convictions is excluded by the testimony they bear. Abraham J. Heschel remarks: "The consciousness of the prophets that they were inspired by God is the foundation of their vocation. The very right to engage in prophetic activity, the claim of authority for their words, begins with the fact of being-given-ness. . . . They are not bringing to the people the formulation of their own consciousness . . . but that which has been given. The vigorous and emphatic certainty that their messages are not inventions . . . but communications . . . as well as their condemnation of the deceit and error of the false prophets . . . constrains us to regard the form of their proclamation—'God has spoken to me'—as unequivocal explanation of the source of that which is given to them" (*Die Prophetie*, p. 7, quoted by Lou H. Silberman, "Revelation in Judaism").

In the Bible the true prophet wrestles with and even struggles against God's revelation and call almost like a draft-resister. This inner resistance to a divine commission is so characteristic of central biblical personages —Moses, Isaiah, Jeremiah, Jonah and Saul of Tarsus among them—as to be virtually a hallmark of the true prophet. The false prophets, as Barth notes, were by contrast "proclaimers of a self-grasped revelation which for that very reason is not revelation at all" (*Church Dogmatics*, I/1, p. 380). The false prophet boasts a sense of familiarity with the divine, acts as if he has free control over his spiritual gifts, and regards himself as an autonomous bearer of God's Spirit (cf. 1 Kings 22:24; Isa. 28:9; Jer. 23:21–22, 30–32). But the true prophet waits in dependence upon the spirit of revelation, and frequently lacks an immediate answer (1 Sam. 28:6, 15–16; Jer. 42:4, 7). Even the early Elijah stories contain no intimation that the living God "is in any way at the prophet's beck and call" (Eichrodt, *Theology of the Old Testament*, p. 319). While the pagan priests of Baal try to "call up" their god as if linked to some dial-a-manifestation answering service (1 Kings 18:26–29), Elijah beseeches God on a notably different basis: "Lord God of Abraham, Isaac, and of Israel, let it be known this day that thou art God in Israel, and that I am thy servant, and that I have done all these things at thy word. Hear me, O Lord, hear me, that this people may know that thou art the Lord God" (1 Kings 18:36–37, KJV). Much of the force of the narrative is lost unless the reader realizes that in answering Elijah by fire Yahweh appropriated to himself the means which the pagan priests had specially associated with Baal.

Revelation has both its basis and its limits in the will of God and in his own preferred means of mediating his Word. Human beings universally have no native resourcefulness for delineating God's nature and will. Not even gifted persons of special capacity or notable religious endowment can by their own abilities divine the secrets of the Infinite. Not even regenerate Christians—be they award-winning clergymen, influential ecumenists, prominent evangelists or eminent theologians— however sanctified they may be, are spiritually endowed with any private organ or internal channel whereby they on their own power and initiative may clarify the mysteries of eternity. Karl Barth rightly adds even a further restriction: even if by an appeal to one's religious consciousness or some other human norm one should arrive at statements about God compatible with the Bible, we ought not to be misled into the notion that the Christian faith has been served because God conforms to "our well-founded convictions" (*Church Dogmatics*, I/2, p. 4). When the apostle Paul declares that "we have the mind of Christ" (1 Cor. 2:16, RSV) and exhorts believers to "let this mind be in you, which was also in Christ Jesus" (Phil. 2:5, KJV), he does not in either case have in view an absolute merging of personalities in a pantheistic mold or even the identical mental facilities that Jesus Christ employed. In the former case he means the ability to judge a situation as God would, in view of the revelation

God has given of his nature and will in Christ Jesus and in view of the truths God has disclosed to the apostles and in which the Spirit illumines believers. In the other case he means the inward bearing and disposition exemplified by Jesus Christ.

God who makes himself known in sovereign freedom in manifestations of his own choosing specially reveals to some what has been hidden from all, and plainly and universally discloses to all what nullifies every last human being's excuse that he or she lacks any spiritual knowledge. The life and destiny of the worldly wise who disdain God's comprehensive revelation contrast markedly with that of the humble novices who become eager recipients of the truth of God. This contrast is graphically evident in Jesus' declaration to the Father: "I thank thee, Father, Lord of heaven and earth, that thou hast hidden these things from the wise and understanding and revealed them to babes; yea, Father, for such was thy gracious will" (Matt. 11:25–26, RSV); this contrast reappears in Paul's letter to the Corinthians where he distinguishes those who cherish the ultimacy of human wisdom from those who receive the revelational wisdom that proceeds from the Spirit of God (1 Cor. 1:26).

These distinctions set the biblical view in sharp opposition also to modern pantheistic and mystical theories of revelation that merge man's reason into an immanent divine Mind. In the biblical meaning the Divine is in and of itself inaccessible to human initiative and the term revelation is not construed as virtually a synonym for human insight and discovery. The Bible does not speak of God's relation to the universe as First Cause, or in terms of uniformly interconnected causal relations; far less does it do so in terms of nature and man as God externalized. The scriptural category is divine locution. Creation is an achievement of God who speaks and by his Word calls into being what was not, and by his Word ongoingly preserves man and the world, and reveals himself to it and in it. Speech is not bound by causal continuity but is personal, free and purposive. In the form of the sovereign Word of God, speech establishes the continuities of the created cosmos without impeding God's liberty as the source and support of all things. Man cannot manipulate God's voice. He is no bigger-than-I puppet upon whom I can project my own thoughts and imaginations as the hidden underside of divine disclosure.

Our word *enthusiasm* comes from the Greek *enthusiasmos* which designates a state of having an inner god, or being inspired by an immanently resident divinity. For this reason Christian scholars have at various times in church history applied the term to those who do not confine special revelation to the biblical prophets and apostles but claim themselves to stand in a special relation to the Holy Spirit. During the Reformation it was used of Schwenkfeldians and certain Anabaptists who claimed divine inspiration apart from the Scriptures. The Swedenborgians are their twentieth-century cousins in this respect. Spiritualism claims to give access to the supernatural through modern mediums.

Some Quakers who appeal to an inner light and certain charismatic groups who invoke ongoing spiritual revelation approach the same error. Seventh-Day Adventists consider Ellen G. White an inspired and inerrant prophet.

Their complete dependence upon God in his divine revelation makes it obvious that revelation does not dignify inspired prophets or apostles with divine status. The prophet or apostle is not a manipulator of divine powers but simply a divinely chosen spokesman moved and possessed by the Holy Spirit (2 Pet. 1:21). Man does not need to become God in order to know God; he does not need to be omniscient in order to have authentic knowledge of the Divine. We do not know as God knows. Revelation does not enable us to see everything *sub specie aeternitatae*. We are human beings, not usurping divinities. Only Jesus of Nazareth carries the fullness of the Godhead bodily, and even he in view of his redemptive covenant with the Father was unaware of the final day which remained in the Father's control ("of that day or that hour knoweth no man, not even the angels in heaven, neither the Son, but the Father," Mark 13:32, ASV). No sadder passage occurs in the Old Testament than Adam's snatching at divinity by assuming himself to be competent for defining right and wrong and for carving out his future independent of the Word of God (Gen. 3:1–7).

Humility is therefore as becoming to the Christian theologian whose affirmations are governed by prophetic-apostolic revelation, as to the secular scientist whose explanations are answerable to external phenomena. The theologian may properly remind the scientist that man-made explanations are not universal descriptions that provide an exhaustive reading of reality; the scientist meanwhile may properly remind the theologian that God's divine revelation does not bestow human omniscience. "Theology does not occupy the place of the transcendent mind of God," writes Dorothy Emmet. The reminder is appropriate even for us who are convinced that fidelity to prophetic-apostolic revelation makes revelation more than simply, in her words, "the interpretation by men of their faith in the impingement of divine activity upon them" (*The Nature of Metaphysical Thinking*, p. 154). Because of their confidence in rational revelation and revealed truths, however, evangelical theologians are prone to consider their systematizations and schematizations of those truths as trustworthy as the Scriptures. But Calvin and Luther and Hodge and Strong surely would not disagree as they do, sometimes on rather important issues, were they infallible expositors of the theology of revelation. The inspired Scriptures remain unique and normative over against even the most devout evangelical expositions of the revealed Word of God. If Calvinistic or any other theology is laudable, it is so for a considerably higher reason than that a particular theologian said what he did—a point on which, to their credit, the Reformers repeatedly insisted. A theology is only laudable for its conformity to the written Word of God.

In early church history, Chalcedonian christology had emphasized that the divine and human natures of Christ are inconvertible. It should have surprised no one that later pantheistic exponents of an essential affinity between God and man not only asserted the latent divinity of man but also assailed the Chalcedonian formulation of Christ's two natures. Over against the loss of divine transcendence in modernist theology at the turn of the century, Protestant neoorthodoxy reaffirmed God's supernatural and superhuman reality but did so in a quite nonbiblical way. Barth's *Commentary on Romans* sounded an equally extreme reaction to exaggerated transcendence, that is, "God . . . standing over in infinite qualitative difference to man." The consequences of Barth's position are devastating to an authentically biblical view of divine revelation. Barth properly opposed those who obliterated a qualitative distinction between God and mankind by narrowing the differences only to a matter of degree, that is, quantitatively. At the same time, he erred in expounding God's epistemological transcendence to mean that divine activity in the universe is hidden, that God is not revealed in nature and history, nor even conceptually to the mind of man. This supposed veiling of God he ascribed not only to the masking of divine revelation by human rebellion and apostasy, but also to the wholly conjectural notion—implicit in his exaggerated doctrine of divine transcendence—that the finite cannot know the infinite, that nature and history cannot manifest what is beyond the relative, and that human thought cannot comprehend or convey divine revelation. Barth denies an objective revelation not only in nature but also in Scripture, arguing that the Bible is the Word incognito, and that the hidden divine Word is only indirectly revealed through human words. But against such unbiblical docetism we must emphasize that the purpose of divine revelation is never to remain incognito.

The term *mystery* as used in the New Testament does indeed carry connotations of awe and wonder, but its context is that of imminent disclosure. "Lo!" writes Paul, "I tell you a mystery" (1 Cor. 15:51, RSV). The Christian faith does more than simply evoke astonishment and surprise; it provides a corpus of revealed truths to be accepted with a clear conscience (cf. 1 Tim. 3:9, KJV, "Holding the mystery of the faith in a pure conscience"). In a secular society in which Bethlehem is more likely to suggest Bethlehem Steel than Bethlehem of Judea, it is imperative that the mystery of God be coordinated neither with the unsure frontiers of modern technology nor with the intertestamental Hebrew tetragrammaton (YHWH) that inexcusably forfeited the name of God out of radical reverence. The God disclosed in Christ can control the power and reverse the powerlessness even of a scientific age. His revealed Word declares truth about man and the world that we seem least ready to hear and most to need.

In the controversy waged in the 1940s in the Orthodox Presbyterian Church, Cornelius Van Til argued for a qualitative difference between God's knowledge and man's. Intending to preserve the incomprehensibility of God, he held that human knowledge is at best analogical of divine knowledge and does not at any point coincide with God's knowledge. This view, said Gordon Clark, leads to skepticism. If there is no point of identity in what God and man know, Clark insisted, then man has no truth about God ("The Bible as Truth," pp. 163 ff.). "If no proposition means to man what it means to God, so that God's knowledge and man's knowledge do not coincide at any single point, it follows by rigorous necessity that man can have no truth at all. This conclusion," Clark emphasized, "is quite opposite to the views of Calvin (*Institutes* II, ii, 12–15) and undermines all Christianity" ("Apologetics," p. 159). In other words, if truth is not the same for God and man then it is humanly impossible for man to possess truth about God.

The fact that we now know only "in part," however, does not destroy the validity and trustworthiness of that portion of knowledge we have through divine disclosure. That God does not reveal himself to man exhaustively does not mean that he does not reveal himself truly. To say that man cannot fathom fully all the depths of God's being is not to assert divine unknowability.

It is impossible therefore to erect either God's revealedness or his hiddenness into a speculative principle that expounds God's nature and ways either rationalistically or agnostically. The hiddenness of God is not a premise to which a biblical theologian may appeal in order to relativize revelation. Man "lives and moves and has his being" in God from the beginning of his life. The Bible begins with the self-revealing God. Only on the basis of God's own disclosure, in fact, can we affirm God's transcendence even of his revelation. There is no support for the hiddenness of God in the familiar passage, "For as the heavens are higher than the earth, so are my ways higher than your ways and my thoughts than your thoughts" (Isa. 55:9, RSV), inasmuch as in context this passage appeals for receiving and appropriating God's truth.

At the same time, the emphasis permeates Scripture that man overcomes God's mystery only to the extent that God chooses to reveal himself. "Behold, God is great, and we know him not, neither can the number of his years be searched out" (Job 36:26, KJV). "Such knowledge is too wonderful for me; it is high, I cannot attain unto it" (Ps. 139:6, KJV). We know God's hiddenness only through his revealedness; apart from his revelation no basis would exist for speaking of God as hidden, or for speaking of God at all. There might be a hidden *possibility* of God, perhaps, but certainly not a hidden *God*, not a God who transcends his revelation. God's hiddenness is the obverse side of his free sovereign self-disclosure; revelation is the presence and activity of the hidden One in an unveiling.[1] To Calvin "the presupposition of man's knowledge of God is

---

1. In expounding God's hiddenness, Barth cites Jeremiah 23:23, taking its sense as "Am I a God who is near . . . and not (also) a God far off?" But in view of the context (v. 24, "The heavens and the earth—do I not fill them?") the sense of the passage is more likely that "God is no small local deity from whom one might conceivably hide, but a God who is in heaven and therefore sees all" (John Bright, ed., *Jeremiah*,

the self-revelation of God; and the presupposition of the self-revelation of God is His incomprehensibility" (T. H. L. Parker, *Calvin's Doctrine of the Knowledge of God*, p. 12).

The present incompleteness of man's revelationally given knowledge, therefore, must not be used to support theories of divine incognito or of God's hiddenness beyond all conceptual knowability. For biblical theology the incomprehensibility of God gains its meaning from within the knowability of God, and not on the premise of his supposed unknowability. Biblical theology rules out all characterizations of God as "the unspeakable depth"; such theories of God do not support theism but lead to atheism. No less objectionable is the Thomist theory that on the basis of natural theology man can say *that* God is, but not *what* God is. The *that*ness of a we-know-not-what has nothing in common with the God of revelation. Thomism promotes an artificial disjunction between essence and existence. In a theology of revelation, the existence of God known in his disclosure belongs to his essence. What can be said of God-in-himself, if we are privileged to say anything at all, can be confidently said only on the basis of his self-revelation.

Nor do the revelational limits of our knowledge of God encourage the theory fostered by modern existential prejudices that revelation is paradoxical and cannot be rationally formulated. A "concealed revelation" does violence to the biblical idea of revelation. Contrary to scriptural representations, such a concept makes divine revelation ambiguous and beclouds and veils God's disclosure. We are not bequeathed a revelation as enigmatic as Mona Lisa's smile. Neither the prophets, the apostles, nor Jesus of Nazareth espouse any kind of "paradoxical revelation." Jesus taught in parables, but in no sense did he venture to communicate paradox.

William Hordern connects the idea of God's hiddenness—mistakenly, we think—with the fact that God's revelation can be misunderstood: "the 'hiddenness' of revelation means that it is always possible" to interpret the concrete events in which God reveals himself "as other than a Word from God. The history of Israel may be interpreted as 'Saving history' or as simply a part of ancient history. Jesus Christ may be seen as the Son of God or as a man who is judged to be either great or mad. The Church may be interpreted as the Body of Christ or as another sociological institution. The Bible may be seen as God's revelation or as an interesting ancient book of history, morals and religion" (*Speaking of God*, p. 123). It is painfully true, of course, that this possibility of divergent and mistaken interpretations exists. But its causes lie not as Hordern thinks in the ambiguity of divine revelation but rather in a deficient human regard for scriptural disclosure. Not each and every interpretation can be wel-

---

p. 154), or better yet, that God is a universal rather than parochial god ("Am I a God of near-at-hand . . . and not a God of far-away?" cf. Sheldon H. Blank, *Jeremiah: Man and Prophet*, pp. 170–71, 230).

comed as definitive. Significance is not finally reducible to one's preferred perspective or faith-stance. Man's difficulty with the revelation of the living God is due not to revelation's unintelligibility but to man's obduracy. "If I have told you earthly things, and ye believe not, how shall ye believe, if I tell you of heavenly things?" Jesus asked (John 3:13, KJV). While the apostle Peter acknowledges that the Pauline letters contain "some obscure passages," he adds that "the ignorant and unstable misinterpret" these "to their own ruin, as they do the other Scriptures" (2 Pet. 3:16, NEB). The factors that bear upon human comprehension of the Word of God will be discussed later. Suffice it to say at this point that interpretation and appropriation of revelation are not frustrated by any ambiguity in God's disclosure.

Alan Richardson is another who so intrudes the notion of mystery upon revelation that he clouds the intelligible content of divine disclosure. Richardson writes, for example, that "all forms of revelation are necessarily veilings of the truth and are signs of the infinite condescension of God, who accommodates his divine majesty to the capacity of our human weakness" (*An Introduction to the Theology of the New Testament*, p. 61). That God accommodates himself to man's ways of comprehension is not in question. But that "all forms of revelation are necessarily veilings of the truth" is a highly debatable premise, and one that contradicts Paul's view of *mustērion*, namely, the making known of what was previously hidden. It makes no sense therefore to speak of the God beyond theology or of the God nobody knows, of an absent divinity for whose presence we wait as for Godot, of God who is experienced yet inconceivable, of deity found as by hurling a rope toward some unsure rock while attempting to scale a mountain, an unknowable X to whom or which our minds and hearts must be ongoingly open. One writer has contorted logic to the extent of delineating "the absent God whose presence is felt in his absence," and in recent years a prominent clergyman addressed a seminary graduating class on the God who is speaking in the presence of his absence!

In summary, God transcends his own revelation. We do not have exhaustive knowledge of the self-revealing God, but what we do know about divine things is determined by his disclosure. "It is not for you to know the times or the seasons, which the Father hath put in his own power" (Acts 1:7, KJV). The biblical prophets and apostles did not carry divine revelation on their persons like some gnosis concealed in their loin cloths or folded into their tunics. They were wholly dependent upon God's sovereign disclosure for their knowledge of divine things. Though they were chosen mediators of a Word of God, their knowledge of supernatural realities was only partial. But this partial knowledge was nonetheless revelation and as such an authentic knowledge that cannot be undone, and that will be incorporated into the final eschatological revelation.

In expounding the perfections of his pantheistic God (Nature), the seventeenth-century philosopher Spinoza contended that deity has an infinity of attributes of which, however, we know only two (thought and extension). Were that the case, then surely what little we know of the Divine might readily be subverted by the much that we do not know. But, as Scripture makes clear, the God of self-revelation makes himself known reliably and adequately for man's present well-being and eternal felicity. We have that assurance on his Word. In view of God's intelligible self-revelation and on the authority of the inspired Scriptures, the Westminster Shorter Catechism does not hesitate to define God as "Spirit, infinite, eternal and unchangeable in his being, wisdom, power, holiness, justice, goodness and truth." The matters of which we are necessarily ignorant—since God has not yet chosen to reveal them—are not to be confused with faith, which is knowledge based on and issuing from revelation. That God has chosen not to reveal everything gives to the church and to individuals no license to formulate and require subscription to man-made theories. That man will be finally judged by the light of revelation now accessible to him, and that he is pledged a place in the kingdom of God on the basis of the Word of God now available, and that in Jesus of Nazareth God himself has come in the flesh as "the way, the truth, and the life" (John 14:6, KJV) attest the validity of God's disclosure. The basic emphasis of Judeo-Christian religion does not fall on God's transcendence and man's consequent ignorance of divine things; it falls, rather, on God's transcosmic revelation that conveys truth about himself and his ways.

But God's revelation gives us no basis for turning the revelational knowledge we have into a trend-chart to prognosticate what God is likely to say or do in areas that are presently sealed to us. "O the depth of the riches and wisdom and knowledge of God! How unsearchable are his judgments and how inscrutable his ways!" (Rom. 11:33, RSV).

5.
Self-Transcendence
and the Image of God

MANY PHILOSOPHICAL IDEALISTS who consider the human mind to be part of the Absolute Mind have emphasized that the human self is reflexive upon itself so that it becomes object to itself. Others have described this phenomenon in other ways, noting that man as subject is aware of himself as subject while being simultaneously aware also of objects that confront him.

Recent religious thought has connected the theme of transcendence with the doctrine of man as much as the doctrine of God. Some theological expositions now locate the divine image in the so-called human capacity for self-transcendence, including the activity of imagination. In the presently emerging theology of man, psychoanalytic conceptions of personality stress self-transcendence as an aspect of ego-integration, value-orientation, and language-use.

In his analysis of human nature, Reinhold Niebuhr found the meaning of "spirit" in self-transcendence disclosed in knowing, deciding, acting and interacting within the realm of persons and events. Man has the "ability to stand outside himself, a capacity for self-transcendence, the ability to make himself his own object, a quality of spirit which is usually not fully comprehended or connoted in 'ratio' or 'nous' or 'reason' or any of the concepts which philosophers usually use to describe the uniqueness of man" (*The Nature and Destiny of Man*, 1:4). Niebuhr asserted anxiety to be inevitably implicit in human finiteness, and on that basis correlated self-transcendence with pride, rebellion and sin against God.

Roger Hazelton proposes to shift the focus in theology "from a super-being called God to the examination of those experiences of transcending or being transcended which provide not only the occasions for religious faith but also the testing ground of its interpretation by theology. . . .

58

This may require bracketing the word 'God' for a time at least," he adds, "although my hunch is that what is intended by the word will always remain on the hidden agenda" (address to the American Theological Society, April 11, 1972). Instead of reserving the discussion of transcendence for the doctrine of the attributes of God with which historic Christianity has mainly connected it, Hazelton, in keeping with its recent theological mutation, connects the theme of transcendence primarily with man.

Hazelton thinks that the experiences that prompt us to affirm or deny transcendence are ambivalent and lead inevitably to ambiguous language and reasoning. But "something important," he claims, is nonetheless at stake although it involves a logic all its own. Hazelton argues that human experience is multidimensional and multidirectional; he appeals to "peak experiences," to research in extrasensory perception, to Gordon Kaufman's exposition of "models" of ranges of reality that cannot be confined within experience, and to the new role assigned to "myth" in depicting reality that is conceptually and historically inaccessible. But if, as Hazelton contends, the credibility of transcendence does not depend upon one common set of criteria, and the canons of logic and rational validity are not universally applicable, then not even Hazelton's formulations of what is objectively the case should covertly be used to seek their accreditation; a contrary or even contradictory explanation of the transcendent would be equally admissible. One wonders, in fact, if the transcendence is then any longer capable of intelligible definition.

Whether man "experiences the transcendent" becomes the core of Hazelton's problem. "Transcendence is a constant accompaniment or background of all experience," he says. "I transcend and I am transcended; I even transcend myself, whenever I act and know I act or think and know I think." The "experience of the transcendent," he adds, is that of an imprecise, elusive and mysterious "presence"—an indication of an existing something whose proper name might turn out to be God but about which "premature dogmatism" is unjustifiable.

In the present theological situation, Hazelton considers human self-transcendence "the most basic if not the most central" meaning of transcendence-in-general. "To be a man or woman," he holds, "means to be a self-transcending self with visions of possibility, yet unrealized yet realizable." Human self-transcendence is to be explored and relied on, Hazelton adds, "for whatever meaning God may still have in our epoch."

If the meaning of God in human experience is to be made known, he contends, theologians must forego "patriarchal or monarchical conceptions" of divine transcendence and ask whether man's self-transcending capacity may not properly be expressed as "God's immanent activity in him." Accordingly, he proposes to invert the Reformation emphasis, *Finitum non capax infiniti* (the finite has no capacity for, or is unable to grasp the infinite) by a "much earlier Christian principle: *Homo capax Dei*" (man has the capacity for, or is able to grasp God) which he misinterprets to mean that "God became what we are in order to make us what he himself is"—a misunderstanding of the doctrine of the incarnation of God in Christ.

Let us focus more closely on Hazelton's appeal to human self-transcendence as decisive for the meaning and reality of God. His position represents a reaction to neoorthodoxy which excluded religious experience as the proper matrix of theological reflection, and also emphasized the paradoxical or existential disclosure in divine confrontation of the supposedly "unknowable transcendence" of God. Hazelton carries forward the neoorthodox revolt against the applicability to the sphere of transcendence of reason and the forms of logic, but reinstates religious experience as the context of theological inquiry. While he rejects any correlation of transcendence with the totally Other God disclosed by sporadic divine confrontation to naked faith, at the same time he refuses to abandon superhuman transcendence, as Ludwig Feuerbach did, on the ground that it cannot be defined in terms of human knowledge. Hazelton accepts the anthropological basis of religious experience and proposes to arrive at the meaning of God by an examination of the human experience of transcendence.

While Hazelton insists that transcendence can be experienced, he contends that our conceptions may distort it, since it assertedly has a logic all its own. In short, cognitive and rational considerations are too narrow to cover the entire content of the consciousness of experience. But Hazelton's abandonment of logical criteria in the realm of transcendence leaves us no basis for distinguishing Yahweh from Lucifer who may come as an angel of light (2 Cor. 11:14). If the law of contradiction is irrelevant in the sphere of transcendent ontology, then God and the not-God, the divine and the demonic, cannot be assuredly differentiated.

If human self-transcendence is scientifically accessible, it must be analyzable by controlled techniques. If it is philosophically significant, it must be intelligible and subject to rational inquiry. The insistence that we experience the infinite in the finite and that we can know ever more about the experience then lacks cognitive supports. In what way does one truly bridge the ontological gap, or is one driven rather to deny that it exists? Even the notion that transcendence means "presence" is suspect —an instance of "premature dogmatism"?—and falls, as must every other comment about transcendence, under Hazelton's stricture that the lines to be drawn are very tentative indeed, and without any presumption of universal validity. What one person experiences as "presence" another may in fact experience as "absence." Are we then merely projecting our ignorance on reality, hurling arrows at the unknown and unknowable, and dreaming an impossible dream? If persuasive cognitive credentials are lacking, then no rational considerations remain to exclude Feuerbach's insistence that transcendence involves nothing beyond human experience and that all theology is disguised anthropology, or Freud's disenchantment with the transcendent. What is gained by reinstating the transcendent if no possibility exists of intellectually convincing anyone that his interpretation of self-transcendence is inferior to my own?

In brief, emphasis on self-transcendence as the *imago Dei* and as the clue to the meaning of God is self-defeating whether one relies on the neoorthodox appeal to noncognitive divine encounter or on a humanistic appeal to internal experience of what allegedly falls outside the realm of cognitive intelligibility. Gordon Kaufman tries to surmount these alternatives of experience or revelation by substituting for a naturalistic model based on complex interrelations of natural powers and processes a metaphysical model based on the concept of the self as an analogue of revelation: "Revelation refers . . . to that locus in experience through which men discover themselves in relation to the *ultimately real*" (*Systematic Theology*, p. 19). But apart from an insistence also on intelligible transcendence, one cannot escape the question of how human psychology is to be turned into divine ontology.

Hazelton's approach, moreover, has devastating consequences for moral experience. If one blurs the distinction between truth and falsehood and substitutes another logic in the realm of transcendence, one also dulls the distinction between good and evil. All concerns that pertain to love and forgiveness are shrouded by ambiguity if not illogicality. Hazelton objects to Niebuhr at the wrong point—that man is ruled inordinate if he does not subordinate himself to God—while he perpetuates Niebuhr's basic epistemological error—that the transcendent falls outside the sphere of the rational.

S. Paul Schilling likewise contends that God is present incognito wherever transcendence breaks into our experience; the beyond, the depth, the whole, the not-yet are frontiers of such transcendence best explained, he says, by theistically affirming a creative, dynamic personal love at the center of all reality (*God Incognito*). Although he refers to Scripture where somewhat serviceable to his view, he does not allow the Bible to speak decisively. More influenced by process theology, he is reluctant to espouse biblical theism. But many contemporary writers who similarly claim that transcendence inescapably brackets human life hesitate to find in this experience a firm basis for theistic belief of any kind. In fact, modern philosophy projects the phenomenon of transcendence in support of atheism as often as in behalf of theism. Schilling offers no persuasive considerations for identifying such experience in terms of the sure working of God.

A fundamental objection to recent discussions of self-transcendence remains to be stated. Prominent as the theme of self-transcendence may be in dialectical and existential theology and philosophy of the recent past, the fact remains that human experience exhibits no discernible or describable place where selfhood ends and otherness begins. The idea of self-transcendence—however attractive it may seem—has on reflection all the marks of pure nonsense; a valid definition of transcendence would help score the point. How can anyone transcend himself? The self is never an object in the sense that nature is an object of thought. That man transcends nature sufficiently to make nature an object of thought is one thing; that he transcends himself is quite another claim, one that appears on its very surface schizophrenic. One who presumes to be a Christian theologian faithful to the biblical witness should indicate where in Scripture the notion of self-transcendence, let alone that of imaginative ideas, has any basis. Where is the revelation that warrants the assertion of self-transcendence? To be sure, we can think about ourselves. But the notion that the image of God in the human person is to be found in self-transcendence that demands a logic of its own is a postulation readily ventured by those who refuse to associate the divine image with the forms of logic and fixed moral distinctions. What proper role has it, however, in evangelical theology?

Brand Blanshard relates that when first told that some men have imaginative ideas, a group of scholars scarcely believed it (*The Nature of Thought*, 1:261 f.). To be sure, some philosophers—among them Aquinas and Hume—hold that knowledge requires images, but this implies that we know only representations of the truth but never know the truth itself. Imaginative ideas, in any event, could only be a hindrance to thinking. With ideas the situation is very different. Descartes noted that logic can calculate the area of a thousand-sided figure whereas imagination is powerless to do so.

The great watershed between the biblical and nonbiblical religions is the self-revealing God who, in contrast with the static gods of other religions, speaks and acts intelligibly. Judeo-Christian religion worships the God who takes the initiative—who plans, creates, judges, reveals and redeems—not some divinity, perhaps ultimately unknowable, that man is left to discern by his own ingenuity.

The God of Abraham, Isaac and Jacob, the God of Moses and Paul, the God unveiled in Jesus Christ, is the active, speaking God, the Eternal One who lives and loves, condemns and rescues, who works out his purposes even in fallen human history.

The quest for a "deeper" self is at the heart of many contemporary cults, each claiming an exclusive meditation technique. It should surprise no one that in a technological era, an activistic generation that neglects transcendent realities should reach beyond the scientific-empirical level to the mystical in search of inner serenity. The human person is stamped with the conviction that ultimate reality is not measurable in kilometers or tons or revolutions per minute and that it is the invisible world that somehow preserves personal values.

Esalen emerged in the 1960s as a self-transcendence cult and forerunner of the encounter movement. It seeks to release the unawakened consciousness by various therapies including even nude communal bathing. In the 1960s it inspired the encounter-movement. Arica pursues the "essential" self through Egyptian gymnastics, African ritual dances, and concentration on the colors black and blue and on the planets Saturn and Jupiter. Est confines groups of people for a half-day or more of intense concentration that restricts even toilet breaks. "Perfect master" Maharaj Ji's Divine Light sect promises "enlightenment" through meditation. For guru Maharishi Mahesh Yogi, Transcendental Meditation is the fourth state of consciousness and will usher in the Age of Enlightenment.

Although Hindu symbols and some Hindu prayers characterize the TM initiation ceremony, its sponsors in America emphasize that the meditation cult is not a religion but a tranquilizing and energizing technique usable with all religions. (TM is not the only cult that has had to secularize itself as a technique to gain wide hearing after first coming to the United States as a religion; Sun Myung Moon, Korean leader of the Unification Church, seeks professional respectability through conferences that stress moral values in a scientific age.) Behind the twice-daily twenty-minute TM ritual of silence, the Grand Seer (Sanskrit, *Maharishi*) postulates the imposing but amorphous theory SCI (Astronomy, Cosmology and the Science of Creative Intelligence). For a $125 initiation fee (cut rate for students and children) lecturers, using a "secret formula," assign one of more than a dozen Sanskrit words to different persons—a *mantra* not to be disclosed to others—that the disciple mentally repeats for the prescribed periods anywhere and anytime except at bedtime lest sleep be impaired.

With or without a mantra two extended periods of silence daily would doubtless curtail quite a number of personal problems or weaknesses. The technique therefore seems an expensive and not always successful way of overcoming tension, temper, and other complaints. According to Dr. Herbert Benson of Harvard Medical School, less costly relaxing techniques are equally beneficial to the body (*The Relaxation Response*). TM, moreover, has no moral requirement that initiates must forego drugs or hallucinogens, sexual immorality, alcohol or cigarette addiction or other vices; those who do mend their morals bring a bad conscience with them, and not all initiates do. TM does not make people better persons, even if some are made to feel better. At best it provides a psychological transition opportunity for altering one's ways. Nor has a connection been proved between the recital of particular mantras and the attainment of specific results.

Other meditation techniques promise special benefits to the initiate's spiritual nature. Most Hindu gurus combine contemplation rituals with some form of union or yoking (Sanskrit, *yoga*) with Brahma or the Absolute. Both Zen and Tibetan Buddhist meditation, for example, aspire to nirvana or cessation of self-consciousness by union with ultimate reality.

Such quasipantheistic approaches conjecturally postulate an all-inclusive Absolute of which human beings secretly are aspects or parts. By contrast, Judeo-Christian revelation openly affirms the supernatural Creator who is ontologically other than humans. Yet, despite their now sullied moral and rational nature, these humans nonetheless reflect his image.

The revelation of the living God is disclosed in the form not of disjointed *mantras* but in intelligible sentences or propositions that require mental assent and voluntary appropriation. The revealed Word of God is openly published in Scripture and can be known by all who read or hear. Christianity emphasizes that transcendent mystery is intelligibly revealed in Christ the creative and redemptive center of the universe, and that the Word of God given in Scripture is not to be artificially apportioned but made universally available and recognized as universally valid.

Meditation, of course, has an indispensable role in biblical religion, but Christian meditation centers on the Mediator. The Psalmist (1:2, KJV) declares that the blessed man "meditates" in "the law of the Lord" (not simply on an isolated mantra) and does so "day and night" (not simply a twice-daily ritual). The term *meditate* here carries the secondary meaning of half-aloud recollection of the written Word. "I will meditate in thy precepts," the Psalmist writes elsewhere (119:15, KJV; cf, 23, 48, 148); "I meditate on all thy works" (143:5, KJV). The term *meditate* also occurs in the King James Version in 1 Timothy 4:15 where the apostle Paul exhorts Timothy as a young minister diligently to practice (*meletaō*) public reading, teaching and preaching of the revealed Word of God. Here the reference has a view to sharing God's Word with others. In Philippians 4:8 the apostle urges Christians to calculate (*logizomai*, "think on logically") the criteria of right action—whatever is just, pure, lovely or to be held in honor—as a test and stimulus of proper conduct. Moral fulfillment is never irrelevant to or isolated from Christian meditation; love of God requires love of neighbor (Matt. 22:37–39).

Ancient efforts to bring humans into transactional relationships with the Divine through dramatic or unconventional symbolism or ritualism beyond words, along with their modern prototypes, are more self-confusing than self-illuminating. The attempt to find the significance of the human self not through the revelation of the transcendent living God and his purposes but in some mystical dimension of human "self-transcendence" in which God may perchance be found, leads to a repudiation of any ontological or moral reality transcendent to the self, and beyond that finally to self-divinization. Peter Marin reports on this trend toward "a deification of the isolated self" in "The New Narcissism" (pp. 45–56). Frontier therapeutic seminars promise both personal efficiency and self-fulfillment through an assertion of the sovereignty of the individual will. One is himself or herself God, the only deity there is. In a report on the human potential movement est, the acronym for Erhard Seminars Training sponsored by founder Werner Erhard, Ned Scharff reports: "Theologically, *est* participants learn, there is no god outside their own consciousness. For that matter, according to *est* doctrine, there is no one else in the universe except the individual. Everyone else is a figment of the imagination" (*Washington Star*, Jan. 18, 1975, p. C-15). One's own ideas are held to be beyond criticism or refutation by others.

Patrons of these expensive psychoanalytic clinics revel in what they delight to hear—that truth is whatever one believes, that the self is creatively all-powerful and wholly determines one's fate, that guilt and shame are arbitrary notions, that human misery is simply an accompaniment of distorted consciousness. The est cult teaches that life is perfect just the way it is, just as each of us has made it. We should therefore not try to change it, but accept it willingly. This philosophy is highly compatible with unregenerate dispositions.

A remarkable shift in values—one might say also in ontological perspective—underlies the tendency today to consider selfishness an evidence of psychic health and enlightenment, and to regard self-survival as the only good. Such calculated disinterest in others is reflected in a "lifeboat" approach to major problems of the modern world. It advocates in effect "survival of the fittest" as the best way to resolve overpopulation, hunger and famine. The felt presence of other selves is dwarfed by emphasizing unfeeling impersonal cosmic processes from which only one's own self-reliance can guarantee private exemption. Those who remain trapped in disabling circumstances are said to have only themselves to blame. By feeling guilt or shame over the plight of others like the poor or the hungry one simply demeans his or her true self.

Marin sees in this attitude "a retreat from the worlds of morality and history, an unembarrassed denial of human reciprocity and community" and "the dead end of generosity." The new therapies, he notes, replace the moral and historical concerns of the past by redefining morality through a defusing of conscience. This therapy provides adherents "with a way to avoid the demands of the world, to smother the tug of conscience . . . to remain who and what they are, to accept the structured world as it is . . . with the assurance that it all accords with cosmic law. We are in our proper place; the others are in theirs. . . . The traditional measures of justice or good vanish completely. The self replaces community, relation, neighbor, chance or God."

This affirmation of the ultimate and intrinsic divinity of the isolated self cancels any call for regeneration of the self or for essential self-improvement. By shrouding the transcendent Creator God, it also clouds the *imago Dei* in created human beings; it empties even the bare interest in self-transcendence into self-assertion. If Jesus depicted the Good Samaritan as one who responds to the beleaguered neighbor, says this self-assertive life-style, that was "his thing." It had more relevance for him than for others. Each of us has his or her "private" destiny, we are told. By death and rebirth the "enlightened" modern must venture to desensitize a troubled conscience, dismiss transcendent morality, disavow any supernatural source of objective truth and eternal commandments. In the name of the self all other claims upon the self are repudiated. Faith is deprogramed from a religious context and viewed as a human phenomenon; any emergence of love is subordinated to self-assertion.

The high tragedy of this affirmation of self-sovereignty lies not in its absolutizing of individual indifference to community concerns as a virtue

—that, unfortunately, already characterizes large pockets of modern urban society. Its devastating calamity, rather, lies in evaluating man's essential nature as a paralytic existence that ideally is insensitive to God and to all claims of transcendent truth, morality and justice. Narcissistically it confuses with liberating divine grace the subjective repression of all that regenerate mankind has come to prize as divinely desirable and humanly ideal, and thus repudiates what it means to be normatively human and free. To speak of God not on the basis of divine speech and action, but only in terms of silence and symbols, leads finally to arbitrary claims of divinity by the subjective ego.

To understand why inner-consciousness theory now empties into self-affirmation, we must recall that Western thought across many centuries has progressively obscured the biblical emphasis on the transcendent God. The medieval mystics were already blurring the supernatural; while recognizing God's transcendence, they forsook objectively mediated revelation, and presumed to draw the divine Spirit into every man for direct intrapersonal disclosure. Earlier notions of the Spirit's exaggerated immanence were not as radical as later forms, but they led nonetheless to loss of interest in the unique incarnation of the Logos. Then, in turn, Feuerbach and Marx made the transcendent God simply a projection of man's highest ideals. That thereafter a death-of-God theology should consequently emerge in concessive Christian circles was highly predictable.

As a fruit of this trend, the modern outlook forfeits both the classic Greco-Roman philosophical awareness of transcendent reality and the Judeo-Christian clarification of God in his revelation. The soul is intentionally shut off if not sealed off to the supernatural, and interest in human destiny beyond nature and history is dissolved.

Feuerbach and Marx had contended that our decisive turning point in history now required man to draw his earlier projection of a transcendent God back into himself so that he recognizes himself as God. Consequently man is transformed into superman (cf. Eric Voegelin, *The New Science of Politics*, p. 125). Nietzsche asks why modern man should humiliate himself by admitting any need of divine love and grace. Man, he says, can act out in himself the whole drama of redemption as well as the fall, and no longer needs God (cf. *Morgenröte*, § 79; English, "The Dawn of Day"). So he declares God dead, and even reports the news that deity has now been murdered.

In this climate a new man arises, a self-luminous anthropoid who stifles sensitivity to the transcendent and abolishes its significance for the modern comprehension of human nature. This creature is no longer ideally motivated by love of God but by love of self. A new empirical psychology connects his basic drives with the passions, fixing attention on man's assertive power over nature and history, and then finally over his fellow man. Supposed freedom from answerability to the Divine now downgrades the importance of intellectual and moral conflicts. Preoccupied with changing contemporary concerns, this secular and relativistic outlook on life breeds impatience with theoretical principles and distrust of rational persuasion; intellectual discussion is viewed as dispensable. Criticism of this stance as intellectually vagrant is considered irrelevant. The convictions of great minds of the past and all the wider wisdom of the ages it scorns as unenlightened or envelopes by vituperative propaganda. Psychological commitment to the modern *gnosis* runs so deep that reason and logic are allowed almost no role except as instruments for rationalization.

The theoretical fallacies on which modern *gnosis* thrives, whether in its appeal to self-transcendence or in its exaltation of self-consciousness, result from a volitional dismissal of transcendent reality revealed and known as the living God. Contemporary man fences himself in from rational discussion about the supernatural, not because supernatural theism lacks persuasive intellectual supports, nor because modern man lacks a capacity for understanding the transcendent, but because he has so encased himself within contemporary prejudices that just to raise the subject seriously seems to compromise his modernity. Current slogans wield a secret authority over his life, and so replace the hold and cloud the relevance of the scriptural disclosure, that the contemporary spirit is given over to unbelief. Reinterpreting the structure of reality and essence of history and of social processes on principles counter to revelational theism, the unregenerate dismiss the transcendent world as illusory or view it as simply responsive to human determination.

For all that, daily existential reminders of this unacknowledged objectively transcendent world mock these biases—the bold witness of believers, the bad conscience, the contemplation of immortality and final judgment when friends and loved ones die, all taunt him in times of personal crisis when the consideration of what is otherwise repressed emerges to the fore. Just as amputees who feel pain at the knee continue to refer these sensations to a foot now absent—not because they are victims of cruel illusion but because the missing appendage belonged to their normal existence as humans—so the consciousness of contemporary man is frequently pierced by instinctive references to God despite ready dismissal of the supernatural as a fiction. The human species cannot hope by repression of the transcendent to alter the structure of reality or of ideal humanity.

Because these gnostic modern versions of life and history misrepresent reality and falsify man's actual life situation, they not only invite final disaster but also implant the seeds of historical disillusionment. The modern cultist psychology of personality distorts the human situation by its nonrecognition and suppression of man's proper transcendent relationships. Neglect of the soul can lead only to an abortive psychology. An adequate psychology is explicit about the soul's reality and relation to the eternal world.

Only the shock of divine confrontation, of God's revelation in his Word, can remove the terrible deformity of the human psyche and fully overcome the illusion of an amputated invisible transcendent world. Contemporary man must now be pressed to ask when and why he deceived himself into thinking that this spiritual amputation actually occurred. "They refused to have God in their knowledge" (Rom. 1:28, ASV) says Paul of man's suppression of the supernatural. Nowhere, however, does Paul grant that this deliberate closure of the soul implies the destruction of God, or the demolition of the soul, or the effective elimination of all human rendezvous with the supernatural, whether overt or covert. Given the actuality of God in his revelation, neither man nor society can be truly comprehended by isolating the soul from the supernatural. Although they mistakenly viewed the individual self as its sensorium, even the classic ancient pagan philosophers coped with the reality of the supernatural. These speculative theories were purified by the Christian revelation of the Logos which provided deeper foundations of knowledge concerning the truth of the supernatural and the nature of the soul. That revelation impinges with inescapable force upon the thought and life of a culture willingly open to transcendent reality. The re-creative power of that same revelation can also liberate into the truth of the eternal Word a generation that barricades itself against the supernatural, shuns transcendent truth, and curbs the soul's profoundest experiences.

THESIS FOUR:
The very fact of disclosure by the one living God
assures the comprehensive unity of divine revelation.

6.
The Unity
of Divine Revelation

THE GOD WHO REVEALS HIMSELF is the source of a comprehensively unified revelation. He is no schizophrenic spirit or vagrant voice in a hierarchy of contending gods.

Polytheistic paganism played off its mythological divinities against each other, identifying this or that favorable or calamitous turn of events with one or another of the many gods. The moment-by-moment outcome of ongoing rivalry between the gods was made to account for every fortune or misfortune. In such a setting of competing and conflicting divinities the very possibility of a unified revelation is frustrated. In the context of ancient Mesopotamian religion no god would make a decision on his own lest he be taken to task by other gods. An invisible world rent with chaotic strife offers no hope for coherently interrelated and comprehensively interconnected divine disclosure.

How different is the case where the living God freely discloses his nature and will and unites in himself everything that appertains to deity! The Hebrew Shema, as Walther Eichrodt reminds us, may be read: "Yahweh our God is one single God" (Deut. 6:4), "that is to say, he is not a God who can be split up into various divinities or powers, like the Baals of Tyre, of Hazor and of Shechem, etc." (*Theology of the Old Testament*, 1:226, n. 2). In contrast to the Mesopotamian view where the counsel of the village elders is projected upon the polytheistic gods, Yahweh alone is Lord, Ruler, King, Lawgiver, Judge. The prophet Jeremiah rebukes those who turn to idols as creators and protectors (2:27). Malachi 2:10 (RSV) reads: "Have we not all one father? Has not one God created us?" While the emphasis on God's progenitorship and authority here applies to the Hebrew people or nation, in view of his creatorship it can be universally extended, consistent with prophetic revelation, to all mankind. "There is no God but one" affirms Paul (1 Cor. 8:4, RSV) in adjudicating the controversy over eating food. One corollary is that pagan gods—even if certain persons look upon them as real divinities and even address them as *lord*—are not actually divinities at all. Another corollary is that "the earth is the Lord's, and everything in it" (1 Cor. 10:26, RSV).

Hebrew-Christian confidence in a comprehensively unified divine disclosure rests upon the revelational presupposition of ethical monotheism. Wilhelm Schmidt's studies into comparative religions (*The Origin and Growth of Religion*) confirmed his conviction that the many secondary gods ranged alongside a high god reflect pagan deterioration of primitive monotheism in which particular attributes of the one God in time became postulated as separate divinities.

From the very first, Old Testament monotheism appears in the living context of divine revelation as a dynamic experience of God's reality; it was never merely a philosophical projection sprung from pious reflection on man and the world. The Bible indicates that, even before the fall, finite man lived in a relation of necessary dependence on supernatural revelation. The divine image in man was not of itself fully adequate as a moral guide, nor was general revelation. Even in the Garden of Eden, God addressed Adam directly and communicated statutes and precepts to him by special external disclosure. Biblical religion has its origins in ethical monotheism, a foundation not speculatively constructed but identified with the revelation of the one Creator God who holds final authority over all life and is mankind's ultimate refuge. So insistently does this monotheistic awareness obtrude throughout biblical thought that by way of contrast A. C. Headlam characterizes even the boldest approaches of the Greek poets and philosophers as "imperfect and partial conceptions which seem to show glimpses of truth rather than attainment" (*Christian Theology*, p. 157).

"To some extent bursting and transcending" all the paraphernalia common to ancient religions, "a new and unique revelation is given to Israel," writes Albrecht Oepke, its peculiar feature being that "Yahweh, the God of Israel, is the living God . . . in distinction from empty idols" (cf. Deut. 5:23; Ps. 96:5; 97:7; Isa. 2:8; 37:4; Jer. 10:10) ("Apokaluptō," 3:571 f.). Biblical religion is "faith in one God who is God in the true sense as distinct from all other numinous experience" (p. 572). Prophetic revelation increasingly clarified the fact that Yahweh is not only the one living God beside whom Israel could acknowledge no other, but is also the universal God of all mankind, the living God for all men alongside whom no other gods really exist.

That his conception of God was already monotheistic Elijah attests by his cry "Yahweh, he is God!" (1 Kings 18:39). Concerning Elijah's challenge to the priests of Baal, Os Guinness comments that "in a situation of potential paranoia, he never lifted his hands in holy horror, insecurely calling on the nation to return to God. Instead, believing that God was there, he presupposed that Baal was not there" (*The Dust of Death*, p.

348). Yahweh never becomes Baal; that title is never applied to him. Elijah scorns the Baalists, and uses anything but reverent language about their god: "Either he is meditating or has turned aside (to relieve a natural need) or is traveling or is slumbering and needs to be awakened" (1 Kings 18:27). Here Elijah anticipates the scathing sarcasm which other prophets in their turn directed at the manufactured idols of popular pagan religion (Pss. 115; 135; Jer. 2:26–28; 10:1–16; Isa. 40:18–20; 41:4–7; 44:9–20). Never does Elijah assert Yahweh's supremacy solely over Israel. In similar fashion Isaiah time and again reminds his readers that the living God's sovereign rule over all the earth and in history implies the powerlessness of the idol gods of pagan nations (cf. 40:26; 41:1–2, 21–24; 43:9–13; 44:6–8, etc.).

Where the one living God makes known his all-comprehending will and purpose, nothing—not even the most adverse turn of events—can be referred to alien gods except by way of apostasy. No one convinced of the reality of the one God's self-revelation will infer from God's seeming absence and abandonment that God has been bested by invisible powers. Jesus' cry was: "My God, my God, why hast *thou* forsaken me?" (Matt. 27:46, KJV). In responding to the revelation of the living God the choice is either obedience and consummatory blessing on the one hand or disobedience and final punishment on the other. The one God's comprehensive, unified revelation is foundational to the biblical doctrines of divine grace and judgment. When human beings bow down as in ancient Athens not only to gods professedly known, but even to "an unknown god" who has yet to be heard from (Acts 17:23, RSV), then the possibility of unified divine revelation is forfeited.

It is in fact through the revelation of the living God and his purpose in the creation of man in responsible freedom that we know, as Robert J. Blaikie reminds us, that history is "one and undivided" (*"Secular Christianity" and God Who Acts*, p. 146), or for that matter, that nature is one and everywhere interrelated. The Bible depicts the entire creation as the sphere of his lordship and rule and this providentially bracketed world and history of mankind as the central arena for the redemptive acts of God.

Whatever other distinctions are required by God's revelation—such as the progressive character of special revelation in terms of promise, fulfillment and the future end-time—its comprehensive unity is assured by the fundamental fact that revelation is the disclosure of the one living God. We must therefore resist any tendency, even by theologians, to press differentiations to a point that threatens the unity of divine disclosure by presumptively imposing speculative categories upon the reality of revelation. Serviceable as the distinction has been in theological studies, not even the terms *general* and *special* arise in biblical history to describe God's revelation. In expounding the one revelation of the living God, this frequently asserted contrast of general and special divine revelation can be appropriately maintained only by deriving the content and meaning of the two terms from the nature of God's disclosure itself, and not from notions of the Divine postulated conjecturally and promoted independently of the actual course of God's self-revelation. In no way can the distinction between general and special revelation imply dual or rival revelations. The essential continuity of general and special revelation is a pervasive biblical assumption. Special revelation does not annul general revelation but rather republishes, vivifies and supplements it. The prohibitory commandment-form "thou shalt not" in the redemption context of the Decalogue presupposes God's positive and comprehensive "thou shalt" addressed to man on the basis of creation in Genesis.

Although their motivation and intention may be quite otherwise, speculative theory and rationalistic exposition have arbitrarily limited the scope and nature of divine disclosure and prejudged God's freedom in his revelation, and have subverted even the affirmation that there is one comprehensively unified revelation of God. Some evolutionary immanentists, for example, assimilated divine revelation to religion-in-general, supposedly incorporating a spiritual essence common to every historical religion that has developed in a variety of unique ways. Others, however, contend that no such common religious essence exists, yet that every historical religion expresses a unique and ongoing spiritual revelation that cannot be grasped in shared ideas. Such speculative approaches negate what is meant by the unity of divine disclosure; they arbitrarily restrict God in his revelation to some single track—be it general revelation apart from special, or special revelation apart from general, and more recently one or the other apart from cognitive divine communication. Such a course postulates in advance a pattern of revelation which, in the one case, cannot be particular, and in the other, cannot be universal; and even these terms in turn are now frequently redefined in novel ways.

Historic Christianity has always insisted on both the continuity and the distinctiveness of special and general revelation. In recent times, however, the nature of both their continuity and their difference is being increasingly misstated in novel thrusts toward universality and particularity in expounding human experience of God. Such discussions do not examine the reality of revelation as it factually occurs and on its own assumptions, but impose constrictive theories upon the very course and character of divine revelation. The arbitrariness of this procedure is especially apparent when all the great world religions are discussed in terms of a presupposed universally operative revelation of God, whereas some of these very religions, notably Buddhism and Confucianism, do not even affirm the indispensable corollary of divine revelation, that is, the existence of a personal God.

The comprehensive unity of divine revelation may be threatened in still another way, that of adducing an additional independent source of revelation alongside the disclosure of God. To assert a second source of the knowledge of God—be it reason, or nature, or tradition—is to devalue and jeopardize the only legitimate source of divine revelation. Roman Catholic theology has traditionally sponsored a *natural* knowledge of God; this, it is said, comes from the light of human reason in advance of any revelation of God in Jesus Christ. In 1870 the Vatican Council formulated as infallible doctrine the teaching that by man's contemplation of the universe God can be known with certainty "through the natural light of reason." God can be known independently of any recourse to divine revelation and simply by inference from the existing world and man—that is, by reflection upon experience. This natural theology was then expanded to assert that not only can we know God by the natural light of reason, but we can also prove his existence without any appeal to divine disclosure. The notion of a natural knowledge of God derived not from revelation yet accessible to human reason was perpetuated by the Second Vatican Council (cf. *The Documents of Vatican II*, pp. 35, 219, 221, 679, 686).

Whatever else the Bible affirms about divine revelation and its relationship to reason, it nowhere considers the natural light of reason per se as a source of true knowledge of God. Apart from divine revelation neither human reason nor human experience as a whole is a source of divine truth. Neither mankind nor the world is a source of the knowledge of divine realities. Human reason is an instrument for knowing the truth of God, but it is not the originating source of divine truth. The Bible acknowledges only God and God alone as the giver and source of divine revelation. Not even the so-called nature-Psalms (e.g., Pss. 8, 19, 65, 104) depict natural revelation. While the universe mirrors God's revelation, it is ontologically *other* than God and therefore cannot be the source of divine revelation. The Bible nowhere espouses a "natural theology" but insists rather that God reveals himself and his ways in and through the created universe. General divine disclosure has sometimes been somewhat ambiguously described as a "revelation in nature." The Westminster Confession points to the "light of nature and the works of creation and providence" as manifesting "the goodness, wisdom and power of God" in a way that leaves all humans inexcusable. The Belgic Confession speaks more specifically of "the invisible things of God" which are on view in the created universe (Article 2).

While God's revelation is one, the forms of divine revelation need not be so. God does not reveal himself only in one way. Various forms of divine revelation—e.g., the universal revelation in the creation, the revelation in Christ, the final eschatological revelation—convey a miscellaneous content. But the "history" of divine disclosure derives its inner unity in the first instance from the fact that the one self-revealing God is sovereignly at its center. The God who meets mankind in revelation addresses us through the creation, in Jesus of Nazareth, and finally at the End of all historical end-times when we shall see him "face to face" and "know even as [we] are known" (1 Cor. 13:12, KJV).

For all that, the unity of divine revelation is not solely a unity of divine act and address—that is, a unity of divine action—for the Scriptures convey divine revelation as a logically interconnected content, as the Word of God revealed in divinely given truths, as an intelligible unity. The unity of revelational content is not to be found only in the living God who stands at the center of all revelation, as indeed he does, but also in the truth conveyed by the God of revelation. Diversity must not be exaggerated, nor the forms of revelation reformulated, with the intention of stripping divine disclosure of its rational unity. Given in sundry times and in different forms, the revelation of the truth of God is interdependent; the revelation in Jesus of Nazareth presupposes the revelation in creation, and the final eschatological revelation presupposes the revelation in creation and in the incarnate Christ. Those who know nothing of the revelation of God in Jesus of Nazareth are nevertheless called upon to repent, for even the worst heathen have the light of conscience and of nature and are in revolt against it. Like all other human beings, those who have the light of the gospel are judged for what they have done with the revelational light bestowed upon them.

It was to "his own" that Jesus Christ came—that is, not merely to his own world and to mankind lighted by the Logos (John 1:9) but in particular to his own people, to the Hebrews, who had the prophetic promise of redemption (John 1:11). While the historical differences between the Old Testament and the New Testament revelation must be preserved in expounding the unity of biblical truth, progressive revelation is in no way destructive of unity. The full unity of God's revelation will not be wholly apparent, of course, until the climactic end-time disclosure, but the continuity of the revelation in creation and in Scripture, and within Scripture between that in the Old Testament and that in the New, is an intelligible unity. The Old Testament does not reveal God as irreducibly triune, although there are hints of this which the New Testament illumines. The Old Testament does, however, reveal God only and always as one God. It speaks, moreover, of God's promised Messiah, but not by name as later did John the Baptist who identified the Israelite from Nazareth as God become flesh. Yet the Old Testament reveals the same God as the New Testament and affirms the same central message of God's redemptive grace. Jesus could say openly that "Abraham rejoiced to see my day" (John 8:56, KJV) and that in the coming judgment his Jewish contemporaries would be accused for rejecting him, not by Jesus but by Moses (John 5:45–47). While to the unbelieving, revelation in creation does not reveal God's mercy, it does disclose to them his "everlasting power and deity" (Rom. 1:20, NEB). The God of Sinai and of Zion is the same God who reveals himself as Yahweh-Elohim. The revelation in Jesus Christ, biblically attested and conveyed, discloses Christ himself standing at the center of all divine disclosure: he is the divine agent in creation, in redemption, and in judgment.

Emil Brunner's notion that the unity of revelation can only be dialectically represented "by the use of contradictory schemata of thought, the schema of identity and the schema of becoming, and of movement within time" (*Revelation and Reason,* p. 199) gratuitously sacrifices the intelligible content and rational consistency of divine revelation; it focuses instead upon God's recurring encounter in which we assertedly meet him by faith. Brunner considers the doctrinal elements to be humanly contributed interpretations that "cancel each other out" and whose "only use is that they direct our attention to the actual reality which we grasp in faith" (p. 199). "It is because we are concerned with this 'encounter,' and not with the content of a doctrine, that the historical variety of the various forms of revelation constitutes their genuine unity, namely, the unity of the divine attitude" (pp. 200 f.). For Brunner, in short, God in revelation gives us only himself; hence "the unity of revelation does not lead to a unity of doctrine" (p. 201).

Brunner's repudiation of intelligible revelation is accompanied by intemperate outbursts in which he grossly misrepresents the views of those who reject his theory of dialectical divine disclosure: "Where the effort is made to conceive the unity of revelation as a unity of doctrine—as all orthodoxy tries to do—there, without noticing it, history is changed into idea, and the Living God of the Bible becomes the absolute Being of speculative philosophy" (ibid., p. 201). Suffice it to say that it is precisely a rationally intelligible and logically consistent divine revelation that enables us to reject reducing biblical history to merely an idea and turning the self-revealing God into a philosophical Absolute. It becomes necessary, as we shall see, vigorously to disown as conjectural and nonbiblical the notion of dialectical disclosure and instead to validate the unity of divine revelation as an intelligibly significant affirmation. Brunner not only bows to radical higher critics who seek to demolish the intellectual unity of the Bible and the trustworthiness of its doctrines—except of course where Brunner's own doctrines are made out to be those of Scripture!—but also contends that not the unity but "precisely the variety of doctrine in the New Testament, and still more in the Old Testament" indicates that God himself is the unity of revelation. The great difficulty with Brunner's doctrine—if we can learn from recent history as well as from the ancient Scriptures—is that it so assimilates the reality of God to internal psychological considerations that it leaves the very existence of the living God in doubt.

Because of his anticonceptual theory of revelation, Brunner's early mentor Karl Barth also leaves much to be desired in several of his comments concerning the unity of Scripture. He does concede, however, that "if the Church of Jesus Christ wants to recognize its Lord as such; if it wants not merely to affirm the connexion between nature and grace, existence and faith, cosmos and community, not merely to conclude and postulate it on inner grounds, but to practise it as the truth of God's Word; if it wants to live consciously and peacefully in this truth, it cannot possibly overestimate the witness of the Old Testament. It will not be afraid, but rejoice, to allow the Old Testament history of creation to speak as a true and time-fulfilling history of the acts of God the Creator and in its connexion with the history of the Covenant; to give it the freedom to say what it has to say" (*Church Dogmatics*, III/1, p. 64).

A later chapter will discuss more fully the doctrinal unity of Scripture. At this point we need only to emphasize that the Old Testament prophets speak in conscious unity with the Mosaic revelation, which in turn presupposes the patriarchal, and that the New Testament speaks in conscious unity with the Old. Both Old and New Testaments attest the moral purpose of God in the universe and in human affairs, the fall of mankind in Adam, and the universal revelation of God in nature and man. Albrecht Ritschl's (1822–89) modernist notion that the Old Testament expounds a God of wrath different from the New Testament God of love has fallen on hard times; the law and the gospel belong to both Testaments. The electing God and his covenant-people are central to the whole Bible. The Messiah of New Testament fulfillment is the Messiah of Old Testament prediction. The coming Son of Abraham and David, the future birth and crucifixion and resurrection of Christ are not unknown to the prophets. As the Old Testament foretold, the church gathers its community of faith from Gentiles as well as from Jews. The God of the Bible is everywhere the living God of commandment, of promise, and of warning. He is the God who in kingly rule draws ever nearer those who trust him. Proclaiming in the Old Testament his universal sovereignty, he comes in person in the New Testament to remove Messiah's incognito, and in the soon-dawning end-time openly to manifest his victorious rule and reign as King of kings and Lord of lords, King of the earth and of the universe. He is the God who decrees and elects from eternity, who creates *ex nihilo*, who works out his purposes in nature and history. He is the God who pledges and provides redemption in Christ Jesus, the Nazarene who as King of Israel not only fulfills the divine election and calling of his people but also grafts upon them the Gentiles. He is the God who will subordinate all things to his righteous, everlasting rule.

The revelation of the living God is therefore one comprehensively unified revelation. Its basic unity derives from the purposive initiative of the self-revealing God, and not from a harmony superimposed by philosophical manipulation or theological projection. The strands of that divine revelation exhibit no rivalry or competition. Distinctions within God's revelation imply no discontinuity or rupture in the unity of divine disclosure. To postulate alongside his revelation any additional source of the knowledge of God only beclouds the unity of God's disclosure. God is known only in his self-revelation, a revelation that gains its comprehensive unity from the fact that the God of revelation is the one sovereign living Lord.

THESIS FIVE:
Not only the occurrence of divine revelation
but its very nature, content and variety
are exclusively God's determination.

7.
The Varieties
of Divine Revelation

FROM START TO FINISH, the forms, no less than the actuality, content, and recipients of God's disclosure, are solely a matter of divine determination. "Who will say unto him, What doest thou?" (Job 9:12, KJV). The apostle Paul's reminder that human beings cannot dictate divine prerogatives—"Shall the thing formed say to him that formed it, Why hast thou made me thus?" (Rom. 9:20, KJV)—can be extended rhetorically into "Shall the creature that God addresses say, 'Why hast thou revealed thyself *thus*, and not *so?*' " "Who has been his counselor?" (Rom. 11:34, RSV), the apostle asks. In the Ephesian letter Paul writes of "the breadth, and length, and depth, and height." Dean Henry Alford refers this passage to "all that God has revealed or done" and intends for us to know (*The Greek Testament*, on Eph. 3:18). As Roger Hazelton remarks, the living God "himself sets the terms on which men may come to know Him" (*Knowing the Living God*, p. 15).

God might have imparted to mankind revelation of one variety only or of numerous very different kinds. The angelic hosts might have been made the beneficiaries and ambassadors of redemption (1 Pet. 1:12). Salvation might have been confined to the Hebrews, and not proffered to Gentiles also, or it might have been offered to Aryans and not to Jews. Jesus might have welcomed rather than refused the intervention of legions of angels when his foes moved to destroy him (Matt. 26:53).

To tie divine revelation to human expectation or prognostication would jettison God's freedom in his revelation. Neither the most astute philosopher nor the most enterprising theologian—even if secretly armed with advanced CIA intelligence techniques—can postulate the nature and form of divine disclosure. The methods and means of divine revelation are not to be limited by any a priori foreclosing or prescribing of ways

77

by or in which the God of revelation might reveal himself. Jürgen Moltmann's reminder is wholly appropriate that "the question of the understanding of the world in the light of God and of man in the light of God
. . . can be answered only when it is plain which God is spoken of, and
in what way or with what purpose and intention he reveals himself"
(*Theology of Hope*, p. 43).

In certain passages where A. H. Strong writes of "marks of the revelation" that man may expect God to provide (*Systematic Theology*,
1:115), he presupposes a knowledge of God already somehow derived
"from nature," and the reasons he adduces for expecting a "special
divine revelation" must be understood within this assumption. Not even
"nature," however, gives man any assured basis for anticipating special
divine disclosure. Neither poet nor philosopher, neither cultist nor
moralist, even if he or she be Joseph Smith, Mary Baker Eddy, Emanuel
Swedenborg, Ellen G. White, Augustus H. Strong or Carl Henry, has
authority to confuse human postulation and predication about the invisible world with God's revelation.

In approaching the variety of God's revelation, questions about scientific credibility, historical continuity, linguistic peculiarity, and so on,
must be reserved as second-priority questions. However important they
are in their place, they are not to be introduced in an a priori determinative role. While the concerns of critical investigation have their rightful
role, they are not by subtle intrusion to be allowed to cancel in advance
even the possibility that God alone in his sovereign initiative determines
the actuality, direction, nature, content and diversity of his self-disclosure.
When contemporary conjectural theories so penetrate the discussion of
the theology of revelation that the living God cannot be conceived as
revealing himself in nature because of either the inner continuity or
pervasive chaos of cosmic reality, or in history because of the finiteness
or interdependence of events, or in conscience because of its answerability to culture, or in human concepts and words because of the supposed
relativity of truth or empirical origin of words, then it should be clear
that the matter of God's initiative in revelation is being avoided on debatable assumptions and not being faced and argued in terms of inherent
merit. Few theories in the recent past have been so pejoratively influential as the one that all religions are evolutionary differentiations of a
common underlying essence conceived and responded to by different
persons in different ways. In this case human beings and not God are
decisive for the "varieties of revelation."

In previous generations it was idealism which found identical divine
revelation everywhere that imperiled theology. Today, naturalism, which
acknowledges no divine reality and revelation whatever, is the ogre.
Between these extremes there are mediating theories that uphold selected
facets of the comprehensive revelation of God. These compromises at-
tach excessive theological significance to one or another fragment of the
totality of revelation and in so doing forfeit the unity of the revelation

of God who has nowhere "left himself without a witness" (Acts 14:17). In order to compensate for obscured facets of divine disclosure some venture even to discover divine revelation where it does not exist. The demonic too becomes a welcome reflection of the invisible ultimate.

For us to require God to make our lifetime his time of special revelation on our terms and at our convenience—instead of accepting revelation given in God's time and way when and where he wills—intrudes creaturely conceit and arbitrary preference upon the God whose "ways are not our ways" (Isa. 55:8-9). Such a requirement would cancel both past and future revelation by circumscribing the realities of divine revelation within the here and now; it would telescope into the late twentieth century all the revelation of creation, that of the years 1-30 A.D., and that of the prophetic-apostolic Word. The arrogance of attempting to confine revelation to John Doe in Quarter Four of Century Twenty detaches revelation from any necessary or definitive connection with a "year of our Lord" let alone the biblical writings. Already in Quarter One of this century, Auguste Sabatier had voiced this mood: "Every divine revelation," he said, "every religious experience fit to nourish and sustain your soul, must be able to repeat and continue itself as an actual revelation and an individual experience in your own consciousness" (*Outline of a Philosophy of Religion Based on Psychology and History*, pp. 62 f.). Fortunately, however, God in his revelation is not waiting for daily conference calls initiated by human beings, not even when they gather in Rome or Geneva for high-level dialogue.

Mormon claims about heaven-gifted divine tablets are incredible, not because the God who freely reveals himself could not have manifested himself in that way, but because they fail the tests of truth and verification, and because Joseph Smith's fantastic claims assimilate to God's disclosure what the living God of revelation elsewhere voluntarily and specifically precludes, namely, a special revelation outside the New Testament revelation consummated in Jesus Christ. No less foreign to the revelation of the living God than Mormonism is the secular "theology of revolution" which allegedly hears God speak, as nowhere else, in the social upheavals of the day. By declaring this social ferment to be revelatory, it actually forfeits any objective standard for distinguishing the divine from the demonic, for if God speaks in revolution per se, no distinction remains between good and bad revolutions. The theology of revolution is actually a sophisticated version of spiritism, since it knows divine disclosure only in terms of vagrant voices that penetrate the chaos of modern life and culture.

The Bible itself attests the considerable variety in God's revealing activity by depicting divine disclosure not by one particular term but by a vast range of descriptive concepts. We read in Scripture of different times, of diverse modes, and of various aspects of God's disclosure. Brunner notes the "great variety of words . . . facts and processes" that pertain to the scriptural account of revelation. "God reveals himself through angels," he writes, "through dreams, through oracles (such as Urim and Thummim), through visions and locutions, through natural phenomena and through historical events, through wonderful guidance given to human beings, and through the words and deeds of the Prophets. Above all the New Testament stands the person, the life, the sufferings, death and resurrection of Jesus Christ, the Son of God, as the final self-manifestation of God. . . . Holy Scripture . . . does not only speak of the revelation; it is itself the revelation" (*Revelation and Reason*, p. 21).

In speaking of God's disclosure the New Testament uses such words as *apokaluptein, dēloun, phaneroun* and *deiknunai*, terms whose related ideas include the concepts of "word," "oracle," "inspiration," "scripture." John's Gospel especially uses the terms *witness* and *testimony* to emphasize the decisive significance of Christian revelation. God has revealed himself in numerous modes—in nature, conscience and history, in prophetic and apostolic utterances and writings, in theophanies, in the plagues of Egypt and the parting of the Red Sea, in the larger history of Israel, and in the life and death and resurrection of Jesus of Nazareth. He clearly retains the right to select the times and ways of disclosing himself to his creatures; he alone determines revelation in a striking variety of ways. "The Lord appeared" unto Abraham (Gen. 18:1, KJV); he "came down in the pillar of the cloud . . . and called Aaron and Miriam" (Num. 12:6, KJV). Abraham is called to establish a new nation while still a citizen of the heathen land of Chaldea; Moses is commissioned to lead Israel from Egyptian bondage while still a shepherd in Midian. The risen Christ confronts Saul of Tarsus amid his persecutions of the church. The God of the Bible is the God who revealed himself in dreams and visions, in theophany and incarnation, in words and writings. His multiform ways of revelation defy simplistic reduction.

God has been pleased to disclose himself through his created universe in a different manner than through prophets and apostles, and in yet another manner through Jesus Christ of whom they wrote; in the promised end-time he will reveal himself climactically in still another way. Even evangelical orthodoxy by extreme fundamentalist statements that identify God's revelation exclusively with the Bible has at times obscured the full range of divine disclosure. While this particular emphasis, that the Bible is the only revelation man has, aims to preserve a much neglected and decisively important phase of the revelation of God, it is too simplistic a reading of divine disclosure. By obscuring equally indispensable elements of divine revelation it defeats even the best of intentions and does not truly represent classic evangelical doctrine. The charge that evangelical Christianity propounds only one kind of revelation is much more pertinent to Barthian neoorthodoxy which regards the transcendent Word as the only revelation and dismisses all else as at most "witness" to divine revelation; evangelical Christianity acknowledges both the living Word and the written Word as revelation.

A certain reluctance to approve God's sovereignty in regard to modes of revelation sometimes characterizes evangelicals in their attitude toward the casting of lots in biblical times to ascertain God's will. Numerous Old Testament passages and at least one reference in the New attest that lots were cast to determine the will of God in quite important matters. There was the allotment of Palestine after the conquest, for example (Josh. 14:2; 18:6; 1 Chron. 6:54–81); determining the guilt of suspected criminals (Josh. 7:14; 1 Sam. 14:42); selecting the first king of Israel (1 Sam. 10:20–21); assigning duties in the temple (1 Chron. 25:7–8; cf. 26:13–16; Neh. 10:34); and even choosing a successor to Judas (Acts 1:26). Some scholars regard the Urim and Thummim (Exod. 28:30; Deut. 33:8; Ezra 2:63) as two small stones that signified affirmative and negative decision.

A defensive attitude toward use of the lot in the Bible is doubtless influenced by the prevalence in pagan religions of divination by lot. Many commentators stress that the New Testament records only one resort to the use of lots and, as Floyd E. Hamilton emphasizes, with "no indication that this procedure was approved by God" ("Lots," 3:988). Others consider the instance in Acts to be "a very primitive Old Testament note." This judgment, however, glosses over the Old Testament distinction between Yahweh's authorized prophets and diviners of all kinds (Deut. 18:10–11), as does G. H. C. Macgregor who thinks it "just possible" that the phrase in Acts 1:26 means the apostles "gave their votes" (*The Interpreter's Bible*, 9:35). Deuteronomy 18 in its sharp condemnation of the forms of witchcraft makes no mention of the lot; in fact, as Isaac Mendelsohn notes, "the use of the lot was not considered a practice bordering on magic (cf. Josh. 18:6, 8, where the lot is cast 'before the Lord our God')" ("Lots," 3:164). Sometimes Scripture uses the image of casting lots of Yahweh's determination of human destiny: "He it is who has allotted each its place, and his hand has measured out their portions; they shall occupy it for ever and dwell there from generation to generation" (Isa. 34:17, NEB).

To be sure, lot-casting has a limited role in the Bible, from Aaron's resort to it on the Day of Atonement to choose a scapegoat that symbolically bore the sins of the people into the wilderness (Lev. 16:7–10, 21–22) to the apostolic replacement of Judas by Matthias, the last recorded instance in Scripture and notably pre-Pentecost (Acts 1). The Bible records some examples of lot-casting in a merely pagan mood: there was Haman, villain of the Book of Esther, who sought by lot to discover the hopefully lucky day for his proposed pogrom (Esther 3:7); there were the Roman soldiers who cast lots for the garment of Jesus (John 19:24) in fulfillment of Psalm 22:18. It is always possible, moreover, that Hebrew lapses into idolatry in Old Testament times involved syncretism not only with pagan gods but also with pagan practices in casting of lots.

That is something very different, however, from attributing pagan beliefs and practices to Yahweh's divinely mandated spokesmen. In the New Testament, prayer preceded the use of lots to determine Judas's successor; and the Old Testament clearly states the principle safeguarding the use of lots: "The lot is cast into the lap [that is, a fold in the garment at the breastline from which the lot was shaken out], but the decision is wholly from the Lord" (Prov. 16:33, RSV). Some evangelical scholars aware of these considerations do not draw the theological implications. The land is given by lot in the Old Testament not because the will of "the gods" is presumed to prevail, but because Yahweh had led the Hebrews out of Egypt into his promised land as their sovereign creator and ruler. Israel is herself Yahweh's "lot" or portion (Deut. 9:29; cf. 32:8-9). It is noteworthy that Philo, while speaking of God as the lot of the Levites, writes skeptically of the lot; in biblical context the sovereignty of God so overarches the idea of lot that no need for skepticism exists concerning it (Werner Foerster, "Klēros," 3:762 f.). Modern science further illustrates the difference between the nonbiblical and biblical views of chance. For it, chance is that which cannot be humanly predicted, whereas the God of the Bible determines or disposes the lot and nothing happens by chance.

Although the customary Greek word for determination by lot is klēros, the verb lagchanō appears in both John 19:24 (of the Roman soldiers) and Luke 1:9 (of Zacharias's lot to offer temple incense) as well as in Acts 1:17 (of Judas's role with the apostles as a divine appointment). Lagchanō is used also in 2 Peter 1:1 where the Gentiles are said to be divinely appointed to faith of equal value to that of believing Jews. Both Greek terms emphasize divine determination. In Colossians 1:12 (RSV) the meaning of "the inheritance (klēros) of the saints" is more properly "the lot of the saints." Commenting on this passage, Francis W. Beare remarks: "At first the meaning is the lot that is cast; then that which is distributed by lot—the allotment; finally, the idea of 'lot' practically disappears in the sense of 'assigned portion.' In the O.T. story the Promised Land was divided by lot among the tribes of Israel (Josh. 14–19); and a part of a tribal allotment might be assigned to an individual . . . (Josh. 15:13). Now the idea is spiritualized; the 'lot of the saints' is no earthly territory, but an eternal abiding place in the presence of God" (The Interpreter's Bible, 11:159). In respect to revelation, the role of the lot seems to have been eclipsed by the post-Pentecost scriptural proclamation of the apostles that the will of God is to be appropriated in spiritual freedom. It was by the Holy Spirit—not by lot—that the apostle Paul himself was turned to Macedonia and prevented from preaching in Asia (Acts 16:6).

No one has private license to exalt any of these varieties of divine revelation above another, or to dichotomize God's disclosure, or to isolate one strand from the others. No liberty is given to fragment or belittle any of it and thereby to weaken the import of the whole and perhaps even unwittingly nullify it. Yet nothing is more characteristic of recent neo-Protestant theology than the tendency to prize and proclaim only certain facets of divine disclosure, and to demean Scripture as the form of revelation divinely authoritative in our time. Hence the debate over divine revelation in the Christian community today centers not only on the nature of revelation but also on its forms and content. Presumably to enhance Christianity's appeal to the modern mind, theologians in the recent past rested the case for theism especially upon selected slivers of God's comprehensive revelation—whether personal, historical, cosmic, or whatever. Invariably this selective approach spelled disaster for artfully constructed modern schemes. Carl E. Braaten's comment is to the point: "The pendulum swings back and forth, and nowhere more conspicuously than in German theology. School after school has hastily and short-windedly constructed its theological position on one principle. The ultimatum 'either/or' is more exhilarating than the balanced 'both/and.' Disciples of these schools languish under the tyranny of a single principle" (*History and Hermeneutics*, p. 51).

One can readily understand, of course, how a selected feature of the comprehensive disclosure of God might hold special fascination for this or that system of theology, or seem specially significant in some particular philosophical context or historical situation. But when other equally important facets of divine revelation are neglected or deleted, the resulting imbalance and distortion soon incite mayhem in manipulating the content of revelation. Amid the failure of recent theologians to recover the full panorama of divine revelation, much of the turmoil in contemporary theology can be traced to the continual readjustment of concessive and compromised projections of divine revelation by mediating scholars of the recent past. Paul Althaus said concerning the frenzied internalization of revelation by some neoorthodox theologians that he "could never understand how one could wish to be responsible to the Church and to theology for abandoning the whole world of nature and history to scepticism and secularism, and to parrot what atheistic philosophy has done towards taking God out of our life—and to claim at the same time that the glory of Christ was maintained" (quoted by Heinz Zahrnt, *The Question of God*, p. 63). A similar protest against subjectively eclipsing unpalatable facets of revelational content or eliminating one or another of the revelational varieties may be directed equally well against theologians who by isolating nature or history or conscience as preferred carriers of divine disclosure shatter the impact of the manifold fullness of God's comprehensive revelation. "What God hath joined together, let not theologians put asunder" is a timely warning against the modern manipulation of the divinely determined varieties of revelational disclosure.

A general revelation of the Creator in his creation is integral to Christian doctrine founded upon Scripture and beyond that upon the factualities of the universe. Anyone who denies this doctrine places himself not only in unmistakable contradiction to the Bible and to the great theological traditions of Christendom that flow from its teaching, but also against the living God's disclosure in cosmic reality and in mankind to which Scripture testifies (Rom. 1:19–21). While Roman Catholic doctrine conflates general revelation into natural theology—unfortunately the theology of Thomas Aquinas divorced the observation of nature from revelational considerations—medieval theology never intended any denial that the universe bears the marks of dependence upon the eternal. Although they rejected scholastic misconceptions, the Protestant Reformers vigorously affirmed God's revelation in creation. Calvin and Luther alike emphasized that God makes himself known in his works, a theme that occurs repeatedly in their writings. Recently even some influential theists have denied this universal revelation, doing so in deference to the epistemological theories of Kant and Ritschl, and to dialectical-existential misconceptions that revelation is solely salvific and internal.

Psalm 19, often considered the classic Old Testament text on God's disclosure in the creation, may be taken as a summary statement of what many so-called "nature psalms" affirm. New Testament passages that emphasize the doctrine are not difficult to find; among them are John 1:4, 9; Acts 14:17; 17:26–28; Romans 1:18–20, 28–32; 2:14–16. The apostle Paul emphasizes that "all that may be known of God by men lies plain before their eyes; indeed God himself has disclosed it to them. His invisible attributes, that is to say his everlasting power and deity, have been visible, ever since the world began, to the eye of reason, in the things he has made. There is therefore no possible defence for their conduct; knowing God, they have refused to honour him as God, or to render him thanks" (Rom. 1:20–21, NEB). While he stresses in Romans 1 that the natural man suppresses the truth, Paul leaves no doubt that it is revealed *truth* that is being thwarted. God's invisible being has been *clearly seen* ever since the creation through his created reality; it is here that God universally confronts man. According to George Vanderlip, "the Greek words are, literally, 'his invisible *things.*' The Revised Standard Version puts in the word 'nature.' The New English Bible adds 'attributes,' the C. B. Williams translation has 'characteristics,' and Weymouth has 'perfections.' All these are interpretations" (*Paul and Romans*, p. 32). Whatever the wording may be, there is no alternative, as even Brunner recognizes, to "revelation given to man as a rational being . . . perceived in a rational act" (*Revelation and Reason*, p. 63) and continuing as such even at the present time. Man's reason is therefore the endowment which enables him to be a recipient of divine revelation; creatures lacking reason do not share the universal disclosure. Everywhere mankind in all ages is given "some clue to his nature" (Acts 14:17, NEB).

That the Logos "lights every man," that God did not leave the heathen "without a witness," that he has written divine law even upon the conscience of the Gentiles, that he is "not far from every one of us" (Acts 17:27, KJV) are integral features of the New Testament message. In addition to the external revelation in the cosmos, man's moral conscience relates him internally to the God of revelation: "When the Gentiles, who have no knowledge of the Law, act in accordance with it by the light of nature, they show that they have a law in themselves, for they demonstrate the effect of a law operating in their own hearts. Their own consciences endorse the existence of such a law, for there is something which condemns or excuses their actions. We may be sure that all this will be taken into account in the day of true judgment, when God will judge men's secret lives by Jesus Christ . . ." (Rom. 2:14–16, Phillips). In other words, no one anywhere at any time can escape the inner, secret, guilty knowledge of the true God and of his demand for spiritual submission and moral obedience. The Logos of God "enlightens every man" (John 1:9, RSV); no one can pull the curtains on the God of revelation. Paul puts it bluntly in Romans 1:21–28 (Phillips): "They knew all the time that there is a God, yet they refused to acknowledge him as such" (1:21). They "deliberately forfeited the truth of God and accepted a lie" (1:25). "They considered themselves too high and mighty to acknowledge God" (1:28).

Since human beings are culpable sinners because of revolt against light, to deny general revelation would destroy the basis of moral and spiritual accountability. Such denial, moreover, would obscure mankind's original relationship to God, a fellowship which redemptive revelation aims to recover by telling us what changes are necessary to restore us to the will of the Maker and Redeemer of human life. All mankind is called upon to understand the meaning of this primal revelation of God's wisdom and omnipotence in the created universe. "Not only *may* we, but we *ought* and *must* . . . learn to see Him in His works of creation," writes Brunner (ibid., p. 77, n. 24). The doctrine of God's revelation in the created universe is integral to comprehensive divine revelation.

This primal revelation is not limited simply to the Adamic era, but is a presupposition of ongoing individual and collective existence in all times and places. It is not something that had actuality only in the remote past. As Paul emphasizes, the Creator God's testimony to himself in creation continues daily and hourly and moment by moment. Fallen man in his day-to-day life is never completely detached nor isolated from the revelation of God. His frustrating of divine revelation is attested in part by the fact of human guilt, which presupposes revolt against the light of revelation. For this revolt against God's disclosure he is held responsible and not without guilt (Eph. 4:18). His revolt is attested also by the moral struggle that characterizes human existence (Rom. 2:15). Man's predicament in his estrangement from God is therefore not that of an absence of light; forever and always he stands in continuing relationship to the Logos whose brilliance he constantly bedims but cannot extinguish. Never and nowhere are the heathen or any of us left without a witness to the living God, however much man deflects and ignores this revelation.

God's general revelation is presupposed not only because the revelation of Scripture declares it to be the basis of man's moral and spiritual responsibility to God. In an even deeper sense it is mankind's revolt against this general revelation, both in Adam and on each one's individual account, that constitutes human beings sinners. The universal revelation in creation makes all humans responsible and frames their guilt. Rejection of God's general revelation is what makes men and women heathen.

Unlike special revelation, general revelation does not exhibit or shelter from the consequences of sin—its guilt, corruption and penalty. General cosmic-anthropological revelation is continuous with God's special revelation in Jesus Christ not only because both belong to the comprehensive revelation of the living God, but also because general revelation establishes and emphasizes the universal guilt of man whom God offers rescue in the special redemptive manifestation of his Son. Indeed, only through special revelation do fallen human beings know the full implications of general revelation and of human sinfulness. This is not to say that general revelation is obscure or unintelligible or known only to faith; scriptural revelation publishes the content of general revelation to all men regardless of their personal faith. While regeneration kindles interest in both special and general revelation, and illumines subtler nuances of revelation, it in no way qualifies persons to perceive that revelation, any more than faith alone automatically discovers the content of revelation.

To be sure, neither Scripture nor human experience warrants the notion that, as a recipient of God's general revelation, man in sin can translate that revelation into undiluted truth about God, that is, into a "natural theology." God declares that his general revelation to man has a wholly different outcome. It is not into "proofs" of the living God's existence, but into an occasion of revolt and estrangement that man the sinner turns the general disclosure of God. The Bible connects the universal or general revelation of God not with "natural theology" but with man's guilt (Rom. 1:20). The emphasis is not that man as fallen can no longer discern God's truth in general revelation; Paul the apostle connects the universal revelation of God in nature "since the creation of the world" with God's anger because man ongoingly suppresses the truth in unrighteousness (Rom. 1:18).

The terms *general* and *special* revelation are preferable to the terms *natural* and *supernatural,* since the term *natural* suggests a type of revelation that is not supernatural in source and content (as all divine revelation must be) and thus implies that the revelation in nature, history and mankind is independent of God's initiative. Louis Berkhof observes: "The distinction between natural and supernatural revelation was found to be rather ambiguous, since all revelation is supernatural in origin and, as a revelation of God, also in content" (*Systematic Theology,* pp. 36 f.). Nor does the term *general* as readily convey the notion—as might *natural* revelation—that mankind before the fall had no need of special revelation. Before the fall Adam indeed had a better grasp of general revelation, but he was vouchsafed special revelation as well in the Garden of Eden.

Alongside the cosmic-anthropological revelation stands God's soteriological revelation, addressed to the whole world through a chosen people and climaxed in the incarnation of God in Christ. God need not have addressed this particularistic redemptive revelation to the Hebrews or to anyone; the Hebrews were not a people of special merit but simply the object of God's sovereign election. Moreover, God's special revelation might have been addressed exclusively and finally to the Hebrews. The God of revelation was not obliged by any internal necessity to extend his offer of mercy beyond Israel. His redemptive disclosure is a revelation of grace, conferred upon the Hebrews for the purpose of demonstrating to the world the blessings of serving the one true God (Mic. 4:2; Isa. 55:4–5). When at his incarnation God the Son is forsaken by his own chosen people, the redemptive offer is extended to all men everywhere by divine mandate.

Because God willed to make himself known thus, he provided a universal revelation in the cosmos and in history, a general anthropological revelation in the mind and conscience of man, and to the Hebrews as a chosen people a particular salvific revelation consummated in Jesus Christ as the promised Messiah and head of the church. God is universally self-disclosed, therefore, in the created world; in man who bears the remnants of the divine image even in his moral rebellion; and in the whole sweep of history that repeatedly falls under God's moral judgment. In redemptive revelation, God discloses himself in the once-for-all saving acts of Judeo-Christian history, particularly in Israel's exodus from Egypt and the consequent founding of the Hebrew nation, and in Jesus' resurrection from the tomb and the consequent founding of the Christian church. And he is disclosed in Jesus Christ the incarnate Logos. He is revealed, moreover, in the prophetic-apostolic Word, in the whole canon of Scripture which objectively communicates in propositional-verbal form the content and meaning of all God's revelation. In Scripture, moreover, God forewarns mankind of his final eschatological disclosure and reminds the world that the resurrection of Jesus Christ supplies an actual sample of a future resurrection of men everywhere from the dead.

God therefore has communicated the truth about himself in a surprising variety of ways. As B. B. Warfield writes, "In whatever diversity of forms, by means of whatever variety of modes, in whatever distinguishable stages it is given, it is ever the revelation of the One God, and it is ever the one consistently developing redemptive revelation of God" (*The Inspiration and Authority of the Bible*, p. 96).

Does the affirmation by evangelical orthodoxy that Scripture is God's Word then encroach upon and conflict with recognizing Jesus Christ as supremely the Word of God? There is no question here of equating the Bible with Jesus of Nazareth, or vice versa, for God wills each and every variety of revelation for a distinct purpose. Therefore, neither the revelation in Jesus nor that in the Bible nor that in conscience nor that in nature can replace one another. Each is an indispensable and individual facet of God's comprehensive disclosure.

Although God alone determines the forms and diversity of divine revelation, certain ingenious dogmaticians, however well-intentioned, have in God's name projected novel forms of revelation that have served, unfortunately, to associate God with forms that do not properly belong to his revelation. Is Barth in his exposition of "the Word of God in its threefold form" (*Church Dogmatics*, I/1, pp. 98–140) faithful to the truth of revelation, or in order to commend his own special theory of revelational forms does he unjustifiably appeal to the Protestant Reformers' insight "into the dynamics of the mutual relationships" involved in divine revelation (I/1, p. 139)? Is his reproach of evangelical Christianity for supposedly "freezing up the connection between Scripture and revelation" defensible? Again, is Brunner on solid theological ground when he speaks of both the Old and New Testaments not as revelation but as mere pointers or testimony to divine revelation? The emphasis on Scripture as witness to revelation—or more ambiguously as "revelation in the form of witness"—is a neo-Protestant formula for denying that Scripture has revelational status; but does Jesus Christ really share this denial?

In order to be true to the self-revealing God, the exposition of divine disclosure must do full justice to all the varieties of revelation which the living God has used to make known his comprehensive disclosure. His surprising confrontation of the human race in remarkably diverse ways, and the wonder of his comprehensive disclosure, call for untrammeled consideration of the whole of God's diffuse manifestation of himself and his purposes. Inattention either through indifference or distortion to the many ways in which God has conveyed his Word leads to the theological tragedy and trauma of veiling from mankind what God himself plainly discloses.

Among the most influential early twentieth-century reductions of this comprehensive revelation is the dialectical theology of Karl Barth. Barth denied God's universal divine disclosure in nature, history and human reason, and limited revelation to special personal confrontation.

Barth was doubtless right in rejecting natural theology. For the Protestant Reformers the "natural theology" elaborated from the universe by the scholastics was a pagan distortion of the revelation in the creation. God's revelation in created reality results not in theological truth but rather in the unregenerate man's misconception of God and, in view of the sinner's revolt against light, inevitably in a pagan notion of God. Only special redemptive revelation remedies this predicament. Paul declares that man "holds down the truth [general revelation] in unrighteousness"; through his sinful response he, in fact, transforms it into idolatrous alternatives. Brunner puts the contrast succinctly: "Biblical and natural theology will never agree; they are bitterly and fundamentally opposed" (*Revelation and Reason*, p. 61).

Barth's controversy with Brunner turned on several considerations. For one thing, Barth insisted that all divine revelation is special or salvific, while Brunner insisted that man's sense of responsibility and guilt as a sinner presupposes the fact of universal revelation. Barth differed from Brunner also in contending that general revelation necessarily implies natural theology, or a "testimony catechized out of the heathen." In *Natur und Gnade* (1934; English translation "Nature and Grace") Brunner had declared for a "Christian natural theology" over against scholastic natural theology. This view Barth repudiated as Thomistic, anti-Reformation and pro-Enlightenment. Brunner replied by emphasizing the biblical texts that support general revelation, and showed that he was therefore very much in line with the Reformers. Barth, in turn, issued his now famous *Nein!* ("No!"). Knowledge of God not derived from Christ, he said, is antichrist; to seek revelation in nature is like staring at a poisonous snake which will soon hypnotize one and bite. It was Brunner's biblical verification of general revelation alongside a vigorous rejection of natural theology that provoked Barth to pursue the distinction between "natural theology" and "Christian natural theology" (*Church Dogmatics*, II/1, pp. 107–141). While acknowledging that men universally have always stood in a positive relation to God's truth in creation, even while they denied and betrayed it, Barth erodes the impact of this comment by channeling Romans 1:19 into special revelation as alone enabling man to recognize the original revelation. From the fact that only redemptive revelation enables fallen man properly to interpret general revelation, Barth infers that man becomes a sinner only by rejecting redemptive revelation, and that general revelation does not, in fact, exist. The Bible, however, clearly declares man culpable because he transmutes and rejects a primary universal revelation.

Barth's denial and repudiation of general divine revelation was just as costly an error as the scholastics' espousal of natural theology. G. C. Berkouwer is absolutely right when he insists that the exposition of God's "general revelation"—if it is to be true to the announced disclosure of God himself—must not rule out the special or particular revelation of God any more than God's special revelation in Christ dare obscure general divine revelation ("General and Special Revelation," pp. 15 ff.). To repudiate general revelation nullifies the very biblical witness which, while insisting on God's special revelation, at the same time insists also upon the reality of general divine revelation. Likewise, to repudiate special revelation would challenge the claim of Jesus of Nazareth to be *"the* way, *the* truth, and *the* life" (John 14:6, KJV), but who depicted God as also sending rain upon just and unjust alike (Matt. 5:45). To speak of a general divine revelation that in principle excludes a special divine revelation is to superimpose in advance a limitation upon the pattern of God's disclosure that cannot be drawn from the fact and nature of God's revelation itself. Any legitimate discussion of varieties of divine disclosure in the context of the comprehensive revelation of the living God must therefore encompass the harmony between special and general revelation. Special revelation must not be demoted to an inferior position within general revelation, nor may general revelation be stripped of universal significance by special revelation. As Berkouwer remarks, "The confession of God's revelation in all the works of His hands does not demean the revelation of God in Christ to relative or lesser importance, but, on the contrary, *serves rather to point toward* that revelation in its saving character amid human estrangement from God" (ibid., p. 16). The relation of general to special revelation is, first, that general revelation is the presupposition of redemptive revelation. This interdependence of revelation is a unique feature of God's disclosure; the final eschatological revelation presupposes the Old and New Testaments, and special revelation in its entirety presupposes general revelation. Through scriptural revelation the content of general revelation in all created reality can be properly comprehended even by man in revolt. Indeed, it is the Bible alone which enables man to assess fully the revelation in God's created works.

So diverse are the ways and means of divine revelation that the self-revealing God may be said to have ventured almost every pattern of disclosure short of his final eschatological confrontation of man. But not until God is all and in all (1 Cor. 15:28) and "dwells with" men (Rev. 21:3) will all distinction of ways and times of God's revelation be transcended. Already now the language of praise anticipates a coming day when the one all-encompassing revelation of the living God will everywhere surround man. Religious worship anticipatively gathers up into a single climactic act of devotion the revelation of God in creation and in the cross, the marvel of his presence and disclosure in all human and redemptive history, and the joy of man's coming heavenly home. For the sake of those related to God's revelation only by way of revolt and who in their guilt remain exposed to his wrath, we may be grateful that God's final eschatological revelation has not yet been given, and that divine forgiveness and new life proclaimed by God through his Holy Son and the Holy Scriptures are still accessible to all who come by faith.

The God who reveals himself is still addressing murmuring nomadic hearts that refuse to enter his promised land; he still calls vagabonds out of a modern wasteland to redemptive fellowship. As the Spirit of eschatological revelation presupposes the Old and New Testaments, and God ongoingly convicts men of sin and imparts new life to all who believe, his self-disclosure in the world takes its free course daily and hourly, even moment by moment, in a galaxy of revelational witness that renders mutinous man an inexcusable rebel.

8.
Divine Revelation
in Nature

WHEN NEO-PROTESTANT THEOLOGY lost the biblical doctrine that God is universally revealed throughout his creation—not only in man's internal being and in external historical events but through nature as well—it soon found itself espousing the case for theism in novel and abortive ways. Modern interpreters who opted for a variety of alternatives helped shape a wide cleavage between nature and human history as the locus of divine revelation.

This deflection of revelation from nature to one or another sphere or spheres—whether to history and/or to man's inner psychological processes or to some more exotic channel—was partly an overreaction against the excessive claims of speculative theologians like Aquinas for whom the existence of God rested solely on sense observations from the universe. It was stimulated further by certain modern philosophical theories. Hume limited man's knowledge solely to sense perceptions and memory images, while Kant believed that the knower's creative contribution accounts for the orderly structure of nature in our experience. Naturalistic evolutionists contend that all phenomena are wholly explicable in terms of evolutionary emergence, while technocratic scientism limits external reality to mathematically connectible sequences. Each and any of these premises requires a sharp dichotomy between nature—in such circumstances necessarily nonrevelatory of the Divine—and any purportedly revelational sphere.

To proclaim the reality of general divine revelation and yet to abandon the possibility of cosmic revelation requires correlating God's universal manifestation with some other arena than nature. In recent years varied and contradictory channels have been proposed as such carriers of revelation, among them superhistory, paradoxic confrontation and exis-

91

tential encounter. Alongside such novel notions, others emphasized broken fragments of the historic Christian view that God reveals himself intelligibly in external historical events as well as to everyman's mind and conscience, particularly over against Barth's dialecticized revelation and Bultmann's existentialized revelation that excluded external nature, objective history and human reason as channels of transcendent disclosure.

Since the post-Cartesian era, Western thinkers have in fact sharply distinguished *nature* and *history*, whereas the Hebrew Old Testament and New Testament writers viewed them as a unified sphere of God's sovereign purpose and action. This unity of nature and history in serving God's purpose and plan is an inescapable biblical motif. Both the creation and the flood narratives are stark reminders of the dependence of history upon nature's God. The creation account, the exodus account, and the Gospel records of Jesus' life and ministry clearly and repeatedly coordinate so-called natural and historical events in which Yahweh actively works out his purposes. The great Hebrew psalms echo not only God's sovereign power as Creator but also his lordship over the nations and all mankind (cf. Ps. 33:6–9).

Some critical scholars assert that the Hebrews had no distinctive view of nature, or that they simply shared the outlook of the ancient Semitic nature-religions. This claim has been made not only by those who completely disown any distinctive Hebrew conception of revelation, but also by some who, although conceding and championing such a concept, nevertheless correlate it one-sidedly with historical events only and not with cosmic revelation. Edmond Jacob comments that "Israel's conception of the world is so little influenced by religion that it was rather an obstacle than an aid to faith" (*Theology of the Old Testament*, p. 146). Similarly Victor Monod had earlier contended that the Hebrews considered the material universe only a temporary setting and removable background for the divine-human drama (*Dieu dans l'univers*, p. 16).

To deny that the Hebrews had a distinctive view of the material universe, and to reduce their outlook to that of other religions of the ancient Semitic world, is possible only by neglecting the biblical sources or by forcing alien and unnatural views upon them. H. Wheeler Robinson (*Inspiration and Revelation in the Old Testament*) has noted the sharp contrast between Babylonian astrology which influenced much of the Near East and in some respects anticipated modern conceptions of natural law, and the Hebrew conception of nature. "The regular rising and setting of the sun, moon and the constellations," he points out, "together with planetary movements amongst the signs of the zodiac, supplied a pattern of fixed order. This was believed to impose itself upon both natural phenomena and human actions, because of the cardinal premise of astrology that the world above supplies the key to the conduct of the world below" (p. 1). For all its parallel emphasis on God's general revelation both in history and to the human mind and conscience, the biblical exposition in no way excludes the cosmic universe as a realm of ongoing divine disclosure (particularly in view of the unity of God's creation). In fact, it stresses God's revelatory activity through nature. Despite his emphasis on the priority of historical revelation, Robinson notes: "The conception of a God who works in history is inseparably linked to his manifestation in natural phenomena. He is what Nature, as well as history, reveals himself to be, and Nature is his peculiar language" (p. 4). Every reader of the Old or New Testament is familiar with the special speech that nature's God speaks. The heavens declare God's glory, writes the Psalmist (19:1), while the apostle Paul declares that created reality from its beginnings has made known the invisible attributes of God's everlasting power and deity (Rom. 1:20).

Rudolf Bultmann contends that the ancient Hebrews did not see God's revelation in the ordered course of nature, this being but a later emphasis of Greek philosophers (*Primitive Christianity in Its Contemporary Setting*, pp. 17 f.)—a theory compatible with the existential concentration of revelation in internal confrontation. The 19th Psalm proclaims abundantly to the contrary.

The Bible's intimations of a divine activity in nature are far more explicit, in fact, than in many ancient Near Eastern cults. Indeed, one cannot escape the irreducible contrasts between Israel's view of man's natural environment and that of other ancient religions. Gerhard von Rad emphasizes for one thing the vastly different attitudes toward images of deity. The Hebrews were divinely enjoined from fashioning any pictorial representations of God, from worshiping him in the guise of "any likeness of any thing that is in heaven above, or . . . in the earth beneath, or . . . in the water under the earth" (Exod. 20:4, KJV). Yahweh is transcendent Creator; he cannot be likened to creaturely things (Isa. 40:15–28), least of all to man-made idols that would materialize and spatio-temporalize the infinite and invisible deity. The pagan Semitic religions, however, assigned a central role to cult-images, assuming that their divinities were somehow present in images. The material representations were thought to supply a direct means of contact with deity and to mediate blessing and salvation to the worshiper. Von Rad explains "the extraordinary tolerance which idol-cults extend to one another" by the fact that the pagan mind finds "an infinite variety of points at which divinity shines through, and every point in which man's world is at least potentially a point of divine intrusion, an expression of deity, and to this extent a means of communication between God and man" ("Some Aspects of the Old Testament World-View," p. 147).

All this might seem to count against the view that the Old Testament emphasizes the revelation of God in the created universe. Nonetheless the Hebrews indubitably declared that the heavens and earth reveal God's glory. As Bernhard Anderson reminds us, however, they "refused to say that the universe is a direct self-revelation of Yahweh, as though it were an emanation of his being or as though he were a power within it" ("Man's Dominion over Nature").

In further contrast with the pagan religions, man in the biblical outlook is not immersed in nature nor a mystical participant in it. Here the scriptural representation differs both from the monism of ancient Asian religions, which considers man a mere appearance of nature (Brahminism) or so correlated with it that the self has impermanent significance (Buddhism), and from modern Western romanticism.

Loss of the biblical perspective nourishes a reactionary contrast not only of nature and history as rivals but also of man and nature as such. This mind-set encourages man to detach himself from nature lest it trap him. Since nature is thought to be outside man and wholly different from and inferior to him, man who transcends nature feels free to manipulate and exploit it for his own ends.

It should surprise no one that man, who tends to play the role of God over nature, should go to yet another extreme and come to view nature as in some sense the divine source and support of his existence and an object of devotion. Both approaches are in fact nonbiblical ways of deflating the tension, consequent upon the fall, between man and nature and are truly overcome only in the context of redemption. The latter predilection, the worship of nature, issues in extremely divergent misconceptions. Spinoza, for example, identified the mathematical network of nature as God, while Albert Schweitzer espoused a pantheistic "reverence for life." Personal idealism and process theology regard nature as part of God's life—the former sees it as God's externalized thought and the latter as a necessity to God's becoming.

While in earlier decades such pantheistic representations were at times confused with biblical perspectives, today the contrasting view, which pits assertive man against nature like some divinely designated conqueror, is more often than not attributed to the Bible. In this sense modern secular theologians like Gerardus Van Der Leeuw (*Sacred and Profane Beauty*) "credit" Christianity with fanning the technocratic revolution. Biblical religion is held responsible for man's autonomous and manipulative control of nature and all the baneful consequences of scientism (cf. Lynn White, Jr., "The Historical Roots of our Ecological Crisis," pp. 1203 ff.).

Somewhat on the edge of ecological concerns the conviction is growing that contemporary theologians have concentrated revelational interests too much upon history as a realm of divine disclosure at the expense of nature. Instead of abandoning the cosmos to the natural sciences, the current situation, we are told, demands a "theology of nature." Evident is a resurgence of literature that correlates man and nature. There is a renewal of interest in "natural theology," and sometimes an infatuation with Oriental religions more geared to nature than to history. Even today's drug subculture and horoscope faddism are probing the transcendent in ahistorical ways. Contemporary literature and life thus try to overcome any threat of polarization between man, history, culture and nature. Nature increasingly becomes decisive for all other facets of creaturely existence.

Too often, even in theological discussion, we forget that most moderns use the term *nature* as a very specific conceptualization, one that excludes a great deal once considered integral and indispensable to any serious discussion of spatio-temporal realities. The point is not that *nature* is but an empty form-category or—as Kant regarded the term *world*—merely an organizing principle of the human mind. To be sure, the term in its philosophical intention designates the powers and processes of the universe comprehended as a unified whole. But does this schematization include or does it exclude personal thought and agency—specifically, the distinctively human? Is man to be considered part of nature or distinct from it? Obviously we do not perceive or experience nature as a whole, any more than we do culture or life. Nonetheless, nature is much more than simply a concrete reality that yields to sense experience. Human beings stand in many diverse direct relationships to nature, carry nature in themselves, and are in some way part of nature —as is evident enough from experiencing a blizzard, or a throbbing headache, or physical death. The *Oxford English Dictionary*'s fifteen definitions of *nature* surely attest that it evokes a much more flexible universe of discourse than we think.

Nature is in fact always viewed through one of several possible conceptual models. The African primitive reads it one way, the Western secularist another. Men of biblical outlook read it in still quite another. Many persons fail to realize that the modern technocratic view represents but one of many possible ways of conceiving nature. They are unaware not only of its sharp antithesis to the biblical view of nature, but also its sweeping differences from other earlier views. Until just the last few centuries, not only Judeo-Christian theology but the main traditions of Western philosophy as well grounded the natural order in the supernatural and viewed nature as an intelligible context in which man and his purposes are meaningfully ensconced. If we begin with God's creation we comprehend reality in a way very different from that in which naturalism professes to "see" it, and the term *nature* itself becomes too ambiguous a category to serve us well. Creation covers all that is not-God, and views man and the cosmos in divinely established reciprocal relationships that are mutually dependent upon the Creator. The not-God is a realm of dependent reality sustained by God's purposive will; all its possibilities of order and uniqueness are grounded in him.

The modern intellectual tends to take the physical sciences as the referent through which he understands nature. Although his conceptualization of nature is often proclaimed by its sponsors to be nonmetaphysical, it presupposes in actuality a concealed and highly arbitrary metaphysics. It finds in natural processes alone a paradigm for interpreting the whole range of life and experience. Naturalism is its credo, and this presupposition wholly transforms and, in fact, deletes any Christian understanding of reality. Not only is one who lives in the late twentieth century continually confronted by this view, but as part of the mood of the times it almost inevitably influences him in every area of life. Contemporary culture views man as a part of nature, and not in any sense outside nature. Defined as perceptually experienced structures and events, nature is considered to be the indispensable source and context of man's being and life. All human concerns are set within natural processes alone; the central concerns of human meaning, value and purpose have no intelligible grounding in the externally real world.

This naturalistic view of nature shapes not only the Western philosophical tradition as inspired by Descartes and Kant, but also the theological tradition deriving from Ritschl, Barth and Bultmann. In contrast to the biblical outlook, it sees nature only as mechanical and nonteleological, and by an inner necessity of this misconstruction excludes from nature the very possibility of divine revelation. The same antithesis of impersonal nature and personal reality underlies most modern evolutionary interpretation, which sees in man's rationality, morality and purposive determination features to which nature is alien. While compromising nature and history into spheres void of objective purpose and meaning, neo-Protestant theology remains confident that Christian categories and principles can be preserved if only they are filled with new possibilities. This requires, however, locating personal thought and agency outside or above nature, compatible with the modern technocratic view of nature and life. It is remarkable, indeed, that such reconstructions were considered specially commendatory of Christianity to irreligious devotees of the modern world view. Actually, of course, this recasting of biblical doctrine covertly eroded the truth of theology among young intellectuals in the churches and offered those outside no persuasive reason for altering their foreign allegiances.

The real need is to present the Christian revelation as the compelling even if neglected alternative. A reversal of the recent past with its sad compromise of Christian convictions will not of course be achieved simply by propagandizing remnants of an earlier tradition. The death of theological compromise with technocratic scientism, with its erosion of personal significance and moral imperatives, is long overdue. To say that nature is an arena of the living God's intelligible and purposive disclosure is, of course, as easily said as that nature is the ultimate reality. Why it is said—and what is meant by this—is the critically important thing. The biblical doctrines have been so long restated and adjusted to modern conceptual frameworks that their inner power has been lost through interpretative mutation. Simply to repeat Judeo-Christian motifs therefore means very little. Not even evangelical Christians can hope to liberate modern men from their misconceptions about nature, unless they exhibit the modern view's inevitably nihilistic outcome alongside a persuasive statement of the biblical truth. Christianity must surely accuse Western scientific reductionism of having shut out God, purpose, meaning and value from the externally real world. Still further adjustments to "technocratic nature" can only escalate even more the sense of conflict between man and the perceptible world and worsen the turbulence of the human spirit.

Seen in the light of the biblical representation of nature, this naturalistic conceptualization of external reality not only arbitrarily eclipses the supernatural but it also falsifies the natural world, both in its reductive exposition of human nature and in its explication of the cosmos. It presumes to illumine nature by blacking out the Creator's presence and power in created reality, but actually obscures all ultimate metaphysical significance of the personal, rational, moral and purposive. The scripturally attested revelation of God is a revelation not only to and in man internally but also specifically in external nature. Further, it is given not merely alongside and supplementary to man, but in fact is intelligibly correlated with, and an aspect of, the revelation to and in him. Nature is not some theologically insignificant material context in which man lives and works. While nature has no will of its own, no capacity for moral choice, its forms and structures are nonetheless given and sustained by the Logos of God. Pervaded by God's divine presence and power it is an intelligible order serving moral purposes and a realm of providential fulfillment.

In brief, the living God reveals himself in and through nature. The Old Testament repudiation of the Canaanite divinities in the name of Yahweh turned essentially on a controversy over the identity of what is metaphysically ultimate. The Hebrews rejected the ultimacy of the natural processes of nature, and proclaimed instead the revealed personal and moral will of the sovereign Creator of nature and Redeemer of men. The Genesis narrative opens with an unqualified reference to "the absolute beginning of the world" (cf. Walther Eichrodt, "In the Beginning," p. 17). George S. Hendry reiterates that the creation language of the Bible "unquestionably connotes origination" ("Eclipse of Creation," p. 420).

Today's conceptualization of the real once again so anchors the totality of existence in natural processes that it erodes any final significance for personal reality, divine or human.

Irreducibly at stake in this contrast of the biblical and scientistic views is whether the ultimate ontological order is personal or impersonal, whether the principle of Creator-creation or that of natural process best accounts for life and experience—in short, whether God is truly known in his self-revelation or is mere fiction. If modern secularism's explanation of reality as a complex differentiation of space-time events and relationships is adequate, if all conceptualities are to be viewed in deference to evolutionary relativism as mere nets to catch the wind, then the concept of God is no longer serviceable. Or does the theory that reality is only a complex of natural powers and processes do violence both to the external world and to man as a knower and personal agent? Either one must abandon the Hebrew-Christian view of the universe or one must repudiate contemporary naturalism and its radical misrepresentation of reality. One must uphold either the biblical emphasis on the ontological priority of the intelligible Creator or opt for the contemporary reduction of ultimate reality to natural processes. The issue is that precise and that clear-cut.

God, who speaks in nature as the transcendent Creator, declares not only that nature is dependent upon him but also that he is the sovereign (his "eternal power and divinity," as Paul writes) on whom man likewise depends. He is sovereign in and over all relationships involving the created cosmos. The biblical view does not dispute that man's personal existence as a psychosomatic self is so bound up with the organic and physical orders that he is inconceivable in total separation from them. But insofar as modern theory implies that nature and man can be adequately explained through an exclusion of transcendent divine power and moral will, the revelation of the Creator-God working out his rational-moral purposes in created reality demands the inversion of this view. Man, in whom the elements of nature focus in a special responsible rationality, exists in a divinely established reliance on both God and created nature. He either ignores this relationship as an ingrate or gratefully acknowledges it and honors God. If indeed there is divine revelation in and through nature, then man acts culpably and not in ignorance whenever he misidentifies the externally real world in terms only of impersonal mathematically connectible sequences. He also acts culpably and knowingly when he fails to find evidence for God's order in nature whenever the external world forces him to revise hypotheses or when its behavior fulfills his expectations, no less than when he shares in wantonly destroying and polluting nature and in grafting the technological monstrosities and the ugly scars of alien conquest upon nature's visage. The Christian apostle's verdict—"they glorified him not as God, neither were thankful" (Rom. 1:21, KJV)—is as equally appropriate to the modern age of technocratic scientism as it was to the ancient pagan religions.

God's speech in nature is not to be confused with the notion of a talking cosmos, as by those who insist that nature speaks, and that we must therefore hear what nature says as if nature were the voice of God. "Hear God!" is the biblical message, not "Listen to nature!" Nature is God's created order, and in nature God presents himself. While this view runs counter to the naturalistic and pantheistic conceptualizations of nature, it involves no theological antagonism to nature as such, for the Bible sees the whole activity of nature as God's work. Within this activity the Hebrews recognize both the mighty acts of God, or special events associated with his creation and redemption purpose, and his more routine providential activity. While both general and special manifestations of God's holy will are displayed in his created cosmos, they are melded and seen as functioning within one comprehensive divine purpose. Both the regularities of nature and once-for-all events reflect the faithfulness and dependability of the Creator; they are not to be explained simply in terms of a self-consistent cosmos. The regularities of nature—summer and winter, seedtime and harvest, cold and heat, day and night—are a commentary on Yahweh's relationship to his creation (Gen. 8:22). He has a covenant with day and night (Jer. 33:20–21); indeed, there is an "everlasting covenant between God and every living creature of all flesh that is upon the earth" (Gen. 9:16, KJV).

God has much more in mind and at stake in nature than a backdrop for man's comfort and convenience, or even a stage for the drama of human salvation. His purpose includes redemption of the cosmos that man has implicated in the fall. Today the ecological problem is often stated in a way that accommodates the divorce and alienation of history and nature by exaggerating the importance of man and downgrading the importance of nature; the ecological problem thus becomes one of *man's* survival. Seldom are pollution or destruction faced out of concern for safeguarding the cosmos itself except as they threaten man's own future, even if environmentalists speak of preserving a world man can love. Because God considers the human more important than the subhuman it becomes easy for prideful man to conclude that external nature is not only less important than man but also of no value apart from him. He sees nature intended solely for his preferred use as he autonomously manipulates it, as lacking beauty except as he pronounces it beautiful, and as having value only as and if he can channel it to human welfare. The same polarization may be involved in pleas over other living creatures —the vanishing buffalo or polar bear, for example. Here this generation is presumably concerned for our ancient kin, even if in this case a reactionary loving of our "brother animals" momentarily preempts the commandment of neighbor-love. Such concern over the extinction of vanishing species has its place in a Christian outlook, but in a naturalistic view it hardly has in it a vestigial remnant of reason. If man himself is only a passing phase of the evolutionary process, how can a wholly unknown future burden him with moral obligations for lesser species of life?

Ecological experts readily concede that appeals based on human survival lack motivational power unless they also involve immediate self-interest. Anguished by the repeated collapse of post-Christian perspectives, social critics call for imaginative approaches and for moral vision, without really knowing how to mount an effective platform. Those who argue that if self-interest got us into the difficulty, self-interest will also extricate us from it, seem to forget that interest in the species's future differs considerably from one's individual present interest. Without a persuasive metaphysics, human beings will simply pursue their own immediate advantage or desires. Process philosophers attempt to confer divine ontological significance on the whole evolutionary process by seeing it as an expression of God's becoming. Few scientists or theologians are enamored of such speculation, however. The ecological problem obviously cannot be disjoined from the conceptual problem, that is, the conception of nature that man ought and must hold as part of a unified metaphysical and moral perspective. To be sure, simply changing man's concept of nature will not solve the problems of ecology—waste, pollution, destruction—inasmuch as decision and action are imperative. But neither will they be solved without adequate alternative conceptualities that confront inordinate self-interest. The basic issue in ecology, as in every other human problem, is not only the nature of man, nor even the nature of nature, but ultimately also the nature and will of God.

Some critics have recently charged Christianity with promoting the present misunderstanding and misuse of nature because it emphasizes that man is the divinely delegated overlord of the world as an orderly law-governed creation. These presuppositions were basic and important for the rise of scientific confidence in nature as an arena of orderly behavior compatible with human well-being. They are not, however, the source either of positivistic science or of ecological insensitivity. Others argue that human beings universally, whatever their religious outlook, display the same callous indifference toward preserving natural resources and the environment. Unfortunately this charge cannot be wholly denied; it nonetheless fails to appreciate the long-standing interest of evangelical Christianity in humanitarian reforms. It is unfair to blame Christianity for the ecological crisis; what's more, Christianity is best able to arrest it. The Bible has timeless relevance for ecological problems; neither heirs of nor strangers to the Judeo-Christian outlook can afford to overlook its message.

The stripping by secular man of revelational content and ethical priorities from the cultural deposit of an inherited religious viewpoint is what nourishes an irreligious neglect and exploitation of nature. Scientific naturalism, not Christian theism, nurtures man's disposition to desecrate the cosmos. Disinterested abuse of nature is a fearsome by-product whenever scientific abstraction assesses external reality without cognizance of personal moral will. If nature is defined merely as a nonteleological and nonaxiological material realm, and man himself creates whatever values are associated with it, then he will obviously deploy nature only to the realization of his own ends. If ecology is a moral concern, that concern can hardly be supported or enlivened by a merely scientistic conception of nature whose methodology is intrinsically blind to ethical norms. The scientist declares that nature's destiny is entropy, that it is running down. If this is so, why should not man *use* it while he can? If B. F. Skinner is right, that man is but a cog in a mechanistically determined universe, what difference can he make in it even if he wanted to, and why would he want to? The present indignation over the ecological crisis is simply an emotional surd, unless contrary to technocratic scientism it presupposes mankind and human culture to be not simply functions and reflexes of the natural world but also somehow distinct from the cosmos and responsibly related to it. The human species has already done much to upset the earthly balances which sustain life; the biblical revelation provides the most persuasive reasons why mankind can and ought now to take a very different course.

Some speak of the ecological crisis not in terms of man's folly but of nature's revenge: man has so long villified and raped nature that at long last she is angrily taking vengeance. Such poetic representations may have their place. But less imaginative and more biblically based is the fact, now almost wholly absent from ecological considerations, that God who reveals himself discloses not simply his common grace but also his wrath in nature as well as in history. Not only in earthquake and flood, which insurance statisticians readily salute as acts of God, but in ecology also, the hand of God points an indignant finger at man's obliviousness to God's purposes in the cosmos. In the so-called cruel and destructive acts of nature, the scientific technocrat sees only a challenge to escalation of human power and control over nature. But if the heavens declare only the prevalence of industrial smog, if day unto day uttereth only the chatter of mass media, then the glory of God as veiled by technocratic scientism is conceivably indeed a form of judgment.

It seriously distorts both the Old and New Testaments to say that man alone matters to God. From the creation account onward the Bible boldly correlates the fortunes of the cosmos with those of man. Even if man made in his image is declared "very good," God identifies the created gradations of existence that precede man as "good." The earth was not made for man to manipulate as he pleases. Indeed, he is given the vocation of keeping and dressing the garden (Gen. 2:15).

The fall of man has dire consequences also for nature. Man once given dominion over unspoiled nature now copes with a terrain cursed because of him. Nature becomes embroiled in the sordid aspects of man's experience (Rom. 1:22–32); the whole natural world is drawn into the tragedy of man's history (Rom. 8:22–23).

The messianic vision comprehends a restoration of the unity of man and nature. In the Old Testament and in the Gospels as well one finds a profound correlation between phenomena in nature and God's salvific agency in redemptive history. Jesus likened God's kingdom to parables taken from nature; even the birds and flowers provide an example to man (Matt. 6:26–30), and bread and wine become the symbolic elements of Christian communion. From the birth of Jesus to his crucifixion and resurrection the provision of salvation in him is coordinated with awe and veneration in view of what is happening in nature. The terrible imbalances that man's inordinate will has introduced into the natural realm can be solved only if the question of existence is once again set in its proper context. Only the knowledge of God and its implications for man's true self-understanding and for the cosmic implications of redemption can restore order and beauty.

While Scripture may not articulate specific lines of ecological action, it does affirm those principles upon which such action should and must rest. The doctrine of God and his purposes in creation needs to be taken seriously. It faces the question of responsibility not abstractly in the context of human and cosmic concerns, but in view of God revealed as the eternal transcendent Creator. God's eternal power and divinity: this is what the apostle Paul declares to be the message of God's general revelation to mankind. Man must deal with the givenness of God as well as the givenness of nature.

Only the theological perspective will overcome also that sentimental reactionary view which speaks of what *man* can do for nature, as if some new burst of human generosity will guarantee fresh concern and tolerance for nature's long-neglected minority interest. The imperative need is for man to do what is right. The right is what God wills, and God's will embraces man and nature alike. God did not create the world a waste or chaos (Gen. 1:2) but a place to be settled (Gen. 1:3–30; Isa. 45:18). God's purpose in nature is correlated with his purpose for man. It envisions obedient human sonship as attested by the incarnation of the God-man, the divine agent in creation of the cosmos and of man. Though man's welfare, properly understood, is indeed a legitimate criterion in approaching nature, this must be comprehended through a restoration of nature and man alike to their divinely intended purpose.

Hendrik G. Stoker's contrast between man's relationship to God's plan or order as revealed in created reality and man's knowledge of God's self-revelation in the *imago Dei* and in Scripture which man's inordinate will veils and alters, is noteworthy. Through common grace, he suggests, the sinner may periodically pierce the veil, as the givenness of cosmic order forces a revision of one's explanatory theories. The evidence one marshals for an externally given order at one and the same time attests an irreducible plan of God. An interest in created reality that is deliberately restricted and methodologically limited to observational concerns offers only a broken response to the call of man's larger environment.

The setting of human life from its beginning to the present time is far more comprehensive than can be expressed in quantitative mathematical computations. Intelligible implications of its enormous hinterland are borne by the revelation of God that penetrates intuitively and internally the mind and conscience of man and simultaneously witnesses through external cosmic reality and history. The careful observer of nature repeatedly betrays his eagerness to move beyond the mere observational to "observations" about the kind of order he considers implicit in nature. Nowhere is the desire to fashion Homeric gods as evident as among modern scholars who strenuously adduce the scientific method as the only source of truth; scientism becomes their primary god, a prejudice within which other false gods soon seek and find refuge. But every conjectural philosophy of nature is an oblique response to revelational realities. Langdon Gilkey has called attention, for example, to "the rather surprising set of unexperienced things that exist in the Whiteheadian world: prehensions, subjective forms, initial aims, and those omnipresent feelings, are simply assumed without further ado to be *real*, and this complicated picture to be the deepest and most certain form of truth" ("A Christian Natural Theology," pp. 530 ff.).

9.
The Rejection
of Natural Theology

ACCORDING TO SOME PHILOSOPHERS and theologians the existence of a supreme and supernatural being can be reasonably inferred from the data of observation and experience. The empirical substantiation of theism has taken several forms, now often designated as the cosmological, teleological, and moral or anthropological arguments for God, arguments sometimes coordinated into one comprehensive case for theism. More recently, scholars approving this approach have isolated and emphasized one or another of these prongs as being more decisive than the others, but these individual expositions are not always developed in quite the same way.

The cosmological argument first appears in Plato's *Phaedrus* and reappears in his later dialogues, particularly in the *Philebus*, in the *Laws*, and also in the *Timaeus*. It was, however, the form that Aristotle gave this argument in his *Metaphysics* that became influential, particularly through its development by Thomas Aquinas. In popularizing the so-called proofs, Thomas at the same time also complicated their ongoing discussion because of scholastic reliance on Aristotelian terminology. According to many modern critics the traditional exposition depends on built-in subtleties that improperly guarantee the argument's success; on the other hand many defenders of the argument insist that it be divorced from its correlation with Aristotelian conceptions. Several modern expositions are more dependent on the eighteenth-century philosopher Samuel Clarke or on Leibniz than on Aristotle.

Now often summarized under the rubric of "natural theology," Aquinas's influential version of the cosmological proof is still vigorously espoused by many if not most Roman Catholic philosophers as the quasi-official philosophy of their church. Interpreters have differed over whether Aquinas presents a single comprehensive argument or several correlative arguments. Many Protestant thinkers, while unpersuaded of the argument's validity in its Thomistic form, find in it nonetheless some core of truth. Others, including such evangelical scholars as Norman Geisler (*Philosophy of Religion*), Stuart C. Hackett (*The Resurrection of Theism*), and Bruce Reichenbach (*The Cosmological Argument*), insist on its validity.

Aquinas claimed that proper and valid deductions from an empirical observation of man and nature demonstrably prove the existence of God. In developing the empirical case for theism Aquinas's larger aim was to prepare the natural man, once convinced of God's existence by his own reason and apart from divine revelation, to accept supernaturally revealed truth.

The Vatican Council of 1870 gave unqualified support to the Thomistic exposition of natural theology by declaring: "The same holy mother Church holds and teaches that God, the beginning and end of all things, can certainly be known[1] by the natural light of reason from created things. . . ." Pope Leo XIII in the later encyclical *Aeterni Patris* (1879) also commended Thomism as the philosophy of the Roman Catholic church. In his 1948 debate with Bertrand Russell (aired over the British Broadcasting Corporation) Jesuit philosopher Frederick C. Copleston championed Thomism against Russell's agnosticism. "We have to argue from the world of experience to God," affirmed Copleston; "it is only a posteriori through our experience of the world that we come to a knowledge of the existence of that being." The existence of God, moreover, "can be proved philosophically" (the debate appears in *The Existence of God*, John Hick, ed.).

Aquinas's intricate fivefold proof of God appears in the *Summa Theologica* (I, 2, 3), a statement that easily runs a thousand words. Let me summarize it here and give the customary interpretation.

According to Aquinas, sensation gives men an immediate knowledge of things in motion. From this experience, and without epistemological dependence on supernatural considerations, the natural man can elaborate concepts and arguments that logically demonstrate God's existence. Aquinas's proof proceeds from (1) motion, (2) the formality of efficient causation, (3) possibility and necessity, (4) the gradation found in things, and (5) the governance of the world. The first four arguments begin with man's ordinary perceptual experiences of a moving thing, a new object, the mutability of finite realities, the graded perfections of creatures. The arguments in turn set these considerations in the context of teleology or purpose.

The first argument, in brief, is that we perceive things in motion and,

---

1. The phrase "certainly be known" suggests logical validity, as against contemporary Thomists who insist that Thomism argues only for the "existential undeniability" of the fivefold argument. Frederick C. Copleston's brief for "philosophical" proof suggests logically valid proof.

since no body moves itself, the cause of this motion must be external. Now if by way of explanation we introduce another moving body, the same considerations can lead only to an ongoing infinite regression that is unable to account for the production of motion. There must, therefore, be a first mover.

The second argument proceeds similarly from our perception of external cause-effect sequences to a first efficient cause; it does so on the ground that without this first cause no intermediate causes would exist in a causal series.

The third argument is that anything capable of nonexistence (as the universe is in view of its contingency) is not self-sufficient and has its ground elsewhere. For an explanation of itself the contingent requires what necessarily exists—indeed, it requires an inherently unending form of existence. In brief, whatever is not self-explanatory demands what is necessarily eternally existent as its explanation.

The fourth argument is that no perfections can arise in anything except through a cause that displays these qualities in equal or infinite amount; the ultimate cause of the universe, moreover, must exhibit all the varieties of perfection or goodness in infinite degree.

The fifth argument differs from the others by beginning not with universal perceptual experience but with the behavioral adaptation of many observed objects. Blind mechanism, Thomas argues, cannot explain this complex adjustment toward ends; required are a controlling intelligence and providential wisdom.

Taken in order, the arguments, if valid, establish (1) an unending source of all change; (2) a first cause of all productive efficiency in the universe; (3) a necessary ground of all contingent beings and events; (4) an infinitely perfect cause of all excellences in the finite universe; and (5) an intelligent, providential governor over everything. Aquinas insists that the arguments demonstrably prove the existence of God— that is, a single, initial, unchanging, infinitely perfect intelligence.

The argument from motion, many critics emphasize, lacks force in an age which presupposes the dynamic nature of all empirical reality. Aristotle admitted an infinite series of motions in time, but held that this series requires a first mover, equally everlasting. Moderns who view the universe as inherently in process do not consider an infinite series of motions to be irrational and see no need to explain motion transcendently. Thomas's conception of motion is, of course, broader than that of modern science, but this very comprehensiveness complicates the problem posed by his view of causality. Early modern science mechanically linked all causes and effects in a spatiotemporal series that was to be explained only within the finite series, to which our experience is confined. Contemporary science is much less prone to assume such objective causality in nature and, with greater empirical propriety, tends to speak simply of mathematically connectible events. By concentrating on prediction and verification, contemporary scientific interest has no need to resolve the debate over an original productive efficiency, or whether such efficiency underlies the continuities of nature; in fact, many scientists now insist that such issues really fall outside the scope of empirical determination. The Thomist argument that all effects require an ultimately superior causality clashes head on with empirical scientific method. In the interest of precise scientific formulas, the modern devotees of empirical scientism first insisted on merely a proportional equivalence between effects and their postulated causes (to project causes more potent or perfect than necessary to account for their effects impedes technological accuracy), and then questioned the very existence of causes and hence of effects.

Thomas's teleological argument aims to demonstrate God's personal providence but only multiplies the overall difficulties. The problem is not that Thomas affirms the metaphysical status of the good, but rather that (with Aristotle) he insists that evil is only a privation of the good and not a positive reality. He holds, moreover, that by empirical observation one can discern a striving by the entire creaturely realm to embody its appropriate perfection, can decipher the essential nature of goodness, truth and beauty, and can find their unity in an absolute and universal goodness, that is, in God himself. Such claims put an intolerable strain on empirical method, to which Hume looked in vain for evidence of God. The problem of evil leaves us in any event with a finite God at best, although Hume admits that if somehow one could show that there is an omnipotent God, the problem of evil could still be solved. The Thomist reply that, since everything finite needs a cause, a nonfinite cause is needed, loses force when we deal with the deity. Many critics also doubt that an empirical approach can lead to a single ultimate cause. While the interrelationship and interdependence of the several arguments seem to suggest one and the same explanatory principle, do the arguments necessarily point to one and the same single being as their ultimate explanation? Paul Edwards ("The Cosmological Argument," p. 139) emphasizes that the cosmological argument does not prove "a *single* first cause," but rather supposes that "all the various causal series in the universe ultimately merge." Edwards does not comment on what they would merge into, however, if not into a single something.

Was Thomas's elaboration of natural theology influenced subliminally or otherwise subjectively conditioned, rather than derived logically from empirical observation of the world? Do his philosophical critics fall into the same error when elaborating alternative views? While modern secular philosophers like Marxists, existentialists, and process philosophers, for example, welcome Thomas's nonrevelational starting point—many appeal to experience—they espouse quite different categories and criteria for understanding man and the world. Some psychological determinists contend that all philosophical perspectives—their own usually exempted!—are subjectively grounded. Unless champions of alternative views exhibit logical weaknesses in the Thomistic proofs and sustain rational credibility for their own philosophical options they will merit little hearing. The basic issue in assessing Thomism is whether a logically demonstrative case can be made for inferential empirical information about God. The most frequent rejoinder to any statement of the cosmological argument is that if everything must have a cause, then so must God (according to Schopenhauer, advocates of the argument maneuver the law of universal causation like a hired cab that one discharges when a desired destination is reached). But Thomas does not, of course, claim "everything has a cause," but only that "finite, changing and/or contingent things have causes." Supporters of his argument, like E. L. Miller, protest that its critics wrongly assume that God is but one of a series in a chain of causes, rather than transcendent cause and necessary being (*God and Reason*, p. 55). Many Thomist scholars emphasize the distinction between a first cause in time (or at the beginning of a temporal series) and a first cause in the order of being (the ultimate ontological cause); they insist, moreover, that Thomas like Aristotle espoused the latter form of First Cause argument and not the former. Some interpreters, however, think that Thomas's argument to an ultimate efficient cause behind all cause-and-effect relations cannot be so easily detached from the notion of temporal sequence and origin. Yet Geisler emphasizes that eternal causality is possible while all existential causality is simultaneous (*Philosophy of Religion*, p. 221). Be that as it may, for Thomas the proofs do not verify creation *ex nihilo;* he looks to them rather to demonstrate that the world is not self-sufficient.

The argument merely to a first cause in time reasons that if the universe existed from eternity, then an infinite span of years has already elapsed, and we could not have arrived at the present point in time;[2] hence the universe must have had a beginning. Since something cannot come from nothing or be its own cause, we must posit a transcendent God as first cause of the whole spatio-temporal series. Many Thomists,

---

2. E. L. Miller (*God and Reason*) remarks that the conceivability of an infinite series of spatio-temporal states does not count against the inconceivability of their having already elapsed. He refers also to recent scientific theories favorable to the temporality of the universe: the Lemaitre-Gamow concept of a "Big Bang" origin of the universe is currently preferred to the "Steady State" theory. Since the second law of thermodynamics (or law of entropy) affirms that energy is constantly being depleted, the universe would now have completely run down if it were not eternal. These considerations do not, of course, apply to an alleged series of here-and-now (conserving) causes of the existence of finite beings. The concept of the conservation of energy in modern physics is sometimes opposed to Thomas's "third way": while particular configurations of matter do indeed come and go, energy itself—it is emphasized—abides ongoingly. But Miller responds that were the conservation of energy incompatible with its creation, then no Christian could subscribe to the concept. The principle asserts only that once energy exists, its total amount in a closed system will remain constant and cannot be destroyed of itself (p. 57). Yet Miller concedes that one cannot move from the present configurations of matter to conclusions about an absolute beginning; the present universe may be but one stage in a more comprehensive cyclical expansion and contraction (p. 50). The second law of thermodynamics can be arrived at as only a segment of a sine curve.

while conceding its weaknesses, carry this argument as far as they can and emphasize that Thomas argued not for a first cause in time but rather for a first cause in the order of being.

Followers of Aquinas now stress that the Thomistic proofs concern not the age of the universe but rather its transcendent cause. Thomas indeed believed on the basis of supernatural revelation that the world has a temporal beginning, but his empirical argument in no way challenges the notion that it has always existed. If there were no ultimate ontological cause, then the universe—whether temporal or eternal—would have no reason for being; that reason, Thomas argues, is supplied by a self-subsisting necessary being. In Rem B. Edwards's words, "when St. Thomas denies the possibility of an infinite regress of causes, he is not denying the impossibility of an infinite series of causes *in time*, but rather an infinite series of causes in 'the great chain of being' " (*Reason and Religion*, p. 257).

The concept of "necessary existence" has stimulated a wave of controversy. Paul Edwards insists that Aquinas in no way demonstrates that an infinite series of causes is impossible; moreover, his arguments are quite compatible with a supernatural being that is caused and that lacks "the attribute of first cause" ("The Cosmological Argument," p. 139). Logical positivists, of course, hold that only *propositions* of logic and mathematics can be viewed as "necessary"; necessity attaches only to analytic statements, and not to metaphysical entities. Over against J. N. Findlay and J. C. C. Smart, John Hick nonetheless defends the notion of factual necessity ("God as Necessary Being"). Richard Taylor argues that "if it makes sense to speak of *impossible* being" (e.g., a square circle or formless body), then it is "hard to see why the idea of a necessary being, or something which by its very nature exists, should not be just as comprehensible" (*Metaphysics*, p. 93). The argument is curious: a square circle is logically impossible by definition. Should not Taylor then say, it is necessary that any existent exists—true by definition; and that is not what he means. After contrasting dependent being, which has its reason for existence in the causal efficacy or nature of another being, with "independent being," which has within its own nature the reason for its being, William L. Rowe then speaks of "necessary being" as one whose nonexistence is a logical impossibility ("Two Criticisms of the Cosmological Argument," pp. 20 ff.).

To two criticisms of the premise that he considers the most important element of the cosmological argument, Rowe responds that "not every being can be a dependent being." In other words, the existence of an infinite collection of dependent beings must find its explanation—if it has any—"either in the causal efficacy of some being outside the collection or it must lie within the infinite collection itself." In his debate with F. C. Copleston, Bertrand Russell held that the concept of cause is inapplicable to the universe conceived as a totality. David Hume argued the opposite view, that the intelligible explanation of the existence of the whole is adequately given in the explanation of its parts (*Dialogues Concerning Natural Religion*, Part IX).

Russell attributes the fallacy of composition to the Thomistic view; it argues, he affirms, from the premise that everything in the universe has a cause to the conclusion that the universe as a whole has one. Ronald Hepburn similarly insists that we are not permitted to argue that "*because* things in the world have causes, therefore the sum of things must also have *its* cause" (*Christianity and Paradox*, pp. 168 f.). Rowe ignores this objection, since Hepburn connects the comprehensive causal explanation with a *because* in the properties of things in the universe. He acknowledges, moreover, that it makes no sense to apply to a collection of things some properties which it is sensible to apply to parts of the collection. Rowe points out that the fallacy of composition is merely an *informal* fallacy. Reasoning from what is true of the parts to what is true of the whole never automatically commits this fallacy; one must examine each case on its own merits. Sometimes reasoning of this kind is not invalid (e.g.: Each brick in the wall is red; therefore, the wall is red).

Rem B. Edwards (*Reason and Revelation*) also emphasizes that not every argument from the parts to the whole is fallacious. The validity or invalidity of reasoning from the parts to the whole must in every case rest on the truth or falsity of the premises. Against the naturalistic contention that nature is self-sufficient he propounds the syllogism:

> If each of the parts of any whole is contingent,
>   then the whole itself is contingent.
> Each of the parts of nature is contingent.
> Therefore nature as a whole is contingent.

Earlier naturalists escaped this line of reasoning by contending that the fundamental parts of nature—atoms, matter, and energy—are eternal, self-sufficient and indestructable. But now that science has split the atom, electrons and protons can be generated, can be destroyed, can be converted into formless natural energy, can be reconstituted. If the naturalist contends that "pure, formless energy too amorphous and elusive to be empirically meaningful" and not easily distinguishable from "pure potentiality" is eternal, self-sufficient and indestructable, then, asks Rem Edwards, "what is the difference between it and the primordial nature of God?" (p. 269). (The answer is, the former lacks intelligence and foresight.) He adds that a philosophical naturalist may prefer "to identify the necessary ground of our contingent existence with nature as a whole" (p. 270). But naturalist Paul Edwards ("The Cosmological Argument") emphasizes that one who rejects the cosmological argument is not therefore compelled to declare that there is "a *natural* first cause, and even less . . . that a mysterious 'thing' called 'the universe' qualifies for this title. . . . If I reject the assertion that God is a 'necessary being,' I am not committed to the view that the universe is such an entity" (p. 148).

The second objection to which Rowe responds is Hume's contention that the explanation of an infinite collection of dependent beings is found within the collection—in brief, that to explain the existence of the whole we need only explain the cause of the parts. He insists that it does make sense to ask why an infinite collection or succession of dependent beings exists. Whereas Russell, in view of his positivist propensities, would dismiss the question as meaningless, Rowe emphasizes that at the very least it makes sense to ascribe the property of having a cause or an explanation to an infinite collection of dependent beings. This is true, he avers, particularly if the question is not asked about an abstract or infinite "set" of finite beings but concerns a concrete collection, such as: "Why does A have the members it has rather than none at all?"

Rowe denies that the Thomistic argument involves transferring what is true of every member of an infinite collection to the infinite collection, viz., an explanation of its existence. Rowe's emphasis is on Samuel Clarke's appeal (*A Demonstration of the Being and Attributes of God*) to the principle of sufficient reason (which some modern Thomists insist Thomas does not use): whatever exists (including an infinite succession or collection of dependent beings) has an explanation of its existence. The principle of sufficient reason, says Rowe, requires an explanation of the existence of an infinite collection of dependent beings. For Richard Taylor the principle of sufficient reason is a presupposition of reason itself, rather than a form of logical argument: "it is hard to see how one could even make an argument for it, without already assuming it" (*Metaphysics*, p. 86). He adds that the principle "does not appear to be itself a necessary truth, and at the same time it would be most odd to say it is contingent . . . (yet) all men, whether they ever reflect on it or not, seem more or less to presuppose" it.

Paul Edwards has restated Hume's criticism in a way that probes the cosmological argument from many sides. He strikes not only at the concept of first cause, but also at that of necessary being; the temporal cause argument does not establish "the *present* existence of the first cause . . . since experience clearly shows that an effect may exist long after its cause has been destroyed" ("The Cosmological Argument," p. 139). He acknowledges that the distinction between a first cause *in fiere* (which helps bring an effect into being) and a first cause *in esse* (which helps sustain effects in being) requires "the present and not merely the past existence of a first cause" (p. 141).

For Edwards, however, there are difficulties of another kind in the argument. Glossing over Mill's pointed observation that "only *changes* require a causal explanation" (rather than all phenomenal objects as such), he emphasizes that "it is far from plausible . . . to claim that all natural objects require a cause *in esse*." "To those not already convinced of the need for a supernatural First Cause," the expositions appear in some respects "merely dogmatic and question-begging." The major difficulty still remains: one who insists rather on an infinite series of causes need not deny the reality of the first cause *in esse* or the first cause *in fiere;* he simply denies a privileged status, that of "first-causiness" (ibid., p. 141). Thomists readily argue that a finite series collapses when carried back to a first unsupported member, and here they invoke a first unmoved mover. But, says Edwards, an infinite series eliminates also a first unsupported member, and therefore dispenses also with the need for an unmoved mover. Anyone who defends the cosmological argument can still insist that the entire series needs an explanation beyond that of its parts, but if the cause of each member of a series has been found "it does not make sense to ask for the cause of the series" (p. 143). Edwards argues that when we have provided an explanation for each particular member of a class, we have thereby explained the class as a whole. Rowe agrees in the case of *finite* sets. He replies, however, that what is true of a finite set of dependent beings need not be the case when a set has an infinite number of members; in the latter situation the existence of the set is not necessarily explained by explaining the existence of every member of an infinite set ("Two Criticisms of the Cosmological Argument," p. 38). Rowe's only contention is that the cosmological argument is not guilty of the two main criticisms leveled against it—a confidence unshared by many. It is noteworthy that Rowe does not, however, claim that the cosmological argument is demonstrative.

To the notion that the demand for explanation of the entire series is no demand for cause, Paul Edwards replies that, whether finite or infinite, the series "is not 'intelligible' or 'explained' if it consists of nothing but contingent members" ("The Cosmological Argument," p. 144). This is essentially Copleston's argument, which Rowe in principle defends: the existence of contingent beings implies the existence of a necessary being. (There can be no empirical support for "a necessary being," of course. In Anselm's sense, necessary means logically necessary, not necessary to explain the world—that is, a being who cannot be conceived not to exist. This excludes empirical factors.) Here Edwards first of all falls back on Kant's controversial refutation of existence as an attribute, and insists that since existence is a category of thought it can never be contained in a concept. Fortunately he does not stop there; the Kantian argument has been refuted by Alvin Plantinga (*God and Other Minds*). Like Russell, Edwards insists that one misconceives what explanation is and does, and what makes phenomena "intelligible," if one seeks more than its cause or some other uniform or near-uniform connection between it and something else. The alternative to this is an obscure and arbitrary redefinition of *explanation, intelligible,* and related terms.

But this approach illumines the issues no more than does the appeal to Kant. Explanation merely in terms of predictable mathematical sequences may be no less arbitrary than alternative models that do not exclude these. The weakness of the Thomistic view, we would say, lies not in its refusal to taper intelligibility and explanation solely to near-term contingencies. It lies, rather, in its inability to validate a viable alternative by the empirical considerations to which it appeals, and its formulation of an alternative in subbiblical categories. Edwards is disposed not simply to set aside the argument for necessary being, but with Russell he thinks that the explanation of phenomena in a special sense over and above tentative scientific explanation has no basis; he doubts that "explanations in this sense . . . *exist*" ("The Cosmological Argument," p. 146), and declares that the Thomistic hypothesis gains an unearned plausibility from using the term *explanation* in two crucially different senses" (p. 147). Norman Geisler remarks that Thomists who defend the argument by an appeal to sufficient reason do Thomas poor service. He insists that Thomas rests the cosmological argument on cause as an existential ground, and not on an appeal to theoretical or rational explanation (*Philosophy of Religion*, p. 181; cf. John E. Gurr, *The Principle of Sufficient Reason in Some Scholastic Systems, 1750–1900*, p. 130). But is it possible, as Geisler insists, that never the twain shall meet, that is, that causal and rational concerns must be ongoingly compartmentalized?

It is here that Thomism serves the Christian cause least of all. As an alternative to secular empiricism it encompasses too many concessions to empirical method to turn that method skeptically against its naturalistic devotees, and as a harbinger of Christian theism it formulates a prolegomenon that more obscures than unveils the self-revealed God. Thomism proffers a scheme of inferential metaphysics that even brilliant philosophers interpret in diverse ways so that Thomists themselves frequently differ in their views. One distressing feature of Thomism is the repeated claim by its exponents that its critics misrepresent or improperly understand the argument and draw wrong inferences from rejoinders. Does Thomas claim that the proofs are logically demonstrative or merely existentially undeniable? (There is much to commend the view that Aquinas opposed Augustine's arguments as based on harmony and beauty and sought to replace them with strict proof, i.e., logical demonstration; otherwise Thomas is not Aristotelian and his distinction between philosophy and revelation fails.) Does he use or avoid the principle of sufficient reason? Are the proofs to be considered several correlative arguments or simply one comprehensive argument? (Thomas says the first proof is more obvious. Does he claim that each singly is valid, or that taken cumulatively they are demonstrative?) On and on run the differences among Thomistic interpreters, each claiming to champion the authentic Thomas. Needless to say, any rational demonstration of God's existence on which human felicity depends deserves better comprehensibility. God merits a more lucid press than the *Summa Theologica*. Evangelical Christians rightly champion a revelational alternative.

Surely no one can afford the luxury of thinking that the cosmological argument is demolished simply by objections which hinge on peculiar theories of cognition and of reality, theories that in themselves are highly vulnerable and that on close examination turn out to be logically untenable. No evangelical Christian can afford to borrow a theory of knowledge that leads only to metaphysical agnosticism, especially if he hopes to avoid that outcome in replying to Aquinas. Criticisms built on faulty commitments are serviceable to no one. Unless a contrary position is viable, it can hardly indict other views on its own premises. By this we do not mean that the Thomistic view is internally invulnerable to certain of Hume's and Kant's specific criticisms, especially when it appeals to empirical considerations. Thomism has long been challenged in fact, not only by philosophers hostile to a theistic view, but also by revelational theists who consider the fivefold proof demonstratively invalid and also highly unsatisfactory and even objectionable for presenting the case for the God of the Bible. Viewed epistemologically, the Protestant Reformation was in some respects a protest against the Thomistic demotion of divine revelation as the controlling axiom; the qualification is required by the fact that many Lutherans carried forward the cosmological argument.

Traditionally the most destructive critics of the Thomistic proofs were Hume and Kant, who centered their attention on the nature of causality, one of the basic and most problematic concepts in the history of philosophy. That these thinkers were ignorant of the Thomistic proofs —as some contemporary Thomists imply—is hardly tenable. (E. L. Miller, for example, writes: "The Cosmological Argument defended by the great scholastics was, in fact, unknown to Hume and Kant—not that it would have mattered," *God and Reason*, p. 62).

The British empiricist David Hume analyzed causality in the context of his phenomenalistic theory of knowledge by which the content of the mind is reduced to sense impressions and to memory-images of these. In terms of sense perception, causal relationships reduce to contiguity and succession. In brief, causality is not then an explanatory metaphysical principle, that is, a basic law of cosmic reality, but rather a psychological necessity that arises in the mind. Since one cannot be sure that events depend upon metaphysical causation, the notion of a cause of the world is irrelevant and the cosmological argument is unpersuasive.

Immanuel Kant anchored causality more firmly, not in the external world but in the mind of man himself, in the "transcendental ego," as one of the means by which the human knower necessarily conceptualizes reality. He thus rescued causality from merely psychological significance, considering it an a priori category of human understanding and intelligible experience. But he too limited its application to the sensually perceived world so that causality has no relevance whatever for God. Kant consequently dismisses the cosmological argument as unsound, inasmuch as causality is held to be applicable only to the phenomenally perceived world and not at all to the transcendent metaphysical realm.

The question here at stake is not merely whether causality has metaphysical significance. (An evangelical Christian convinced on revelational grounds that the universe is Logos-structured and Nomos-ordered may insist that it does, although Christians would be horrified if God were identified as a cause in Kant's sense of an event which is also an effect in a series.) The issue is rather whether the empirical epistemology approved by Thomism can escape diluting or evaporating it. Even contemporary empirical science avoids causality as irrelevant to the mathematical continuity of events, or, better, devoid of empirical meaning.

Thomism centers so crucially on the human reason's competence in metaphysics (unaided by special revelation) that it unwittingly lent new impetus to speculative rationalists who, with no recognition whatever of supernatural revelation, rested the whole case for theism on conjectural grounds. At the same time, despite vigorously promulgating the fivefold proof, Aquinas so limited human intellection concerning God that agnosticism seems to many of his critics almost inevitable: we know God not as he knows himself to be, but only by way of negation and analogy. When, for example, we affirm God's eternity and infinity, we simply deny to him the limitations of temporality and finitude predicable of the creaturely world. But when we ascribe positive attributes, we do so analogically (not univocally or equivocally); that is, while we attribute to God in an infinite degree perfections exhibited in a limited way in creaturely existence, divine predication carries a meaning not identical with that of creaturely attribution. In the *Summa Theologica* (I, 13, 5) Thomas asserts: "Univocal predication is impossible between God and creatures." His several reasons for this rejection of univocal knowledge of God may be summarized as follows: Essence and existence are identical in God, but obviously not so in the case of creatures, so that even the word *is* does not hold the same meaning in the case of God as it does in the case of creatures. Since *is* does not mean the same thing, then "God is good" cannot mean the same as when the term *good* is used of creatures, both because of the *is* and because of the *good*. Thomas concludes that "no name is predicated univocally of God and of creatures." This denial of univocal predication seems to many scholars to result not in analogical knowledge but rather in equivocal assertion, and hence excludes valid knowledge of God. The metaphysical boldness with which Thomas initially promotes the fivefold proof seems therefore finally to channel into theological agnosticism.

Protestant Christians are more at home with a natural theology less dependent upon Aristotelian concepts and not encumbered by the notion of analogical predication. Although the cosmological, teleological and moral or anthropological arguments, as they are usually designated, are important in post-Reformation Protestant theology and religious philosophy, their significance varies considerably. Those who agree that the arguments are invalid, or as some put it "mathematically" incorrect, disagree as to whether and to what extent they may be considered plausible or probable. They disagree also, and for different reasons, as to whether all three arguments, or only one or two, are significantly decisive.

One highly influential form of theistic argument was propounded around the turn of the century by James Orr, professor of apologetics in the divinity school of University of Glasgow. His Kerr Lectures were read by English-speaking evangelicals in many parts of the world. "It is not one line of evidence only which establishes the theistic position," Orr wrote, "but the concurrent force of many, starting from different and independent standpoints" (*The Christian View of God and the World*, p. 111). While Orr defends theism "not in dissociation from revelation" (p. 77), his correlation of empirical observation and revelational information is ambiguous.

On the one hand, Orr asserts: "I do not say that reason could have reached the height of the Christian conception for itself; I do not even think it can hold to it unless it accepts the fact of Revelation and the other truths which Christianity associates with it. But I do say that, with this view as given, reason is able to bring to it abundant corroboration and verification" (ibid., p. 111). One would glean from this that Orr proposes to begin with revelation as an epistemic axiom and looks to empirical data only 'for corroboration and verification. Yet he also expounds the theistic arguments as if they have independent value, not indeed as logically demonstrative, but as anticipating revelation and making it compelling.

In depicting the cosmological argument "from the contingency and mutability of the world . . . to an infinite and necessary Being as its ground and cause" (ibid., p. 95), Orr concludes that "Reason . . . itself points us to the need of a First Cause of the universe, who is at the same time a self-existing, necessary infinite Being" (p. 96). Concerning teleological considerations he remarks that "a world so full of evidences of rational purpose can only be the work of a wise and intelligent mind" (p. 98). Of the moral argument, Orr says that God's "existence is implied in the very presence of a morally legislating and commanding Reason within me" (p. 110); "the moral consciousness is one of the most powerful direct sources of man's knowledge of God" (p. 110). "It is the moral consciousness particularly which safeguards the personality of God" (p. 111).

The ontological argument, Orr adds, in an exposition which gives it an a posteriori rather than a priori cast, is needed "to show us in the clearest and most convincing manner that this Being and Cause of the universe is infinite, self-conscious Reason" (ibid., p. 103). "Strict and sober analysis of what is involved in such knowledge of existence as we have" leads us to conclude that "thought is the necessary *prius* of all else that is" (p. 104), that "the existence of an Eternal Reason is . . . involved in the very thinking . . . of any thought . . . not simply my thought, but an Absolute Thought, and with this the existence of an Absolute Thinker" (p. 105). "The voice of reason is confirmed by the soul's direct experiences in religion," Orr writes. "At the very least these considerations show—even if the force of demonstration is denied to them—that the Christian view is not *un*reasonable; that it is in accord with the highest suggestions of reason applied to the facts of existence" (p. 111). "Theism . . . needs revelation to *complete* it" (p. 77). In binding together "the two ideas of God and Revelation" the Christian view "has its strength against any conception of God based on mere grounds of natural theology" (p. 77).

While Orr does not regard the arguments from man and the world as logically demonstrative of a God living, personal, ethical and infinite, he nonetheless assigns them a positive evidential role preparatory to theistic belief; he does not introduce them merely as corroborative or compatible with a revelational axiom. In some moods he even sanctions the empirical proof of God, declaring "that there are necessary acts of thought by which we rise from the finite to the infinite, from the caused to the uncaused, from the contingent to the necessary, from the reason involved in the structure of the universe to a universal and eternal Reason, which is the ground of all, from morality in conscience to a moral Lawgiver and Judge" (ibid., p. 95). He speaks approvingly therefore of empirical theistic argumentation by which man's thoughts naturally rise to God.[3]

This line of argument would have seemed to Reformation Protestantism, or in the larger light of the New Testament, as demoting of God's initiative in revelation, and as not adequately reflective of finite man's epistemic correlation with revelation. Had Adam even before the fall pursued this line of argument he would have erred; the argument is invalidated by the laws of logic. God's universal disclosure in nature, history and to the human mind and conscience is not in dispute. What is rejected rather is the expectation that fallen man will translate general divine revelation into a natural theology that builds a secure bridge to special revelation; in that event special revelation has significance only as a crown that caps natural theology elaborated by man in sin. Those who expound the theistic proofs often do so not expressly in view of general revelation at all, but simply on the basis of empirical observation, and look to man's inferences from experience to prepare the way for

---

3. By using the term *cosmological* in "a wider and more original sense," Charles H. Malik proposes "to identify and exhibit the biblical cosmological argument" and to refute Kant's dismissal of "any intimation we may get about God from the world or the cosmos under any and all of its aspects" (*The Wonder of Being*, p. 36). This not only blends teleological and anthropological and cosmological arguments, but also seeks to hold together the inner and outer aspects of general revelation as they impinge upon man's experience. Malik argues for a universal a priori awareness of God, so that man as man is intuitively and intellectually in touch with an external essence independent of the ego, even of Kant's transcendental ego. He deplores the "epistemologically-existentially denatured mind" (p. 49), and emphasizes God's revelation of himself. But instead of relying on the epistemic principle of God in his revelation, normatively disclosed in Scripture, Malik turns to an Aristotelian-Thomistic approach to develop his argument (p. 43). To get from the eternal "givenness" of the universe to the God of the Bible with no appeal to God in his revelation and simply by intuition and inference, however, is to expect more than man in sin achieves.

any and every clue to divine reality. Their stance is not that "God in his revelation attests his existence and power in the created universe," but rather that "we have a basis for affirming God's existence in observational data" and that "without empirical evidence no basis remains for affirming his existence." In this way a denial of empirical evidence becomes tantamount to a denial of God's reality.

Such apologists intended to prepare the way for supernatural revelation and miraculous redemption. Their approach, however, left biblical theism suspended grotesquely in midair when philosophers not only exposed the inability of merely empirical analysis to provide the expected theistic supports, but also readily correlated the data with nonrevelational speculative premises that led to contrary inferences.

As noted above, Hume held, on the basis of sensory observation, that causality has only psychological necessity and has no objective relation in the world. But, granting its objective significance simply for the sake of argument, he asked what *experience* we have of the origin of worlds to enable us confidently to assume that the present universe was caused rather than resulted in some other way. But even if we grant causality as a transcendent explanatory principle, Hume emphasizes that the terrors of natural evil allow us to infer empirically a god of only finite power, since a deity who is good (as Christians assume) would prevent such destructive occurrences. The scholastics inferred an infinite cause to account for the finite universe. Hume, however, anticipated the modern scientific requirement of strict proportionality between cause and effect as the only premise serviceable for prediction and control. The dependence of scientific inquiry on strict equivalence in cause-effect relationships weighed against invoking a greater cause to account for any phenomenon. Post-Darwinian evolutionary philosophy carried this revolt against the concept of an infinite first cause still further: it related all effects to simpler rather than to more complex causes, and the very categories of reason and morality, long considered evidential of theism, it dismissed as evolutionary emergents.

The present secular mood, as Langdon Gilkey notes, is marked by its "posture of metaphysical modesty" resting on "a rejection of philosophy as a form of genuine knowing that can proceed by implication alone far beyond immediate experience not only to talk of the real but the real as a coherent whole" (*Naming the Whirlwind*, p. 223). The widely divergent strands of contemporary philosophy—whether Edmund Husserl's phenomenology, John Dewey's empirical instrumentalism, Jean-Paul Sartre's existentialism, A. J. Ayer's logical positivism, and some forms of linguistic analysis as well—all agree in their common denial of speculative metaphysics and in the "consequent universal rejection of those rationalistic assumptions on which a natural theology is necessarily based" (p. 224).

Gilkey thinks this philosophical concurrence attests that "metaphysical discourse, and so *a fortiori* theological language predicated on it—is itself unintelligible to modern man," so that nothing is gained by translating God-language and Word-language into contemporary philosophical categories (ibid., p. 224). Indeed, those who do so may be charged with simply trying to clarify beliefs they already hold on "religious grounds." This does not mean that "these rationalistic assumptions are untrue," but merely that they are almost "as alien to the secular mood as is the assumption of the divine Word received in religious faith" (p. 224), and that neither culminates in intelligibility and validity. Hence to the modern secular mind secular metaphysics seems as religious as revelational theology, and revelational theology as irrelevant as secular metaphysics. "The rationalistic assumptions, essential to *all* forms of speculative metaphysics relevant to natural theology, are as strange in our age as are the assumptions of revelational faith" (p. 225). "Metaphysical language and Biblical language face very much the same problem—despite their manifest scorn of one another" (p. 226).

What this development attests is that the failure to predicate argumentative theism on intelligible divine revelation as a significant epistemic principle has had costly consequences for both modern theology and modern philosophy. The attempt to concentrate the case for theism upon observations from the not-God, while neglecting the reality of God in his revelation, has led to more than the erosion of the power of God in modern life; it has also betrayed modern philosophy and theology into a time of intellectual sterility.

No one more deliberately disowned the deduction of theological truth from divine revelation than did Friedrich Schleiermacher (1768–1834), the father of Protestant modernism, who substituted religious experience for revealed theology as the source of Christian beliefs. As far back as Origen (about 250 A.D.) the procedure in writing systematic treatises on Christian theology had been to begin with the conception of God given by revelation, and to deduce from this the content of faith. In *De principiis* (the Greek title was *peri archōn*), Origen rests theology firmly on authority (although he supplements his appeal to scriptural teaching by apostolic tradition). From the doctrine of the self-revealed God he derives the divine attributes and through these expounds all other Christian themes. Although Aquinas, as we have already noted, in the thirteenth century compromised this dependence on revelational authority, the Protestant Reformers restored the ancient precedent and expounded Christian theology by deduction from revealed first principles. Thomas believed that man was God's creation, and that God had given him sensory perception to use with the God-given abilities of the active intellect. Over against empirical philosophy, which presumes to derive the knowledge of God from an examination of nature or from an analysis of the cosmos or of history, the Reformers insisted on the basis of Holy Scripture that Christian theology has a wholly different foundation, namely, divine revelation. Affirmation of the living God, they insisted, rests not on inferences from man and the world but on God's supernatural disclosure. When, under Kant's influence, Schleiermacher assumed that we can have no objective knowledge of God, and that any final definition of divine nature is therefore impossible, he concentrated instead on empirical evidence of God's reality.

Whereas Roman Catholicism and evangelical rationalism resorted to natural theology as preparatory to specially revealed religion, Protestant modernism appealed solely to religious experience to validate its commitment to Jesus Christ. This anthropocentric approach to Christianity won the loyalties of many theologians, church administrators and clergy during the first quarter of the twentieth century. The modernist movement took its direction from Schleiermacher rather than from the prophetic-apostolic witness and adopted the Enlightenment motif that Christianity and the church are phases of a much larger movement of thought and life, and that the progress of civilization as a whole is the expanding kingdom of God. Influenced by the Renaissance, many Protestant scholars turned their interest from the Beyond to man and nature, and sought to understand man through general anthropological truths acquired by empirical observation. Theological methodology centered in examining the religious nature of man; scriptural teaching about human nature fell by the wayside. In line with Gotthold Lessing's (1729–81) attribution to human nature of an immanent power to discern the coincidence of revelation and history, Schleiermacher held that faith has its possibilities in the nature of man as he is, that is, in human possibilities.

Not only had modernism, like Thomism, replaced God by man as a theological starting point but, as Karl Barth protested, it had also in effect deified man himself. It recognized no point of reference outside man in establishing theological truth. Its main speculative ally, philosophical idealism, wholly forfeited the unconditionally transcendent, and depicted the divine Spirit as immanent in all men. Modernism in principle therefore forsook theology for anthropology and for humanism.

By his devastating critique of modernism as a "heresy" whose "final and almost unavoidable logic would be blasphemy" (*Church Dogmatics*, I/2, p. 403), and by his alternative emphasis on transcendent divine disclosure, Karl Barth became the twentieth century's most influential theologian. In the preface to his voluminous *Church Dogmatics* Barth indicates that he can only see "in the line Schleiermacher-Ritschl-Herrmann, and in any thinkable continuation of this line . . . the plain destruction of Protestant theology and of the Protestant Church" (I/1, p. x). Modernist Protestantism, as Barth put it, found its criterion in "the modern consciousness of being civilized" (I/1, p. 288), not in the Word of God. The Christian faith was reinterpreted through "general anthropology," not identified by a revealed Word transcendently addressed to man. Adolf von Harnack (1851–1931), who clung to this illusion to the end of his life, voiced the neo-Protestant credo as follows: the "proper object of faith is not God in his revelation, but man himself believing in the divine" (I/2, p. 368).

Some modernists insisted that God bestows upon every man as man an independent possibility for experiencing and knowing God. Others, however, among them Georg Wobbermin and Robert Winckler, rejected the notion that God bestows this possibility as a universal religious capacity, and held rather that God imparts it from the divine side in synthesis with human faith, and only on this basis is the divine Spirit known in consciousness.

Barth thunderously disapproved both formulations: the modernist elaboration of the actuality, or possibility, of theology on the basis of man's inner resources, even as a special divine endowment, he said, has nothing in common with a theology derived from God's transcendent Word. To imply that man has a spiritual capacity for properly expounding the content of theology from his own consciousness reflects the modernist refusal to anchor revelation in the transcendent disclosure of God.

Barth disavows any general anthropological capacity in man to formulate theology, any possibility of deriving knowledge of God from man's inner resources. If man stipulates the content of theology by standing upon himself, even upon some special endowment he professes to have, he merely ventures to derive theology from his own possibilities. There is in man under no circumstances any source of authentic theological knowledge. No possibility exists of stipulating a priori "what revelation must be, may be, and ought to be" (ibid., I/2, p. 4). It is impossible to rise from experience of the space-time universe, from revelation-as-human-history, from independent anthropology, to a revelation of the living God. Divine revelation is neither a distillation of history nor of the spirit of man, but a transcendent disclosure of the Lord of history and man. It is not evolved by man but addressed to him. Revelation has its free and independent ground solely in the divine Revealer, in the Creator who is other than both man and the cosmos.

Barth stresses that even the biblical prophets and apostles are not exempt from these strictures. The affirmations of the inspired writers and the declarations of Scripture are not to be considered the statements of men, not even of specially chosen men who on the basis of anthropological possibilities expound the mysteries of the invisible world. Rather, Scripture testifies to the transcendent initiative of the living God in his self-revelation.

God is therefore the personality who in the actuality of his self-revelation precedes all legitimate human predications about him. He is not, as modernism had come to view him, an infinite religious reality postulated by man, a reality whose nature man defines, and to whom any ascription of a self-consciousness different from man's could only jeopardize human self-realization in correlation with the divine (on idealistic premises God was the totality of all human values). Theology as a discipline of learning and study does not depend upon the insights of men, not even upon those of the most brilliant philosophers and theologians, nor does its essential support or justification stem from any conjectural thought system whatever.

No recent theologian more vigorously than Barth repudiated the modernist attempt to distill revelation from empirical considerations, whether anthropological, cosmological or historical. For him the transcendent self-revealing God alone is the source of authentic theology. Significantly enough, Barth was invited to give the Gifford Lectures (1937-38) despite his candid declaration (echoed in the introduction and conclusion of his series, *The Knowledge of God and the Service of God*) that he could not directly fulfill Lord Gifford's stipulation that the lectures reflect natural theology and not "any supposed special, exceptional, or so-called miraculous revelation." Theology must above all else have its ground in the Word of God, Barth insists; theological methodology must appeal to the divine Word as its center and not to an independent anthropology or cosmology.

To say that special revelation loses its reasonableness unless the validity of natural theology is maintained is fallacious, although that has been the view of Roman Catholic scholastics—indeed, it is the official Roman Catholic position—and that of some other philosophers as well. At present there is an impressive attempt to rescue natural theology from the discredit into which Hume and Kant brought it. Certainly no one ought to think that Hume and Kant destroyed the case for theism, nor even that they invalidated general revelation, even though Hume met head-on the manner in which Thomists forged their theory. Charles Hartshorne may be quite right that "Hume and Kant argued against natural theology from premises which not only begged the question, but are today highly controversial," and that professional philosophers have nowhere performed so poorly as in their "mostly careless, sloppy or unfair" statements and evaluations of the "proofs" ("Can There Be Proofs for the Existence of God?," pp. 65, 68). To expose the partisan biases of philosophers like Hume and Kant does not by and of itself, however, establish the validity and coherence of the views of Bergson, Whitehead, Hartshorne and other process theorists whose speculative constructions are no less vulnerable. Nor in fact does special revelation depend for its intelligibility upon natural theology; what special revelation presupposes, rather, is general revelation.

To reject the validity of natural theology—as an enterprise that presumptively underestimates the epistemic predicament of finite man—in no way requires the rejection of the role of rational argument in theology, or abandoning the intrinsically rational character of special divine revelation. Modern champions of natural theology have in no way embarrassed Reformation theology when, contrary to the promoters of paradox, they argue for the rationality of revelation, or when they insist that even apart from special revelation all men have ineradicable knowledge of God. These issues are not at stake. The essential issue is rather the validity of natural theology. Hartshorne protests that to invalidate natural theology by appealing to the fall of man and the corruption of man's reason is comprehensively destructive since despite their appeal to a certain revelation even theologians are then under the fall. This complaint loses merit, however, because there is no logical necessity for distorting divine revelation. The history of religious and philosophical thought doubtless indicates that, except as special revelation has insinuated itself as a corrective, man volitionally—and invariably so—distorts the disclosure of God in the cosmos and in history. But the question is not over the relevance of reason to theological realities, but over the disposition and ability of the finite sinner to expound general revelation accurately, even if he has the logical competency to do so.

While Hartshorne admits that philosophy cannot concoct a formal proof for God that only witless or dishonest persons would sidestep, he insists that it can establish conclusions whose rejection is possible only at "a logical price." What he claims for the theistic proofs—that they make "the logical price of unbelief seem unbearably high"—cannot therefore conceal his apparent disregard for the "proofs" in any form as demonstrably valid, although to deny them may "seem counter-intuitive to some" and although the argument is "for us . . . a valid one" (ibid., p. 68).

A faith in God which tries to establish its case on any proposition derived from general anthropology or philosophy of history or any other basis than the revelation of God in his Word is in no sense on the road to monotheism but is already on a one-way street to atheistic humanism. The Christian revelation of the living God propounds information about God on the basis of the Word of God, and not on what is professedly derived by analytico-synthetic examination of human experience. We reject natural theology not for the reasons that Hume or Kant or the Darwinian evolutionists did, and despite the claims of contemporary process philosophers. We reject natural theology because of the express nature of supernatural revelation, because of man's epistemic nature and because of the invalidity of empirically based arguments for theism.

10.
The Image of God in Man

REVELATIONAL THEISM AFFIRMS that the human person as divinely created bears the image of God.

This biblical emphasis differs greatly, to be sure, from theories of a rational a priori that fuse the divine and human minds and discount man's finitude and fall. Metamorphosing "created image" into "divine participation," pantheists and idealists typically consider man's spirit as part of an all-inclusive divine Spirit and as immediately reflective of divine life and thought. While philosophical rationalists may distinguish God ontologically from man, they nonetheless, simply on the basis of its immanent epistemological capacities, consider the human mind competent to formulate sure answers to ultimate questions. These exaggerations of man's rationalistic competence not only neglect the fall of man, but they also misstate man's epistemic capabilities on the basis of creation before the fall. Such philosophical hyperbole virtually implies the rational omnicompetence of the human knower and has encouraged a number of later expositors to exclude rationality from the religious a priori (Rudolf Otto) and finally even to eliminate the rational from the revelational entirely (existential theology).

The divine prohibition of graven images in the decalogue may well have had in view not only the spirituality of God but also man as the divinely designated image-bearer, and God's messianic Son who would manifest the holy image forfeited by Adam and to which penitent humanity will ultimately be conformed. Something may even be said for the view that man was created *as* the image of God, and not merely, as commonly asserted, *in* the divine image. After fashioning other living creatures by graded classifications, God announced his solemn intention to make man "as" (or, "according to") our image (*selem*), and "after" our likeness

124

(*demuth*). The prepositions *as* and *after* are reversable (cf. Gen. 5:3), and the Old Testament employs the former (*be*) in several senses. If its intention, as Koehler-Baumgartner think (*Lexicon in Veteris Testamenti Libros*, pp. 102 f.) and von Rad also (*Genesis*, p. 56), is to indicate "the quality or manner in which an entity shows itself," then "as" is preferable.

The Bible does not define for us the precise content of the original *imago*. But this gives no ground for viewing the *imago* as having only a vague and indefinite content or form before the fall. From the beginning, man in the Bible is depicted not as an evolved animal but as a uniquely endowed creature specifically distinguished from the lower animal world and specially related to God by the divinely bestowed image. From his very creation man is constituted a personal being in self-conscious spiritual fellowship with his Maker. Traditionally God's image in man has been identified centrally in terms of man's rational and moral aptitudes; these are presuppositions not simply of human civilization and culture, but of meaningful and responsible personal fellowship with God as well. In his original condition of moral rectitude, man loved God in total self-devotion and gladly gave himself to all that God requires. He knew the truth and did it. His created dignity consisted in knowledgeable and responsible relationships to the supernatural world and to fellow humans. His life was intended to consist of intelligible and dutiful devotion to God who is himself the truth and the good, and of service to his earthly neighbor. His mental capacity transcended the changing sensory realm; it included general ideas conducive to intelligible conversation and fellowship with God.

Alongside man's rational and moral aptitudes, his capacity for self-transcendence, his exercise of will, and his immortality have also been considered as elements of the divine image. In recent years more emphasis has been placed on physical aspects as well (e.g., sexual differentiation in unity as symbolic of a dynamic love relationship; and surrogate-rule over nature). Preeminent over the animals, he was given dominion over the earth. To Adam was delegated the Creator's privilege of naming the animals; in this task he readily discriminated their nature from his own, and found no helpmeet for himself among them.

The divine image, a cohesive unity of interrelated components that interact with and condition each other, includes rational, moral and spiritual aspects of both a formal and material nature. We may isolate these various facets abstractly and examine them independently. Man's ethical responses are not disjoined from intellection, however; his comprehension of truth is not sealed off from conscience, nor are his knowledge of the truth and his moral insights divorced from an awareness of answerability to God.

But in contemplating the divine image in man, it should be clear that the rational or cognitive aspect has logical priority. The Johannine Prologue declares that man by creation is lighted by the Logos (John 1:4, 9), that is, logically lighted. The apostle Paul, moreover, exhorts Christians as their "logical service" (literal) to present their bodies "a living sacrifice, holy and acceptable to God" (Rom. 12:1, RSV). The restoration of sinful man to his created image includes logical considerations. *Light* in John's Gospel has both rational and moral connotations.

Whatever ethical factors formally structure the divine image, man without rationality—or the basic forms of reason—could never intelligibly discriminate God from the not-God, right from wrong, truth from untruth. Only if man is logically lighted, and not simply morally or spiritually involved independent of intelligence, can he be meaningfully aware of responsible relationships to God and other selves and to the cosmos. If man made any sense of his own experience, the laws of logic must intrinsically have qualified the *imago Dei*. From the first, man as man possessed reasoning capacities and rational discernment on the basis of creation. All distinctively human experience presupposes the law of noncontradiction and the irreducible distinction between truth and error; man cannot repudiate these logical presuppositons without sacrificing the intelligibility of what he says and does and his own mental coherence. Reason illuminates divine revelation by furnishing the concepts for truth not only about man and nature but also about God, and by discriminating the true God from false gods, revelation from pseudorevelation, and true from false religion.

The divine image includes also the structures of morality, that is, an awareness that the distinction between good and evil and between right and wrong is irreducible. In the Genesis creation account, having declared the earlier successive stages of creation to be "good," God uses the superlative "very good" (Gen. 1:31) of man fashioned in his own image, and thereby attaches profound moral significance to man's appearance as the divine *imago*-bearer. Man's very self-constitution is stamped with the conviction that the distinction between good and evil is not merely an arbitrary and optional contrast but is genuine and objective. Moreover, he was endowed with conscience—with the "good conscience" which approves what is right and disapproves what is wrong; he did not as yet have a "bad conscience" because of moral disobedience. Anyone who demotes all ethical distinctions to relativity and considers conscience an irrelevancy is not only morally perverse but also a candidate for insanity.

Just as important, the *imago Dei* stamps man by nature with the conviction that the distinction between God and the not-God is ultimate and undiminishable. No man can live a human existence who considers God to be everything that is or might be, and who does not discriminate between ultimate loyalty and that granted subordinate competitors. Even if he denies the existence of God, he knows that this is something very distinct from denying his own existence.

Although we have thus far been considering only the formal elements of the divine image in man, their importance should be evident. Humanistic anthropologists are prone to view man simply as a developing animal, and to regard all his basic dispositions as mere distillations of evolutionary experience. In deference to the theory of cultural relativity they deny that any common principles or practices can be discerned in the history of humanity. According to Edmund Leach, "morality is specified by culture" and "universal morality gets no further than" the fact that nobody "has yet met with a society in which it is considered proper for a man to have sex relations with his own mother" (*A Runaway World?*, pp. 48 f.). Oswald Spengler declares, moreover, that only diverse cultures exist, each holding meaning only for itself, and that there is no comprehensive culture as such. If this is so, then true meaning remains in doubt. Christianity has never denied the vast range of moral relativity in fallen human history. But it explains those perverse notions of the good and the failure of those who truly know the good to do it (Rom. 7:19–23.) by a principle far superior to ethical relativism—man's moral revolt against his holy Creator. Christianity, moreover, specifically rejects the notion that man's nature as man bears no structures other than those derived from evolutionary development. The forms of logic and morality are not derived from experience; rather they are what make human experience possible. As the Psalmist puts it, the horse and the mule "have no understanding" (Ps. 32:9, KJV); it is patently obvious that animals have no religious propensities while on the other hand human history is replete with rational, moral and religious concerns.

Karl Barth vigorously denies that the divine image is especially to be seen in the rational and ethical features of human existence. "The biblical witness makes no reference at all," he declares, "to the peculiar intellectual and moral talents and possibilities of man, to his reason and its determination and exercise" (*Church Dogmatics*, III/1, p. 185). While his emphasis on transcendent divine revelation commendably rejected the modernistic postulation of a possibility in human nature per se for knowledge of God independent of divine disclosure, Barth went much further than this, indeed beyond all biblical warrant. He dismissed any general divine revelation whatever and insisted rather that men universally have only vague and ambiguous impressions of divinity, and that suggestions of divinity known to sinners are in no sense divine revelation. To be sure, if the revelation-event is a sporadic and noncognitive personal confrontation, and if all revelation is salvific and exists only for faith, then what the Bible affirms about general revelation and the image of God in man is dispensable. In that case we have done profound violence, however, to the biblical witness to divine disclosure. Barth considers any survival of the original *imago* after the fall as covertly preparing the way for natural theology, that is, for knowledge of God accessible to man independently of divine revelation, and he rejects every effort to associate the original image with considerations of reason and cognition. But Barth's dismissal of general revelation and of any divine preforming of man by creation for ongoing cognitive relationships with his Creator, and hence his rejection of any intelligible formal and material content of the *imago* in man, was motivated not by the necessary issuance of these views in natural theology—for that is not their inevitable outcome—but rather by Barth's insistence that divine revelation is personal and paradoxical and internal and not rational and objective. Were Barth's views valid, the categories of thought even in a revelational context would be impotent to yield universally valid knowledge of God; this is precisely the outcome of Barth's religious epistemology.

Emil Brunner emphasizes that the fall does not erode all human consciousness and he differentiates man in sin from the animals in view of the *humanitas* surviving the fall. The recognizability of God is "marred" by sin but not destroyed. Certain formal aspects survive the fall, he maintains, to distinguish man's life and experience from that of brute animals, and in this formal accessibility lies the "point of contact" for divine grace. He limits the *imago* to merely formal aspects, holding that the fall has disordered only its material content. Over against historic evangelical orthodoxy, however, Brunner associates the formal *imago* onesidedly with conscience. Concentrating on man's sense of guilt, he minimizes cognitive facets and conforms them to the nonintellective notion of revelation as championed by dialectical theology. As bearer of the *imago*, man must form an idea of an absolute, yet as sinner in revolt against God he conceives God only in empty or abstract terms or fills these with a perverse content. God is "truly" known only in a hearing of the Word in faith. In all this, the cognitive content of general revelation as well as of special revelation is eclipsed in deference to a dynamic view of divine disclosure. An authentically biblical exposition of the divine image, and even of conscience as an aspect of it, must instead preserve cognitive knowledge as the essential basis of moral responsibility and of meaningful religious experience. Contemporary process theology assigns larger scope to rational considerations in formulating man's relationship to God, but it likewise veers toward noncognitive interpersonal revelation and agrees with contemporary interpretations of the *imago* as a dynamic love relationship (cf. Daniel Day Williams, *The Spirit and the Forms of Love*, pp. 131 ff.).

Is the divine image in man merely formal, as Brunner contends, or does the image of God surviving the fall also involve some material content? The apostle Paul's broad indictment of Gentile religions in Romans 1 is sometimes used to contravene the view that man universally possesses authentic knowledge of the living God. But this is a misunderstanding. This view overlooks the apostle's unequivocal assertion, in this very context, of a general or universal revelation of God: "that which may be known of God is manifest in them; for God hath showed it unto them" (Rom. 1:19, KJV). While properly insisting on general revelation, Brunner's anticognitive theory of revelation shapes his exposition of the *imago Dei* no less than of general revelation. He connects the fact that general revelation has no saving significance with the dialectical theory that it is not salvific because in it God meets man impersonally rather than personally. Yet the passage in Romans speaks of the disclosure of God's divinity and eternal power through the created universe. There are Old Testament passages as well, although they may be few in number, which categorically assert that man as such knows God. Daniel 5:22, for example, attests that knowledge is an essential basis of moral responsibility (cf. Luke 12:47–48 and John 15:22).

Two Johannine passages are sometimes adduced to oppose representations of a general knowledge of God because they assert human detachment from God. The texts are John 1:10 ("He was in the world, and the world was made by him, and the world knew him not," KJV) and John 17:25 ("O righteous Father, the world hath not known thee: but I have known thee, and these have known that thou hast sent me," KJV). But these verses do not really justify either the agnostic theory that God is essentially unknowable or the notion that God is universally unknown. At first reading these passages might seem to globalize the Athenian altar to an unknown God. A second look, however, will indicate that they supply no firm basis for denying a general or universal knowledge of God. The Fourth Gospel teaches that as God's creature man is meant and made to know him and that God is everywhere present through the Logos (cf. C. H. Dodd, *The Interpretation of the Fourth Gospel*, pp. 156 f.). In John 7 and 8 the Jews are in fact said to know much about God, before they are accused (8:54–55) of not knowing him. The exhortation to "receive" the Logos in John 1:10–12 and to "know God" in John 8:54–55 does not basically have in view the intellectual apprehension of the truth of God's reality, but rather the experiential knowledge of God as a liberating power found in a life commitment to his holy will. Unbelievers are not God's children, not because they have no knowledge of him, but because they lack spiritual commitment and vocational obedience. That the Jews do not "know God" here means not that they lack all cognitive information about him, but that they reject God's ethical demand and disobey him. The Old Testament prophets, in the same vein, attribute man's ignorance of God (Isa. 1:3) and failure to worship him (Jer. 10:25) to man's own stupidity and ethical misbehavior (Isa. 5:12).

The New Testament affirms that even the demons possess a belief in one God (James 2:19). Since unembodied spirits cannot derive their knowledge from sense experience, how but through divine revelation could they have acquired the truth of monotheism? While any determination of anthropological considerations from demonology involves high risk, doubly so in a generation whose intellectuals do not believe in demons even while the public probes demonology, it is noteworthy nonetheless that in the New Testament even demons tremble in anticipation of final doom because they possess explicit knowledge of God, and that unregenerate humanity likewise pursues the paths of death despite ineradicable knowledge of the Creator and his coming judgment (Rom. 1:20, 32).

The Bible considers human reason and conscience a divinely given instrumentality for man's responsible existence in relationship to God and his fellow human beings. Men have inescapable knowledge of God on the basis of God's self-revelation through nature (Rom. 1:20), and God is, moreover, nowhere in the external course of things without a witness (Acts 14:17). Mankind, to whom the revelation is addressed, is lighted by the Logos (John 1:9) and the moral law is "written on their hearts" (Rom. 2:15, RSV) so that men know that the self-revealed God justly punishes those who flaunt his will (Rom. 1:32). The revelation of God invades and penetrates the very mind and conscience of every man, despite the fact that, in face of this very revelation, men do not *choose* to know God (Rom. 1:28). To say that man's very religious idolatry attests his revolt against light and right is to say no more about the human religious condition than Scripture says. Paul writes that even the Gentiles, who lack the Mosaic law, "show the work of the law written in their hearts, their conscience also bearing witness, and their thoughts accusing or else excusing one another" (Rom. 2:14–15, KJV). Conscience is a second "knowing," a "knowing alongside" what is otherwise revealed, and it hails men anticipatively before God's judgment bar.

Protestant theologians who disavow natural theology as strenuously as does Barth have insisted that, however serious were the moral and intellectual consequences of the fall, the divine image in man after as well as before the fall embraces both a formal aspect and a material content. To say that the divine image in man after the fall ongoingly includes both formal and material elements, in no way requires a regard for human reason as an inherent source of truth about God. Rather, by dependence upon and fidelity to divine revelation, the surviving *imago* assures the human intelligibility of divine disclosure, preserves the universal validity of human knowledge, and correlates God's inner revelation to man in the mind and conscience with God's external revelation in nature and history. It qualifies man not only as a carrier of objective metaphysical truth about God's nature and ways, but more particularly as a receiver of the special revelational truth of redemption.

Immanuel Kant had validated the universal validity of human thought on the basis only of innate forms of thought. But because he arbitrarily ruled out the divine preforming of these innate categories, he sacrificed the metaphysical objectivity of man's knowledge and forfeited transcendent divine revelation that conveys cognitive knowledge of the supernatural world. Precisely because Kant did not recognize the formal aspects of human knowing to be elements of the divinely created *imago*, he correlated the categories not with metaphysical reality but only with sense perceptions. In contravening Humean skepticism, he insisted that simply as formal elements of the human understanding, the innate categories make human experience possible, and assure the universal validity of human knowledge. He preserves in principle an intrapersonal objectivity of knowledge; the human mind in effect is a transcendental ego universally structured by common categories and forms, so that all human knowing stands under the same epistemic necessity. Contrary to Hume's reduction of knowledge to individual percepts and psychic responses, Kant believed that the inherent categories and forms of the human mind structure man's thought universally. Human knowledge is therefore possible because of the a priori epistemic thought equipment by which man comprehends experience. This emphasis on innate a priori categories is congenial to the universal validity and necessity of human knowledge.

But God's existence or nonexistence then remains for Kant intellectually problematical in view of the nonconnectibility of the categories with the supersensuous and metaphysical. Kant consequently assumed the autonomy of the human mind, and compromised the objectivity of human knowledge in respect to God and the supernatural in yet other important respects:

(1) We cannot know things-in-themselves, or noumenal reality as independently existing or structured. We know phenomenal appearance only (or the impression made upon us by reality) grasped in a certain necessary way. We know nature and history only as determined by our innate concepts, and hence solely under the conditions of human knowing. Therefore we do not know the objective phenomenal; we know only the subjective phenomenal, which is not decisive for the nature of things-in-themselves.

(2) We can have no objective knowledge, or even conceptual knowledge of God, since the limits of man's knowledge are such that sense experience supplies the only content of human knowledge. God becomes for Kant a mere postulate with no cognitive grounding.

(3) It is not clear, in fact, how Kant could on his theory have acquired objective knowledge of the categories. Since he declares all knowledge to be a joint product of innate forms and sense conduct, how did Kant learn of these forms as isolated from sensation and given a priori? How could the categories alone become for him an object of knowledge?

(4) Kant presupposes that God was not the source—in terms of the *imago Dei* conferred on man at creation—of the categories of thought structuring human knowledge. He ignores the transcendent Logos as the indispensable ground of universally valid knowledge. Yet for all that, he violates his epistemic theory by attributing to human knowledge some relation to an objective world. If metaphysical reality lies beyond all cognitive knowledge, the question remains how sense perceptions can assuredly relate to the thing-in-itself. If we know nothing beyond phenomenal impressions or inner perceptions structured in a given way, then any rational conclusions about the thing-in-itself are inclusive and indeed impossible. Things-in-themselves cannot be the *cause* of our impressions because causality is a category of the understanding valid only for phenomena (things as they appear). *Cause* cannot be used to *account for* the experience since causality is declared to be valid only within the experience.

(5) If not even sensation can be traced to some independent *cause*, then the whole process of knowledge must originate in subjective factors; consciousness is merely this necessary process of knowledge, and no basis exists for affirming either an underlying *ego* or self or an independently real existent. Knowledge is thus reduced merely to the flow of consciousness; indeed, here one finds a clue to Johann Fichte's notion that all that exists is the many finite consciousnesses or the *human ego*.

(6) But how can we say that the *ego* exists when not even my own consciousness is given in sensibility? The ego, self or person, too, must therefore be only an idea.

(7) And if the human ego itself is a mere subjective representation, can we then even argue for the necessity and universal validity of our ideas or representations, despite Kant's assumption that this form of experience is common to the human race? Indeed, for all of Kant's valiant effort to overcome Humean skepticism, his Critical Philosophy sinks at last toward solipsism (we know nothing independent of our experience), illusionism (we know nothing beyond our representations) or nihilism (not even the ego is knowable, not even I exist).

In summary, Kant's view is that we can have no objective knowledge except under the conditions necessarily imposed by our minds. While he rejects skepticism, his alternative leads nonetheless to an overthrow of the knowledge of objective truth; our affirmations have no metaphysically objectifying significance. What gives the representations of human knowledge their only objectivity is their subsumption under the categories as necessary forms of all thought. But these categories, on Kant's premises, are found solely in the human understanding and not in external reality, nor are they grounded in the supernatural or metaphysical sphere. Hence the categories confer no metaphysical objectivity on human knowledge; no objective knowledge of a reality outside and independent of our consciousness is affirmed, no knowledge of the constitution of objects as they are in themselves, no affirmation about the nature or essence of things as they exist apart from our own representations. The constitution of our knowledge by the universal and necessary forms of human cognition provide no basis for any inference concerning the nature of things-in-themselves. None of man's knowledge-claims can be considered definitive of external reality as it inherently is; the innate categories of thought supply no rational basis for insisting or expecting that the actual nature of metaphysical reality will conform to human knowledge and experience.

Kant's theory of knowledge retained such elements of the biblical view as that the mind itself has inherent structures of rationality, and that these structures are constant rather than changing. But because he forfeited the Judeo-Christian revelation of man's creation in the image of God, he was unable to derive these premises from his own epistemology, and was required simply to postulate them. His retention of some aspects of a biblical view of man, alongside his loss of the creation of man in the divine image for responsible cognitive knowledge in a Logos-structured universe, involved his theory of knowledge in overwhelming inconsistencies.

Gordon Clark moves us beyond the emphasis on merely formal a priori elements of human knowing by insisting that the very forms of reason and morality may and must, in fact, be viewed as belonging also to the content of the divine image in man. The Bible disowns the vulnerable feature of Kant's theory of innate categories of thought, namely, the autocracy of creative human reason. It precludes viewing the categories of understanding merely as subjective forms of consciousness or as simply human determinations of knowledge, whose objectivity consists entirely in their validity for mankind. Were the laws of thought not valid for nonhuman reason, that is, for the Supreme Intelligence, as well as for all other intelligences, then not even the laws of identity and contradiction which govern all human thought would hold everywhere and always. Human thought would then reduce to subjective assertions valid only in relation to finite individuals constituted to think in a special way.

In revealed religion the forms which govern thought and the objectivity of knowledge have their basis in the transcendent God. The laws of reason and the forms of morality have been prescribed by the Creator, upon whom all created reality depends for its origin, continuance and intelligibility. Only the content of God's intelligible revelation can properly combine reason and fact, inasmuch as God is the source of all meaning and the author of all facts. All men have the same formal laws of thought and conceptualize in the same way.

The image of God, moreover, is not to be located only in conscience, or freedom of the will, or even in self-consciousness or self-transcendence nonintellectively defined; it specially embraces all psychic elements that elevate man above the animal world, although, of course, any beclouding of the rational in human experience will confuse everything else.

The consciousness of God is necessarily posited along with the consciousness of the human self, not because man's spirit is a finite part of the infinite Spirit, nor because man's reason is an omnicompetent source of ultimate truth, but because God himself ongoingly confronts man by addressing him to, through and in the creation-bestowed image which distinguishes man as a creaturely reality. Self-consciousness, the immediate certainty of my own being, is involved in any and all comprehension. But neither existence nor the ego is intelligible unless much more is the case than that I exist. Divine revelation is the starting point of all human knowledge. Consciousness of God is not merely an inference from consciousness of the finite by way of a negation of the finite; it rises in man's inner being in such a way that man is conscious of himself in relation to God, in his knowing God as the not-me and me as the not-God. The existence of God is no less an original and immediate certainty than the certainty of one's own existence. The sinner may assume that self-consciousness is possible without God-consciousness or that self-consciousness is God-consciousness, but such assumptions already incorporate, from the standpoint of revolt, a modification of divine revelation.

Man's perception in his inner life of the Sovereign to whom he is morally accountable, and whom he somehow unpreventably knows, is accompanied from the first by a perception also of God in the cosmos; it is widened, moreover, by man's dealings with his fellow men to whom he knows himself obligated in a certain way and from whom he has certain moral expectations. General divine revelation embraces God's disclosure in all of created reality; to this man stands in moment-by-moment relationships alongside direct *imago*-relationship with the Creator and is thus hedged in on every hand—outside and inside—by God's unyielding claim.

That man as created bore God's unblemished image does not mean, however, that before the fall man manifested or mirrored all the divine attributes. The Creator alone determines the respects in which man as his privileged creature images the Divine. Man never was nor will he ever be omniscient or omnipotent, nor was he ever fully free and independent as God is. To speak properly of "image" requires that we respect the difference between the prefatory *omni-* appropriate only to all of God's perfections and what is reflected in created beings in a qualified way. Man is not gifted with divinity or eternal power which God self-discloses in his revelation through the created universe (Rom. 1:20).

Yet both before and after the fall, man is endowed not merely with a formal likeness to God; the *imago* also has material content. On the basis of creation man had more than a mere capacity for knowing God, for discerning good from evil, for discriminating truth from error. He not only knew that God is not the not-God, but he also knew Elohim his Maker personally, truly and intimately. He not only knew that good is contradictory of evil but he knew also that God's revealed will defines the good, and he knew specific elements of that will that placed him under God's command. He knew not only that truth and falsehood are antithetical, but also that the truth is what God thinks and says, and by divine communication he also knew and treasured in his heart certain truths enunciated by his Maker. Indeed, man in God's image knew God himself to be the truth and the good, the Creator and Lord of all; he knew reason and conscience as God's enablements to recognize and approve the true and holy Lord. Created man knew God's revealed truth and declared will, and loved, trusted and obeyed him. His fellowship with God was unbroken; he lived a moral life in truth, a life consonant with God's revelation pulsating through the *imago Dei*. To God he gave his whole heart, his undivided self; God's light and law were his highest fealty and felicity.

The fall of man was a catastrophic personality shock; it fractured human existence with a devastating fault. Ever since, man's worship and contemplation of the living God have been broken, his devotion to the divine will shattered. Man's revolt against God therefore affects his entire being; he is now motivated by an inordinate will; he no longer loves God nor his neighbor; he devotes human reasoning to the cause of spiritual rebellion. He seeks escape from the claim of God upon his life and blames his fellow man for his own predicament. His revolt against God is at the same time a revolt against truth and the good; his rejection of truth is a rejection of God and the good, his defection from the good a repudiation of God and the truth.

The consequences of man's fall, therefore, are far more serious than Thomas Aquinas and Roman Catholic theology allow. According to Thomas, the fall neither affected the natural gift of reason nor impaired the natural light of reason in relation to God; man in fact is even thought capable of demonstrably proving the existence of the one true God without dependence on revelation. *The Documents of Vatican II* reaffirm this position. Vatican II declared that "the Gospel is in harmony with the most secret desires of the human heart," that the natural reason is unspoiled, and that God can therefore be known by the natural light of reason.

Calvin, on the contrary, in championing God's general revelation, held that sin obscures almost everything about God except man's knowledge that God exists and that he executes moral judgment. Man cannot work himself up to the standpoint of special revelation or to the full vision of original general revelation because even in his best moments he is constantly in revolt against revelation and involved in the consequences of that revolt.

Luther believed that the fall totally destroyed the moral *imago* because it corrupted man's will. Since his time, Lutheran theologians have been divided over whether the *imago* was totally destroyed, but they have not castigated each other as heretics in this disagreement. None of them exempts the intellect from the effects of the fall; all insist that the fall impairs and disrupts the image in its entirety. The doctrine of total depravity asserts that no function of man whatever escapes the effects of Adam's fall. Some Lutheran and Calvinist theologians insist that human reason is now completely defective in respect to the truth of God, others contend that despite the fall man possesses a capacity for rationality and knowledge as an ongoing aspect of the divine image.

Gordon Clark emphasizes that the fall affects the functions of the reason and of the will in different ways; his argument is persuasive. "While no act of will can be moral in the unregenerate man," says Clark, "it does not follow that no intellectual argument can be valid" ("The Axiom of Revelation," p. 75). Clark distinguishes sin's noetic effect on the content of man's thinking, that is, on his philosophical premises, from its effect on his mental activity or the components of logic and reason. Whereas sin affects man's psychological activity, and hinders his ability to think correctly, it does not affect the laws of valid inference. True propositions are universally true now, as they were before the fall and as they always will be. "Logic, the law of contradiction, is not affected by sin. Even if everyone constantly violated the laws of logic, they would not be less true than if everyone constantly observed them" (ibid., p. 75).

Two important considerations underlie this debate over whether rational powers are completely defective in consequence of the fall of man. If fallen man cannot know the truth, then he cannot have knowledge of God, and is therefore reduced to skepticism about spiritual ultimates. But skepticism is self-refuting, since it claims to know that we cannot know. Moreover, Scripture refutes the view that men have no knowledge of God; it considers all men guilty sinners in consequence of a revolt against light. Had man's rational competence not survived the fall, he could neither know nor communicate intelligible truth, nor could intelligible revelation be appropriated by him or meaningfully addressed to him.

However serious its consequences and however far-reaching its effects, the fall of man, therefore, did not involve man's total loss of knowledge of God, nor of his rational competence or ethical accountability. Although sullied by the fall, the divine image in man was not totally shattered. Despite man's loss of moral integrity and the threat to the integral unity of the *imago* posed by an inordinate will, even after the fall man is marked off from the animal world by facets of the original image, and lives out his creaturely existence within the forms of reason and morality that distinctively structure human experience. He stands ongoingly in responsible relationships to God and society.

This denial that the fall has destroyed the elements of rationality in man means that modern existentialists misconceive the human predicament when they affirm that he can have no cognitive knowledge of God, and that the reality of God and the content of the moral claim are distorted when formulated in rationally consistent propositions. Man's situation is not one of natural agnosticism, nor is he called to trust God in the absence of cognitive knowledge; rather, sinful man violates what he knows to be true and right.

In view of Paul's Epistle to the Romans, Calvin insists that man's universal sense of divinity embraces the knowledge that God exists, that he is a God of glory and majesty, that he is omnipotent, and that he justly punishes all who disobey him. Calvin also finds in unregenerate mankind "some notions of justice and rectitude . . . implanted by nature in the hearts of men. . . . For though they have not a written law, they are by no means wholly destitute of the knowledge of what is right and just" (*Epistle to the Romans*, commentary on 2:14). By the phrase "implanted by nature" he means, in context, implanted by God in the divinely given form and content of the *imago*. Calvin points to man's sense of shame over wicked deeds as attesting the survival of this imprinted knowledge of right and wrong, and asks, "Why were they ashamed of adultery and theft except that they deemed them evils?" (ibid., on 2:15). He even says that "the internal law . . . suggests to us in some measure the same things which are to be learned from the two tables of the Decalogue" (*Institutes*, II, viii, 1). Edward A. Dowey, Jr., too much ignores the qualifying phrase "in some measure" when he ventures, on the basis of Calvin's writings, to depict the Reformer as affirming on the basis of creation an ongoing moral content which includes not only the obligation to worship God and to honor parents and rulers, but also to practice monogamous marriage, and to observe property rights, benevolence to the needy, respect for the aged, and preservation of human life (*The Knowledge of God in Calvin's Theology*, p. 71).

Philosophical theists who deny the reality of special revelation sometimes escalate the responses of mankind to general revelation in a way that suggests that even atheists are disguised believers. But only volitional trust in God as a cognitively known reality constitutes genuine personal faith. The Bible does not say that atheists are believers in disguise; it affirms, rather, that while all men have cognitive knowledge of God, fools "say in their hearts" that God is nonexistent (cf. Ps. 53:1), that is, they do not yield themselves to him. Atheism is, of course, possible not only as a conjectural hypothesis, but also as a preferred philosophy of reality held by many naturalists. Logical positivism reduced atheism to nonsense on the wrong premise; since it declared the statement "there is a God" to be unintelligible, the contradictory "there is no God" would then be equally meaningless. Tillich argued that atheism is impossible; he defines belief in God so broadly, namely, as ultimate concern, that anyone absolutely devoted to atheism is thereby marked as a believer. Evangelical Christianity insists only that everyman has inescapable knowledge of God even in the course of rebellion; were he to suppress that knowledge even to the point of speculative atheism, he would not succeed in destroying significant cognitive relationships to God within which he remains spiritually and morally accountable. Paul Edwards remarks that "a person is an atheist if he *rejects* belief in God, regardless of whether his rejection is based on the view that belief in God is false" ("Some Notes on Anthropomorphic Theology," p. 242).

Whatever may be the unregenerate man's philosophical credo, he can neither live as a human being nor understand himself without adhering to some ultimate loyalty and concern; in this sense no one can existentially be an atheist. Everyone has his private god or gods and everyman is a religious man, though most men are religiously devoted to false gods and do not trust the living God.

Recent interpretation of the *imago*-passage has moved away from what is now often called a spiritualizing view (that the image consists in man's spiritual capacities such as reason, moral consciousness, conscience, self-transcendence, will, freedom, immortality, etc.) to a corporeal understanding of *selem* (image), which the parallel term *demuth* (likeness) somewhat softens.

Barth locates the image in mankind's sexual differentiation in unity ("let us make man . . . male and female created he them") as a reflection of dynamic interpersonal relationships in the three-in-one God. Instead of finding God's image in rational and moral factors, he locates the image in human creation as male and female, a "relationship in differentiation" supposedly reflective of the triune God (*Church Dogmatics*, III/1, p. 184). The theory deserves less plaudits for exegetical fidelity than for ingenious imagination. On the surface it is more compatible with binitarianism than trinitarianism; moreover, as Clark notes, it implies that in heaven where marriage relationships are irrelevant man will forfeit God's image ("The Axiom of Revelation," p. 108). Barth correlates his view with the modern population crisis, contending that the command to "be fruitful and multiply" is effective only during the Old Testament period when barrenness is considered a reproach in view of woman's hope that she might be mother of the promised Messiah. After Jesus' birth, Barth argues, the command lost force. More recent theories correlate the image rather with the ecological crisis and emphasize man's God-given responsibility for his environment.

Some theologians, e.g. Ludwig Koehler, locate the image in man's upright walk, which equips him for dominion over his environment by elevating him above the beasts and nearer to God (*Old Testament Theology*, p. 147). Gerhard von Rad finds corporeal *imago*-reference rather in man's entire historical bodily function on earth as God's representative: "Just as powerful earthly kings, to indicate their claim to dominion, erect an image of themselves in the provinces of their empire when they do not personally appear, so man is placed upon earth in God's image, as God's sovereign emblem . . . God's representative . . . to maintain and enforce God's claim to dominion over the earth" (*Genesis*, p. 58).

The fact that the word for image (*selem*) is used for a statue and similar material objects (Num. 33:52; 2 Kings 11:18; Ezek. 7:20; Amos 5:26), and is used also to designate a copy of an original (1 Sam. 6:5, 11) or a sketch of man drawn upon a wall (Ezek. 23:14) shows, says Bernhard W. Anderson, that the ancient world did not sharply distinguish "between an original and its copy, that is, a copy was something more than a mere resemblance" ("Man's Dominion over Nature," p. 14). But all theories of a corporeal likeness founder not only on the lack of biblical confirmation, but also on their inconsistency with the Judeo-Christian insistence that God is Spirit, incorporeal and invisible.

Von Rad's theory that the *imago Dei* has a functional or representational character has recently been supported by extrabiblical texts from the ancient Near East, both Mesopotamian and Egyptian. The word for image (*salmu*) is used in Akkadian to describe the king's relationship to the deity. But Werner H. Schmidt (*Die Schöpfungsgeschichte der Priestschrift*) links the Genesis passage to Egyptian rather than to Mesopotamian ideas because, he thinks, it reflects the court style of ancient dynasties in which Pharaoh was called the "image of Re" and "likeness of Re" in relation to the Lord of the universe.

Schmidt contends that Genesis 1:26–28 "democratizes" this motif by depicting mankind (adam) as the image-bearer. Bernhard Anderson also supports this view, despite its rejection by Claus Westermann (*Genesis*, fasc. 3, pp. 209 f.). Presumably the democratization of the image is supported by the correlation of singular and plural pronouns in the *imago*-passage: "Let us make man in our image, after our likeness: and let *them* have dominion" (Gen. 1:26, KJV). That not only the individual Adam but also mankind as a collective social group is in view gains further credence, it is said, by both the execution of God's resolution: "So God created *man* in his own image; in the image of God created he *him*; male and female created he *them*" (Gen. 1:27, KJV), and by the blessing, "be fruitful and multiply, fill the earth and subdue it, rule" (Gen. 1:28, NEB).

Several factors weigh heavily against the notion that the Adamic-image is a universalization of the Pharaoh-image. One is the gratuitous derivation of the narrative motif from Egyptian sources, another the fact that, contrary to the ancient pagan regard for rulers as incarnations of divinity, the Old Testament consistently represents Yahweh as the only divine king. Moreover, the ban against any visible image would seem to exclude entirely the idea of corporeal representation by creaturely man (Jesus' reference to magistrates as "gods" or as standing in God's place in no way suggests the notion of mankind as the divine image, cf. John 10:34–35).

According to Anderson the Genesis writer so extensively reinterprets the earlier myth that "not much" of the original is left. Not only does the writer "democratize" the image universally, but he also "stresses the transcendent majesty of the Creator and thereby establishes a sharp differentiation between Creator and creature" ("Man's Dominion over Nature," p. 15). The reluctance of the Old Testament to speak of a divine king except in messianic terms nonetheless weighs against the theory that mankind is installed as the agent of divine rule on earth. Anderson notes that unlike Genesis, the Egyptian myths nowhere affirm that Pharaoh and his wife bear the divine image. That does not settle the point at issue, however, for the Old Testament never speaks of Eve as the first queen nor of woman as the coagent of divine rule on earth.

We need not and do not at all question that man by creation is God's own legitimate image, or that mankind collectively somehow shares and in some respects even retains the originally imparted image. But we do question the following notions, as unproved assumptions, and as highly speculative: (1) that the biblical representations of the *imago Dei* are mythical rescensions of Near Eastern religious myths; (2) that they locate the divine image in corporeal likeness as God's representative kingly ruler over the earth; and (3) that in expounding the divine image with respect to man's relationship to nature the Adamic fall may be virtually disregarded.

The biblical emphasis that man as God's image has a divinely delegated dominion over the earth is clearly an aspect of the Genesis teaching, one which in current literature more and more monopolizes discussions of the *imago*. Secular scholars, alert to the ecological crisis, increasingly blame this biblical emphasis for the rise of technocratic scientism and its manipulative exploitation of nature for human convenience, comfort and profit—with no regard to the permanent welfare of the race and none for the independent claims of nature itself. For all that, man in the Bible is not identified as having a mystical affinity with nature; rather, he is given dominion over his earthly environment. The restrictions on man's dominion are very specific, however. He is given neither autonomous sovereignty over God's creation nor the right to selfishly exploit it.

It may mean very little to emphasize that Genesis speaks only of man's dominion over the earth, and not over the whole of cosmic reality, a point that some have raised in opposing moon-shots and exploration in outer space. While Genesis contains no explicit statement concerning man's comprehensive dominion, and concentrates rather on his immediate territorial environment, Scripture does view the entire space-time universe as God's creation, and more than that, as somehow embraced in his redemptive program. Nonetheless on the earth is where the Bible locates the human drama; here is the arena of man's fall and of God's salvific rescue, and here we are reminded that man is not infinitely extended in time and space.

Although Genesis 1:1–2:4 as an account of origins has no suggestion of a cultic setting and evinces theological reflection rather than hymnic praise, a number of scholars nonetheless believe it may once have served a liturgical purpose. Psalm 8:5–8 and Genesis 1:26–28, which both relate man's high position in God's creation with man's power to exercise dominion over the animals, Bernhard Anderson interprets as liturgical reflections of the Jerusalem cult. He thinks it probable that Psalm 8 is older and influenced the formation of the Genesis *imago*-passage. He considers it possible, however, that the latter may be older and existed in the form of a cultic legend in the Jerusalem temple ("Man's Dominion over Nature," p. 8).

Although Anderson gives import to the Genesis narrative concerning man's dominion, he classifies this Hebrew account within the same category of myth about "the creation of individual man or the creation of the world as a whole" that characterizes Canaanite religions generally. He writes: "Undoubtedly these myths, mediated to Israel through Canaanite culture or through the cosmopolitan atmosphere of the Davidic-Solomonic court, belong to the prehistory of Genesis 1–3 and of other literature of the Old Testament: cultic, prophetic, and sapiential" (ibid., p. 6). While he notes that Psalm 8 places the theme of man's coronation in the context of Yahweh's transcendent sovereignty, he thinks it "draws upon mythical language, perhaps Canaanite in origin, to portray Yahweh's sovereignty in the cosmic sphere."

Instead of taking "crown" in a general sense (as in Ps. 103:4), Anderson argues that the language of Psalm 8 suggests royal investiture, and that man's dominion is here regarded as a consequence of Yahweh's elevation of him to royal status. Whereas in Genesis 1:28 "man's dominion is based upon a divine blessing which empowers him to multiply and subdue the earth," in Psalm 8 "man is invested with a royal splendor that not only raises him above the animals but draws him into the sphere of God's kingly rule" (ibid., p. 10). Anderson contends that Psalm 8 should not be messianically interpreted, as by some modern scholars who apply it to the "son of man" as corporately representative of "man." He suggests rather, since the royal dominion there in view is not over enemies or over both men and animals, but solely over animals, that it refers instead to mortal man or everyman, although "perhaps the myth of the Kingly First Man is in the background" (p. 12). He concedes, however, that Genesis 1:26–28 nowhere reflects a "coronation of man" motif. Some Scandinavian scholars contend nonetheless that the Genesis *imago*-passage depicts the first man as "the first king of the world" (Aage Bentzen, *Messias, Moses redivivus, Menschensohn*, p. 12).

According to Anderson "ancient mythical views lie behind Genesis 1:26–28, just as they lie remotely behind the opening picture of chaos (Gen. 1:2)"; the writer uses "mythical language" he says, to stress that man stands closely related to God and is the earthly agent of divine rule ("Man's Dominion over Nature," p. 15). Anderson thinks that Psalm 8 and Genesis 1 evidence the new situation when, in David's time, Israel "accepted the alien institutions of temple and king and came under the influence of the royal theology which prevailed in the ancient Near East" (p. 16). In different ways and degrees the two passages, he contends, modify the existing myths in the context of Hebrew faith which emphasized Yahweh's incomparability and prohibited any material image or likeness. Psalm 8 declares man (perhaps represented by David the king) to have a status just *below* that of the divine beings, and as making God's name illustrious and glorious throughout the earth by the exercise of his divinely bestowed dominion. But Genesis 1:26–28 democratizes this royal theology further: man is differentiated into male and female, to emphasize the plurality of mankind in God's image.

Anderson contends that the Genesis writer reinterprets the Egyptian myth of Pharaoh as God's image to stress the Creator's transcendent majesty, and universalizes the image to depict man generally (cf. Gen. 5:3, where Adam's son bears Adam's image).

Now if it is indeed the case that Genesis gives us a recension of ancient Near Eastern myths in mythical language, while it incorporates unique conceptions to be contrasted with Egyptian sources, then a critically important question is whether Genesis 1:26 belongs to the genre of religious literary myth or whether it reflects divine truth. All that is said about the moral qualities of divinely delegated dominion loses its universal validity and ethical compunction if, like some modern Old Testament scholars, one regards the biblical representations simply as distinctive mythological accounts, and adduces no ground for viewing their content as transcendent divine revelation. One cannot logically contend that the distinctive ideas of the Genesis passage are objectively valid and carry a moral imperative in contrast to ancient religious myths if the content of Genesis 1:26–28 has no epistemic basis to support it over against the ancient myths. Anderson's insistence that all man's religious views are cast in mythical form disallows any special truth-claim for the biblical representations. One is left with the impression that the Genesis writer was inspired by Egyptian sources, and that the passage more assuredly reflects a redaction of an Egyptian motif than that Adam (whether the first man or all men represented in him) reflects the divine image.

If the Genesis creation account supplies us only with a myth, and not with revealed truth, then it is merely another interesting literary turn in the mythology of a comparatively primitive people, and its importance is limited to a few learned scholars, whether historians, anthropologists or comparative religionists, interested in fragments of literature from remote ages. If Scripture matters only because it reflects the myth of a particular covenant-community, or only because its special form of a given myth has been more influential than others, then no case can be made for God's saying anything decisive in the Genesis *imago*-passage. If, on the other hand, Genesis is a distinctive revelation of truth, it is an enormously significant disclosure of the mind and will of God and of the Creator's purpose for man in relation to the universe. If the *imago*-passage carries an authoritative message it can do so only if it expresses transcendent divine revelation. But one can hardly support this latter claim on the thesis that all religious assertions are mythical in form and content, however much one distinguishes between the ideas of competitive myths. Mythology encompasses as many absolutes as myths, and anyone who simply lumps the biblical representation with all others as mythical forfeits any basis for differentiating between them in respect to truth.

The same negative result obtains, even where interpreters emphasize that the divine image consists in man's visibly exercised dominion, if the inner rational and ethical aptitudes traditionally associated with the *imago* are excluded. One can argue vigorously, as Anderson does, that dominion in the context of the Genesis *imago*-passage implies a situation of paradisaic harmony and peace devoid of violence, even though in some other Old Testament associations *rada* (subdue) means "to trample" and *kabash* (have dominion) refers also to such acts as rape. If the forms of reason and morality do not in fact belong to the *imago Dei* but rather are environmentally derived, then no final reason can be given why dominion may not as legitimately be expressed in nonbenevolent as in benevolent ways. Indeed, precisely the Pharaohlike dominion—man in the role of the "trampler"—may be expected if man by creation is not bound to criteria of logic and morality. No objective reason can be adduced for deploring such an alternative as unreasonable unless the law of non-contradiction belongs to the very givenness of human existence.

11.
Recent Conjectural Views
of Revelational Forms

NUMEROUS THEOLOGIANS IN the twentieth century have recovered a significant interest in divine revelation. In the absence of scriptural controls, however, some novel theories have emerged concerning the forms of divine disclosure.

No exposition has been more formidable than the threefold form of revelation expounded by Karl Barth, to whom the contemporary religious scene largely owes its renewed regard for special revelation, now often defined in a quite unorthodox way.

Barth identifies revelation in its primary and continuing form with the Word of God which he expressly distinguishes from Scripture. He depicts revelation as a prior divine activity, to which he then assimilates both Scripture and church proclamation. "Revelation is the form which establishes the other two" (*Church Dogmatics*, I/1, p. 136). "We do the Bible a poor honor," he writes, "when we directly identify it with . . . something else, with revelation itself" (I/1, p. 126). For Barth, Scripture and proclamation are not simply derivatively suspended upon this primary form of revelation, but become revelation in correlation with it only contingently, that is, only on the occasion of sporadic divine confrontation and personal trust.

In one sense, although this is not at all what Barth maintains, there is indeed divine revelation prior to Scripture, that is, the general or universal revelation of God. Evangelical orthodoxy has long distinguished general from special revelation, insisting that God is revealed and in some respects known even where special redemptive revelation is unknown. But Barth repudiates the reality of general revelation. When he contends for revelation as an event superior to Scripture, he has in view not general revelation but a primary form of special revelation.

Just what Barth means by this revelation superior to Scripture is not wholly clear. By "revelation" that is other than Scripture, he obviously does not mean the divinely inspired thoughts and words of prophets and apostles who spoke as well as wrote the Word of God. For he causally and essentially distinguishes revelation from both Scripture and proclamation (even prophetic-apostolic proclamation), declaring that "revelation engenders the Scripture which attests it" (ibid., I/1, p. 129), and arises "out of Scripture." Does he then perchance mean to equate his superior revelation with Jesus of Nazareth? Certainly not the historically manifested Jesus, despite such statements as that "revelation in fact does not differ from the Person of Christ himself" (I/1, p. 134), or that Jesus Christ is "the pure event in relation to which everything else is not yet an event or has ceased to be one" (I/1, p. 131). Simultaneously with his reference to Jesus Christ, Barth insists that "revelation is not conveyed in secular history" and that "revelation is itself the divine decision which takes effect in the Bible and in proclamation" (I/1, p. 133). In some passages he states that divine revelation never meets us abstractly but only in the specific form of Scripture and proclamation. As he puts it, "Revelation never meets us anywhere in abstract form, of it precisely our knowledge is only indirect, arising out of Scripture or in proclamation. It is just the immediate Word of God which meets us only in this twofold mediacy" (I/1, p. 136).

Gordon Clark thinks that Barth's obscurity in formulating the identity of revelation must be traced to his uncompromising insistence that the Bible is not revelation. As a consequence, revelation for Barth is "some sort of event or events" that is "wordless" and "not a series of sentences." But if this is so, asks Clark, "how does Moses or a theologian today get from a dumb, unintelligible event, to articulate and definite theological belief?" (*Karl Barth's Theological Method*, p. 173). Barth's extraneous form of the Word, Clark remarks, "solves nothing; it merely creates problems, useless problems, insoluble problems" (p. 175).

When Barth, for example, declares that "revelation . . . makes proclamation possible" (*Church Dogmatics*, I/1, p. 136), what is rather the case, Clark emphasizes, is that Scripture makes proclamation possible. Again, when Barth asserts that we know "the written Word of God only through the revelation," it would be more accurate to say instead that we know the written Word through the reading of Scripture.

Barth's superadded form of nonintellective revelation is actually extraneous and dispensable. His appeal to the Protestant Reformers and to a few other influential theologians of the past to find prestigious precedents for his exposition of "the threefold form of the Word of God" is unconvincing. He relates this threefold form to an exposition of the doctrine of the Trinity and says much that evangelicals would approve. But his schematic correlation of the Trinity and revelation is something else; it is a novel creation that provides no coherent explanation of the three revelational forms he espouses, nor does it exhibit any secure basis in revelation for his trinitarian affirmations.

It remains a colossal mystery how Barth himself can arrive at doctrinaire illumination of the inner secrets of the Godhead on his view that the Christ-event communicates no universally valid truths and occurs in divine history rather than secular history. Barth sacrifices biblical leverage for trinitarian doctrine by insisting that the revelation quality of Scripture is not to be found in its cognitive-verbal teaching but solely in Scripture's accommodation of a confrontation with the transcendent Word of God. That the Father is disclosed in the Son and communicated by the Spirit is indeed, as all evangelicals insist, an objectively valid statement about what is actually the case. But on his revelational formula which considers Scripture to be a quite fallible propositional witness to a superior nonintellective revelation-event, Barth cannot firmly relate what he says about the Trinity to the eternal nature of God, nor escape suspicion that he is overworking a fertile theological imagination when he makes such claims.

Clark thinks the motivations underlying Barth's view may lie in the desire to find an analogy between revelation and the Trinity (*Karl Barth's Theological Method*, p. 176). Insisting that the *ordo essendi* precedes the *ordo cognoscendi*, Barth correlates his emphasis that the eternal Word is the *prius* of revelation with the declaration that Jesus Christ is himself the event of revelation; this, in turn, he connects with God's speech in eternity. He says, "In the fact that for revelation, Scripture, and proclamation, we can substitute the divine 'Person'-names of Father, Son, and Holy Spirit, and *vice versa*, that in one case as in the other we shall encounter the same fundamental determinations and mutual relationships . . . we may see a certain support for the inner necessity and rightness of the present exposition of the Word of God" (*Church Dogmatics*, I/1, pp. 136 f.). This highly speculative excursus equates revelation with the Father, Scripture with the Son, and proclamation with the Spirit—an arrangement which, as Clark insightfully notes, "breaks the previous identification of revelation with the Son" (*Karl Barth's Theological Method*, p. 176).

To reinforce the unity of the threefold form of revelation, Barth resorts finally to the concept of contemporaneity. Here he adduces the notion of three times, or varieties of times, in which God speaks. The importance that Barth assigns to this correlation of three differing times and the threefold form of revelation is clear: "If we drop the orderly variety of the three times . . . we must drop the concept of the Word of God itself" (*Church Dogmatics*, I/1, p. 167). What then is involved in this emphasis on the difference of times? Barth sees in it a safeguard against dissolving revelation, Scripture, and the church into the general movement of history, and therefore a means of preserving supernatural revelation from immanental reductionism. As he explains, "If we insist that the concept of the Word of God means precisely that the Church does not stand solitary . . . then we must abide by the orderly distinction between the times, and the present day proclamation with Scripture and with revelation can certainly not be regarded as a thing to be introduced . . . by incorporating Scripture and revelation into the life of humanity" (I/1, p. 167).

Yet it remains to be seen whether the complex notion of contemporaneity that Barth introduces to achieve the unity of the so-called threefold form of the Word of God clarifies or confuses the issue. The Word of God in all three forms is depicted as God's contingently contemporaneous act. Barth distinguishes (1) the time of the original revelation, that is, of God's original utterance, as the time of Jesus Christ, which is the time of Abraham (John 8:56) no less than of the Gospels; (2) the time of apostolic attestation or of the canon; (3) the time of the church and derivative proclamation (ibid., I/1, p. 164). These three times and forms require the same subordination of proclamation to Scripture and of both proclamation and Scripture to revelation or the time of Jesus Christ. Thus far in his system Barth has not shown how the postulated difference in times really assures or guarantees apostolic superiority over proclamation, or the superiority of revelation over Scripture; we have, in effect, merely his assertion that "that's the way it is!"

In the "revelation-faith event," says Barth, the time of Christ as the Word of God becomes contemporary with the time of the apostles and with our time. In this way of putting the matter, something remarkable has clearly happened either to the notion of time or of contemporaneity, although what has happened may not be immediately apparent. The "step from one time to another" takes place when "the Word of Scripture in its quite different time area, with its quite different content compared with the Word of revelation . . . simultaneously utters the Word of Christ Himself" and when "Church proclamation becomes real proclamation; because in it Holy Scripture, and in Holy Scripture Christ Himself comes to expression" (ibid., I/1, p. 169). On Barth's premise, it seems that conformity to Scripture does not make proclamation real proclamation, nor does Scripture utter the Word of God when it attests the incarnation and resurrection of the crucified Logos; the real thing exists only when "the Biblical Word . . . makes a place for itself in a quite different period" and "the Word of God in this step from revelation to Scripture and to Church proclamation . . . is contemporaneous" (I/1, p. 169).

Barth's confident declaration that this formula unravels the secrets of the Word of God and exhibits the unity of the Word in its allegedly threefold form has all the marks of a Roman priest giving assurance of transubstantiation during mass. It is perhaps worth quoting him again: "The problem of the Word of God is thus from time to time a perfectly definite, once-for-all, peculiar problem, and of this problem we must say that it is solved by the Word of God itself, spoken by the Word of God, being contemporaneous *illic et tunc* and (i.e., exactly as spoken *illic et tunc*) *hic et nunc*" (ibid., p. 170).

But Clark is certainly right in insisting that two time periods separated by centuries are surely not contemporaneous; Barth's failure, moreover, to begin with levels of authority—God's, prophetic-apostolic Scripture as his inspired written Word, and the church's proclamation of this inspired message—misleads him into this impossibility by an emphasis on contemporaneity of justifying the superiority of the apostles over modern men. "In all these details," Clark comments, "not only 'contemporaneity' but also 'revelation' fails of intelligible definition. This leaves the unity of Barth's three forms unclear and obscures the identity of the Word of God" (*Karl Barth's Theological Method*, p. 184).

However earnestly Barth strives to present a theology of the Word of God, however magnificently architectonic his framework of revelation may be, he frequently says less or more than the Bible says and at times other than what it says. Such speculation may be motivated by legitimate concerns—in Barth's case, to connect revelation with the doctrine of the Trinity and to preserve some priority for the apostolic testimony. But the dynamics of divine disclosure are inevitably blurred where divine revelation is not allowed to indicate its own framework for an exposition of its forms.

If we are to expound the varieties of divine revelation, it is therefore imperative that the exposition proceed from the nature and content of revelation uncompromised by speculative considerations. The Bible is indeed a form of revelation, and not only holds epistemic priority over church proclamation but is also the communicated form of God's special revelation and not dependent on some prior nonintellective form. There is indeed a general revelation of God in the universe, but this revelation too is cognitive, and not nonintellective; the biblical writers characterize it as God's daily "speech" (Ps. 19).

Jürgen Moltmann likewise sponsors a novel form of divine revelation. Insisting that the Old and New Testaments contain "no unequivocal concept of revelation" (*A Theology of Hope*, p. 139), he then attempts to exhibit one whose "peculiar dynamic" is messianic in kind and implies a history of promise. Moltmann rejects every attempt to derive the theological content of revelation from the meaning of the term *revelation* (to unveil, etc.) and contends that Scripture attaches "a meaning of a different kind . . . mainly determined by the events of promise" (p. 45). For Moltmann the correlate of faith is not revelation but the *permissio Dei*, an eschatological outlook in which revelation is "the promise of truth" (p. 44). If God reveals *himself*, says Moltmann, "revelation does not then open up a future in terms of promise, nor does it have any future that would be greater than itself" (p. 46). *Deus dixit* is a divine promise which discloses and guarantees an outstanding future" (p. 58).

Moltmann as well as Barth and Bultmann holds that statements made on the basis of revelation may not be objectified; they give us no valid information about God in himself. To define revelation merely as "apocalypse of the promised future" forfeits its universally valid cognitive content as fully as does the surrender by Barth and Bultmann of objectifying knowledge of God. Moltmann warns against reading the meaning of revelation in terms of the God of Parmenides. His meaning, however, becomes also a polemic for a new and tenuous view of revelation in which he elevates to priority and converts into conjectural principle what in the Bible is but one important aspect of divine revelation, namely, emphasis on the future in which God's promise will find comprehensive fulfillment. Although Moltmann loosely shares with Bultmann an emphasis on the eschatological orientation of revelation, he deplores any understanding of God's futurity as something constant; if this were the case, God's futurity would accommodate a revelational "epiphany of the eternal present" (ibid., p. 68) even if anthropologically interpreted, instead of being simply faith in "the eschatological perspective of promise" (p. 69).

It is clear that Moltmann turns revelation into a predicate of eschatology and does not correlate it unambiguously with the self-disclosing God who intelligibly communicates his purposes to man. Promise alone determines what is to be said of the revealing of God. This approach replaces the evangelical-orthodox theology of scriptural revelation with a revelational theology of history viewed eschatologically. In Moltmann's scheme, revelation loses its Logos-determined character as reliable information about God's nature and purposes for man, and becomes simply promise or hope. Its cognitive vacuity is evident: " 'Promise,' " says Moltmann, "announces the coming of a not yet existing reality from the future of truth. Its relation to the existing and given reality is that of a specific *inadaequatio rei et intellectus*" (ibid., p. 85).

It would therefore seem quite impossible to distinguish promise from fantasy and miracle from myth; indeed, to say that we are here dealing with revelation of God—even of the future of God—seems more a private reverie than a publicly defensible actuality. To be sure, Moltmann insists on the resurrection of Jesus Christ from the dead as proleptic of the Final End, and hence as providing in history open to the future an anchor for revelatory promise and fulfillment. But if the future wholly relativizes the past and the present, it is unclear just how the resurrection can escape these same consequences. If the resurrection of Jesus Christ in about A.D. 30 is not relativized by revelation as the history of promise that looks to the End, then the comprehensive relativization of revelational truth and deed must be abandoned. Moltmann's emphasis on promise and fulfillment as the only form of revelation is too narrow to survive logical scrutiny and biblical verifiability.

Some neo-Protestant scholars, prominent among them Schubert Ogden, prefer Schleiermacher's view of "original revelation" to the traditional evangelical representation of general or universal revelation. According to Schleiermacher, the feeling of absolute dependence on God carries with it also immediate self-consciousness of God. Such an approach to universal revelation bypasses, among others, the questions whether all divine revelation is mediated, and whether noetic consequences of sin involved in the fall of Adam impinge on general revelation. It focuses, instead, on everyone's absolute dependence on God as the basis for affirming the reality of the Divine (the precise definition of God is for Schleiermacher an empirically open matter). Thus redefined, original revelation strips away the sense of revelation that is *temporally* or *chronologically* prior from a universally given revelation that is *logically* prior to special revelation. In expounding universal revelation, moreover, the quasi-pantheistic context in which Schleiermacher formulates his understanding of original revelation avoids the traditional insistence on the supernatural and concentrates instead upon unqualified human dependence on the divine, an emphasis more congenial to process philosophy than to biblical theism. While Ogden therefore affirms general revelation to be a form of divine disclosure, he redefines it in a manner that eclipses the channeling of all divine revelation through Christ the Logos of God. He also evades the issue of the noetic consequences of the Adamic fall for general revelation, and compromises the essentially supernatural character of divine disclosure.

Ogden does not stop here, however. He champions a novel revision of particular divine disclosure. Preferring the term "decisive revelation" to that of "special revelation," he emphasizes that this "decisive revelation" and not "original revelation" has since New Testament times constituted the primary sense of revelation in Christian theology. For Ogden special revelation is the clarification of general revelation in a particular way. Special revelation is necessary simply to add something "more" to general revelation, and not, as in historical biblical theism, to add also something "other," namely, the redemptive dimension. Ogden does not believe that special revelation, that is, the particular revelation centered in Jesus Christ, serves to complete natural or original revelation. As he sees it, the role of special revelation is to clarify rather than to complete. Special revelation, he maintains, gives point (existential urgency) to the universal revelation.

But if the role of decisive revelation is merely to supplement and clarify, then, it should be noted, it need not be an exclusive revelation; in fact, several such clarifying revelations might far better satisfy the criterion of understanding. It becomes obvious that Ogden's view leads to more than simply a novel definition of special revelation; it opens the door to many varieties of decisive revelation. He reduces the absolute need for Christian revelation into simply a generalized need for clarifying it, something that may take different turns in different times and places. Unless Ogden defends the tenet—and he apparently does not—that the exclusive truth-significance of the Christian claim is alone decisive, he is merely commending a multiplicity of claims to religious decisiveness. Properly understood, the Christian truth-claim embraces all other legitimate revelatory claims and on its own incomparable basis of special once-for-all disclosure shows itself to be both more accurate and adequate.

If special revelation is unqualifiedly necessary for any reason—even for clarification—can it any longer be considered a gracious revelation? Ogden forfeits the cognitive clarity of general revelation and obscures the redemptive once-for-allness of special revelation preserved by evangelical theism. As he sees it, the Christian revelation conveys nothing new; all it does is to make explicit those truths already but merely implicitly known to man at every moment of his existence. If, as Ogden contends, special revelation does not convey a peculiar content not found in general revelation (in the objective form of Scripture), then why is Ogden's "special" revelation not subject to the same fate as "original" revelation, that is, defeat by sin? The fact is, however, as incontrovertibly attested by the history of Christian thought, that Christian revelation does indeed convey a new content—for example, the truth of divine incarnation in Jesus of Nazareth, his substitutionary atonement and bodily resurrection for sinners, and the divine triunity. The Christian revelation does not offer itself as one of many varieties of "decisive" disclosure: "There is no salvation in anyone else at all, for there is no other name under heaven granted to men, by which we may receive salvation" (Acts 4:12, NEB). What Ogden does, therefore, is to distort the Bible by moving behind it to alien and restrictive presuppositions which dull the supreme revelation in Jesus Christ and the objective authority of Scripture.

Ogden goes beyond simply rejecting the two traditional forms of divine revelation—general and special—in their biblical understanding. While it is true that he abandons the eschatological orientation of revelation propounded by Bultmann and Moltmann, and yields quasi-objectifying significance to revelation, he nonetheless rejects the historic view that revelation is primarily a communication of cognitive information, a view that Ogden declares to be contrary to the New Testament. But surely the prophets and apostles proclaim as revelation not what is implicit in everyone's faith-response but rather the Word and truth of the God who has appointed them carriers of his revealed message.

By rejecting special propositional revelation objectively given in Scripture, the way is opened, in Ogden's as in Moltmann's case, for espousing a cognitive clarification in which process philosophy assumes the stature of revelation.

THESIS SIX:
God's revelation is uniquely personal
both in content and form.

12.
Divine Revelation
as Personal

REVELATION IS PERSONAL communication. Its personal originator is God, and persons are its recipients; it involves personal thought and speech as when God addresses Abraham and Moses; sometimes in addition to God's direct address it involves also personal agents as bearers of revelation. Here one thinks especially of the Angel of Yahweh during the Old Testament era (Gen. 16:7; 18:4–5, 22–23; 21:17; 32:24–30; Exod. 3:2; 14:19; Isa. 63:9), of the inspired prophets and apostles, and supremely of Jesus Christ.

At the center of revelation stands the God who names himself; his self-disclosed Name is a distinctive feature of that revelation. He is not simply a magical power inhabiting some local cultic site, nor some artfully embroidered literary fiction, no flimsy and elusive Mystery at the outermost limits of knowledge, no impersonal principle speculatively postulated to make human sense of the universe. God who makes himself known by name is the ultimate Spirit that peoples the invisible world which bounds and defines human destiny.

God's declared purpose in disclosing his Name is to fully apprise man of his divinity. The formula for divine self-presentation (*Selbstvorstellungsformel*), "I am Yahweh," indicates this, especially when taken alongside the fuller "recognition-formula," "and they will know that I am Yahweh" (e.g., 1 Kings 20:13, 28).[1] The emphasis falls, as Walter Zimmerli remarks, "on the naming of Yahweh's proper name, which

---

1. We need not more than note the divergent conclusions to which textual critics are driven by their presuppositions. Walter Zimmerli contends on form-critical grounds that the shorter expression "I am Yahweh" is original and is alone decisive for God's self-presentation, whereas Rolf Rendtorff considers it a late reduction of longer statements that additionally characterize Yahweh's name.

contains within it the whole fulness and glory of him who here names himself" (*Gottes Offenbarung*, p. 11, quoted by Moltmann, *A Theology of Hope*, p. 113).

Yahweh's stern disapproval of any visible material representations dramatizes the centrality and indispensability of his self-presentation in his own way—that is, by the audible disclosure of his name. His followers dare not dilute this invisible presence and audible presentation into visible material forms. The entire religious history of the Hebrews is shaped by the prohibition of material images representing God the invisible and immaterial Spirit. The audibly given divine Name and revelation of God in his Word replaces for the Hebrews the need for a visible material image to identify the living God. A material representation could only denigrate the self-revelation of God who makes himself known by his own personal manifestation in his audibly spoken Word. The Hebrews knew that the spatially localized and perishable idols, man-made and man-named, are antithetical to the invisible God who himself speaks his own Name and Word.

This Hebrew presentation of Yahweh solely by his revealed Name utterly baffled those whose religion centered in visible images. The Roman general Pompey, for example, was completely confounded when, in the first century B.C., he entered the Holy of Holies and found in the sanctum of God's special Presence no visible representation. To the Hebrews, God's revelation meant Yahweh's utterance of his Name, and Hebrew religion consisted of hallowing that divinely revealed Name.

Implicit in this restriction to God's authorized Word and the total disallowance of material misrepresentations was the incomparability of Yahweh—indeed his absolute uniqueness. Admittedly, Israel was not alone in the religious *Umwelt* of the ancient Near East in depicting deity as incomparable. In a general way, of course, every asserted divinity can be described as unique, or it would be indistinguishable from other concepts of the Divine. But over and above this, specific claims of incomparability were explicitly attached to Egyptian, Sumerian, Babylonian and Assyrian gods. Does this mean, then, that we identify Hebrew concepts with these apparently corresponding ideas or derive biblical from pagan motifs? Might not separate religious traditions formulate claims that appear to be outwardly similar but on a quite distinct and independent basis? It is not established that the Hebrews simply borrowed a commonly used religious formula, but if it were, the question would still remain: did they also borrow the meaning it expresses in their own very different situation? Or do they despite verbal similarities affirm something far different about Yahweh than do their near neighbors about pagan gods?

G. Ernest Wright contends that the ascription of incomparability was transferred to Yahweh from a pagan background, and that it is merely an honorific term and therefore lacks any truly comparative content (*The Old Testament against Its Environment*, p. 34, n. 49). But C. J.

Labuschagne stresses that attention given to biblical theology as well as to the nonbiblical religions will best answer the question of whether the Old Testament asserts the incomparability of Yahweh in some wholly unparalleled way.

Assyro-Babylonian prayers and hymns much more frequently imputed incomparability to Marduk, god of the city of Babylon, than to other gods, but in this polytheistic milieu they readily ascribed incomparability also to several other deities as well, regardless of their rank. The very same hymn can ascribe, in fact, incomparability to both Marduk and another god. Since the ascription does not as such exalt one god above another, Labuschagne concludes that incomparability functions as a stereotyped label to express profound adoration (*The Incomparability of Yahweh in the Old Testament*, p. 3). It is equally significant that in Assyro-Babylonian religion this same quality of incomparability is readily transferred to earthly kings on the premise of their divinity.

Labuschagne notes however that incomparability was not attached indiscriminately and universally, but was reserved for particular gods; hence it originally must have had some comparative intention. He finds no evidence, however, that Assyro-Babylonian religion first applied the concept to one particular god, and then only later distributed it among several gods. The comparison may from the first have been based on the rivalries said to exist among the polytheistic deities, or on an identification of respective gods with various natural phenomena. But "the idea of incomparability did not include any notion of exclusivism. . . . Supremacy was never reckoned at the expense of other gods" (ibid., p. 53). "The application of the attribute did not imply any trend towards real monotheism" (p. 54). Instead, says Labuschagne, the ascription of incomparability is "an emotional, effective hyperbole, expressing the profoundest praise to the god who happened to be the object of worship" (p. 54).

Egyptian religion not only depicted various gods as unique and incomparable, but also asserted the existence of still other gods worthy of worship. Incomparability was ascribed as well to the pharaohs who were viewed as divine rulers. There is no evidence that Egyptian religion merely imitated Mesopotamian religion in thus ascribing incomparability to several gods as well as to earthly kings; the practice seems to have arisen independently.

Is it possible then to identify any features by which the Old Testament revelation presents Yahweh as incomparably different from the gods of the ancient Near East? Contrary to G. Ernest Wright, Labuschagne emphasizes that the incomparability ascribed to Yahweh contrasts sharply with the absence of radical dissimilarity and exclusiveness characteristic of polytheism. In the Hebrew Scriptures, Yahweh alone is said to be unique and unrivaled; incomparability is asserted only of Yahweh and denied all others, whether polytheistic divinities or early rulers. Israel interprets the incomparability of Yahweh as meaning the worthlessness of all other gods (Deut. 32:39; 2 Kings 19:18; Isa. 37:19; Jer. 10:12;

51:15). That Yahweh is unique and unrivaled is stated not only positively but negatively: "There is none . . . like Yahweh" (cf. Exod. 8:6; Deut. 33:26; 1 Sam. 2:2; 2 Sam. 7:22; 1 Kings 8:23; Ps. 86:8; Jer. 10:6-7). The Hebrew Scriptures, moreover, do not apply uniqueness to earthly kings, and thus avoid any suggestion of their divinity; according to the Old Testament Yahweh is the only divine King (Jer. 10:7, 10).

It is important to reemphasize that Yahweh's incomparability is affirmed not simply as a philosophical conclusion, but is integral to his self-revelation. Only on this basis has it monotheistic significance repudiating idolatry; especially noteworthy is 2 Samuel 7:22, RSV ("There is none like thee, and there is no God besides thee") which B. Hartmann insists is a monotheistic affirmation. Yahweh himself asserts his incomparability when he says: "I am God unrivalled, God who has no like" (cf. Isa. 46:9, JB); the same disclosure appears in a rhetorical question to which Yahweh expects a negative answer: "Who is like . . . ?" (Jer. 49:19; 50:44; Isa. 44:7). Labuschagne remarks, "In the mouth of Yahweh Himself our rhetorical question appears in its shortest form, without any qualifying adjectives or nouns. This is most significant, for it implies that Yahweh need not justify His claim to incomparability, because He really is the Incomparable One" (ibid., pp. 20 f.). Both the positive ascription and the rhetorical question carry over into Hebrew worship in prayer, praise and confession (Exod. 15:11; 2 Chron. 14:11; 20:6; Pss. 35:10; 71:19; 89:9; 113:5; Mic. 7:18). In some instances God's superiority is further expounded in terms of some particular divine perfection (Job 36:22; Deut. 3:24; 4:7; Ps. 77:14; Mic. 7:18).

Yahweh's self-revelation and his incomparability are therefore theologically correlative; he is the absolutely incomparable God known in self-disclosure. He introduces himself audibly through his Word; he designates himself explicitly by name; he declares his own incomparable uniqueness; he is practically and decisively engaged in the cosmic and historical sphere; he is not to be and cannot be visually represented by graven images.

Where discussion of the Divine deletes the category of personal revelation, it should come as no surprise that the special Old Testament form of self-manifestation represented by the theophanies, or appearances of the Angel of Yahweh, constitutes a special embarrassment. Wolfhart Pannenberg, for example, because he allows only God's indirect revelation through historical acts, argues that "For us as non-Israelites, the divinity of Yahweh is not convincing on the basis of those self-manifestations attested to in the Old Testament. Many religions tell of appearances of deities and of the communication of the divine name—how will one decide from this that precisely the God of Israel is the true God?" (quoted in James M. Robinson and John B. Cobb, Jr., Theology of History, p. 232, n. 12). The question at this moment is not whether we can vindicate the case for biblical theism solely on the basis of divine self-revelation as an undefined category, appropriate as this question is. But if like Pannenberg one forfeits all interest in God's self-revelation, and therefore in the theophanies, on the restrictive premise that God's disclosure is given only indirectly in historical deeds, then one embraces presuppositions that frustrate even the biblical understanding of historical revelation.

As direct appearances, the theophanies no doubt could immediately convince only the recipients of those manifestations, but they do not on that account lose their larger importance.[2] Theophany is a special mode of revelational miracle, a supernatural appearance in which God directly communicates his message. It therefore anticipates, however dimly, a climactic visual manifestation of God in his own time and way, one which the messianic promises expectantly await. The theophanies therefore have a special significance in the theology of revelation in that they prepare, amid the prophetic concentration on the auditory disclosure of God, for the coming momentous visual manifestation of Yahweh in Jesus Christ (John 1:18). The New Testament channels all interest in the theophanies of God into the divine manifestation in Jesus Christ; the Old Testament (Septuagint) term for theophanic appearances is, in fact, used of the resurrection appearances of Jesus Christ (*ōphthē*, 1 Cor. 15:5-8).

All this contrasts unmistakably with the *epiphany* appearances in the Greek myths. Despite the latter's claims of sudden manifestations of divine Being, their underlying assumption represents man's being as essentially congruous with eternal Being and the temporal-historical world as unimportant for disclosure of the Divine, along with an intransient deity. The entire exposition of divine manifestation therefore rests on a transcendental misunderstanding; the mystery of the Divine is unraveled only as man's supposed secret divinity is unveiled. But the self-revealed I who is the manifested Thou of revealed theology discloses his character not as an extension of the human self on the premise of man's hidden identity with eternal Being, but as the transcendent Other, the absolute Creator of men and things. The self-disclosed and absolutely incomparable God is not simply our cosmic Big Brother, not simply *more* than

---

2. In Gen. 16:7-13 the *malach* (messenger) who appears to Hagar is identified as Yahweh by power and by name. Similarly Yahweh is said to appear to Abraham (Gen. 18:1, 13, 22, 33) and to Jacob (Gen. 32:22-32). Further appearances include those to Moses (Exod. 3:2-6; 33:11). Some commentators consider the theophanies of Yahweh preincarnation manifestations of Christ the mediator (note John 8:56-59; 1 Cor. 10:1-5). Calvin comments on the Corinthian passage: "The angel who appeared first to Moses, and was always present with the people during their journey—was the Son of God, and was even the guide of the Church of which he was the head" (*First Epistle to the Corinthians*, loc. cit.). In the *Institutes*, moreover, he remarks that "The Word of God was the supreme angel, who then began, as it were by anticipation, to perform the office of the Mediator" (p. 118). The New Testament does not hesitate to identify the preincarnate Logos as active agent in Old Testament revelation; words, works and relationships attributed to Elohim or Yahweh in the Old Testament are applied to the Logos in the New Testament (cf. Gen. 1 and John 1; Isa. 8:13-14 and Rom. 9:33).

man, but is ontologically Other. There remains on the basis of the self-revealedness of Yahweh no option but to reject Greek epiphany-constructs that presuppose the secret divinity of man and the nonrevelational significance of history.

Yet it will not do to distinguish Yahweh's revelation solely in terms of an emphatic contrast between I-thou and I-it relationships. Some expositors seem wholly to forget that during the long history of religion, multitudes have mistakenly worshiped nature as "Thou." Not only has this been the case in pantheistic misunderstandings of the universe as a cosmic Self, but also in misrepresentations in secular philosophical theory and in pagan religious worship of one or another aspect of the world as being intrinsically divine. It is also a fact that, contrariwise, many influential philosophers have degraded deity into an "it," into an impersonal first principle supposedly explanatory of the universe.

These misguided speculations do not, of course, annul the truth that the living God centers his disclosure in personal relationships very different from man's correlations with nature as a realm of impersonal objects, even if the cosmos is an arena of divine revelation. Nonetheless, the incomparability of God does not ultimately rest on our subtle Thou-it distinctions; rather man's own personal distinctiveness rests on the divine "Thou shalt . . ." and "Thou shalt not . . ." which refuse to excuse man as a dumb beast of the field or as mere dust of the earth. Through his own personal initiative and self-disclosure, Yahweh makes himself known as the divine Other whose incomparability far transcends the truism that he is not an impersonal "it" like the physical world. In his own right Yahweh views his creation through the personal purposes for which he intended man and the cosmos, and in final expectation of which the whole creation is said even now to "groan and travail" (Rom. 8:22).

If man understands the indispensable priority of God's self-revelation for his knowledge of God, he will blanket modern philosophy of religion with a huge question mark because it virtually denies that God as personal Subject takes any significant initiative in revelation. Only because it unjustifiably dismisses divine revelation as a category of religious knowledge can modern philosophy of religion discuss deity as an enigmatic cosmic X to be deciphered by human initiative and ingenuity. Or it perceives him as an object whose personality is demoted under our probing to just another quantifiable impersonal thing to be known solely by methods appropriate to our knowledge of man and the world. Insofar as emphasis on God's self-revelation supersedes both man and nature or history as the indispensable factor by which we are to answer the question of God's reality, there is every reason to insist that God is the preeminent Subject; the case for theism has a solid basis only because God discloses himself. A self ontologically other than the human self, a reality wholly different from the universe, stands at the center of the truth of God. The case for the reality of God begins not with human experience or speculation about the ultimately real but with God's self-disclosure, with *Deux dixit*. When discussing divinity, God in his self-revelation is not a deferrable or disposable consideration; it is the *sine qua non* without which all God-talk is but human chatter.

In emphasizing the personal form and content of divine revelation, we therefore view God as the active thinking Subject whose personal initiative is the indispensable presupposition of all knowledge of him. He sovereignly discloses the names properly applicable to him, and in so doing proclaims his absolute incomparability. Even in the patriarchal era his theophanic appearances foreshadow his climactic manifestation in Jesus Christ.

But even more needs to be said, lest the prejudiced theological context of our day spawn gross misunderstanding and delusion concerning God's self-revelation. For neo-Protestant theologians currently expound divine self-disclosure in a prejudicial manner that turns it into one of the most misunderstood themes in contemporary theology. The difficulty is not one of precise terminology that lacks biblical precedent, although Werner Elert and G. Gloege ("Offenbarung dogmatische") profess to find none. Considerations of terminology aside, there can be little doubt that in some decisively important sense the personal revelation of the living God is a central scriptural motif. But the assertion of God's self-revelation is today so correlated with dubious theological emphases that any significant view of divine disclosure is sadly eroded. That God personally reveals himself is made to imply, among other things, that revelation is nonintellectual and nonpropositional; that God is never an object of conceptual thought; that theological assertions are nonobjectifying; that personal faith in God excludes mental assent to theological doctrines. Such assertions not only derive their inspiration from modern philosophical speculations alien to the biblical view, but they in effect also destroy divine self-disclosure in the scriptural understanding.

What is involved in such modern restatement of God's self-revelation may perhaps be best understood if we briefly indicate several major developments from Hegel to Herrmann to Barth and then to Bultmann (cf. Moltmann, *A Theology of Hope*, pp. 52 ff.). Hegel saw the Absolute manifested everywhere directly and immediately, although his thesis that the divine Mind is the totality of all finite minds left many followers unsure about the separate personality of the Absolute. Wilhelm Herrmann, Barth's most revered teacher, stressed divine self-revelation, an emphasis that imparted to the twentieth-century theology of revelation a distinctive slant over against that of the nineteenth century. Like Kant, Herrmann insisted that metaphysical affirmations are nonobjectifying, and held, therefore, that revelation cannot be grounded objectively nor approved to the theoretical reason. As a consequence he rejected not only orthodoxy which insisted on subscription to revealed doctrines, but also liberalism's disavowal of any special revelation whatever. Herrmann's position was, to use Moltmann's words, that "we cannot say of God what he himself objectively is, but only what effect he has on ourselves" (ibid., p. 54). He stressed, however, that we know God only because "he himself reveals himself to us ourselves by acting on us" (*Gottes Offenbarung an uns*, 1908, p. 76, quoted in ibid., p. 52).

Ritschlian influences lurk in the background of Herrmann's insistence that God's unique revelation in Jesus of Nazareth is comprehended only in our inner response to divine grace and issues in a new kind of thinking, willing and feeling. Faith begins with the recognition that we lack true selfhood: only in complete surrender does the self find its authentic freedom. Herrmann criticizes Schleiermacher for failing to grasp the dynamic nature of faith as a response to revelation that involves personal surrender because he posited "the feeling of absolute dependence" as being universally present in man. But Herrmann himself attributes to man "the possibility of . . . grasping the reality of his own situation and of making this knowledge the starting point from which he moves to the Knowledge of God" (James D. Smart, *The Divided Mind of Modern Theology*, p. 35). If one asks what happens to past biblical events as a fulcrum of revelation, Herrmann answers that "any communication whatever we can call a revelation only when we have found God therein" (*Der Begriff der Offenbarung*, 1887, pp. 10 f.). Consequently all else but God's present action on us is only the permanent possibility of revelation. Herrmann thus fixes the interest in revelation on subjective individual experience. He assimilates objective revelation only to what directly and potently affects us "not as a historical event in the distant past, but as a personal experience in the immediate present" (A. E. Garvie, *The Ritschlian Theology*, p. 197).

Herrmann's formula therefore emphasized (1) God's self-revelation; (2) the inner secret experiential correlation of the human self and the divine self; (3) the nonintellective nature of divine revelation and the nonobjectifying nature of our knowledge of God; and (4) dynamic personal actualism that links revelation, action, and a special religious knowledge in an ongoing event.

Barth expounds his doctrine of God's self-revelation initially in the essay on "The Principles of Dogmatics according to Wilhelm Herrmann" in *Die Theologie und die Kirche* (English: *Theology and Church*, pp. 238 ff.). Herrmann had developed revelation in terms of man's subjective experience grounded in the Divine; that is, he affirmed a hidden correlation between God and the human self. This experiential correlation of God's self and man's self Barth rejected; he appealed not to man's consciousness but rather to supernatural divine revelation, emphasizing that ungrounded religious experience cannot provide revelation. He reinforced the importance of divine self-revelation by interposing the supernatural act of *Deux dixit* between the nonobjectifiable subjectivity of God and the subjectivity of man. At the same time Barth carried forward Herrmann's tenets that special divine revelation is neither a mental concept supplying intelligible instruction, nor is it confined to chosen prophets and apostles but is, rather, an ongoing sporadic event. In essence, then, Barth's view declares (1) God's supernatural self-revelation, (2) known through God's internal action, and not through the reflection of man's faith upon his own inner experience, (3) viewed as redemptive communication and not as propositional disclosure, (4) yet viewed as an ongoing sporadic event in which the ancient prophets and apostles hold chronological priority. As for Herrmann, so for Barth, God reveals only himself and not information, propositions, truths. Moreover, his self-revelation cannot be objectively defended in terms of any external divine relationship either to the cosmos, to history, or to man in general, but must be believed solely in view of personal divine confrontation. This ongoing sporadic inner revelation of God becomes necessary only because Barth rejects objective intelligible revelation. If there is to be divine revelation at all, his philosophical premises leave no option but *"self-revelation,"* and that in terms of dynamic actualism.

Barth struggles to make this divine self-revelation to man reflect what is actually the case regarding God "himself." He does this by developing the idea of God's self-revelation first in the context of a doctrine of the Trinity (the threefold form of the revelation), and then further in the context of God's lordship. In each case, he attempts to learn the content of revelation from concrete divine action upon man. Yet shorn of any grounding in the objectivity of God and precluding all objectifying statements about him; shorn of intelligible propositional character and of verbal mediation by chosen prophets and apostles; shorn of every connection with an external divine activity in nature, history, or a universal *imago Dei* in mankind, God's revelation must here necessarily mean something very different from the biblical understanding. What God is this, whose self-revelation demands as a condition of "knowing" him that I refuse to make him an object of thought, must forego all objectively valid reasons for obedience, and must believe simply because he presses upon me a totalitarian claim of lordship? In this context does it even make sense to speak of God revealing his Name? Or of divine *self-revealing*? Or of God at all?

Rudolf Bultmann also shares the premises handed down through Herrmann, namely, that theological assertions are nonobjectifying, that revelation is cognitively uninformative, and that special divine revelation is an ongoing event. His exposition centers, however, upon the *human* self as the locus of divine disclosure—in the "us ourselves" to whom, according to Herrmann, God reveals himself by acting on us; all statements about God in his action or revelation can be spoken of only in relation to the human self. One recalls Barth's words in the essay "Rudolf Bultmann—An Attempt to Understand Him": "All I want is to understand Bultmann as best I can. After all, he learnt his theology from Wilhelm Herrmann, and he is fond of quoting him. In justice to Bultmann, we must remember all he could have learnt, and probably did learn from Herrmann long before he ever heard of Heidegger" (2:122–23). Bultmann writes, "Theology speaks of God by speaking of man as he is confronted by God" (*Glauben und Verstehen*, 1:25). In contrast to and in criticism of Barth, Bultmann's view involves, as Moltmann remarks, "the rejection of all objective statements about God which are not existentially verifiable but are derived from the realms of mythology and world-picture without regard to our existence—indeed, it is only arrived at in the light of the antithesis that has continually to be stated anew between *Weltanschauung* and self-understanding, between objectified statements and the non-objectifiability of God and of existence" (*Theology of Hope*, p. 60). This is doubtless why Robert T. Voelkel comments that "whereas Barth deviates consciously from the intentions of his teacher, Bultmann self-consciously attempts to salvage Herrmann's notion of faith" ("Introduction" to Herrmann, *The Communion of the Christian with God*, p. xliii).

Divine self-revelation as Barth expounded it—objectively ungrounded either in God as an object of knowledge, or in the cosmos and history externally, and lacking intelligible cognitive content and propositional validity—could offer no persuasive resistance to this further existential reductionism; Moltmann rightly labels it the defenseless self-revelation of God (*Theology of Hope*, p. 55). If Barth could speak strenuously of supernatural revelation, Bultmann could reiterate the nonobjectifiability of theological assertions. For Bultmann the supernatural and miraculous belong to the category of myth in view of the supposedly closed network of cause and effect in the objective world of nature and of history (*Kerygma and Myth*, 2:196 ff.). It is not at all surprising that whereas kerygmatic theology in Barth's version emphasized the Christ Word only in terms of personal supernatural confrontation, and eclipsed the importance of the words of revelation, Bultmann's exposition, in fixing upon divine confrontation eclipsed most of the historical data about Jesus and subordinated the Nazarene. All claims made on the basis of revelation find their nonobjective verification in man's existential coming to himself.

Herrmann had not only rejected the possibility of objectifying affirmations about metaphysics, but by vitalistic tendencies in his later thought also supplied a bridge between Kantian idealism and Bultmannian existentialism. Along with Barth, Bultmann maintains the nonobjectifiability both of God and of the human self; over against Barth, however, he reaffirms the view of a hidden correlation of God and the human self, albeit on the basis of existential faith. James Smart's observation is to the point: "Herrmann held fast to the conviction that man's coming to his true life depends upon the unique and decisive revelation of God in Jesus Christ. It is not difficult then to see why Barth in 1925 could say that he was not conscious of any 'conversion away from him' but only that he had to say differently what he learned from him. . . . When we hear Herrmann say, 'God reveals himself to us only in the inner transformation which we experience. . . . The religious man is certain that God has spoken to him, but what he can say of the event always takes the form of a statement concerning his transformed life . . . since religion is the transition from what only seems to be life to what is truly life,' we seem to be hearing the voice of Bultmann" (*The Divided Mind of Modern Theology*, p. 36, quoting Herrmann, *Gesammelte Aufsätze*, p. 159).

Rather than objective empirical experience, Bultmann advances existential experience through man's freedom as a personal subject to transcend the closed system of causally determined reality, and to find self-fulfillment through subjective decision. Subjectivity is nonobjectifiable because transcendental. To speak of God's action or of myself is existentially to transcend the causally determined external world; the religious ingredient stems from Bultmann's emphasis that God is personally encountered in this inner realm of personal decision and response. Presupposed in our responsive acts of obedient faith are the inner transcendent acts of God. Only by obediently hearing the Word of God that confronts him can man find real freedom and authentic existence. For both Bultmann and Barth, therefore, no objective evidence or attestation is to be, nor can be, adduced for the existence of God. Bultmann insists that "when we say that faith alone . . . can speak of God, and that therefore when the believer speaks of an act of God he is *ipso facto* speaking of himself as well, it by no means follows that God has no real existence apart from the believer or the act of believing" ("Bultmann Replies to His Critics," 1:199). But precisely here, as Robert H. Ayers remarks, "Bultmann the theologian is compelled to set the limit of demythologizing for it is difficult, to say the least, to speak of an act of God as an objective reality in existentialist terminology. All that one could do would be to give a phenomenological account of what it means for human beings to live as if there were a god" ("Religious Discourse and Myth," p. 85). For Bultmann only authentic self-existence confirms God's transcendent address to us in Christ.

Bultmann unmasked a deforming weakness in Barth's theology: despite a theory of revelation and knowledge that in principle renounced objectifying metaphysical assertions, Barth had ventured to make quasi-objectifying statements about God-in-himself; moreover, Bultmann considered Barth's affirmation of miraculous supernaturalism wholly incompatible with the assertedly modern scientific world view. Bultmann was challenged in turn by more radical neo-Protestant theologians for making much the same mistake at another level. Even if Bultmann turned the resurrection into cryptic apostolic language for man's prospect of new being through an inner faith-response to God's address to us in his Word, on what basis, they asked, could Bultmann insist that God addresses us only in Christ? And if the self gains whatever authenticity it has through subjective decision (cf. *Glauben und Verstehen*, III, 1960, E. T., p. 79: "faith itself belongs to the revelation"), what basis is there for speaking of anything more than simply man's higher selfhood? Why must we speak of a transcendent Word of God that confronts us? Why does man need transcendent divine revelation, "that opening up of what is hidden which is absolutely necessary and decisive for man if he is to achieve 'salvation' or authenticity" (ibid., p. 59)? Marxists and others propound a wholly different self-understanding of man. Bultmann had called for the demythologizing of Barth; and now critics of Bultmann called for the demythologizing of Bultmann. Bultmann had tapered revelation to simply the event of preaching and faith ("The preaching is itself revelation and does not merely speak about it," ibid., p. 78). It required more credulity than a reflective modern man can muster to take seriously such "preaching-revelation."

Divorced from objectivity, conceptuality, and external reality, and predicated solely on inner confrontation, Bultmann's exposition of divine self-revelation collapsed under the crushing weight of both internal inconsistency and external criticism.

Although Bultmann professes to replace speculative world views by transcendent revelation, he does so by a specious religious theory that actually evaporates any recognizable form of divine revelation. He does not achieve a contrast between "self-understanding" and "Weltanschauung." As Moltmann remarks, Bultmann espouses "a definite Weltanschauung, a definite view of history and a definite analysis of time, according to which man has become questionable to himself in his social, corporeal and historic relations to the world and attains his selfhood by differentiation from the external world and reflection upon his objectifications" (Theology of Hope, p. 67). Bultmann identifies man's authentic selfhood as the receiving of individual inner subjectivity wholly from God and independently of all relationships to objective rationality, to external history and to the outer world. This stratagem actually achieves the very opposite of what it intends, that is, man's authentic existence. A true self-understanding of man is impossible on premises that becloud conceptuality, man's cognitive relations to the external world, to history and to society, and that expressly forfeit God's purposive activity in the cosmos, his redemptive deeds in history, his intelligible revelation in Scripture and indeed, his very objective existence. Bultmann's sharp antithesis between God and the inner self on the one hand, and the whole realm of external reality on the other, harks of gnosticism and of mysticism. Such speculative schematization of divine self-revelation has little if anything in common with the scriptural exposition.

What philosophical roadblocks detoured the neo-Protestant concept of revelation in this manner over the roadway of internal existential confrontation? Obviously the fault lies in philosophically abandoning the external world completely to scientific empiricomathematical definition and neglecting the Christian view of revelation. Already at the threshold of modern philosophy Descartes had radically segregated the thinking self from outer reality, and had bestowed upon the science of mathematics the prerogative of illuminating the external world. Later Kant deprived the self of cognitive knowledge of metaphysical reality as it objectively is, and held that man's own a priori thought-forms alone structure the phenomenal world. External events, he said, are experienced by us only through the mesh of an unbroken causal continuity, for causality is one of the indispensable categories of knowing.

Most contemporary scientists no longer postulate external cause-effect relationships, and speak more guardedly of predictable connections between observable events. But the empirical methodology they employ, by which external reality is mathematically quantified, affords no basis for discussing nature and history in the context of personal decision and activity, that is, in terms of conscious, rational and purposive acts. Stemming in modern philosophy from Locke and Hume, such impersonalistic reading of external reality has, to quote M. Polanyi, "almost entirely dominated twentieth-century thinking on science" (*Personal Knowledge*, p. 9). The arbitrarily limited presuppositions of scientific empiricism preclude any recognition of psychological referents such as mind and will; methodological consistency requires that even persons be comprehended merely as impersonal entities.

Only one consequence is possible where external reality is deemed ideally expressible only in mathematical formulas that state predictable successions of events: such views eliminate from nature and history any observable significance for transcendent personal will, freedom, thought, and activity, be they divine or human. If external reality is identifiable in terms of mathematically quantifiable propositions about predictable sequences, then the possibility of special or once-for-all transcendent revelation in external history or nature is excluded in advance. For the theologian who accepts this nineteenth-century view of science there remains no room for free divine agency in history or in the cosmos. The only possible channel for divine revelation is then man's inner selfhood. Whether it be universal, once-for-all, or sporadic, divine disclosure must be detoured over the avenue of internal confrontation. The existential correlation of faith in God with man's internal freedom and self-assertion therefore requires this kind of theology to completely abandon the world of "objective reality" and consequently to turn away from external acts of God, since free purposive action is connected solely with inner existential response.

Existential theology can formulate the Word and Act of God only in this peculiar internal way. By assigning to God only the reality of Word and Act in inner divine confrontation, it forfeits the objective being of God. Since it regards the observable world either as a wholly closed causal network or sphere of mathematically predictable sequences, existential theology must disallow the free action of God in external nature and history. Since God's transcendental reality is assertedly experienced only in inner personal encounter, the correlation of God as *super*natural vis-à-vis nature and history is, in fact, irrelevant. While God's being, action and word are considered coincident, with "Christ" at the center, the existential theory of revelation totally excludes any presupposition of

God as a supernatural Being. The "Christ" at the center of the Word and Deed of God is not the Jesus of history, but rather the "Christ" affirmed in a faith-response. The "Christ of faith" exists not as an objective reality but only as a subjective-existential reality through the "Word" of the gospel.

The Christian factor in Bultmann's theology is supplied by the cross as a historical happening and by the resurrection of Jesus Christ as apostolic proclamation. The cross—to which Bultmann assimilates virtually all that may be said of Jesus of Nazareth—must for him be itself an event in the causally determined network of the observable objective world—and therefore, as Robert Blaikie acutely notes—is not an "act of God" in the sense of a purposive divine act. The resurrection, for Bultmann, exists only for subjective faith in response to the inner "Word of God" ("Secular Christianity" and God Who Acts, p. 95). As David Jenkins remarks, the existential representation is that "God has always and only acted in his Word, whereby men who have heard this Word have been set free for authentic existence. . . . There has been no act of God as an historical event but only . . . the hearing of God's Word in historical events" (Guide to the Debate about God, p. 62). The revelational activity of God therefore centers in subjective-existential experience, and is detached from the external saving acts which are of first importance for biblical theology. Only at the point of the cross of Christ, regarded not as a supernatural, purposive and objective disclosure of God but as a happening within the causal determinism of the observable world, does the Bultmannian theory impinge upon external history. The apostolic proclamation of Christ's death and resurrection becomes, for Bultmann, merely a verbal cryptogram for authentic existence available to every man through faith-response to an internally experienced "Word of God."

The "acts of God" have therefore been attenuated to an inner "Word" which supposedly frees man, in obedient response, for the resurrection faith of authentic existence. Since the transcendent "act of God" in his Word has no objective reality or external import in the observable world of nature and history, it confronts man internally with a noncognitive demand for a responsible "act" of trust. Man is called to decision, and in faith receives new self-understanding.

The realm of inner subjective experience in which existentialism seeks revelational refuge from the supposed monopolistic encroachment of causal determinism makes of Christian theology a speculative shambles. The relationships between God, man and the world are here so obscured that no consistent and coherent basis remains for any universally significant correlation of man's will and acts with the transcendent reality of God and the outer world of nature and history. Man as the Bible knows him does not live his spiritual life only in subjective-existential relationships, nor is the living God debarred from purposive activity in nature and history.

Scientific empiricism must of course remain silent about God's personal reality and activity, and about purposive human behavior as well, since its methodology can recognize only observable events in the external world. As John Macmurray emphasizes, the fact that human behavior is explicable in terms of conscious purposes and personal intention is a transempirical postulate that empirical science cannot validate (*The Boundaries of Science*, pp. 144 f.). If the empirical scientist makes empirical science the measure of all reality and the source of all knowledge, he necessarily finds himself in the peculiar position of having to deny his own reality and activity as a personal self, and that of other selves, let alone that of the living God. Advance allegiance to the sovereignty of a restrictive methodology cancels out any recognition of God's reality as Agent and his purposive acts in history and nature. Indeed, such methodological commitment in principle excludes acknowledging any personal agency or purpose whatever. According to Blaikie, "Only the self-indulgent inconsistency of most would-be 'secular theorists' permits them to imagine that, having disposed of God as a supra-empirical or supernatural figment, they can still properly retain man, as free and personal, in their world-view. There is room only for man as an automaton, a sum of events" (*"Secular Christianity" and God Who Acts*, pp. 80 f.).

K. Z. Lorenz and others who increasingly see the human mind only in terms of "computer thought," insist that if rigidly applied, the empirical scientific method would exclude not only divine intervention but also man's purposive actions in nature and history. On the other hand, observes Blaikie, some computer theorists predicate intention and purpose of specialized mechanisms as much as they do of human beings (ibid., pp. 81 f.). If their theory has any meaning, behavioral theorists who reduce all truth to necessary relational connections must themselves forfeit all claim to truth in an objective sense. Blaikie is surely right when he observes: "If the rationality and freedom of men are real, if the terms truth and error, right and wrong, really mean what they have always been taken to mean—involving the view of man as the morally responsible person assumed not only in biblical theology but in human relations universally—then the secular presupposition with its *exclusive* devotion to the empirical method must be ruled out as false" (p. 83).[3]

Loss of the intellective dimension of God's self-disclosure has therefore

---

3. Blaikie rejects the attempts by C. A. Coulson and others to escape this dilemma by their appeal to the concept of "complementarity" to justify the propriety of both the behaviorist and personal explanations of human response; he shows that physicists apply the complementarity principle to observed data capable of divergent explanations, whereas mind, will and purposive action are not observable by empiricist methodology (*"Secular Christianity" and God Who Acts*, pp. 84 f.). The distinction Coulson offers between the mind and will as observed from without and within (in the latter case personal and purposive and in the former mechanistic and impersonal) (*Science and Christian Belief*, pp. 96 f.) is hardly more than a subjective postulation of freedom unless one vindicates the validity of transempirical knowledge and maintains the invalidity of an exclusive empiricism.

had shattering implications for theology, cosmology, history and anthropology. Not only has it issued in exiling God from nature and history, not only has it led to serious doubt over the very reality of God, but it has also fostered an inability to preserve the significance and worth of man himself as more than a passing speck of inanimate cosmic dust. An impersonal external world has cast its flattening shadow over all reality and in reducing all existence-claims to one dimension has overtaken and veiled both God and man.

The self-revelation of the living God is therefore not to be defined and curtailed by special theories that declare God to be "off limits" in the world of "external reality" and that seek to debar him from any objective revelation to man. Only the superimposing of arbitrary views concerning the externally real world is what restricts God's self-revelation merely to internal confrontation. Only alien views concerning the nature and limits of human knowledge are what confine revelation to the inner non-intellective existential surd championed by recent neo-Protestant religious theory. It should be readily apparent that the one-sided neo-Protestant stress on divine self-revelation dims rather than illumines what actually constitutes revelational truth-data. The intelligible content of divine disclosure becomes unmistakably obscure when we are told, as by William Temple, that "there is no such thing as revealed truth" (*Nature, Man and God*, p. 317) but that "the living God himself" (p. 322) is alone at the center of revelation. Such theories create widespread confusion about the nature of revelation because of the conjectural bias that divine self-disclosure is best preserved by the exclusion of divinely revealed truths. In this misconception neo-Protestant theology does not stand alone. As Carl E. Braaten remarks: "Roman Catholic theology today is catching up with Protestant theology; it is no longer sure of what it means by revelation" (*History and Hermeneutics*, p. 117). Legitimate emphasis on divine self-revelation cannot compensate for illegitimate debarment from revelation of its truth-content.

13.
The Names of God

IN THE MATTER OF NAMES for God, biblical theology does not "stand alone"; the history of philosophy and of comparative religions also makes its "contribution." The whole history of unbelief may be summarized as a "calling God names"—sometimes blasphemous, sometimes ridiculous, always somewhat derogatory—indeed, as a refusal to identify him by his true name. The subject of theology (in its narrower reference to the nature of God) might even be approached through a dictionary of divine "names" since every age has added to "sacred nomenclature" by the coining of new God-names. Over against the human misnaming of God— both by the coarse caricatures of atheism, the earthy epithets of secularism, and the polite profanity of speculative philosophy—biblical theology insists on a self-named God.

The Misnamed God of Speculative Philosophy and of Nonbiblical Religions

1. *The long sweep of philosophy,* throughout centuries of interaction with problems of the supernatural, has wavered between the contention that God is Nameless and the ascription of specific names to him.

On the one hand, speculative thinkers have contended that all finite conceptions are irrelevant to deity, that divine Being is beyond predication and wholly attributeless. Not only some Greek philosophers and later Western mystics, but Hindu mystics as well (Yajnavalkya, for example), have insisted on a wholly negative theology. Here all names for God are disparaged as merely a misnaming of deity by human aliases, a pretentious misuse of finite dialect in the realm of the Infinite.

The theology of negation knows God only as the Nameless One. Along

167

with the ancient Athenians, it embraces an unnamed (and unknown) God. Or with modern agnostics like Herbert Spencer (1820–1903), it is prepared to acknowledge the Divine only as the Unknowable (to which, remarkably, Spencer nonetheless inconsistently ascribed such qualities as infinity, eternity, energy). Or with religious philosophers it speaks reverently of the Unconditioned, as did Paul Tillich, who dissolved into mere symbolism all other names and attributes of divinity including the perfections "living" and "personal" (*Systematic Theology*, 1:149 ff.). Heinz Zahrnt says, "It is no accident that when Tillich speaks of God he prefers impersonal expressions: 'being,' 'the divine,' 'the unconditional' (and uses the neuter gender in German: *das Sein, das Göttliche*, etc.)" (*The Question of God*, p. 335). Tillich retains the notion of God's name only to substitute his own philosophical nomenclature: "The name of this infinite and inexhaustible depth and ground of all being is *God*. That depth is what the word *God* means. And if that word has not much meaning for you, translate it, and speak of the depths of your life, of the source of your being, of your ultimate concern, of what you take seriously without reservation. Perhaps, in order to do so, you must forget everything traditional that you have learned about God, perhaps even that word itself. For if you know that God means depth, you know much about Him. You cannot then call yourself an atheist or unbeliever" (*The Shaking of the Foundations*, p. 57). Death-of-God theologians understandably considered Tillich a forerunner of their views. For Thomas A. J. Altizer and other "secular theologians," any nameable God is not only transcendent but also unknowable and unthinkable.

But the great philosophical traditions of the past are studded nonetheless with names for God. The speculative approach has not been content by any means with an innominate God; it has busied itself instead with a removal of divine anonymity. With some justice, the major traditions in philosophy can be catalogued by the divergent names they employ to designate Ultimate Reality. Names for God are indexes to philosophical approaches and systems, whether one thinks of Plato's *Idea of the Good*, Aristotle's *Prime Mover*, Plotinus's *One*, Spinoza's *Causa Sui*, Hegel's *Absolute*. Since for Hegelians the Absolute was impersonal, the divine Name was merely an imaginative way of contemplating a logical Universal inherent in all things.

Modern theology attests its speculative conditioning by the avoidance of biblical names for God, and the deliberate substitution of philosophical alternatives: Schleiermacher's Infinite, Otto Pfleiderer's world-controlling Power, and so on. Barth takes contemporary theologians to task for losing the self-named God of revelation in their speculations about "the World-ground or the World-Soul, the Supreme Good or Supreme Value, the Thing in Itself or the Absolute, Destiny or Being or Idea, or even the First Cause" (*Church Dogmatics*, I/1, p. 210). He scorns religious philosophers who shun the language of Scripture and prefer to speak of God "in abstract terms as 'the highest good' or 'the absolute' or 'omnipotence' or 'omniscience' or as 'the world-spirit,' or world cause or the like" and thereby avoid prominence for God as a person, "the knowing, willing and acting I" (II/1, p. 286).

In representative modern thought, no proper names for God occur at all. A *naturalistic* philosophy, obviously, cannot introduce God in person, but only—if at all—in terms of impersonal stuff. Idealistic traditions, to the extent that they espouse ultimate personality rather than ultimate impersonality, have at least an option on the use of proper divine names. But naturalists, who deny that any living mind and will is ultimate, can only take proper names of God in vain. The naturalistic gods, where such are insisted upon, are really antigods. In this twilight of the gods all divine names are recalled and retracted, and sophisticated utterances translate vivid dreams into divine reality. When naturalism speaks of gods, there is simply confusion of tongues and babel. The real God loses capital letters, and false gods are capitalized: Space-Time, Energy, Neutral Entities, Creativity, Nisus. This "pious naturalism" rails against the true names of God, which are then "naturalized" into earth-bound entities. The familiar words are retained as colloquialism and lingo, as merely symbolic names for a symbolic Divine. But all genuine interest in the divine names is gone, since naturalism no more involves a real name for deity than it involves a living God.

But even the *supernaturalistic* philosophers adduce a heterogeneous plurality of names for God; they cancel each other out. Their speculative names exhibit no inner unity, but reflect diverse ways of interpreting reality. They witness to the fact that where God is humanly named, he is readily misnamed. They are largely a conglomerate aggregation of objectionable nicknames, names imposed at a distance upon deity by strangers who stand outside the family of special divine revelation but who feign intimacy.

To be sure, God has at times been depicted in the history of philosophy as "personal." Plato in some passages represents God as living Mind. Christianity, however, gave Western philosophy its main incentive for comprehending God in personal terms. William Hordern remarks, "The philosophers' God is . . . always spoken about as an 'it,' a hypothesis to explain the universe" (*Speaking of God*, p. 156). The philosophical names for God are titles ascribed on the basis of a humanly initiated effort on man's part to introduce himself to God. In the final analysis, they reduce to personifications of philosophic abstractions—neat formulas by which speculative thinkers aim to depict pithily that postulated first principle which appears to them necessary in order to explain the universe and man. They depose the anonymous deity of philosophical negation only by substituting gods competitive with the living God, competitive not alone because of their plurality—although the history of philosophic monotheism exhibits its own cumulative polytheism—but because they are gods who, since they never speak for themselves but are mute except as speculative philosophers become vocal for them, might just as well be nameless because they are lifeless. That is why philosophical theism, insofar as it considers the naming of God its own special task, trafficks in stillborn divinities, and has moved closer to atheism than it knows.

2. *The history of world religions* witnesses abundantly to the fact that the pagan religious gods too have their special names. In ancient non-biblical religions especially, a striking use of the "name" comes to the fore: sometimes the gods or demons are summoned into the worshiper's presence by the use of their names in incantations. A correct pronunciation of their names in invocation not only assures their accessibility, but places them in a relationship whereby the worshiper can exercise power over them. The gods named in the pagan magical rites thus bear the marks of human control both in their behavior and nomenclature.

Some critical scholars misrepresent the biblical use of the divine Name as an extension of this pagan demonology. The peculiar biblical interest in the names of God was dismissed by Wellhausen scholars as merely a "theurgic formula" which Hebrew-Christian religion shares in common with ancient heathen magic (cf. F. C. Conybeare, "Christian Demonology"). During periodic lapses of Israel into idolatry, some such magical efficacy may from time to time have been attributed to the divine Name. But this is by no means decisive for its normative use. The standard Old Testament use of the Name is not derived from such heathen practices. Hebrew theology does not propose utterance of the divine Name for magical human control of the deity. Precisely such a magical misuse of God's Name is prohibited by the divine command not to take God's Name in vain (Martin Buber, *The Prophetic Faith*, p. 23). The Old Testament use of the Name expresses a higher idea entirely than that found in popular superstition, whether in the Palestinian milieu or in the later Greek mysteries. Harry Blamires pointedly writes of God in his self-disclosure that "his Name does not head the list of contributors to the fund for extending our empire of mastery; rather his Signature seals the death-warrant of our egotism" (*The Christian Mind*, pp. 146 f.). What centers in the Name is not human control of the Divine, but rather the gracious divine provision of merciful access to the Lord of life.

Yet even in the world at large God's Name is more misread and mis-pronounced than wholly censored. The generic term *God* has a recurring place even in the vocabulary of unbelievers, and this bare name remains on the tongues of men and women in every age and land. When translating the Bible into other languages, scholars often retain the foreign name for God (e.g., Allah) when the term is generic rather than specific. God has not left himself wholly without witness even amid the galaxy of the false gods. Calvin asserted: "It is true, indeed, that the name of the one supreme God has been universally known and celebrated. For those who used to worship a multitude of deities, whenever they spoke according to the genuine sense of nature, used simply the name of God, in the singular number, as though they were contented with one God" (*Institutes of the Christian Religion*, I, x, 3).

But the generic name is swiftly misconstrued through its acquisition of a speculative content. The major emphasis in Islam on the names of Allah can only be construed as a distorted reflection and expansion of the biblical names of God. The ease with which man in sin further remodels the divine features into patterns of polytheism or pantheism is attested by the history of religion. Misconceptions of the nature of God are all too obvious wherever the generic name is articulated outside biblical theology: deities are multiplied, or deity is blended with nature and man. As written outside the Hebrew-Christian movement, the Name of God is misspelled. The false religions therefore only stammer God's true Name. Apart from special revelation, mankind in sin articulates the divine Name in an alphabet of false gods (Ashtaroth, Judges 10:6; Baal, Judges 2:11; Chemosh, Num. 21:29; Dagon, Judges 16:23; and so on through Zeus, Acts 14:12)—a panorama of pagan divinities that biblical theology exposes to the lash of divine wrath in prophetic-apostolic denunciation. The gods marshaled by the pagan religions do not differ from the gods adduced by the speculative philosophies in respect to their rivalry with the God of the Bible. They differ only in names and nature from the philosophical contenders (Absolute, Being, *Causa Sui*, Daemon, First Cause, Value, World-Soul, and so forth).

Yet the fact that the Bible itself associates the Name of God with general revelation warns us against escalating the predicament of the pagan world into complete ignorance of the living God. Although the divine Name is much more frequently associated with special revelation (e.g., the glory cloud, Deut. 12:11; the temple, 1 Kings 8:29; the incarnate Christ, John 17:6), Scripture emphatically enunciates God's Name in the context of cosmic creation and universal history. While the universal garbling of God's Name attests that it is not known in true communion and personal fellowship, the Bible insists that God's revelation has not been mangled. The Psalmist writes: "How excellent is thy name in all the earth" (Ps. 8:1, KJV; cf. 89:11–12).

3. Curiously, however, some *early church fathers* spoke also of the Christian God as nameless, thus reflecting Greek rather than biblical emphases. A remark by Clement of Alexandria near the beginning of the third century illustrates this unfortunate development: "The first principle of all things cannot be named. And if we give it a name, not properly calling it either One, or the Good, or Intellect, or the Very Existent, or Father, or God, or Maker, or Lord, we speak as not declaring its name, but by reason of our deficiency" (*Stromata*, v. 12). Clement's dismissal of the legitimately biblical names along with speculative philosophical projections is really due to his notion, alien to scriptural theology, that "the Divine Nature cannot be described as it really is" (ii, 16). The fifth-century pseudo-Dionysian writing on "The Names of God," attributed to Dionysius the Areopagite, reflects the teaching of Philo and Neoplatonists that divine Being is wholly without attributes.

One may also refer in this connection to the medieval scholastics, particularly to Thomas Aquinas whose insistence that we have only analogical but not univocal knowledge of God became a hallmark of Roman Catholic theology: "We cannot so name God that the name which denotes Him shall express the Divine Essence as it is, in the same way as the name *man* expresses in its signification the essence of man as it is" (*Summa Theologica*, i, XIII, 1). Barth ascribes to medieval scholastic expositions of the nature of God—in superlatives to be sure, but in neuter superlatives: *ens perfectissimum, summum bonum, actus purus, primum movens*—a shaping influence that prepared the way for the emphasis on the impersonality of God in nineteenth-century philosophy of religion and its reduction of God to a neuter. Paul Heinisch, the Catholic Old Testament scholar, today follows this same objectionable path: "Since God far transcends all human comprehension, He can, strictly speaking, have no name—He is 'Nameless,' 'Unutterable,' as the Fathers of the Church have declared" (*Theology of the Old Testament*, p. 48).

When one surveys the multiplicity of divine names in the realm of philosophy and world religions, and senses the impossibility of reconciling them, this reluctance to venture names for God may seem to have much in its favor. But the total refusal to speak of divine names signifies actually a surrender to philosophical fancy in its rejection of any fixed or final divine revelation, rather than any deference to biblical theology. Where no interest at all remains in the divine names, not only is the lesson taught by the history of secular philosophy and world religions lost, that is, the futility of attempting to name God outside of his self-revelation, but the truth of revelation and the biblically accredited names for God are also needlessly forfeited.

Nowhere does systematic theology, as a discipline of study, move nearer the heart of the Bible than when it expounds the revealed names of God. For salvation-history discloses not merely that the God of the Bible *also* possesses names, as if to say that in this respect the gods of the pagan religions have no special advantage, but that the living God is truly known only where he introduces himself by name, and that everywhere else God is either inadequately named or misnamed. Insofar as names for the one true God are legitimate, they are disclosed to mankind through God's own initiative attested in the biblical revelation. Without vital interest in the revealed names of God, therefore, no theology can claim to be authentically biblical; biblical theology and lively interest in God's names stand or fall together.

Significance of the Name in Biblical Revelation

Consider then the significance of God's self-given names in the context of Hebrew-Christian revelation.

1. The Bible not only records the authorized names of God, but it frequently speaks in the singular of *the name of God*. Here "the name"

represents "the whole manifestation of God in His relation to His people, or simply . . . becomes synonymous with God . . . in His self-revelation" (Louis Berkhof, *Systematic Theology*, p. 47). It is "a succinct expression for the revealed character of God, for all that is known of Him" (G. B. Gray, "Name," 3:478b). The divine Name thus serves as a medium of revelation of the first magnitude, and denotes the self-revealed God as he desires to be known by his creatures. "All that which can be known of God by virtue of his revelation is called by Scripture: God's *name*" (Herman Bavinck, *The Doctrine of God*, p. 83).

This identification of the divine Name with the divine nature is in strict accord with the biblical usage: "As is thy name, O God, so is thy praise" (Ps. 48:10, ASV). "The *one* name . . . is the very being of God with which the names have to do" (ibid., p. 86). The Name is thus often used for God's entire reality; it is equivalent to the totality of his attributes. C. H. Dodd remarks: "The name of a person is the symbol of his personal identity, his status, and his character; and so, for the Hebrew monotheist, the Name of God stands as a symbol for His sole deity, His glory, and His character as righteous and holy" (*The Interpretation of the Fourth Gospel*, p. 93).

We shall note later that the divine Name is also applied to various particular attributes definitive of the nature of God (e.g., his might, Ps. 54:1; 76:1; mercy, Ps. 20:1–2). "He leadeth me in the paths of righteousness for his name's sake" (Ps. 23:3, KJV). "Behold, the name of the Lord cometh from far, burning with his anger, and the burden thereof is heavy" (Isa. 30:27, KJV). His name is "holy" (1 Chron. 29:16) and "everlasting" (Ps. 135:13).

In the tradition of the Orient, a name is not merely a vocable having its own distinct sounds and letters, but expresses the inner nature of its intended object. The ancient biblical world recognized an inner relationship between reality and language, and particularly between name and character. The name not only serves the purpose of identification, as do personal names in the Western world, but also serves a descriptive and definitive function in the disclosure of inner nature. The recognition of a connection between name and character, which the writer of Genesis traces back to man's earliest history, had become so much a cultural phenomenon of the ancient Near East that both divine and human names were regarded as an extension of the personality of their bearers. The name audibly introduces or presents a person whose character would otherwise be unsure or unknown.

Since the name penetrates to the inner secret of one's nature and discloses what is hidden from mere external knowledge, some ancients avoided use of their real or proper names in public. The Israelites, however, shunned the use of secret names. In pagan religions, the summoning of gods or demons by magical incantation of their names led to the further belief among some groups that even among human beings one can gain power over another individual by a subtle use of his or her name. This superstition survives among certain primitive tribes which are still for this reason reluctant to disclose the names of their members to strangers.

Modern exponents of a naturalistic evolutionary theory of religion suggested that this "close relation . . . supposed to exist between the name and the personality" in the pagan rites was simply borrowed and modified in the Hebrew use of " 'name' as almost an equivalent of the 'personality' or 'character' or nature of the person or thing named" (Gray, "Name," p. 478a). But the use of names to express the character of persons and objects has its origin in the earliest history, and the theology of revelation views the pagan rites as a corruption and loss of the true Name.

The Old Testament frequently notes the close connection between the bearer of a name and the nature it attests in the case of ancient biblical characters. Scripture finds an ontological intention in the ascription of their particular names to Eve (Gen. 3:20), Cain (Gen. 4:1), Seth (Gen. 4:25), Noah (Gen. 5:29), Ishmael (Gen. 16:11), Esau and Jacob (Gen. 25:25–26), Moses (Exod. 2:10), and others. In the Genesis creation account Adam is represented as naming the animals according to their nature (Gen. 2:19–20). This passage is striking for its suggestion of an inherent relation between logic and life and language. Not only does it imply a connection between reason and reality, but it also supplies hints of a theistic view of language. A name in the Old Testament is not "a mere label, nor just an external description" but rather, as H. Michaud comments, "expresses the profound reality of the being who carries it. That is why creation is not completed until the moment when everything brought into existence has a name." Michaud calls attention to Isaiah 40:26, "see: who created these (stars)? . . . He who calls them all by name" and notes that whereas the Name of God "is the name *par excellence* (Zech. 14:9) on which the reality of all other names depends (Isa. 56:5) . . . 'Adam' is a 'human' being, for having been made from the humus his reality is earthy" ("Name," pp. 278 f.).

This is not to deny that proper names are frequently based on paronomasia, or a play upon words, and not on ontological intention. This would explain why *Babel* (Gen. 11:9) does not really mean "confound" and why *Jacob* is explained in two ways (cf. Gen. 25:26, 27:36). Andrew F. Key notes that where the explanation of names occurs in the Old Testament, such explanation is commonly based on the meaning of the name, although names sometimes bear a symbolic meaning associating the person with what is yet to happen, especially in the prophetic books (e.g., Hos. 1:9). Key thinks "the practice of giving and explaining the name grew up fairly early in Israel's history, lasted a brief while, and fell into disuse (perhaps in the period of the exile)" ("The Giving of Proper Names in the Old Testament," pp. 55–59).

The living God is nameable according to his true nature only because of his divine initiative, his self-revelation, whereby man is taught to name

God accurately as God names himself to man. As Karl Barth has remarked, "It is the revelation of the name by which He wills to be known and addressed by us . . . the name and the criterion and the truth . . . of His innermost hidden essence" (*Church Dogmatics*, II/1, p. 273). For biblical theology, therefore, any surrender of interest in the Name of God implies a cessation of interest in the living God. The Name of God, in brief, is the revelation of his true self. Study of the divine Name is therefore indispensable to theological inquiry into the nature of the true and living God.

This identity of God's Name with his self-revelation led early Christian theologians to expound the doctrine of God in its entirety under the comprehensive major theme of the Name of God. The divine attributes which constitute his essence, the divine personal names embraced in God's triunity—indeed, all the divine appellations—were discussed under this topic. Following the lead of older Hebrew scholars (who listed as many as seventy divine names) the attributes of God were expounded as an aspect of the revealed names.

In modern times, this coordinated treatment of divine appellatives and attributes has been less frequently followed. The Dutch theologian Herman Bavinck, however, divided his noteworthy exposition of the divine names into three sections: God's proper names, God's essential names (attributes), and God's personal names (Father, Son and Holy Spirit), but his English translator modified this plan.

2. The one divine Name is made known in a series of divine self-manifestations, and the variety of names through which God identifies himself give an enlarging revelation of God's nature. Our use of more than one name in addressing God gains its propriety from God's self-introduction alone. In Barth's words, "When we do call God by a name, we must keep to the name which He gives Himself" (ibid., II/1, p. 59). Through the diversity of divinely authorized names, we come to know God's full Name. Finite man cannot, by a single act of comprehension, grasp the divine nature in its simplicity. Sinful man adequately knows God's true nature only through remedial redemptive revelation in which God has taught us his first, and middle, and last names. So Bavinck comments: "The *one* name of God, as inclusive of his entire revelation both in nature and grace, is for us resolved into many, very many names. Only in that way do we obtain a view of the riches of his revelation and of the deep significance of his name" (*The Doctrine of God*, p. 85). Berkhof remarks: "For us the one general name of God is split up into many names, expressive of the many-sided Being of God" (*Systematic Theology*, p. 47). That we know the divine Name only in a plurality of names, therefore, reflects our finiteness and sinfulness, while the remarkable fact that we know God's true names attests that divine revelation and redemptive love have progressively overcome our broken knowledge of man's Maker.

The names of God are obviously part of an earthly vocabulary, "borrowed" from human language. Otherwise they could not be uttered intelligibly to and by man at all. Would it at all have served the purpose of intelligible revelation had God named himself a colossal cosmic X, to stimulate modern scientific curiosity, or simply applied to himself only initials as the content of his Name? The names are intelligible names, to be uttered in the language man knows and speaks, and not in some unknown tongue fit only for an unknown god. If it is improper to speak of God anthropomorphically, that is, to apply such names to him, then, as Bavinck replies, "the only logical alternative is not to speak about God at all" (*The Doctrine of God*, p. 90).

And yet, despite this anthropomorphism, the names are in no sense to be considered human inventions gratuitously applied to God. Precisely this use of divinely sanctioned anthropomorphic names, rather than of artificial linguistic constructs (which differ from abstract mathematical symbols mainly through an imaginative content contributed by creative philosophers), is an aspect of the Bible's revelational uniqueness in contrast to speculative religious philosophies. Barth rightly stresses the danger of overemphasizing the "impropriety" of anthropomorphism. This prejudice, he notes, can provide "a basis and occasion for the pitiful transition from theology to philosophy, or from the theology of revelation to natural theology. . . . But, if it lets itself be guided by its object, theology ought to try to evade these anthropomorphisms least of all" (*Church Dogmatics*, II/1, p. 222).

The biblical names, in fact, offer themselves as intentional alternatives to names which are humanly applied to deity. Bavinck rightly asserts that we derive the right to apply these names only because "God Himself . . . has put in our mouth His glorious names" (*The Doctrine of God*, p. 95). "Only because God has revealed Himself in His name," because divine self-revelation actually emboldens us, "we can now designate Him by that name in various forms" (Berkhof, *Systematic Theology*, p. 47). The biblical names for God are sustained not by human hearsay but by divine demand. "Left to ourselves we would be altogether silent" with respect to the legitimate divine names, Bavinck asserts. "We would deny every one of his names. . . . We continually protest against all his names or attributes: against his independence, his sovereignty, his justice, and his love. . . . But it is *God himself* who reveals all his excellencies and puts his names upon our lips. It is *he* who gives himself these names, and it is *he* who defends them against every attack" (*The Doctrine of God*, p. 130).

The speaking God thus makes human language his divine language. But he does not do so as one for whom human language is a wholly foreign tongue requiring superhuman adaptation for its effective use. God's creation of man for interpersonal communion anticipated his condescension and initiative in the use of human language as an instrument of divine disclosure. He is God in whose nature the Word eternally inheres, and the Word, active in the creation of the universe and of man in the divine image, became incarnate and inscripturate in human flesh and language. Properly guarded, there is truth in Jacobi's statement that man may rightly anthropomorphize God because God theomorphized when creating man. The universe is not a sphere essentially opposed to God, but owes its creaturely form, preservation and final destiny to God, who fashioned it to manifest its Creator.

3. The various divine names do not imply that the divine essence is hidden from man. God's names are not so numerous that just any name will do. Although he is infinite he is not known by an infinity, but rather by a severalty of names. And this range of names does not disguise his essential being, but rather defines it. Because they are no longer one the names are not, on that account, no longer intimately revelatory. The God of Israel is one God, whose true identity was neither lost nor obscured in any superabundance of names.

The Babylonians had fifty names for Marduk, and the Egyptian Re has been called "the god with many names" (von Rad), the plurality being due to the combination of old traditions. Albright reminds us that "the Babylonians listed thousands of divine names and appellations. Hundreds of them are mentioned in the earliest lists from before 2500 B.C." (*History, Archaeology and Christian Humanism*, p. 99). This multiplicity itself begot uncertainty, so there exists a Babylonian penitential prayer "to the god whom it may concern," which presupposes ignorance of the name. The public confusion resulting from this multiplication of names disposed a religious inner circle to keep the supposedly "real name" a secret.

But for Israel, as von Rad notes, the divine Name "never became a 'mystery,' to which only the initiated could have access. On the contrary, each and every Israelite was at liberty to avail himself of it, and once she had become fully aware of the distinctiveness of her worship, Israel did not hide this name of God from the Gentiles in fear, but rather felt herself in duty bound to make it known to them (Isa. 4; Ps. 1–3). Indeed in the end YAHWEH is to be revealed to the world in such a way that all worship of idols will vanish, and every knee bow to His name alone (Zech. 9; Isa. 24). . . . It is of great significance that Israel never had any idea of piling as many names as possible upon YAHWEH. YAHWEH was, in fact, one" (*Old Testament Theology*, 1:185).

Israel's use of differing names, when these were not employed simply as synonyms, did not introduce into the understanding of deity a conflict of function or a plurality of beings, but more precisely expounded the self-revealed nature of the one God.

Bavinck and Berkhof appear rather too hesitant on this score. For Bavinck asserts that "the name of God . . . does not designate him as he exists in himself, but in this manifold revelation and relation to the creature" (*The Doctrine of God*, p. 85), and that "of all his names not a single one describes him as he is in himself, i.e., in his inner essence" (p. 94). In his revelation, God is "polyonymous, i.e., possessing many names," whereas, Bavinck adds, in himself God is "anonymous, i.e., without name." But God would be thus nameless only had he not introduced himself at all. Since God has stipulated the biblical names, they afford knowledge which, although incomplete, is nonetheless true and adequate. Berkhof too held that the divine Name "is a designation of Him, not as He exists in the depths of His divine Being, but as He reveals Himself especially in His relations to man" (*Systematic Theology*, p. 47).

But God's revelation of himself to man, even though not exhaustive, is a revelation of his essential nature. The names are in fact used as synonyms for divine perfections, such as faithfulness (Isa. 48:9), grace (Ps. 23:3), and honor (Ps. 79:9).

The revelation we have does not cancel every last vestige of divine mystery. But for all that, God's self-revelation is not tangential to his inmost essence. However far short our knowledge falls of infinite comprehension, God's self-revelation of his names affords us genuine knowledge of his true nature. Even Berkhof is driven to affirm that the names "contain in a measure a revelation of the Divine Being" (ibid., p. 47), and Bavinck declares that "the name is not arbitrary, but God reveals Himself as He *is*. Hence God's name stands for his . . . divine essence" (*The Doctrine of God*, p. 85). But once this is granted, the notion that we have knowledge only of God in relation to us, and not as he is in himself, ought to be disowned.

The names for God in the Bible are not employed because of a prophetic transferrence to God of personified symbols of God's activity in the universe or even in his special relation to them, and which symbols are then stripped of improper finite or anthropomorphic connotations. God himself has declared their propriety and adequacy. Had God not made himself known, had he not actively introduced himself by name, then Hebrew theology would need to confess that, like those polytheistic religions it deplored for their misnaming of the living God, it too had propounded names for the Divine as a merely human effort and given God an alias. But biblical religion is born and nourished in the conviction that the living God allows himself to be named only in his own way, and does not now rename himself by the misnomers of speculative philosophy and alienated religions.

The objections voiced by dialectical or neoorthodox theologians against understanding the divine names as inclusive of conceptual knowledge of God rest upon highly prejudicial and vulnerable philosophical presuppositions involving the contrast of revelation and reason. They have given new theological importance to the divine names by their emphasis that God is self-revealed as personal. But they balk at the cognitive implications of the names of God because, contrary to biblical theology, their underlying philosophy disallows intelligible revelation in the form of concepts and words. Despite his rightful insistence that our knowledge of God is wholly dependent on God's making himself known in his self-introduction by name, Barth hesitates to claim universal validity for the knowledge God conveys in his self-disclosure. Barth even summarizes and approves the teaching of some of the Early Fathers: "The words Father, Creator, Lord, Sovereign—even the word God itself—are not in themselves and as such identical with the ineffable name by which God calls Himself and which therefore expresses His truth; and therefore they cannot in themselves express His truth" (*Church Dogmatics*, II/1, p. 195). For Barth, the ineffability of God's Name remains except when and as God sporadically reintroduces himself, and the "meaning" of his Name is given only to individuals by an internal act of grace and lacks universal intelligibility. Barth's religious theory makes knowledge of God dependent on repeated personal decision, and this erodes objective and universally valid knowledge of the one true God even on the basis of divine self-revelation.

Dialectical theology has exploited emphasis on the names of God as an alternative to divine revelation of truths; the revelation of God's Name is unjustifiably made to reinforce an anti-intellective view of revelation. Miskotte, for example, asserts that "the revelation is concentrated in a proper name" and this "bars the way to the theoretical kind of 'monotheism'" (*When the Gods Are Silent*, p. 122). Miskotte scorns the interpretation of revelation as "the communication of supernatural knowledge, of knowledge about the supernatural" as "shallow" and "distortive," although he remarks that this view is "apparently ineradicably ingrained in Western man" (p. 106). The Old Testament, he goes on to say, "can free us from such a shallow, westernized concept of 'revelation' because it shows us that no human word as such is revelation, whether it be profane or sacred, New Testament or Old Testament, the language of the priests or of the great writing prophets. Neither a report about God or what God says can express, represent, much less take the place of the NAME" (p. 107).

We need only comment briefly on the futility of such efforts to retain any intelligible significance for revelation once it is thus defined as nontheoretical and detached from a communication of knowledge. Unless what revelation communicates is cognitively distinct and noncontradictory, one could not know what Miskotte means even by the self-disclosed Name of God; this logical requirement is not simply a Western prejudice, but a universal presupposition of intelligibility. The central importance of the Name to the theology of revelation must not do service for an attack on the rationality of divine revelation nor discredit its verbal formulation, even if such dialectical Western notions have become influential in recent decades. The Name and the intelligibility of revelation stand or fall together; they are not antithetical emphases. The reality of Yahweh as the living God does not in any sense depend upon an anti-intellective religious theory that blurs the Name in superrational mysticism.

Barth's dialectical theology unfortunately encouraged the contrast between the personal and the propositional, and his later efforts to reinforce the cognitive aspects were too long delayed and too guarded to repeal his noncognitive emphasis. "The decisive act of the revelation by which Israel is chosen as Israel, becomes the people of this God, is just the revelation of the name of God. That this revelation of the name (Exod. 3:13 f.) is in fact, in content, a refusal of any name . . . is significant enough; for the revealed name itself by its wording is to recall also and precisely the hiddenness of the revealed God. But still under this name, which itself and as such expresses His mystery, God *does* reveal Himself to His people" (*Church Dogmatics*, I/1, p. 365). This passage so shuttles between mysticism and meaning that it erodes the intelligibility of God's Name, and suspends the rational significance of the Name in mid-air.

The biblical exposition of God's Name does not really shelter the modern antithesis of personality and rationality; in fact, it disowns the current disjunction of revelation from reason and language. In both Old and New Testaments the self-revealing God is the rational God and the speaking God—self-disclosing, self-defining, self-communicating. The writer of Genesis distinguishes him from false gods not only by his eternity, sovereignty, and creativity, but also because he is the self-revealed personal, rational, holy one. The orderly universe exists through his eternal Word; creation is capped by man, the image-bearer of the Divine. The creative Word, John's Prologue pointedly instructs us, is Logos and Light, who in Jesus Christ takes human nature upon himself, unveiling the Divine in human thought and word and life. God names himself in our flesh and thought and language, and reclaims human conceptions and words for the true knowledge and service of himself. Divine incarnation involved no undeifying of the Logos; and divine inscripturation involved no illegibility of his revelation. God need not stutter when he pronounces his own Name nor when uttering any sentence he wills to speak in our language.

The biblical names of God carry divinely authorized information about God's nature and ways, that is, authentic knowledge of transcendent Being.

The History of God's Names

The revealed names of God connect the knowledge of God in a special way with his creation of the universe and with his redemptive deeds in the history of Israel and the founding of the Christian church.

This correlation of God's names with historical developments is susceptible, however, to highly objectionable misunderstanding and misinterpretation. The Bible has no room for the naturalistic account of religion, which contends that God has an earth-bound imaginative "history." It is not the God of the Bible, but the god-theorizing of naturalistic speculation that rises out of space-time factors and owes its origin to human ingenuity.

Nor does the series of divine names imply a multiplicity of gods. The fatal error of polytheism was its departure from God's self-revelation, and its ready postulation of a separate spiritual power behind every sacred name, so that the Divine is both misconceived and misnamed. In the consequent subdivision of the supernatural, divine attributes are isolated and then deified into separate man-made divinities, each responsible for some special province of earthly affairs. With this invention of a plethora of gods the significance of the Name evaporates into a new nomenclature wholly lacking divine sanction. The very first commandment condemns any such setting of false heathen gods alongside the one true God; in effect, such accommodation displaces the self-revealing Lord.

Nor does the severalty of God's names mean that the deity is essentially conditioned by history. There is in biblical theology no tolerance of premises like Hegel's presumptive pantheism according to which universal history directly discloses the interior life of the Absolute, and which regards all biblical representations of God as imaginatively pictorial and not metaphysically definitive. Nor is there any basis for a literary-critical rearrangement of the various divine names in the service of evolutionary theory. This influential but highly imaginative hypothesis takes the various God-names as mirrors of independent or conflicting written traditions, and on its own mythological assumption of a unilinear development of all history derives the most exalted spiritual and moral ideals in the ancient world from the creative ingenuity of literary redactors who falsified the past. Aubrey R. Johnson rightly warns of "a real danger in Old Testament study as a whole of misinterpreting what may be different but contemporary *strata* in terms of corresponding *stages* of thought, which can be arranged chronologically so as to fit into an oversimplified evolutionary scheme or similar theory of progressive revelation" (Aubrey R. Johnson, *The Vitality of the Individual in the Thought of Ancient Israel*, preface).

The truly remarkable factors in the disclosure of God's names are these: that the living God transcendently and absolutely discloses his name in historical revelation, and that the successively revealed names of God signal distinctive epochs in the progressive manifestation of God's redemptive purpose. The fact that the Hebrew people come to know God now by one and then another revealed name bears its own testimony to the enlarging redemption significance of these names. Viewed from the side of human comprehension, no single name wholly expresses God's Being; the many names unveil his perfections, purposes and personal distinctions. Moreover, the progressive character of special revelation imparts to the divine names, as Cornelius Van Til has put it, "a history" through their ever-fuller unveiling of the divine nature and purpose. The divine Name, in Geerhardus Vos's words, serves "to sum up the significance of a period" (*Biblical Theology. Old and New Testaments*, p. 76).

Yet we shall see that the Hebrew-Christian revelation not only periodically unveils new names for the living God, but that in successive periods of redemptive history earlier names of God are retained side by side with later names. Later divine disclosure does not annul the force and significance of the earlier names, for God does not deny himself in the progressive revelation of his names. He can be properly addressed by the earlier or later names. As God manifests his nature and purpose in a profounder disclosure of his Name, the new name may reflect not only this latest revelational climax but the cumulative force of his earlier names as well. Yet, an earlier name may be employed either in its limited original sense, or in a later epoch its connotation may be expanded to embrace also the newer knowledge of God. These varying possibilities remind us that, while their revelational content excludes any reference to "bare names" of God apart from close attention to meaning in context, one can be easily misled, as were the practitioners of the documentary hypothesis, into superficial misconceptions.

ELOHIM, a generic term common to the Semitic religions, serves also in Israel's history and experience as a *nomina propria*. Nothing seems farther from the intention of the Old Testament writers than the notion of documentary critics that the names ELOHIM and JEHOVAH are not interchangeable, as if they did not designate one and the same deity. While not annulling the progressive disclosure-significance of successive divine names, this possibility of alternating usage is fatal for any theory that constructs literary strata merely on the basis of the names for God or that simply equates such literary strands with differing notions of God. The monotheistic emphasis overshadows the whole of Israel's transcendent spiritual relationships; the several names of the God of the Bible appear everywhere as names of the one God. The uncompromising biblical protest against polytheism disallows any other viewpoint. We need not deny that disobedience and relapse into idolatry now and then blurred the significance of the names in various periods of Hebrew history. The prophets of Israel had to recall the chosen people from worship of false gods and the high places to the living God whose name was known alike to the fathers and to the prophets. Yet nothing would offend the Hebrew spirit and undermine its confidence in special divine revelation more than any insistence that the progressive disclosure of the divine names provides the slightest basis for polytheism. Precisely the conviction of God's special and absolute revelation of his Name quickened the Hebrew hostility to polytheism. The names of God yield, one to the other, not in the interest of competing multiple gods, but in the interest of fuller disclosure of the one God who in a unique way reveals himself to his covenant-people.

In the Old Testament, it is uniformly ELOHIM who is self-revealed in the creation of the universe and of man. Yet in Israel's history, ELOHIM gives to the Hebrews the right to name him more comprehensively through fuller disclosures of the divine Name. In the ongoing movement of redemptive history, the names known to God's people are nonetheless sometimes used interchangeably, or combined, as in the case of JEHOVAH-

ELOHIM, or JEHOVAH-ADONAI. On the ground that the ideas associated with each name wholly differ, Gregory of Nyssa argued that it is erroneous to use the names of God interchangeably. But the divine names differ not by way of mutual exclusion, but by way of supplementation. For the several names of God are the way in which the full Name of God is made known to us. Moreover, the feature of parallelism in Hebrew poetry requires corresponding terms or synonyms in the use of names of the God of Israel to convey its message. Circumstances of biblical history sometimes also call to mind the work of God in creation or providence (cf. Ruth 1:20) and, because of the relevance of this to the immediate occasion of faith, the earlier names are retained to emphasize certain divine characteristics which the later disclosure in no wise cancels. Certain names, moreover, are peculiar to certain books, as EL SHADDAI to Job, and ELOHIM to the Wisdom literature.

Yet the names of God are not on this account indiscriminately employed. Their use in the record not only sets the living God over against the man-named gods of the pagan world, but the self-revealed names of God dramatically accord with the turning chapters of divine redemptive revelation. The names of God supply an index to the epochs of revelation in the biblical literature. The disclosure of God as EL SHADDAI constitutes the distinctive patriarchal revelation of God, although this is not yet the high point of Old Testament disclosure. The name EL SHADDAI forms in fact a connecting link, as Vos observes, "between 'El' and 'Elohim,' on the one hand, and 'Jehovah,' the Mosaic name, on the other hand. If the former signify God's relation to nature, and Jehovah is His redemptive name, then El Shaddai may be said to express how God uses nature for super-nature" (*Biblical Theology*, p. 52).

14.
God's Proper Names:
Elohim, El Shaddai

IN THE SCRIPTURES, the Name of God in its comprehensive sense, as already indicated, is identical with the totality of divine self-revelation. The full Name of the one God is self-disclosed in a panorama of names— the proper names, the perfectional names (or attributes), and the personal names.

God's proper names are those appellations by which he is addressed as a specific independent Being.

Generic Terms and Proper Names

In the Old Testament EL, ELOAH (Greek, THEOS) appear as generic terms for GOD, that is, indefinite designations for deity in general, both in pagan and Hebrew use. EL was the general Semitic name for deity.

Although the generic term *God* has become part of the linguistic heritage of mankind, references to deity-in-general do not predominate in the early history of religion; least of all does one find the technically abstract "God-concept." The generic terms for deity or the gods were mostly employed of specific supernatural entities. EL was used not only generically but also, where Semitic religion affirms a pantheon of gods, of the supreme deity. The Old Testament uses EL not only to refer to "deity" in the general Semitic sense, but to describe the God believed in by Abraham and his descendants in a true and vital sense. The people of God had every reason on the basis of the theology of revelation to use the term EL in a specific rather than a merely general sense. EL is not for them the highest god in a pantheon of divinities, but the one and only God whom they worship on the ground of his revelation. The living God is not "a god"—not one of a larger class, not *"a spirit"* as the King James Version wrongly translates John 4:24; he is, as Barth emphasizes, *sui generis*. The

184

Hebrews when they speak for themselves employ the term *God*, ELOHIM, not as a class word, but as a divine name. Moreover they distinguish the Name from the pagan gods by using what we have called the generic terms in a peculiar way and a highly specific sense.

Elohim Comprehends All Deity in Himself

The noun ELOHIM, although a Hebrew plural form of ELOAH, is characteristically used—except when polytheistic heathen divinities are in view (Ps. 96:5; 97:7)—with a singular verb or adjective,[1] in strict conformity with the uncompromised monotheism of Hebrew revealed religion.

In the Bible, ELOHIM is uniquely the one God who concentrates in himself the being and powers of all the gods, comprehending the totality of deity in himself. This explains the assignment to the God of the Old Testament of the epithets used of pagan gods. The God of the Bible insists on taking to himself the abilities ascribed to the many Canaanite and other false divinities. As Charles F. Pfeiffer notes, if Baal is "rider of the clouds" in Ugarit, YAHWEH rides the clouds in Psalm 68; if Baal is a fertility god, the Israelites must know that YAHWEH causes fertility; if Shemesh brings light to the world in Canaanite thought, the Hebrews insist that YAHWEH enlightens the world (*Old Testament History*, p. 346).

A superficially similar phenomenon occurs in the fourteenth-century (B.C.) Amarna letters with a different result. The letters use *ilani*, which as the plural of EL appears frequently in Akkadian for "the gods," with a singular verb in order to designate "the deity," thereby concentrating emphasis on one particular god. But in the Hebrew Old Testament the widespread use of the normally plural form ELOHIM as if it were a singular noun, with a regularity unknown elsewhere in the Semitic languages, reflects neither a tendency to generalize in the divine realm, nor simply an emphasis on a particular deity among many gods, but rather a confident belief in the supreme significance of the God of Israel as the totality of deity. While EL is indeed a generic term, the Bible uses it to emphasize that ELOHIM, and ELOHIM alone, exhausts everything comprehended in the category of divine reality.

Progressive Disclosure of the Inner Secret of God's Being

By this introduction to ELOHIM, Creator and Supporter of nature, we are brought into the arena of biblical revelation, with its progressive dis-

---

1. A qualifying comment is required by a few odd passages. In Josh. 24:19, the usual modifying adjective in the plural is followed by a modifying pronoun in the singular. The plurals in Deut. 5:26, 2 Sam. 7:23 and Ps. 58:11 are perhaps best understood as seen through pagan eyes. Cf. also Judg. 11:24, 1 Kings 11:5, and 2 Kings 1:2 for designation of a single heathen god by the plural ELOHIM. In Israel the term ELOHIM includes a plurality of majesty, the God who is truly and fully God. This emphasis leads consistently to the declaration that the heathen gods are no gods (Jer. 2:11; cf. Isa. 6:3; 41:4; 42:8; 43:10–13; 45:3, 6; 48:11).

closure of EL, not amid the panoply of pagan deities but in the context of a protest against those pretenders: the one God is self-revealed as EL ELYON, the Highest; ELOAH, the Mighty One; and EL SHADDAI, the Omnipotent One. Then follows his fuller self-manifestation as YAHWEH/JEHOVAH,[2] the great proper Name of the God of Israel mentioned 6,823 times in the Old Testament.

With the dawning of New Testament realities, even these proper names for God yield to his self-revealed personal names. In sending his beloved Son, YAHWEH discloses his holy intimacy as Father. The Threefold Name then declares the inmost secret of the self-revealed God, whose followers confess "the name of the Father, and of the Son, and of the Holy Spirit."

Thus the history of humanity discloses a dual movement with respect to the Name of God. Outside the line of special revelation, man in religious revolt turns the proper name of God into more and more improper names, and then seeks to turn the proper name into merely a generic term which man is himself free to fill with whatever content he wishes, or wholly to disown as a merely imaginative God-concept. In his created relationship with the living God, Adam could properly name the self-revealed God and could name the animals in accord with their nature. Contemporary man so concentrates on turning nature to his own devices that he can neither give God's real name nor identify the objective constitution of the external world. It is not at all surprising that "secular theology" and "linguistic analysis" should most of all find difficulty with the biblical emphasis on the Name of God. Paul van Buren, who reduces the biblical interest in the supernatural to a debate over words, notes the avoidance of the name YAHWEH in Jewish speech, and thinks "it might be argued that the Christian Church never adequately appreciated this reticence" (*The Secular Meaning of the Gospel*, p. 4, n. 5).

Meanwhile the God whom the speculative philosophers profess only to

---

2. Although we cannot be absolutely sure, it is quite certain that the divine Name YHWH was originally pronounced YAHWEH. Hence in this presentation YAHWEH is used (except in a few dual references to remind the uninitiated, or in quoted material). Nowhere does Hebrew usage supply a basis for the form *Jehovah*, which is late medieval in origin and an Anglicized form (combining the four consonants JHVH —represented by the sound of J for Y and V for W as in Latin—with vowels from a wholly different word). This is one reason the Revised Standard Version abandoned the term *Jehovah*. The Hebrews came to view YHWH as too sacred to be pronounced, so they added vowel signs designating the Hebrew word ADONAI/LORD (or ELOHIM/GOD) as a substitute. The ancient Greek translators substituted KURIOS/LORD; the Latin Vulgate, DOMINUS. The Revised Standard Version substitutes LORD, following this long-established precedent.

The Hebrew avoidance of YAHWEH was not true to the spirit of Old Testament religion, which does not shy away from the use of the divine names. The development apparently resulted from an exaggeration of divine transcendence that tends to separate God from the life of man (cf. the intertestamental introduction of intermediate beings, the Pharisee's refusal to submit the inner life to God, and the later substitution for ADONAI—itself a substitute for YAHWEH—of "hash-Shem" (The Name). Walther Eichrodt supplies good documentation in *Theology of the Old Testament*, 1:218–220.

know as a generic term, assigning him polite or impolite names of their own and defaming his name through fabulous imagination, nonetheless penetrates the rebellious minds of men through his ongoing self-revelation in nature, history and conscience. And in special redemptive revelation he openly publishes his *proper* names, his *perfectional* names, and his *personal* names.

EL (*Strong and Mighty One*); ELOAH (*Mighty One*); ELOHIM (*Almighty One*); ELYON (*Exalted One*).

ELOHIM, the first form of the divine Name in the Bible, appears in the opening verse of Genesis. Along with a group of kindred names, among them EL and ELOAH, it is common to Semitic languages and religions. It is of prehistoric derivation, although its etymological origin remains in doubt. All three forms, EL, ELOAH, and ELOHIM, are used of the pagan gods, as well as of the self-revealed God.

The name ELOHIM occurs more than 200 times in Genesis alone and 2,570 times in all the Old Testament. Its New Testament equivalent is THEOS. The term is used not alone of the living God and of idols (Pss. 95:3; 96:5), but in certain usages is applied also to men (Gen. 33:10; Exod. 7:1) and to rulers as representatives of deity (Exod. 21:6; 22:8–9; Judg. 5:8; Ps. 82:1). Liberal scholars reject this association of ELOHIM with human beings or judges acting as God's agents, and contend rather that such passages presuppose the real existence of the heathen gods among whom the God of the Hebrews reigns supreme. But this compromises the unyielding monotheism of the Old Testament, attributes to the pagan gods a role of judgment that the Old Testament does not grant them, and ignores other passages (e.g., Ezek. 23:24) that refer to men as YAHWEH's agents in judgment (cf. Leon Morris, *The Biblical Doctrine of Judgment,* pp. 33–36).

Since the earliest details lie outside the scope of historical records, any account of the interconnection of biblical and non-biblical usage involves some element of uncertainty. In view of the fact that EL is the common noun for a variety of gods, and appears also in the Old Testament as the proper name of a particular deity named EL, evolutionary reconstructionists derived the biblical ELOHIM from the pagan EL. But the Hebrew use of the EL-forms does not of itself prove Hebrew dependence on pagan religion; there is a reverse possibility of a pagan corruption of a primitive revelation of ELOHIM. The biblical emphasis on a general divine revelation written on men's hearts, and surviving even the distortion of sin, may itself furnish an important clue to the widespread use of the generic name EL, despite its expansion into many divinities. In the Ugaritic pantheon, EL appears as both head and father of the seventy Elim ("gods"), including Baal.

The attempt of evolutionary philosophers to derive Hebrew religion from religion in general is challenged by the fact that in their biblical character ELOHIM, ELOAH, and EL uniformly indict the pagan divinities.

In biblical religion EL (ELOHIM) not only holds distinctive associations (as does every particular use of EL), but as a proper name it designates not one special divinity in a polytheistic milieu, but rather the one living God who precludes polytheism. Nowhere does one discover confraternity with the localized nature gods in Israel's Canaanite environment. ELOHIM everywhere judges and challenges them not merely as their divine Superior but as their divine Alternative. The scriptural abhorrence of polytheism is evident in its reservation of the most severe condemnation for man's worship of the false gods.

The Bible nowhere encourages or condones the view that Hebrew monotheism emerged by unilinear evolution from various strands of primitive pagan polytheism. Instead, the Old Testament asserts man's original relationship to the one God. It indicates that, outside the line of special divine revelation, this original relationship gradually deteriorated to polytheism and was swiftly degraded. Before Old Testament history was speculatively conformed to modern theories of unilinear evolution, the biblical view was everywhere understood in terms of a primitive monotheistic revelation, which underwent later corruption in the pagan religions. Archaeological attestation of the presence of pagan "high gods" in the early stages of religious worship has now rebutted the claim of evolutionary religionists that these "high gods" were later emergents from primitive animism.

"In the beginning ELOHIM. . . ." "In the beginning . . . the LOGOS."[3] So Old and New Testament alike name Ultimate Reality in the spirit of uncompromising monotheism. Nowhere else in the history of Western thought has scholarship succeeded, as it has in the religious realm, in establishing the idea that historic written sources presuppose the very opposite of what they state—so that in the beginning there was really something else. Any secular scholar who similarly sought to invert and subvert the underlying and controlling principle in the writings of classical philosophers would soon be disowned by academic colleagues. But one of the now deeply embedded delusions of modern religious thought is the critical notion that the Old Testament narrative of human beginnings presupposes actually a prehistory of an absent divinity.

James Barr ("God," p. 334a) stresses that the living God appears at the very outset of human history, and does not first emerge at some late stage in the process: "There is no sign in the Old Testament of any consciousness of a pre-theistic stage, of a time when gods were not yet known, and the texts depict their God as having relations with man from the beginning of history. The question which they do discuss to some extent is not whether He was really a God but by what name He was known." The notion that the ELOHIM of Genesis presupposes pagan myths borrowed by Hebrew writers, who then gradually erased their polytheistic features—whether through developing religious insight or through some ingenious postulation of the supernatural—reflects a bias void of

---

3. Capitals are supplied for emphasis in Scripture quotations.

objective confirmation. Beyond the Bible, ELOHIM is nowhere found in its distinctive monotheistic intention. The EL-forms are everywhere coupled with the names of alien gods reflective of a polytheistic religious environment. The repeated prophetic denunciation of lapses by the Hebrews into the cult of Baalism and of Ashtaroth show that in times of apostasy the Hebrews did not attempt to adapt these idolatrous practices to their own tradition of monotheism, as the developmental hypothesis would encourage one to expect, but sought rather to displace it by them. G. Ernest Wright noted at midcentury the mounting difficulties challenging the now popular notion that religious evolution supplies the key to the Old Testament view of God: "It is increasingly realized today that the attempt to make of the Old Testament a source book for the evolution of religion from very primitive to highly advanced concepts has been made possible only by means of a radical misinterpretation of the literature" (The Old Testament against Its Environment, p. 12).

"The religion of Israel—only one God." So W. F. Albright sums up its uniqueness in the ancient religious world. "This is the view of the entire Old Testament—only one God who reigns over all that exists. In the ancient Orient there were many gods. . . . The gods shade into one another and change form constantly. There is utter confusion, a confusion affecting gods by the scores and hundreds. The Canaanites assumed they had seventy gods, seventy sons of the great god EL and his consort Asherah. . . . But in the Old Testament there is no conflict between the functions of God. He is one God who is over all, one God of morality and human relations, one God of all nations, one God over all nature. There is one God who is in supreme control of destiny, one God who creates man with free will" (History, Archaeology and Christian Humanism, p. 99).

Albright remarks that he is "fully aware of all the conventional arguments against early Israelite monotheism, but I consider virtually all of them as invalid and some of them as quite absurd. . . . No one could have predicted that the First Commandment would be explained in the nineteenth century as henotheistic. . . . As a matter of fact, there is nothing in the earlier sources which sounds any more polytheistic than the words attributed to Solomon by the Chronicler about 400 B.C.—'for great is our God above all gods' (2 Chron. 2:5). Nor is any allusion to the 'sons of God,' to the angels, or to the possible existence of other deities in some form or other (invariably very vague) any more henotheistic than the views of Philo, of Justin Martyr or of the Talmud with regard to pagan deities. . . . If monotheism connotes the existence of one God only, the Creator of everything, the source of justice and energy who can travel at will to any part of His universe, who is without sexual relations and consequently without mythology, who is human in form but cannot be seen by human eye or represented in any form—then the official religion of early Israel was certainly monotheistic" (ibid., pp. 155 f.). We must oppose this verdict to von Rad's contention that "the first commandment has initially nothing to do with monotheism" but rather "is only comprehensible in the light of" a polytheistic background, which von Rad characterizes as "not monotheistic" but rather "henotheism or monolatry" (*Old Testament Theology*, pp. 210 f.). Although von Rad insists that Israel's history must be understood in terms of "the rise of monotheism," he concedes what is really the most vulnerable point in the evolutionary theory of religious origins, that "the last thing we can hope to do is to indicate a particular point in history at which monotheism took its rise" (p. 211).

The premise of original monotheism has been championed anew in our century by scholars of divergent outlooks, among them Andrew Lang (*The Making of Religion*), Nathan Söderblom (*Dieu vivant dans l'histoire*), R. Pettazzoni (*Formazione e sviluppo del monoteismo nella storia della religione*), Wilhelm Schmidt (*The Origin and Growth of Religion*), S. M. Zwemer (*The Origin of Religion*), H. S. Nyberg (*Irans forntida religioner*), George Widengren (*Hochgottglaube im alten Iran; Religionens värld*), Ivan Engnell,[4] H. Ringgren (*Word and Wisdom*), and Alexander Grigolia, the American anthropologist whose work in support of primitive monotheism remains unpublished.

The Bible ascribes to ELOHIM the creation and preservation of the universe. Its uncompromising monotheistic spirit stands in clear antithesis to the polytheistic crudities of so-called pagan accounts of beginnings. Donald J. Wiseman, professor of Assyriology in the University of London, asserts that "no myth has yet been found which explicitly refers to the creation of the universe, and those concerned with the organization of the universe and its cultural processes, the creation of man and the establishment of civilization are marked by polytheism and the struggles of deities for supremacy in marked contrast to the Hebrew monotheism. . . . The Hebrew account, with its clarity and monotheism, stands out unique; there are no struggles between deities or attempts to exalt any special city or race" ("Creation," pp. 272b–273a). Moreover, ELOHIM from the first enters decisively into the life history of the Israelites, disclosing his name and defining their destiny, whereas the so-called pagan "creator"-gods do not really vindicate themselves in the historical process as does the living God.

Abba Hillel Silver reminds us that although Moses "was trained in the

---

4. Ivan Engnell, *Studies in Divine Kingship in the Ancient Near East. Gamla Testamentet, En traditionshistorisk inledning.* Engnell inverts the popular critical view by holding that the supremacy of the God EL represents a point of departure, not a terminus. He contends that this same "high God" was worshiped in the Western Semitic world as EL SHADDAI, EL ELYON, SHALEM and HADAD, and was worshiped as YAHWEH by Moses because of a new manifestation—so that a fusion of EL and YAHWEH takes place at Israel's entrance into Canaan. While this view somewhat exalts the Hebrew EL above the rampant polytheism of the Semitic world, it nonetheless assimilates him objectionably to the pervasive polytheism of Canaanite religion which, for all its recognition of a high god, invited judgment by the God of the Old Testament.

court of Pharaoh and was fully instructed in the creation myths which were prevalent in such incongruous diversity in Egypt and elsewhere in the ancient world and which constituted the very essence of all the naturalistic religions," he nonetheless "refused to make myth a part of the religion of YHVH" (*Moses and the Original Torah*, pp. 5 f.). Silver emphasizes that "all the literary prophets refer, in one way or another, to the Torah of YHVH which was given in the wilderness" (p. 13). "The two primary names for God in Judaism, YHVH and Elohim," writes Silver, "the Rabbis took to designate Him as a God of mercy and as a God of justice" (*Where Judaism Differed*, p. 125).

ELOAH. This singular form of ELOHIM is used predominantly in biblical poetry. It is especially characteristic of the Book of Job, in which it occurs more frequently than the plural ELOHIM, which elsewhere is the preferred form. In fact, ELOAH occurs more often in Job than in the remainder of the Old Testament. The Aramaic parts of Daniel and Ezra use not ELOHIM but the form ELAHA, very similar to ELOAH.

Most scholars hold that ELOAH was originally a generic designation for "the mighty One" rather than a proper name. The root meaning of EL and ELOAH is probably "might" or "power" (Edmond Jacob surveys the evidence in *Theology of the Old Testament*, pp. 33 f.). Hence it designates God as the "mighty" One. The plural form ELOHIM may also suggest plurality[5] of powers, indicating plenitude of strength (hence, "the Almighty").

EL. This primary form of the EL-cognates, commonly taken to mean "the Strong One," is one of the most common terms for a god in the Semitic languages. In Ugaritic literature EL holds venerable and senior status among the many gods, although he is not the central figure in the Canaanite myths. EL appears in the Semitic world generally as a particular deity, in the larger pantheon of divinity, or as a special local deity. In the Old Testament EL is used mainly to designate Israel's God; occasionally it refers to the pagans' "god" (Isa. 44:17) or in the plural to their "gods" (Exod. 15:11). Although found throughout the Old Testament, the term is generally poetical in use; it occurs in Job and Psalms more often than in the remaining books. It is seldom found in the historical books, and in Leviticus not at all.

Frequently EL is juxtaposed with nouns or adjectives that express some particular divine attribute or activity, as ELYON. Thus the generic name is coordinated with a specific divine perfection and the designation gains

5. Some theologians have found here anticipations of the Trinity, of a plurality of persons within a single divine essence. But the revelation that the one God is irreducibly triune awaits the manifestation of the Son and the larger New Testament revelation. To insist on plurality in ELOHIM, and then to expound this in terms of a plurality of persons but not of essence, reflects a retroactive theologizing that nullifies God's progressive self-disclosure of the inmost secret of his Being. Yet the deity of the Messiah is foretold in Ps. 45:7, etc., and we should not deny revelatory intimations of the doctrine in the Old Testament.

the force of a proper name. ELYON, meaning "highest," designates God as the "most high" or by nature "the Exalted."

In view of the role of the names of God in the theology of revelation, we must ask, however, whether one adequately represents the patriarchal uses of ELYON and related names by describing a gradual emergence of a divine name through repeated use of the generic term for God in special associations it held for the patriarchs. We need not doubt that the revelation of the Name is correlated with certain memorable experiences in patriarchal history. But the basic question is whether these experiences, and the use of the Name, are grounded in the revelatory initiative of God. Edward Mack held that the early use of ELYON (Gen. 14:18–20) "points to an unquestioned monotheism in the beginning of Hebrew history" ("Names of God," 3:1267a). The religion of the patriarchs, as J. A. Motyer tells us, "revolves round the worship of EL. Their religious experience found natural expression by elaborating the term EL so as to make it express different facets of the Divine nature which were revealed to them" (*The Revelation of the Divine Name*, pp. 26 ff.).

Motyer lists six such elaborations: EL ELYON (Gen. 14:18, 19, 20, 22); EL SHADDAI (Gen. 17:1; 28:3; 35:11; 43:14; 48:3); EL BETHEL (Gen. 31:13); EL ROI (Gen. 16:13); EL ELOHE-ISRAEL (Gen. 33:20); EL OLAM (Gen. 21:33). These titles, Motyer asserts, reflect several outstanding features of the patriarchal apprehension of God: they associate divine revelation with historical confrontation; they connect God's disclosure with his own nature, not with mere externalities; and they disclose religious worship in the spirit of monotheism. Motyer holds that this general type of EL-revelation, of which EL SHADDAI singles out one significant facet, supplies essential background for the fuller revelation of the divine Name at the exodus.

Genesis 14 bears in an important way on the question of patriarchal knowledge of YAHWEH, not solely of EL ELYON, and poses a special problem for source critics, who postpone all awareness of YAHWEH beyond the patriarchal age. Melchizedek, king of Salem (Jerusalem), attributes Abraham's success to EL ELYON, and pays him homage. Abraham does not dispute this attribution, and gives a tithe of the spoils of war to the high priest of EL ELYON. Yet in addressing the king of Sodom (v. 22, KJV), Abraham identifies YAHWEH as EL ELYON: "And Abram said to the King of Sodom, I have lift up mine hand unto YAHWEH, EL ELYON, the possessor of heaven and earth." Walter Harrelson interprets the passage by rejecting its historical truth while equivocally acknowledging "probably . . . some historical information." He thinks it "fairly clear" that the account is "designed to demonstrate" that "Abraham had long ago worshipped YAHWEH at Jerusalem" (*Interpreting the Old Testament*, p. 44). Harrelson ignores many penetrating criticisms of the documentary hypotheses, and presents "a table of Pentateuchal sources" somewhat embellishing Martin Noth's analysis. Although he discreetly defers his source analysis to the appendix, its "authoritative" shadow determines the exposition of the Old Testament text. Martin Buber refuses to see "a late theological construction" in Abraham's identification of his God YAHWEH with the EL ELYON of Salem, and finds, rather, a basis for "fusion" in the recognition of their identity (*Kingship of God*, p. 34).

EL SHADDAI, SHADDAI (*Omnipotent One*).

The name EL SHADDAI is found especially in patriarchal history, and also in the book of Job, in a number of Psalms, and occasionally in the prophetic literature. It has been considered the distinctive name for God in the patriarchal period in view of Exodus 6:2–3, RSV: "And God said to Moses, I am YAHWEH. I appeared to Abraham, to Isaac, and to Jacob as EL SHADDAI." Its inclusion in the ancient list of names in Numbers 1:5–15 (cf. vv. 6, 12) attests its early use.

The exact etymological derivation remains in doubt. Ludwig Koehler asserts that no explanation of the etymology is satisfactory (*Lexicon in Veteris Testamenti Libros*, p. 950). A variety of meanings have been suggested. Against the evolutionary interpretation that SHADDAI was a mountain or storm-god stands the absence of any hint of this derivation in Scripture, which associates the idea of God standing on the mountains rather with God's almightiness. Much recent scholarship has followed W. F. Albright's derivation of SHADDAI as a divine epithet from the Akkadian *shadu* (mountain), with the sense "he of the mountains" (*From the Stone Age to Christianity*, p. 300; cf. *Journal of Biblical Literature* 54 [1935]: 180 ff.). But this proposal is challenged by E. A. Speiser, editor of the Anchor Bible volume on Genesis, who notes the phonologic difficulties of Albright's view (*Genesis*, p. 124). (It is noteworthy that YAHWEH who manifests himself at Sinai, shows himself not limited to the mountains, as in the Ahab–Ben-Hadad encounters.) *The Scofield Reference Bible* (note in Genesis 17:1) associates EL SHADDAI with the Hebrew *shad* (breast), and God is consequently designated as The Nourisher, The Strength-giver, and secondarily as The Satisfier. This option becomes increasingly hazardous as the meaning is extended, since the tertiary sense of The Provider overlaps an alternate derivation expressing the idea of might. The recent Scofield revision (1967) moderates the earlier emphasis and assigns more weight to "all sufficient" as the sense of EL SHADDAI. The usual translation of EL SHADDAI is "God Almighty." Almost all the older lexicons associate *shaddai* with *shadad* (might), as the Septuagint translators frequently did. Speiser remarks that "the traditional translation of Shaddai as 'Almighty' goes back to an early rabbinic etymology" (*Genesis*, p. 124). But the fact that some Hebrew lexicons list the term *shadad* only with a violent use of might, in the sense of despoiling, tended to disqualify this derivation and to divert recent etymologists from any such association. Since the exact meaning of *shaddai* remains in doubt, exegetes are increasingly reluctant to press an option.

But theological use rather than philological derivation is in any event decisive. Invariably the scriptural use conveys the notion of invincible strength. Both the Septuagint (LXX) and the New Testament translate the term by PANTOCRATOR or "all-powerful" (2 Cor. 6:18; Rev. 4:8). In Ruth 1:20 the LXX translates it in the sense of competence to perform (*hikanos*).

Franz Delitzsch long ago contrasted the revelation content of the name EL SHADDAI with that of ELOHIM by pointing out that whereas ELOHIM reflects God in the role of creating and supporting nature, EL SHADDAI is "the God who so constrains nature that it does His will, and so subdues it that it bows to and subserves grace" (*A New Commentary on Genesis*, 1:32). So, G. F. Oehler finds the Name disclosive of "the God who testifies of Himself in special deeds of power, by which He subdues nature to the ways of His kingdom . . . and who causes that race with which He has entered covenant to experience His powerful presence in protection and blessing" (*Theology of the Old Testament*, p. 91). God's disclosure as EL SHADDAI came with his establishment of the covenant with Abraham (Gen. 17:1–14) and was demonstrated in the birth of Isaac, and in the preservation, guidance and multiplication of his posterity. Hence C. F. Keil remarks that the name EL SHADDAI belongs "to the sphere of salvation, furnishing one element in the manifestation of Jehovah, and describing Jehovah, the covenant God, as possessing the power to realize His promises, even when the order of nature presented no prospect of their fulfilment, and the powers of nature were insufficient to secure it" (Keil and Delitzsch, *The Pentateuch*, 1:223). So Geerhardus Vos observes that God is called EL SHADDAI "because through the supernaturalism of His procedure He, as it were, overpowers nature and, in the service of His grace, compels her to further His designs" (*Biblical Theology: Old and New Testaments*, p. 96). While the previous names portray the mighty God exalted above all creatures, EL SHADDAI emphasizes God's solicitous condescension and singular providence in the creaturely sphere. Not only for his creative and preserving work, for which the Hebrews praised ELOHIM, but for his special activity of covenantal concern the omnipotent One was honored in Israel as EL SHADDAI.

After God reveals his Name to Abraham, EL SHADDAI constantly recurs in the patriarchal period (Gen. 17:1; 28:3; 35:11; 43:14; 48:3; 49:25; Exod. 6:3). In view of the Abrahamic covenant and the birth of an heir in initial fulfillment of that covenant, the patriarchs know that their powerful God is moving toward a goal whose consummation still lies in the future.

God's invincible power now becomes "the guarantee of the fulfillment of his promises and of the fact that he will ever keep his covenant. Hence, from now on God is repeatedly called the God of Abraham, Gen. 24:12; of Isaac, Gen. 28:13; of Jacob, Ex. 3:6; of your fathers, Ex. 3:13, 15; of the Hebrews, Ex. 3:18; of Israel, Gen. 33:20" (Bavinck, *The Doctrine of God*, p. 102). Albrecht Alt theorizes that the God of Abraham, the Fear of Isaac (Gen. 31:42—Albright suggests rather, the Kinsman of Isaac) and the Mighty One of Jacob were originally three distinct deities ("Der Gott der Väter," [1929] 1:24 ff.). But Derek Kidner rightly notes that this rests precariously on the further "gratuitous theory that the three patriarchs were unrelated and unknown to each other," whereas "the patriarchs' father-son relationship . . . is the crux of the middle chapters of Genesis, where all hinges on the promise of a son to Abraham and the election of the younger son of Isaac" (*Genesis: An Introduction and Commentary*, p. 166, n. 2).

The disclosure of God as EL SHADDAI is the distinctive[6] patriarchal revelation of God, and was specially evocative of the divine covenant with Abraham (Gen. 17:1–2). But it is not yet the high point of Old Testament disclosure. The name EL SHADDAI forms a connecting link, as Vos observes, "between 'El' and 'Elohim,' on the one hand, and 'Jehovah,' the Mosaic name, on the other hand. If the former signify God's relation to nature, and Jehovah is His redemptive name, then El Shaddai may be said to express how God uses nature for super-nature" (*Biblical Theology: Old and New Testaments*, p. 96).

Significance of Exodus 6:2–3

In support of their widely divergent views, both evangelical expositors of progressive divine revelation and documentary source-theorists appeal to the names of God. The debate involves many textual considerations, but two passages that represent God as speaking his own Name are specially decisive.

One of these passages is Exodus 6:2–3, which records God's conversation with Moses in these words: "I am the LORD [YAHWEH]: And I appeared unto Abraham, unto Isaac, and unto Jacob, by the name of GOD ALMIGHTY [EL SHADDAI], but by my name JEHOVAH [YAHWEH] was I not known to them" (KJV). The other passage is Genesis 28:13, actually one of a considerable number of texts in Genesis in which YAHWEH occurs as a familiar divine name.

The apparent teaching of Exodus that God's revelation as YAHWEH was not given until the time of Moses, encouraged textual critics to explain the frequent occurrence of the name YAHWEH in the Genesis narrative in terms of later literary revision. By taking the varying divine names as clues to redactors who presumably correlated and synthesized the content of the Old Testament books, the so-called J-E-D-P hypothesis identi-

---

6. The weightiest objection to attaching this significance to EL SHADDAI is that it only occurs seven times in connection with the patriarchs and that in one of these instances it is equated to EL BETHEL (Gen. 48:3; 31:13). On this ground some scholars consider it merely one epithet of God among others, and favor Albright's "God, the mountain" (cf. "God my high tower," Pss. 18:2; 144:2 KJV) (Albright, *Journal of Biblical Literature* 54 [1935]: 180–93, and *From the Stone Age to Christianity*, p. 244). Albrecht Alt also calls attention to the ABIR of Jacob (the mighty God, Gen. 49:24) and the PACHAD of Isaac (Gen. 3:53) (*Essays of Old Testament History and Religion*, pp. 25 f.). But E. A. Speiser remarks that Albright's equation of SHADDAI with mountain (as a divine epithet derived from the Akkadian *šadû*) not only suffers phonologic difficulties, but must cope with the fact that Akkadian religion had hundreds of epithets like it (*Genesis*, p. 124). Kidner emphasizes that study of the use of the term confirms the sense of might, for the name "tends to be matched to situations where God's servants are hard-pressed and needing reassurance" (*Genesis*, p. 129).

fied divergent literary strands. "The clue to the distinguishing of the various documents," A. G. Hebert writes, "was first given by Exodus 6:3 where it is said that God was known to the patriarchs as El Shaddai and not by His Name Yahweh; yet in our Book of Genesis the Name is freely used" (*The Authority of the Old Testament*, p. 30). "The author of these statements" (in Exod. 6:2–3), wrote John Skinner, "cannot have written any passage which implies on the part of the patriarchs a knowledge of the name YAHWEH, and, in particular, any passage which records a revelation of God to them under that name" (*The Divine Names in Genesis*, pp. 12 f.). Skinner considers it "an inevitable inference . . . from the express statement of Exodus 6:2, 3" and in fact "*certain* that at least two writers are concerned in the composition of Genesis. . . . We are well on our way to a documentary theory of the Pentateuch." The "flat contradiction," as H. H. Rowley labels it (*The Biblical Doctrine of Election*, pp. 25 f.), between statements that God was known to Abraham by the name YAHWEH (Gen. 15:2, 7) and that he was not known to Abraham by that name (Exod. 6:3) has long been held to require "the recognition that varying traditions have been incorporated from different sources" (A. H. McNeile, *Exodus*, p. 34).

Evangelical and liberal scholars alike sensed at once that any radical loss of the literary unity of the Bible must involve the question of theological unity as well. Assuming the truth of the documentary hypothesis, the religious unity of the Old Testament is really an achievement of editorial redactors rather than a reflection of progressive divine self-disclosure. Whether the critical use of divine names as a criterion of documentary sources was or was not valid became, therefore, a crucially important issue in discussing both the theological and literary significance of the Bible.

More than two centuries have now passed since the French physician Jean Astruc (1684–1766), fascinated by the fact that Genesis 2 uses mostly the name YAHWEH, first proposed the hypothesis that the names ELOHIM and YAHWEH are clues to separate manuscript sources. Ever since then, the divine names have held a central importance in critical discussions of the biblical documents. But the literary dissection of the sacred texts led in swift succession to a variety of views, concerning both the number of literary sources and their date and character as well.[7]

---

7. Gleason L. Archer, Jr. (*A Survey of Old Testament Introduction*, p. 82), notes these contradictions and reversals in the early development: (1) A different divine name is taken to point to a different author (Astruc, Eichhorn), each with his own circle of interest, style and vocabulary. (2) The same divine name (Elohim) is ascribed to different authors (Hupfeld), while some E passages are acknowledged not to differ greatly from J in circle of interest, style or vocabulary. (3) The Elohist (P) strand which most differs from J in interest and style is held to be earliest (Jahweh being a later name for God than Elohim). (4) On the contrary, P is designated as latest instead of earliest (in conformity with the evolutionary derivation and development of Hebrew religion from the primitive polytheistic to the priest-ridden monotheistic). (5) J is held, of course, to be later than E (all the critics up to Graf); but no, J is really earlier than E (Kuenen and Wellhausen).

The successive source theories were met by vigorous evangelical counterattack. But liberal critics made the Exodus contrast of EL SHADDAI and YAHWEH a court of high appeal in insisting that YAHWEH is a post-patriarchal name of God and that the different divine names infallibly indicate diverse streams of composition. Conservative scholars like William Henry Green skillfully countered the documentary theory even before the end of the nineteenth century (*Unity of the Book of Genesis*, 1895; *Higher Criticism of the Pentateuch*, 1896), but its commanding influence was not arrested. In Europe, in alliance with form criticism, its prestige has been extended into the late twentieth century on a modified basis, while in the United States it remains the operating premise of most liberal scholars. Otto Eissfeldt concedes that the Old Testament nowhere reflects a conflict between EL and YAHWEH (such as that between YAHWEH and Baal), but presents a continuous revelation—first in terms of EL to the fathers, and then of YAHWEH to their children. Yet he considers this a later rationalization of the early history, and finds in Exodus 6:2-3 an unwitting disclosure of what he declares the "actual" state of affairs— a fusion of the Canaanite EL and the Hebrew YAHWEH in which the latter supersedes the former ("El and Yahweh").

Yet the disintegrating supports of the documentary theory are increasingly evident (Cyrus H. Gordon, "Higher Critics and Forbidden Fruit," pp. 3 ff.), and the uneasiness of frontier scholars in face of formidable refutation of the Graf-Wellhausen hypothesis is apparent. "That it [the Graf-Wellhausen theory] is widely rejected in whole or in part is doubtless true," concedes Rowley, "but there is no view to put in its place that would not be more widely and emphatically rejected. . . . The Graf-Wellhausen view is only a working hypothesis, which can be abandoned with alacrity when a more satisfying view is found, but which cannot with profit be abandoned until then" (*The Growth of the Old Testament*, p. 46). Because many biblical critics are reluctant to return to conservative views of the origin of Genesis, Old Testament research amid its eager identification of literary strands is declining into chaotic confusion. Herbert F. Hahn speaks of Old Testament criticism in the last quarter century as "a chaos of conflicting trends, ending in contradictory results which create an impression of ineffectiveness in this type of research. The conclusion seems unavoidable that the higher criticism has long since passed the age of constructive achievement" (*Old Testament in Modern Research*, p. 41). Significant studies now come mainly from scholars who simply accept the records as they stand, on the ground that the supposed redactors must after all have intended that we use the writings as we have them.

Against the validity of divine names as a sure criterion of late literary sources, evangelical scholars have noted that the Septuagint frequently uses names for God (in no less than 180 instances) that do not correspond with the Masoretic Hebrew text; that literary critics violate Israelite psychology by applying modern Occidental techniques for discerning J and E strands in the ancient Semitic narratives; and that even within the supposed sources the names are employed inconsistently with the Wellhausen theory (cf. Archer, *A Survey of Old Testament Introduction*, pp. 84 ff., for a list of such objections).

But what then of Exodus 6:2–3, which explicitly confirms God's revelation to the three patriarchs under the name EL SHADDAI, and apparently by way of contrast adds that God had not previously disclosed himself as YAHWEH, the name by which he was now disclosing himself to Moses? Evangelical scholars have long contended that the passage does not demand the critical view which erodes confidence in the early composition of the narratives and has destructive consequences for Old Testament theology (cf. Robert Dick Wilson, "Critical Note on Exodus vi. 3," pp. 108–119). This contention has recently been reasserted with new force and in a new form. In the Tyndale Old Testament Lecture for 1956, J. A. Motyer appealed for reexamination of the controversial passage, and pronounced Exodus 6:2–3 a reliable theological summary of the content of God's self-manifestation between the call of Abram (Gen. 12) and the call of Moses (Exod. 3) (*The Revelation of the Divine Name*, p. 6).

A series of recent developments in the Old Testament field has shaped a propitious atmosphere for fresh inquiry. Among these are the changing face of Pentateuchal criticism, the cumulative evidence of archaeology, the decline of confidence in religious evolution as the decisive key to the Old Testament. But no less important is the growing uneasiness over regard for the divine names as literary constants, and a larger emphasis on their theological significance. Instead of following the critical theory, steeped in evolutionary motifs, some liberal scholars ask whether extensive pre-Mosaic use of the name YAHWEH may not require a quite different understanding of the Exodus passage. The Norwegian scholar Sigmund Mowinckel, a champion of form criticism, contended that Exodus 3:14–15 ("And God said unto Moses, I AM THAT I AM: and he said, Thus shalt thou say unto the children of Israel, I AM hath sent me unto you. . . . The Lord God of your fathers, the God of Abraham, the God of Isaac, and the God of Jacob, hath sent me unto you: this is my name for ever, and this is my memorial unto all generations," KJV) does not really promulgate YAHWEH as a new name for God, but on the contrary presupposes that YAHWEH was already known to the patriarchs (*Zeitschrift für Altertumswissenschaft*, to which he contributed two articles in 1930).

Mowinckel allots one of the J-strata of the early chapters of Genesis to E, with the result that (since E is author of what was previously attributed to J) E then knew and used the divine name YAHWEH: "It is *not* E's view that Yahwe is here revealing a hitherto unknown name to Moses. Yahwe is not *telling* his name to one who does not know it. . . . The whole conversation presupposes that the Israelites know this name already" (*The Two Sources of the Predeuteronomic Primeval History (JE) in Gen. i–xi*, p. 55). The Swedish scholar Ivan Engnell in 1945 emphasized that the use of different names finds its true explanation in the contexts in which they appear, and that context determines their appropriateness (*Gamla Testamentet, En traditionshistorisk inledning*): "The different divine names have different ideological associations and therewith different import. . . . It is the traditionist, the *same* traditionist, who varies in the choice of divine names, not the 'documents.' " C. R. North summarizes Engnell's application of this principle: "Yahweh is readily used when it is a question of Israel's national God, indicated as such over against foreign gods, and where the history of the fathers is concerned, etc., while, on the other hand, Elohim, 'God,' gives more expression to a 'theological' and abstract-cosmic picture of God, and is therefore used in larger and more moving contexts" ("Pentateuchal Criticism," pp. 66 f.).

We return, then, to Motyer's call for a reassessment of the implications of Exodus 6:2–3, and note his specific proposals: (1) a retranslation of the passage that surmounts the supposed conflict between pre-Mosaic and Mosaic revelation of God's name, and preserves the validity of progressive revelation over against documentary reconstructions; (2) an insistence that YAHWEH is the only genuine divine Name, so that other Old Testament forms usually taken to be proper names are dismissed simply as descriptive terms.

The translation Motyer proposes, and proceeds to justify in detail, is: "And God spoke to Moses, and said to him: I am YAHWEH. And I showed myself to Abraham, to Isaac, and to Jacob in the character of EL SHADDAI,[8] but in the character expressed by my name YAHWEH I did not make myself known to them" (*The Revelation of the Divine Name,* pp. 12 ff.). This translation denies patriarchal knowledge only of the *significance* of the name YAHWEH, but not knowledge of the name itself. Moreover, it preserves patriarchal familiarity with God as EL SHADDAI as distinctive of that period. Not only grammatical acceptability, but contextual suitability also, Motyer argues, supports this rendering. Taken in its larger outlines, the Old Testament indicates "not that now for the first time the name as a sound is declared, but that now for the first time the essential significance of the name is made known. The patriarchs called God Yahweh, but knew Him as El Shaddai; their descendants will both call Him and know Him by His name Yahweh."

For indirect confirmation of this emphasis to Moses on YAHWEH's inner nature, rather than merely on a verbal designation, Motyer turns to the related passage Exodus 3:13 ("And Moses said unto God, Behold, when I come unto the children of Israel, and shall say unto them, The God of your fathers hath sent me unto you; and they shall say unto me, What is his name? what shall I say unto them?" KJV) and notes Martin Buber's comment that the Hebrew interrogative pronoun requires reference of this inquiry not to the *name* as such, but to the reality behind it. "If you wish to ask a person's name in Biblical Hebrew . . . you never

---

8. Motyer's emphasis on Yahweh's expression of his character is found also in the *New Scofield Reference Bible* (see note on Exod. 6:3).

say, as is done here, 'What (*māh*) is his name?' or 'What is your name?'
but 'Who (*mî*) are you?' 'Who is he?' 'Who is your name?' 'Tell me your
name.' Where the word 'what' is associated with the word 'name' the
question asked is what finds expression in or lies concealed behind that
name" (*Moses*, p. 48).

Any effort to dissociate the patriarchs from the use of YAHWEH's name
on the basis of Exodus 6:2–3, and to link them exclusively to the use of
EL SHADDAI runs into formidable difficulty. In an article published post-
humously, G. T. Manley stresses that "although many sayings of Abraham
have been preserved there is not one in which he uses *el shaddai*. . . .
The only place where the words '*el shaddai*' occur in Abraham's life history is Genesis 17:1, and here . . . the speaker is Yahweh Himself. . . .
Genesis 17:1 and the words of Yahweh to Moses in Exodus 3 and 6 form
a good and intelligible sequence if allowed to speak for themselves without being manipulated and dissected" ("The God of Abraham," pp. 6 f.).
Manley defends the statement that Abraham "called upon the name of
Yahweh" (Gen. 12:8) against the documentary theorists' easy dismissal
in supposed deference to Exodus 6:2–3. He notes already in Genesis 10:9
the appearance of a "traditional saying" incorporating the name YAHWEH
("even as Nimrod the mighty hunter before YAHWEH") in a context that
authentically reflects an environment prior to the destruction of Sodom
(Gen. 10:19). In the earlier story of the flood, moreover, the only words
attributed directly to Noah contain a curse on Canaan and this blessing:
"Blessed be YAHWEH, the ELOHIM of Shem" (9:26). Here Manley asks:
"Are we expected to believe that this bit of poetry was an invention of
the post-Mosaic period?" And even if in connection with the naming of
Noah it should be argued that the reference to the ground that "YAHWEH
had cursed" (5:29) must be viewed as a subsequent insertion, he contends, it is more probably from Abraham than from a later redactor.
Concerning the declaration of Genesis 4:26 (ASV), "Then began men to
call upon the name of YAHWEH"—words used later of Abraham himself
at Bethel (Gen. 12:8; 13:4) and Hebron (13:18)—Manley offers the interesting suggestion that this may have been Abraham's way of noting
the beginnings of ceremonial worship, since the previous verses mention
the origin of music and industry.

S. R. Driver's argument, that the consistent[9] use of the double name
YAHWEH-ELOHIM in the creation narrative of Genesis 2 and 3 was introduced by a later redactor, to show that the YAHWEH of Genesis 2 was the
same God as the ELOHIM of Genesis 1, founders on Manley's protest that
"after the exile would seem late in the day for this identification to be
necessary." The skepticism of evangelical scholars over critical positions
is well voiced in Archer's remark: "It requires a tremendous willingness
to believe the unlikely, for an investigator to come up with a conclusion
. . . (that) despite the analogy of Israel's pagan neighbors and contempo-

---

9. Manley notes that the serpent and Eve both use ELOHIM.

raries (who embodied their religious beliefs in written scriptures long before Moses' time), the Hebrews never got around to inscripturating the records of their faith until 500 B.C. or later" (*A Survey of Old Testament Introduction*, p. 94).

In summary, then, the evangelical counterassault on higher critical documentary views holds that a proper understanding of Exodus 6 is consistent with the patriarchal use in Abraham's time of YAHWEH and not simply EL SHADDAI, and that the evidence is not wholly undone even if one takes the patriarchal narrative as source-theorists propose to refashion it.

Alongside this emphasis on the early patriarchal use of YAHWEH's name, we must consider Motyer's other line of argument, that the term EL SHADDAI is not in fact a divine name at all, but simply a descriptive term.[10] Motyer extends this argument to all terms for God except YAH-WEH: "The Bible knows nothing of different 'names' of God. God has only one 'name'—Yahweh. Apart from this, all the others are titles or descriptions" (*The Revelation of the Divine Name*, p. 7, n. 18). If, as Motyer contends, the Old Testament on revelational ground knows only one proper name for God, YAHWEH, then the higher critical denial of pre-Mosaic knowledge of YAHWEH would leave the Hebrews in total ignorance of his name, that is, with a nameless God throughout the patriarchal era.

Motyer supports this claim by his translation of Exodus 6:2–3, which distinguishes the knowledge of God's *character* as EL SHADDAI and of God's *name* YAHWEH from knowledge of God's *character* as YAHWEH. Manley, likewise, would erase any significance of EL SHADDAI as a name of God. "Where . . . is there documentary evidence that Abraham used *el shaddai?* There is absolutely none, whether in J, E or P. He spoke of God as *el Elyon*, and as *el 'olam* (21:33), but never, so far as we are told, as *el shaddai*" ("The God of Abraham," pp. 6 f.). YAHWEH had revealed "to the fathers great promises and Himself as able (*shaddai*) to fulfill them; but had not then, as now, revealed to them all that was involved in His 'Name.' That name is Yahweh, *el shaddai* is not a name."[11] As Manley sees it, God introduces himself successively to Moses as "1) the God (Elohim) of thy father; 2) the God of Abraham, Isaac and Jacob; and 3) Yahweh, the God of Abraham, Isaac and Jacob. There is nothing new in this; Moses is expected to recognize these descriptions. They are to be

---

10. Speiser comments: "Significantly enough, Exod. vi 3 does not call it a name" (*Genesis*, p. 124).

11. "Yahweh opens His word of wonderful promise to Abraham by saying, 'I am *el shaddai*,' which RV translates with 'God Almighty.' But *el* is not the same as Elohim. It is a common noun and the literal translation would be 'an almighty God.' In Ruth 1:20 the LXX translates *shaddai* by *hikavos*, an adjective meaning 'competent' or 'able to perform a thing.' Whatever adjective is used, the expression is not a new 'name.' Indeed, it is not a name at all, but a claim to be able to perform the promise which follows" (Manley, "The God of Abraham," p. 6).

followed by a revelation, not of a new name, but of a new *meaning* to be read into the Name" (ibid., p. 7).

Insofar as this approach emphasizes that God's Name is a revelational unity, and that his progressive self-manifestation unveils the manifold fullness of the divine nature, it is to be welcomed. Moreover, the further question whether EL SHADDAI is or is not truly a divine name is here placed in proper perspective, since Motyer and Manley champion the specially revealed Name of God, against views that sacrifice all names of God to the speculative notion that he is the "Nameless One," or subvert progressive divine self-revelation in deference to secular metaphysics, or see in EL SHADDAI only an extension of the Canaanite divinities.[12] Both Motyer and Manley, furthermore, stoutly insist that the patriarchs had a pre-Mosaic familiarity with the revealed name YAHWEH.

But the denial by Motyer and Manley that the term EL SHADDAI is a divine name seems unnecessarily to complicate the role of the divine names in Genesis and Exodus. Christian theology has traditionally regarded EL SHADDAI as one of the divine names, and in fact considered it the characteristic name for God in patriarchal religion (as presumably attested by Exod. 6:2–3) (J. Barton Payne, *The Theology of the Older Testament*, p. 146). The argument against recognition of EL SHADDAI as a name for God therefore calls for careful scrutiny. In espousing patriarchal familiarity with YAHWEH's Name, does the evangelical as opposed to the developmental view require also the repudiation of EL SHADDAI as a divine name? It seems contextually unnecessary, theologically inconsistent, exegetically unjustifiable, and tactically unnecessary to reject EL SHADDAI as a proper name for God in order to preserve pre-Mosaic use of the Name of YAHWEH.

The larger biblical revelation of God's personal names in principle attests the propriety of more than a single name for God; the use of ELOHIM as a proper name, and not simply as a general term for deity, and the patriarchal worship of God as EL ELYON (as well as EL OLAM, EL BETHEL, EL ELOHE, EL ROI), not to mention EL SHADDAI, indicate that God was known by other names than YAHWEH before the full significance of his name YAHWEH became apparent. YAHWEH is not, therefore, the only name by which God was known in patriarchal times.

The distinctive theological feature of all the biblical names for God is that they are not arbitrary sounds, but specially reveal God's nature. Motyer nowhere disputes, but everywhere insists, that EL SHADDAI is revelatory of the divine nature: "When God revealed Himself 'as' El Shaddai, it was not with a view to providing the patriarchs with a title by which they could address Him, but to give them an insight into His character such as that title aptly conveyed" (*The Revelation of the Divine Name*, p. 14). To contend that because EL SHADDAI describes God's

---

12. Von Rad criticizes the redactor P for taking EL SHADDAI as "the God of the pre-Mosaic period" for, von Rad holds, EL SHADDAI "most probably belongs to the group of originally Canaanite El numina" (*Old Testament Theology*, p. 179, n. 8).

character it cannot be a divine name erects a disjunction which would, if consistently followed, erode the significance of every biblical name for God, YAHWEH included. Some Christian theologians, moreover, compatibly with the biblical connection of name and nature, have considered even the divine perfections or virtues as legitimate divine names, although they distinguish "essential names" (attributes) from proper and personal names. The question over EL SHADDAI is then best expressed in this way: Is EL SHADDAI a *proper* name for God, or an *essential* name?

The argument that EL SHADDAI is not a proper divine name but rather a term descriptive of his nature is unconvincing. Edward J. Young thinks the words EL SHADDAI are used as a proper name not only in Genesis, but also in almost every other occurrence, Exodus 6:3 included. The phrase is similar to EL ELYON, he notes, which in Genesis 14 must be regarded as a proper name, and evidence from Ras Shamra would seem also to support this view.

Exegetical difficulties also cast doubt on the reduction of EL SHADDAI to nothing more than an impersonal descriptive term ("an almighty God"). The term appears six times in Genesis (17:1; 28:3; 35:11; 43:14; 48:3; 49:25). Its use as less than a divine name seems incongruous in the context of the divine address to Abraham at the renewal of the covenant ("I am EL SHADDAI; walk before me, and be thou perfect. And I will make my covenant between me and thee, and will multiply thee exceedingly," Gen. 17:1–2, ASV), and again, in the divine address to Jacob when he came out of Padan-aram ("I am EL SHADDAI: be fruitful and multiply; a nation and a company of nations shall be of thee, and kings shall come out of thy loins; and the land which I gave unto Abraham and Isaac, to thee will I give it, and to thy seed after thee will I give the land," Gen. 35:11–12, ASV). To be sure, the attribute of power (*shaddai*) here stands appropriately in the background of God's intervention in behalf of his people.[13] But just so the revelation of his unique ability to redeem them historically supplies in Exodus 6:2–3 and 3:13–15 the background for the larger revelation of his name as YAHWEH.[14] David W.

---

13. As Motyer comments: "Fourteen years at least had elapsed between the original promise of descendants to Abram and the time when God next spoke to him about the matter. The passing of the years, and the manifest failure of manmade alternatives to God's declared plan, had the effect of underlining powerlessness." In these circumstances God discloses himself in his Name and character as EL SHADDAI, in the face of the capricious power of the Egyptian tryants (Gen. 43:14). EL SHADDAI is the God who "takes over human incapacity and transforms it . . . performs His wonders on the basis of a miracle worked on the individual primarily concerned . . . covenants to the patriarchs' boundless posterity and inheritance of the land of promise. . . . It was the claim of El Shaddai to be powerful where man was weakest, and He exerts this claim supremely by promising to an obscure and numerically tiny family that they should one day possess and populate a land which, in their day, was inhabited and owned by people immeasurably their superiors in number and power" (*The Revelation of the Divine Name*, pp. 29 f.).

14. Why are we to exclude EL SHADDAI from Motyer's own observation regarding the patriarchal apprehension of God?: "These titles . . . show us revelation in terms

Kerr (in personal correspondence) points out that the formula of the prayer "May EL SHADDAI bless thee" in Genesis 28:3 is very similar to that of Numbers 6:24–27, which begins "May YAHWEH bless thee and keep thee" and concludes "and they shall place my name upon the children of Israel and I shall bless them." The use of YAHWEH in this context as a personal name is presumptive evidence that EL SHADDAI is to be similarly understood. In Genesis 48:3, moreover, on the assumption that EL SHADDAI is merely a descriptive title, one would be compelled to read: "One who is an almighty God appeared"—a gratuitous requirement in view of similar passages which are unhesitatingly translated: "YAHWEH appeared."

We need not eviscerate EL SHADDAI as a proper name for God, therefore, in order to enhance patriarchal use of YAHWEH as a proper divine name in Genesis. The objectionable notion in the higher critical reconstruction is its attempted exclusion, on the basis of Exodus 6:2–3, of any patriarchal knowledge of the name YAHWEH, so that the knowledge of the divine name EL SHADDAI in patriarchal times becomes a necessary *alternative* to the knowledge of the divine name YAHWEH. Nobody can minimize the high cost of this theory: forfeiture of the authenticity of the pre-Mosaic YAHWEH-sections involves the loss also of the truth of Genesis at the crucial point of God's revelation-relationship. This consequence alone should be reason enough to prod biblical scholarship into a new searching of the sense of Exodus 6:2–3.

But the higher critical claim that the Exodus account absolutely precludes any knowledge whatever of the name YAHWEH in the patriarchal period also runs amuck on the sticky flats of contrary internal evidence. The Book of Genesis unhesitatingly carries the name YAHWEH back to very early times (Gen. 4:26). Von Rad concedes that "the God who supremely controls all that happens in the history of the patriarchs is Jahweh," but holds that "regarded from the historical standpoint" this theological interpretation "is an anachronism, for Israel's ancestors prior to Moses as yet knew nothing of Jahvism" (*Old Testament Theology*, p. 166).[15] James Barr comments that all the old Yahvistic saga can

of historical confrontation—God meeting people at some point of awareness and revealing Himself more fully to them: the same type of revelation which received its supreme Old Testament exemplification at the Exodus. . . . These titles show us that the patriarchs were interested in the 'quality' of God, and not in some externality about Him. In revelation they saw into His nature, and they gave Him qualitative titles. Thus He is known as everlasting, most high, the God who sees, or lets Himself be seen" (*The Revelation of the Divine Name*, pp. 26 f.). Would not consistency then require either that we also question the propriety of YAHWEH as a divine name or that both EL SHADDAI and YAHWEH be recognized as such?

15. It is noteworthy that von Rad finds it odd that the latest of the "supposed" source documents (P) "most strongly emphasizes" the break in the history of revelation in God's name (ibid., p. 179). And he allows that Exod. 3:6, 13–14 aims to fuse together "the two eras in the saving history, that of the God of the ancestors and to the time of the full revelation of Jahweh," and states that "what came to pass with the revelation of the name of Jahweh was certainly of incalculable importance for

hardly be attributed to the Kenites, and that it is "doubtful whether Genesis would have become so deeply penetrated by the name Yahweh if that name was totally unknown before Moses. It should therefore be considered possible that the name was already circulating in some group of the ancestors of the later Israel, and that it was associated with stories of the old saga brought on the migration from Mesopotamia (creation, deluge, tower of Babel)" ("God," p. 335b).

Speiser thinks that "an acute problem is posed" by the reading of the text ("It was then that the name Yahweh began to be invoked"; not "the name *of* Yahweh") which precisely emphasizes the personal name (*Genesis*, p. 37). This he considers "directly at variance" with Exodus 3:14 and 6:3. Yet as a possible reconciliation he suggests that "The worship of Yahweh was in all likelihood confined at first to a small body of searchers under the aegis of the patriarchs," while YAHWEH later revealed himself to Moses as fountainhead of the distinctive religion that was to be a feature of nationhood. Abraham's use of YAHWEH to Melchizedek (Gen. 14:22), moreover, Speiser considers natural "especially in an oath," and he rejects the suggestion that the textual use of YAHWEH here proves J's authorship (pp. 108 f.). Although Speiser does not carry this break to significant conclusions, his position compromises the critical rejection of patriarchal knowledge of YAHWEH and the critical insistence on a conflict between the source of the Genesis and Exodus accounts.

Virtually all evangelical interpreters insist, against the higher critical assertion of patriarchal ignorance of the name of YAHWEH, that this name was indeed known to the patriarchs, and that speculative reconstruction alone requires its suppression from the ancient history. Compatible with Motyer's emphasis that the name was known to the patriarchs, Edward J. Young asserts that Exodus 6:3 "does not mean that the name Jehovah, as a vocable, was not known before this time. . . . This verse . . . teaches that in His character of Jehovah, i.e., covenant-redeemer God, God was not known to the patriarchs, a statement which is perfectly true" (*An Introduction to the Old Testament*, p. 136). Merrill F. Unger comments similarly: "Certainly the meaning is *not* that they should be told that this was His name, but that they should see the mighty manifestation of God's grace and power in *redeeming* His people from Egypt" (*Introductory Guide to the Old Testament*, p. 252). Oswald T. Allis points out that the expression "and they shall know (or, 'that they may know') that I am Jehovah" occurs many times in the Old Testament, and shows that it is used in Exodus not only

---

Israel, but it was not the beginning of her God's self-revelation. Jahweh is identical with the God of the ancestors" (pp. 179 f.). We believe that the evolutionary documentary bias underlies the refusal to interpret Exodus 6 in the light of Exodus 3, and thus requires von Rad, along with the documentary critics, to dismiss Genesis 4:26, which traces the cult of YAHWEH back to early times, as "an isolated tradition which cannot be harmonized" with Exodus 3 or 6 (p. 180, n. 10).

of the Israelites (6:7; 10:2; 16:12; 29:46; 31:13) but of Pharaoh (7:17; 8:22) and of the Egyptians (7:5; 14:4, 18) in such a way as to involve not the first disclosure of the name YAHWEH but the revelation of his character. "The declaration that *Elohim* was not known to the patriarchs in the significance of the name *Jehovah* may properly be taken to mean that the redemptive significance of the name was not known or had not been made clear to them" (*The Five Books of Moses*, p. 28).

Some evangelical interpreters deliberately move beyond Motyer's view by not only asserting that the bare *name* YAHWEH was known to the patriarchs, but also by insisting that the patriarchs also had some specific knowledge of YAHWEH's character (contrary to Motyer's proposed translation of Exodus 6:2-3: "in the character expressed by my name YAHWEH I did not make myself known to them"). R. Laird Harris thinks the negative in this text is rather a negative of comparison (cf. Prov. 8:10), and contends that the character expressed by YAHWEH may well have been known to the patriarchs, but that a new and striking manifestation of this character was given to Moses.[16] Not simply as a later theological interpretation, but in historical actuality, YAHWEH is seen to have a significant role in patriarchal history.

The higher critical refusal of any knowledge of YAHWEH to Moses' ancestors becomes, therefore, increasingly indefensible. Three arguments forcefully dispute critical contentions that the patriarchal age lacked knowledge of God as YAHWEH and, instead, support the evangelical view that the Mosaic revelation deepened and widened the earlier patriarchal knowledge of YAHWEH.

Assuming documentary redaction of the Pentateuch as projected by the critics, the very prominence of the name of YAHWEH in the pre-Mosaic narratives renders it highly improbable that any redactor could himself have understood Exodus 6:3 as a categorical denial that YAHWEH's name was known before Moses' time. In the use of the names with almost equal frequency in Genesis (where YAHWEH occurs 146 times, ELOHIM 164 times) Allis finds evidence that the name YAHWEH was known in patriarchal times and while still lacking its later importance, had perhaps already gained prophetic significance (cf. Gen. 49:18; *The Five Books of Moses*, p. 28).

Not only does the name YAHWEH occur throughout the Book of Genesis quite as frequently as does ELOHIM, but it appears there not simply in the mouth of the narrator of the events, but on the lips of Noah and the patriarchs. Edmond Jacob notes "several indications" that "the name Yahweh may not have been an absolutely new revelation to Moses"

---

16. In correspondence with me, Harris comments: "I am impressed by the fact that *yhwh* occurs in no names earlier than Moses' mother. Even hers is questionable. Now the house language of the patriarchs was not Hebrew. If *yhwh* has a Hebrew derivation it may well have been a new vocable in the days of Moses or at least, the bondage. In this case all the uses of *yhwh* in Genesis are *anachronisms*—as in the Hebrew language!"

—in particular, Enos's invocation (Gen. 4:26) and Noah's use of the name in benediction upon his sons (Gen. 9:26). Jacob writes: "The link between Yahweh and the gods of the patriarchs, upon which the narrative of Exodus insists, might not be entirely due then to the harmonizing attempts of the redactors" (*Theology of the Old Testament*, pp. 49 f.). More than a century ago, J. H. Kurtz considered this patriarchal use "an absolute proof" that no redactor could have held the view that the name YAHWEH originated with Moses, for otherwise "in Jacob's blessing, which indisputably belongs to him, he puts that name into the mouth of the patriarch" (*History of the Old Covenant*, 2:101). Nor is that all. For YAHWEH occurs in Genesis even *in the very speech of God* ("And, behold, YAHWEH . . . said, I am YAHWEH of Abraham thy father," Gen. 28:13). Any supposed redactor must here either disclose his awareness that an earlier literary groundwork represents the name YAHWEH as existing in the patriarchal age, or he takes liberties with the very speech of God—an unthinkable alternative whose consequences would be devastating to every effort to derive a significant religious point of view from the Old Testament records.[17] Hence this verse must be assigned full weight in any discussion of Mosaic or pre-Mosaic use of the name YAHWEH. Since this passage is antecedent to Exodus 6:3, the latter cannot be properly evaluated without attention to Genesis 28:13.

A second argument is based on etymological considerations. When used emphatically, the Hebrew term translated "I was known" denotes thorough insight into or grasp of the nature of an object (cf. the use of "know" in Exod. 1:8, 6:3). The Exodus passage would, on this reading, mean that the divine Name YAHWEH is now opened to Israel in an intimacy of manifestation unknown to the forefathers. YAHWEH's relationship in the patriarchal era centered more in promise and hope than in fulfillment; the Mosaic era inaugurated a striking transition to comprehensive divine accomplishments.

A third consideration is historical. The critical view makes a shambles of patriarchal history, which is the indispensable background for the Mosaic history. Not only the names ELOHIM and EL SHADDAI, but the name YAHWEH also constantly appear in the early narratives, illuminating the covenant by which God binds the chosen people to himself. Abram was summoned into a special divine relationship wherein covenant and grace would transcend the ordinary expectations from nature. He was to leave his people and family, although himself childless, and find a new home in a new land; he was then himself to become a great nation, and through him blessing and salvation were to flow to all nations. What thus happened in the patriarchal period, in God's special disclosure to Abram, left its permanent stamp upon that later history of Israel for which the patriarchal history prepares and serves as a type.

Martin Buber's appeal to "tradition narratives" as more reliable indi-

---

17. It is remarkable that Speiser simply glosses over the difficulty: "*J* speaks of Yahweh as standing beside Jacob and addressing him directly" (*Genesis*, p. 219).

cators than "literary sources" leads not simply to Mosaic use of YAHWEH but also to familiarity with the name and its connotation among the patriarchs whose personal life stands in a religious connection with the later life of the nation. Buber identifies "JHWH leads us" as the central ancient religious idea of Israel. This is not a matter of "theological metaphorics," for the Exodus account "presents the historical warrant of this leading in insurpassable concreteness" (Kingship of God, p. 23). Against the attempt to inaugurate Israel's relation with YAHWEH at the time of Moses, Buber stresses that "approximately twenty passages" say only what the Pentateuch has earlier said, and not that YAHWEH is known only from Moses' time. The revelation to Moses in Exodus 3 "demands almost a preceding explanation of who is thus speaking to Israel; no other than an already originated God can, even before the establishing of the covenant, even before the direct contact, say 'my people'" (p. 28). The title "God of Abraham, Isaac, and Jacob" becomes the standing designation of the God of Israel; its every use breathes a holy warmth.[18] The "seed of promise" and the "land of promise" which stand at the center of patriarchal expectation henceforth shape the hope of Israel in an ever profounder way.

The patriarchs knew God as ELOHIM, they knew him as EL SHADDAI, they knew his name as YAHWEH as well—but God's powerful redemptive disclosure as YAHWEH waited for the deliverance of his people in Moses' time. Moses' conversation with YAHWEH in Exodus 3:13-15 presupposes the earlier relationship between YAHWEH and the Hebrew patriarchs, not the utter novelty of a divine name. When in Exodus 3:13 he asks how he is to identify God to the chosen people, Moses does not seek some new and wholly unfamiliar name of God. Rather, as Mowinckel contends, "Moses asks for some 'control' evidence that his countrymen may know, when he returns to them, that it is really the God of their fathers that has sent him. . . . The whole conversation presupposes that the Israelites know this name already" (The Two Sources, p. 54). Edmond Jacob, too, writes, "We do not have in the Exodus narrative the revelation of a new name but the explanation of a name already known to Moses which in that solemn hour is discovered to be charged with a content the richness of which he was far from suspecting" (Theology of the Old Testament, p. 50).

What greater irony can be imagined than that the critical world-wisdom of liberal scholarship saw in the use of YAHWEH as an alterna-

18. Abba Hillel Silver comments: "There is no indication in all the early biblical records that in the patriarchal age the Hebrews worshipped any other god or that their God shared His sovereignty with other gods and goddesses. . . . It is to the Patriarchs that the Jewish people throughout subsequent ages invariably traced the origin of their faith—not to Moses or the later prophets. The Bible speaks of the Torah of Moses but never of the God of Moses, only of the God of Abraham, Isaac and Jacob" (Moses and the Original Torah, pp. 24 f.). Moses and Elijah, and Jesus also, support the view that the one and only God to whom Israel belongs is the God of Abraham, Isaac and Jacob.

tive to ELOHIM only two documents or redactors. Merely on the ground of literary evidence it had later to be conceded that the postulated differentiation of names was not preserved throughout the supposedly separate strata, and that each term crosses into the other. The use of different divine names provides no justification for confidently distinguishable documents.[19] Rather this striking feature supplies a clue to what modernist scholarship could miss only because of its bias against transcendent divine revelation, that is, to the living God who progressively discloses himself in fulfillment of his redemptive covenant. It was primarily because Israel's God was different from the gods affirmed by the other religions that Israel knew her religion to be different, and the incomparable uniqueness of Israel's God was known in connection with the self-disclosure of his Name.

---

19. "Whether the name YHWH *elohim* originated from YHWH *elohe elohim* and designated JHWH as chief of the gods (Nathaniel Schmidt, 'Yahwe Elohim,' JBL XXXIII, 1914, 44) or whether, as I assume, it originated from an act of identification, in any case *'elohim'* was understood appositionally by the reader of our texts" (Buber, *Kingship of God*, p. 189, n. 14).

15.
God's Proper Names:
Yahweh

THE DISTINCTIVE PROPER NAME of the God of Israel is YAHWEH.[1] Not only does this name occur more than 6,800 times in the Old Testament, but it alone—in contrast with ELOHIM and ADONAI—is never used in reference to other gods but is reserved exclusively for Israel's God. T. Rees called it "the personal proper name *par excellence* of Israel's God" and said pointedly that "Hebrew theology consists essentially of the doctrine of Jehovah and its implications" ("God," 2:1254b–1255a). YAHWEH's crowning historical manifestation occurs in dramatic special events in the life of the Hebrews: Israel's divine deliverance from Egyptian bondage, Israel's adoption as a chosen nation, and Israel's guidance into the promised land.

The derivation and original meaning of the word YAHWEH are unsure, and critical negation of the biblical testimony has served only to deepen the obscurity of the name. Modern interpreters have suggested a number of etymological derivations, but the resultant meanings are often artificial.

Evolutionary naturalists looked outside the Hebrew movement for the inspiration of almost all its distinctive ideas, but the meaning of YAHWEH will hardly be deciphered by the nonbiblical religions. The evolutionary bias long regnant in comparative religions study encouraged attempts to trace the term to Egyptian or Assyrian sources, or to propose early etymological connection with the Latin *Jove* (*Iovis*), but no objective evidence confirms such dependence. Explanations of the name

---

1. Translators of the Old Testament portion of *The New English Bible* substituted the title LORD for JAHWEH or JEHOVAH to promote readability.

YAHWEH in terms of natural phenomena, such as "He rains," or "He blows," betray their speculative origin at once. R. H. Pfeiffer held "this name . . . is not Hebrew but belongs to an otherwise unknown Semitic dialect" (*Introduction to the Old Testament*, p. 48). The Kenite hypothesis theorizes that Israel at Sinai was converted to the Kenite religion of YHWH as a fire-god (so Lods, *Israel*, pp. 367 ff., and Oesterley and Robinson, *Hebrew Religion*, 1930, pp. 110–14). Kenite derivation is supported by Ludwig Koehler (*Old Testament Theology*, pp. 42–45). Even in the modified form presented by Rowley (*The Faith of Israel*, p. 54) it can be accepted only by sacrificing the Exodus account. Kenite derivation must be considered only a convenient hypothesis until we know more Kenite; meanwhile we must agree with Buber that exegetical justification for the theory is lacking (*Kingship of God*, p. 33).

Edmond Jacob comments that "up to the present we have no attestation of Yahweh as a name for God outside Israel" (*Theology of the Old Testament*, p. 49). Since Genesis 4:26 suggests that men called on the name of YAHWEH long before the Mosaic age, it may be one of the very oldest names for God. Widespread approximations of the name (for example, its presence even in the name of Jupiter—*yu* = *yw* is *piter* = *pater* or father—hardly settles anything about its Hebrew derivation or conceptual content). Some scholars note, in view of the connection of YAHWEH with the verb "to be," that the Egyptian verb "to be" (*iw*) has a sound somewhat similar to YAHWEH. Others suggest that God's special name was taken over from pagan Canaanite neighbors, since the Ugaritic Tablets tell us that the supreme god had a son whose name is written *yw il*, which means "*yaw(e)*—is—god," but this is very meager evidence for the derivation of the Hebrew name of God from Ugaritic materials. Albright asserts that the many attempts to derive YAHWEH from the term *Yahu* have all broken down (*From the Stone Age to Christianity*, p. 259).

Both A. Murtoneau (*A Philological and Literary Treatise on the Old Testament Divine Names*) and von Rad have commented on the difficulty posed by the term YAHWEH, since etymological research "contributes little or nothing towards the theological significance of the name" (*Old Testament Theology*, p. 10). The question of the early significance of the root consonant is still unsure. Also, because the full name occurs thousands of times in the Old Testament, a study of etymological relationships is no minor task. Moreover, the short form YAH is also found in parts of the Old Testament (Exod. 15:2; Isa. 12:2; Ps. 68:18), and scholars are unsure whether this is (1) a poetic contraction (since it is nearly always found in poetical and liturgical composition, (2) an archaic survival in the ritual tradition, or (3) an exclamation of wonder (such as, "Oh!") in the presence of a mysterious divinity.

The crucial passage for the meaning of the term YAHWEH is Exodus 3:14. Quite apart from the etymological difficulty with YHWH, there is the uncertainty whether the Tetragrammaton is a nominal or verbal form.[2] If it is verbal, does it lead to the interpretation (based on the imperfect qal, a Hebrew verb stem), of "the passionate," "the one who loves passionately," as S. D. Goitein ("YHWH the Passionate," pp. 1 ff.) and others contend? Or does it lead to the interpretation (based on the imperfect hiphil, a Hebrew verb stem carrying a causative connotation) of the One who "calls into being," or "causes to be," as Albright contends (*From the Stone Age to Christianity*, pp. 259 ff.)? Or does it have some other significance? In view of the lack of scholarly agreement on the meaning of YAHWEH, Speiser warns that through these rigidly conflicting interpretations, "the name of Yahweh is constantly taken in vain" (*Genesis*, p. 38). But it would be remarkable indeed if the high point of the self-disclosure of the divine Name in revealed Hebrew religion were so obscure that, thirty-five hundred years later, biblical scholars are involved only in a game of blindman's buff.

Happily many scholars are moving beyond the semantic hypnosis that reduced "biblical understanding" to an analysis of word-structures and the derivation of their elements from root-originals. S. F. H. Berkelbach appropriately remarks that such exegesis is much like a historian's demolition of an ancient building into stones and rafters until he can visualize the quarry and forest from which they came, and loses the purpose of the structure (*Handboek voor de Prediking*, 1:37). It is contextual use more than etymological origin that determines the sense of meaning of concepts and words. There may be more truth than error in the somewhat sweeping comment of Morton Smith that "the Israelites and Jews preserved place names and adopted foreign names often without any knowledge of the original meaning, and often, when they did happen to know it, without any concern for it" ("Common Theology," p. 136). We need not suppose that the name YAHWEH was simply emblazoned on the sky; it was likely derived from something, if only from some feature or city that held special significance in the early days of Hebrew religion. We are not even sure it is a Hebrew word; it may, as R. Laird Harris thinks, have been only phonetically equated with the Hebrew verb "to be" (HWH), so that not only would the usual pronunciation be questionable, but all attempted etymological derivation would be unfruitful.

Can we then discern the meaning of the name YAHWEH by sensitivity to contextual considerations in the classical passage in Exodus? Five main

---

2. R. Laird Harris contends in a letter to me that the original Hebrew pronunciation is too uncertain to consider "Yahweh" the authentic pronunciation of the name of the God of Israel. This pronunciation assumes that the name is a verb form, and in Moses' day the pronunciation of such a verb form would not have ended in *h* but in *y*. During the history of the Hebrew language the form of verbs of this class was altered. Furthermore, he emphasizes, the name may not even be a verb form. In Exodus 3:14, the comment based on the name may be a play on words using the similar sounding verb "to be" (*hāyāh*), and not an etymological explanation.

interpretations are now proposed, and it will be well to devote some attention to each.

1. "I am the One who is." This translation has lost favor because of its assimilation by medieval scholastics and modern Roman Catholic scholars to the Greek view of eternal substance, because of the anti-metaphysical activist and existential temper of twentieth-century theology. There is indeed no basis in this text for any philosophy of static divine Being, and one can only deplore the speculative identification of YAHWEH with *ens realissimum* ("most real being"). Surely no abstract notion of *ontos on*[3] is here in view.

If, however, the Old Testament provides no basis for a speculative doctrine of Being, neither does it provide a basis for turning YAHWEH into an antimetaphysical symbol, and for denying that God in his self-revelation communicates some truth about his inmost nature. The Psalmist can call the people to "know that YAHWEH is the Godhead" (Ps. 100:3). If YAHWEH suggests the eternity of his divine Being, the God who is faithful from generation to generation as the One who is, and we recognize that his self-existence and metaphysical independence are less explicit than implicit in this assurance, the interpretation satisfies the rules of Hebrew word-formation which indicate a statement about being rather than about acting. If we derive the sense of YAHWEH from the common Hebrew verb *hayah* ("to be"), an abstract metaphysical sense is not at all precluded. The French version regularly uses *l'éternelle*, and James Moffatt everywhere translates YAHWEH by "the Eternal," the "always being."

When, therefore, von Rad tells us that the text does not envisage "a definition of his nature in the sense of a philosophical statement about his being . . . a suggestion, for example, of his absoluteness, aseity, etc." (*Old Testament Theology*, p. 180), we may surely commend von Rad's desire to differentiate the revelation of YAHWEH from the postulations of abstract metaphysics, yet we shall need to ask whether an antimetaphysical bias or anti-intellective view of revelation underlies this warning. On the ground that such definition "would be altogether out of keeping with the Old Testament," von Rad cautions against overestimating the importance of the words "I am that I am" as "a theological first principle. . . . We are certainly not to assume that the narrator's intention was thus to give the interpretative formula of the name which was theologically fundamental and normative for Israel" (p. 181). Von Rad contends that except for Hosea 1:9 ("And I, I am no longer yours") other Old Testament passages lack any etymological interpretation of

---

3. As proposed, for example, by the Benedictine scholar Paul Heinisch: "The phrase cannot denote that kind of existence which is shared by things in general; it implies that God possesses existence by His very nature, that His existence is from Himself, that His origin is not from some other being. Philosophically expressed . . . He *is* being" (*Theology of the Old Testament*, p. 55).

the name YAHWEH, and that less ambiguous theological alternatives
("YAHWEH, YAHWEH, a God merciful and gracious, slow to anger, and
abounding in steadfast love and faithfulness," Exod. 34:6, RSV, and "YAH-
WEH, whose name is Jealous," Exod. 34:14, RSV) indicate different angles
from which the name YAHWEH was understood. Von Rad therefore
erodes confidence in Exodus 3:14 as "a final axiomatic formula" epitomiz-
ing the nature of YAHWEH's revelation.[4]

But unless we recognize in this revelation of the divine Name a supreme manifestation of the close connection between God's character
and his deeds—an idea von Rad himself considers of "quite fundamental
importance" for the cultic life of the ancient East—we cannot adequately
explain the strategic importance that the revelation at the exodus came
to hold in the Hebrew worship of YAHWEH. The divine presence is today
often misinterpreted in the framework of modern epistemological
theories that exclude the rational significance of revelation and spe-
ciously rule out any possibility of God's disclosure of conceptual truth
about himself and his purposes. In consequence, the revelation of
YAHWEH's presence remains exposed to the crudest religious misunderstanding.[5] We are indebted to Edmond Jacob who, though too hur-
riedly setting aside any revelation of God's self-subsistence in Exodus
6:3, nonetheless puts us on guard against the prevalent modern antimetaphysical bias. "It must not be supposed from the little grasp which the
Israelites had of abstract ideas that they were incapable of understanding the reality of being and it is not attributing to them a metaphysics
too highly developed when we imagine they could define God as 'he who
is' over against things which aie temporary—the succession of days and
seasons, the verdure of the desert which grows and withers, flocks which
are born and die, the successive generations, men whose bodies return to
the dust. The Old Testament is full of statements about the eternity of
Yahweh as over against the ephemeral character of all created things

---

4. It is noteworthy that Jesus' allusion to Exodus 3:14 fits the *I am* into a patriarchal context: "Before Abraham was, I am" (John 8:58, KJV). The statement is emphatic of his eternal divine existence; the "I am" does not take an object but is
absolute and emphatic. It may point also to the fact that in fulfillment of Abraham's
messianic expectation (8:56) he as divine agent (8:28, 40) sent from the eternal order
(8:42) unveils the Father's glory in the midst of Jewry (8:49–55).

5. When, for example, von Rad finds in the striking statements about YAHWEH's
name in Deuteronomy (12:5, 11, 21; 14:24; 26:19, etc.) an obvious attack on "the
older and more popular idea of Jahweh's immediate presence at the place of worship" and the substitution of "the theological differentiation between Jahweh on the
one hand and his name on the other, a severance which is carried through to the
point of spatial separation" (ibid., p. 184), we cannot refrain from asking many questions. Not only does this interpretation objectionably divorce the Name from the true
character of God but its assumption that in earlier disclosures of God's presence the
Hebrews were ignorant of the transcendence of God can only be ascribed to evolutionary views contradicted by the biblical narratives. That the Hebrews periodically
lapsed into pagan ideas and practices is not in dispute; that these were part of their
official religion is quite another matter, and one without warrant.

(Ps. 90:1; 102:27–28), the God of Israel does not die (Hab. 1:12), the terms eternity and Yahweh are sometimes even synonymous" (*Theology of the Old Testament*, pp. 51 f.).

Even if we insist that the context does not permit us to understand YAHWEH solely in terms of the eternality of God, and emphasize that in any event we are here not given a philosophical elaboration of a doctrine of divine Substance, we must wholly resist the notion that the revelation of divine eternity would be "too advanced a metaphysical conception of God for an early nomad people" (Oesterly and Robinson, *Hebrew Religion*, p. 153), or that such a divine revelation is inadmissible because it would imply an extraordinary "break" in the historical development. What else does divine revelation imply but an advance beyond man's own conceptions?

If the emphasis on God's independent divine Being is not wholly adequate to explain the revelation of YAHWEH, the objection must not assume that this conception is beyond the early mentality of the Hebrews, nor that divine revelation has merely a practical and nontheoretical significance, but rather that in context this explanation does not seem fully to correspond to the situation of Moses and the Hebrews.

2. "*I am who I am*" (cf. Exod. 33:19; 34:6). On this view, YAHWEH suspends his disclosure upon his free activity as Israel's sovereign, withholds the full meaning of his Name, and does not commit himself to Moses (lest Moses invoke his Name at will for the demonstration of miraculous power). Barth's dialectical theory of revelation clearly underlies his emphasis that "the great revelation of the name in Ex. 3 consists precisely in a refusal of the name" (*Church Dogmatics*, I/1, p. 370). Von Rad stresses that even in his self-manifestation in Moses' time, YAHWEH reserves his freedom to himself and therefore—so von Rad contends—communicates no fixed knowledge.[6]

Walter Harrelson contends that YAHWEH "both hides Himself and reveals Himself in this encounter with Moses. . . . Moses properly asks for and is given His name. Yet the meaning of the name is not fully explicated: it is to be accepted as—a name! The name of God, in short, does not provide the knower with power over the one named" (*Interpreting the Old Testament*, p. 79). The Catholic scholar A. M. Dubarle argues that Exodus 3:14 marks God's refusal to disclose his name at a mere mortal's request ("La signification du nom de Iahweh") and Gustav Lambert takes essentially the same tack ("Que signifie le nom

---

6. YAHWEH had indeed associated his name "with the free manifestation in history of his self-revelation in history. The formula which occurs so frequently in Ezekiel, 'and they will know that I am Jahweh,' shows this indissoluble welding-together of Jahweh's name and his self-revelation just as clearly as does the preface to the decalogue, which also interprets the name in the light of the redemptive historical act. Thus from the very start Israel . . . was not in a position to appropriate the name of Jahweh and make it an object of an abstruse mythology or of speculation: it was to be understood only in historical experience" (von Rad, *Old Testament Theology*, pp. 185 f.).

divin YHWH?" pp. 897 ff.). Helmut Rosin holds that untranslatableness of YHWH as a name signals its absolute uniqueness and the impossibility of converting it into any general concept or definition in advance of future revelational guarantees (*The Lord Is God*, 1955). Rosin contends there should be no missionary translation of the untranslatable name lest YAHWEH be equated with what he is not, and we conceal his nature as the God wholly free to act.

With any emphasis that God is not exhaustively revealed in his self-disclosure we wholly agree. Surely God's progressive self-revelation has not even yet erased all elements of divine mystery and epistemic transcendence. But this theory fails to do justice to the intimate relationship between the divine Name and nature in biblical theology, and to the divine disclosure of reliable and authentic religious knowledge. It superimposes on the biblical religious situation a dialectical or existential misunderstanding of revelation shaped by recent European theological speculation, and thereby exaggerates divine transcendence at the expense of cognitive revelation. Edmond Jacob's reminder is surely to the point: Moses was "on a Divine mission which demands precise information" (*Theology of the Old Testament*, p. 51). In order to dissociate YAHWEH from all conjuration it is not necessary to existentialize or dialecticize his self-revelation. That the living God cannot be summoned or controlled at man's whim, but establishes his relationship with Israel at his own initiative, is integral to the body of biblically revealed truth: "I will be gracious to whom I will be gracious, and will show mercy on whom I will show mercy" (Exod. 33:19, RSV). But to contend that this sovereign freedom of God demands his "indefinite definiteness" (so Miskotte, *When the Gods are Silent*, p. 176) is nonsense, for then we have no transcendent basis for definiteness even about this interpretation of what was the case.

Ian T. Ramsey holds that God has not revealed his name, and that the ideal religious situation precludes his doing so. According to Ramsey, "the logical structure of the phrase given as God's name" in Exodus 3 "is not at all a personal proper name" but rather it is "a phrase which could be posited by the religious man to do justice to the commitment his religion carries with it" (*Religious Language*, p. 127). "The true logical point," Ramsey contends, lies in the tautology: "I'm I," which discloses a final option. As such it is not even a statement of God's nature or a promise of his faithfulness, however possible these variants may be on the basis of the Hebrew language. "What is given in Ex. 3 as the name of God, is not a 'name' . . . but a phrase . . . men can use . . . of that full commitment in which . . . loyalty to God is expressed" (p. 128).

The turning point of Ramsey's contention that God deliberately withholds his name (in some contexts Ramsey inconsistently says that God does not reveal his name "completely" or "fully") is that all divine mystery would be destroyed and men would inevitably fall into idolatry were God to make his name known. He asserts: "It is a well known fact of Old Testament theology that the Hebrews were nervous about naming God" (ibid., p. 124). Ramsey supports his contention (1) by noting that the sacred Tetragrammaton was never pronounced, and (2) by espousing a philosophical theory of religious experience that in principle would dissolve the cognitive significance of all the divine names.

Quite apart from the question whether Ramsey accurately assesses the attitudes of Old Testament Jewry, there was not on the part of Christians—the early Christian Hebrews included—least of all by Jesus of Nazareth, any reluctance to use the divine Name.[7] Indeed, Christians gloried in the Name, insisted there is "no other Name" whereby mankind could be redeemed (Acts 4:12), and they explicitly baptized converts in the Name. But is it really a "fact" of Old Testament times that "the Hebrews were nervous about naming God"? If Ramsey means that they refused to invent names for God, then his remark defectively understates their disapproval. If he means that they normatively hesitated to use the divinely revealed names, then the comment defectively overstates the situation. For avoidance of the divine Name was not at all characteristic of Israel at her prime. Nonpronunciation of the Tetragrammaton was a late development of the intertestamental period, and was due to scribal superstition.

While those who know God's Name might fall into religious formalism and idolatry, ignorance of the divine Name would seem to make idolatry unavoidable if not inevitable. The Hebrews in their periodic apostasy did lapse into idolatry, not because they knew the Name, but because they forsook the Name. If nonknowledge of the Name precludes idolatry, what, on Ramsey's premises, would account for the periodic lapses of the Hebrews? To argue, as Ramsey does, that "the inevitable elusiveness of the divine name is the logical safeguard against universal idolatry" (ibid., p. 129) inverts the logic and history of Hebrew religious commitment. Moreover, the notion that God's mystery logically requires his anonymity places Ramsey in the peculiar position of peddling secrets about divinity which, on his own theory, ought to be universally hidden.

Furthermore, Ramsey's occasional qualifiers "fully" and "completely" serve to confuse the issue of the revelation of God's Name. Are these terms the opposite of "partly," or of a total withholding of the divine Name? Ramsey helps matters when, elsewhere, he uses the term "approximate." In any event, the notion that the religious situation would be lost unless "only God could know his own name" (ibid., p. 129), presupposes that the religious situation ideally exists in a cognitive vacuity. This modern philosophical premise is grossly out of harmony with the actualities of biblical religion.

With these views, associating the term YAHWEH with the hiddenness

---

7. It is noteworthy that the *Manual of Discipline of the Dead Sea Scrolls* even uses the term *Name* as a circumlocution for the Tetragrammaton. YAHWEH was apparently sacred at Qumran since bowls discovered in the scriptorium were probably used by scribes to wash their hands before copying the Sacred Name in a manuscript.

and sovereign freedom of God, we reach an almost total contradiction of Umberto Cassuto's insistence that when the Hebrews spoke lucidly of God's attributes they used the name YAHWEH, and used ELOHIM when they spoke more generally and obscurely about God (*The Documentary Hypothesis*, 1941). No evangelical theologian has ever doubted that there is more to God than we know. But God either reveals his Name or he does not.

3. *"I will be what I will be"* (cf. Exod. 33:19). Current interest in process theology has encouraged some contemporary religious philosophers to assign the Exodus text an activist, futurist interpretation. But if the rules of Hebrew word-formation are decisive, it must be a statement about being, not acting. The attempt to impose modern process philosophy upon the Mosaic account has no solid basis either in Hebrew linguistics or in Hebrew theology. The Hebrews, moreover, would not have been misled by modern notions that the world is as necessary to God as God is to the world. They knew God as sovereign Creator.

Calvin long ago noted that the future tense here in the Hebrew has the same force as the present: "He is self-existent and therefore eternal: and thus gives being and existence to every creature." YAHWEH is (Exod. 3:15, ASV) "the God of your fathers," The fathers had lived centuries earlier, but YAHWEH is the same.

4. *"I cause to be what I cause to be,"* or *"I cause to be what occurs."* On this view YAHWEH's disclosure is that as Creator of the universe and Maker of the Covenant he is able to fulfill his purpose for his people in Egypt. Albright contends that the enigmatic formula "I am what I am" must be understood by deriving YAHWEH from the verbal stem HWY ("to fall, become, come into existence") and hence, in the third person singular, the meaning in the hiphil (or causative) would be "he causes to be what comes into existence" (*From the Stone Age to Christianity*, p. 261). Albright seeks to justify this rather abstract idea of divine causal action by citing Babylonian, Canaanite and Egyptian analogies from the second millennium B.C. Julian Obermann supports the view by an appeal to Phoenician inscriptions also ("The Divine Name YHWH in the Light of Recent Discoveries," p. 301).

But many scholars consider this interpretation highly vulnerable. Norman Walker, replying to the similar view of David Noel Freedman ("The Name of the God of Moses," pp. 152 ff.), in a critical note in the subsequent issue of the *Journal of Biblical Literature* (p. 277), rejects it as "conjuring up a non-existent hiphil form" (since the existence of the verb *hawah* in the hiphil is nowhere attested). He insists, less convincingly, that "the idea of 'causing to be' is foreign to the Hebrew mentality." R. Laird Harris considers most difficult any verbal derivation of the name and meaning of YAHWEH from outside sources. The *W* of YAHWEH is a problem, he comments. The ordinary verb for "become," "be," in Hebrew is HWH and in Hebrew a *W* at the beginning of a syllable usually turns

to *Y*. What, he asks, is the relation of "to fall" and "to come into existence"? "Cause to be" should be *Yahyeh*.

Although the Israelites long regarded YAHWEH as "Creator of All," this
does not necessarily predetermine the revealed meaning of YAHWEH in
the Exodus account, particularly since the fact of creation had long been
associated with the name ELOHIM. Moreover, Silver notes that the name
EL ELYON, known to the patriarchs, already included the notion of "He
who causes to be" in the sense of Creator. He thinks YAHWEH designates
the "Accomplisher," "He who performs what He promises" (*Moses and
the Original Torah*, p. 25). He quotes Jewish writers who interpret the
meaning of YAHWEH as "I can be trusted" (to make good, or to fulfill
my Word).

5. *"I am present is what I am."* On this view YAHWEH emphasizes his
living active presence, responsive to the needs of Moses and his people,
in whose behalf he is redemptively ready to intervene. YAHWEH speaks
not of "the being of God," writes Miskotte, but of "the presence of God,"
and especially "his presence in his activity," in which he "reserves the
freedom to act as he wills" (*When the Gods Are Silent*, p. 121). "He can
be known only in His acts" (p. 122). YAHWEH is here understood not in
a metaphysical sense but in an active, phenomenological sense as he who
executes his promises ("I will be with you"; "I will be your mouth"; "I
am YAHWEH . . . and I have remembered my covenant" (Exod. 6:2–4).
Koehler contends that because YAHWEH was revealed to Moses by his
divine works, therefore no revelation of the secret of his nature is given
and " 'I am who I am' is . . . *Deus Absconditus* in the strictest sense"
(*Old Testament Theology*, p. 242).

On the surface much may seem to commend a merely phenomenological interpretation. In the context of the Mosaic revelation at the exodus, and frequently also in the larger Old Testament disclosure, YAHWEH
gives unyielding assurance of his personal presence and active deliverance. In context, God's self-revelation of his Name to Moses does not
seem to imply God's disclosure either as eternal unchanging Being or as
Creator of all, but rather as Israel's redemptive Deliverer. This fuller
revelation to Israel thus involves YAHWEH's disclosure, as A. B. Davidson
expresses it, not of an ontological name, but of a redemptive name (*The
Theology of the Old Testament*, p. 47). The preceding contextual stress
is on the words "Certainly I will be with thee" (Exod. 3:12, KJV; compare
2 Sam. 24:16 for the use of the verb *hayah* in the sense of "be [found]
with"). Here one thinks of numerous passages in which the Name of God
signals his presence (Deut. 12:11, 21; 14:23–24; 16:2, 11; 26:2; Neh. 1:9;
Ps. 74:7; Isa. 18:7; Jer. 3:17; 7:10–13, 30).

But can the notion of presence be derived from the root of the word,
or from the term YAHWEH itself, or is this an illegitimate transfer of
meaning? The root *haya* is used, albeit in a secondary sense, for "to
abide," when accompanied by stipulations of place and time. But how-

ever interesting or even plausible in connection with certain theories the etymological study of the name of YAHWEH may be, it cannot supply information conclusive for its meaning and content beyond that indicated in the scriptural source, which does not indicate that etymological analysis provided the spiritual vitality of this dramatic biblical episode.

Martin Buber emphasizes the correspondence of the meaning "I will *be* there" (to vindicate his revelation in person) with God's promise to Moses in Exodus 3:12 (*Moses*, pp. 18, 19, 53). It is noteworthy that *'ehyeh* is used in the sense of "being present" (*adesse*) in 3:12 (KJV), "I will be with thee" and in "I will be thy mouth" (cf. Gen. 31:3, KJV, where "I will be with thee" marks the promise of special assistance and protection for Jacob). Edmond Jacob writes, "To make the people aware of the presence of Yahweh in their midst was exactly the task committed to Moses. . . . The priority of presence over existence gives a new and unexpected aspect to all the interventions of Yahweh; the presence of Yahweh corresponds each time to a new approach and the prophets stigmatize as a grave illusion the faith of those who interpreted the 'God is with us' in the sense of a definite and inalienable possession" (*Theology of the Old Testament*, pp. 52 f.). J. Barton Payne supports the emphasis on God's testamental nature as "faithful presence" in his self-disclosure as YAHWEH (cf. Exod. 6:2, 4; Deut. 7:9; Isa. 26:4) (*Theology of the Older Testament*, p. 148). "God is rather Jahve," asserts Oehler, "in as far as He has entered into an *historical* relation to mankind, and in particular to the chosen people, and shows Himself continually in this historical relation as He who is, and who is what He is" (*Theology of the Old Testament*, p. 95). The revelation to the oppressed people centers in YAHWEH's manifestation in rescuing grace. Thus God identifies himself as that same YAHWEH who in covenantal care singled out Abraham, Isaac and Jacob. There he called out one family and its posterity; now he calls out a nation. God answers the question regarding his name or nature (Exod. 3:13) in verb form: "I am" or "I will be" or "I will be present."

Yet, if we emphasize here God's redemptive revelation, we have really no basis on that account to delete all transcendent ontological or metaphysical connotations from YAHWEH, and to espouse a dynamic view of revelation that leaves to prophetic voices the ingenious discernment of what YAHWEH is doing. It is precisely the Exodus narrative that emphasizes that God clearly reveals his purpose before he acts in redemptive rescue. Although philosophical metaphysical conjecture is excluded, that the living God reveals himself as Creator and as the eternal and independent Lord of all, who in sovereign freedom works out his redemptive purpose in history, is nonetheless integral to the biblical view of divine disclosure. While the forward-looking manifestation of YAHWEH has in view the pledge of redemptive presence, the name YAHWEH accumulates to itself all that the patriarchs had already known about God. The Hebrew verb "to be" had originally to do with absolute existence, not relative relationships. In our view, YAHWEH is the revelation of the Eternal, the independent sovereign of all, who pledges in free grace to come to the redemptive rescue of his chosen people. *The God who is,* who is *eternally there,* will personally manifest his redemptive presence in Israel's midst.

If, Moses asks, when he explains that he is sent by "the God of your fathers," the Israelites should ask "What is his name?" what answer is he to give? God replies to Moses: *"I am that I am . . .* say *. . . I am* hath sent me. . . . say . . . YAHWEH the God of your fathers, the God of Abraham, the God of Isaac, and the God of Jacob, hath sent me . . . this is my name for ever, and this is my memorial unto all generations . . . . say . . . YAHWEH the God of your fathers, the God of Abraham, of Isaac, and of Jacob, appeared unto me. . . . unto the king . . . say . . . YAHWEH the God of the Hebrews hath met with us. . . . Let us go . . . three days' journey into the wilderness, that we may sacrifice to YAHWEH our God. . . . the king of Egypt will not let you go. . . . And I will . . . smite Egypt with all my wonders . . . and after that will he let you go. And I will give this people favour in the sight of the Egyptians . . . . And Moses answered . . . they will say, YAHWEH hath not appeared unto thee" (Exod. 3:13–4:1, KJV).

By the serpent-rod God manifests his presence "that they may believe that YAHWEH the God of their fathers, the God of Abraham, the God of Isaac, and the God of Jacob, hath appeared" (Exod. 4:5, KJV). By the miracle of the leprous hand he again manifests himself, saying, "If they will not believe . . . these two signs" there will follow the changing of the water into blood. A God angered by Moses' hesitancy then dispatches him to his people and tells him to go bearing "this rod . . . wherewith thou shalt do [the] signs" (Exod. 4:9, 17, KJV). This context seems to require for the understanding of "I am that I am" God's special redemptive solicitude and presence in behalf of his people.

We must now focus on etymological considerations. In Exodus 3:14 YAHWEH is said to be the equivalent of *'ehyeh* (an abbreviated form of *'ehyeh 'asher 'ehyeh,*[8] translated "I am that I am"). For good reason the Hebrews connected the name YAHWEH with *hayah,* "to be." For through the striking formula, "I shall be to you a God" (Gen. 17:7; cf. Exod. 6:7; Lev. 11:45; 26:12, 45; Deut. 29:13; Jer. 31:33; 32:38), God manifests himself in the patriarchal period as the covenant God of Abraham, Isaac and Jacob. This "I shall be" finds its expression as a present indicative, "I am," in the revelation to Moses; the God of the covenant relation bares himself redemptively in Israel's present need. The "I shall be," which almost always has a covenantal sense, retains this sense in the divine disclosure "I am," which dramatically connects this covenant relation with the immediate crisis in Hebrew history. And the name YAHWEH is simply the imperfect third person masculine of the same form: "He is." YAHWEH is the God of covenant promise, of covenant re-

---

8. Harris thinks this expression is mere word play.

lation, whose active redemptive concern for his people *is*—is not merely a *memory* of past history, is not merely a *future hope*, but *is*.

In the exodus revelation God "gave himself away" to Israel—within his freedom indeed, yet bound by covenant to historical redemptive deliverance. This pledge of nearness and ready help guaranteed by his word and character assured Israel of access to his heart. The Old Testament scholar William J. Martin notes that the niphal (the passive of the qal stem) form *yechaway* (Jehaweh) would acquire a tolerative sense, "He suffered himself to be" (cf. "Seek the Lord while he suffers himself to be found"). YAHWEH will come to Israel's aid "for his name's sake" (Pss. 23:3; 25:11; 143:11; Jer. 14:7; Isa. 48:9). God's *coming* to man, his special redemptive activity, thus historically vindicates his Name through his free initiative in gracious disclosure to a chosen people.

This Name, this revelation of God as the divine redemptive intervener, is the Name whereby God desires to be known: "YAHWEH . . . this is my name for ever, and this is my memorial unto all generations" (Exod. 3:15, KJV). The tabernacle itself objectively embodies this truth (Exod. 29:43-46) and YAHWEH is used always in the Old Testament as the memorial name of God. The Old Testament associates God's special presence with the Ark of the Covenant which links God's reality with his promises. In the golden calf idolatry (Exod. 32) the Hebrews reintroduced the pagan Egyptian motif of the immanent nature-and-fertility deity, which misconceives divine presence and blurs the transcendent Creator who speaks his Word and publishes his purposes. "In the cult, the divine name was used by Israel at sacrifice, in prayer, in blessing and cursing, and also in holy war," notes von Rad, "and it had been given her for this purpose" (*Old Testament Theology*, p. 183). "To hallow the name of Jahweh was tantamount in itself to acknowledging the uniqueness and exclusiveness of the cult of Israel *per se*. Wherever Israel in any way opened its doors to the cult of another deity, the name of Jahweh was profaned. . . . On the positive side, the name was hallowed by obedience to the commandments, by 'walking in the name of Jahweh'" (p. 184).

The revelation of YAHWEH's will is the main theme of the entire Sinai tradition: YAHWEH has revealed to his people those binding ordinances which make possible human life in his service and communion. The decisive and preeminent factor is not the exceptional position of Sinai or the exceptional role of Moses, but beyond these, the unique history that YAHWEH has made possible. The commandments assert YAHWEH's sovereign rights over man and summarize YAHWEH's holy will for man. The Decalogue is introduced by the words: "I am YAHWEH, your God" (cf. von Rad, ibid., p. 192, n. 11). It was the "glory of YAHWEH" that came down upon Sinai; the "glory of YAHWEH" that came down upon and filled the tabernacle; the "glory of YAHWEH" that approved the first sacrifice offered after the consecration of Aaron and his sons as priests. In short, not only does YAHWEH disclose the fundamental requirements through which Israel may experience life before and with God, but the "glory of YAHWEH" comes to dwell in the very midst of Israel.

Franz Delitzsch asserts that the names ELOHIM, EL SHADDAI and YAHWEH are "the sign-manual of three degrees of Divine revelation and Divine knowledge . . . (the first) the God who so made nature that it exists, and so preserves it that it consists . . . (the second) the God who so constrains nature that it does His will, and so subdues it that it bows to and subserves grace . . . (the third) the God who carries out the purposes of grace in the midst of nature, and at last puts a new creation of grace in the place of nature" (*A New Commentary on Genesis*, 2:32). Oehler notes the displacement of earlier names in deference to the later and larger revelation: "As soon as the name *Jehovah* unfolds its meaning, the name El-Shaddai falls back on the one hand into the list of the *more general names of God. . . .* But, on the other hand, it is still used at times *alternately with the name Jehovah* where God's omnipotence is made prominent in contrast with human weakness" (*Theology of the Old Testament*, p. 91).

In conclusion, we must consider also the divine name ADONAI.

The name ADONAI appears first in Genesis 15:2 and 8. *Adon* is the Hebrew word for "owner," "master," "lord." It is used of both divine and human relationships. When applied to God, it denotes his role as divine ruler (Ps. 2:4; Isa. 7:7) and emphasizes his power over man and the world as the giver of life and death. Hence, like EL and its combinations, ADONAI stresses God's sovereignty. In Malachi 1:6 the usage demonstrates God's claim upon man's service. In some occurrences it is conjoined to ELOHIM and also frequently to YAHWEH.

In the early period the name BAAL was applied to God as a synonym for ADONAI in the sense of "owner" (1 Chron. 8:33), but the prophets later opposed this use when that name became generally associated with the pagan Baalim and thus acquired an idolatrous meaning (contrast 2 Sam. 2:8 with Hos. 2:16–17).

Additional names for God appear in the post-Mosaic era, although some are compounds of ELOHIM and YAHWEH. Some may be descriptive phrases rather than names. Payne mentions EL HAI, "living God" (Josh. 3:10), used synonymously with YAHWEH; ELOHIM Q'DHOSHIM, "holy God" (Josh. 24:19); YAHWEH SEVAOTH, "God of hosts" or "of armies" (1 Sam. 1:3, etc.); and also BAAL (1 Chron. 8:33) (*The Theology of the Older Testament*, p. 150). But new names for deity are no longer found in Israel's consolidation period (Robert Dick Wilson, "The Names of God in the Psalms," pp. 1–39, provides a useful study of the divine names in the literature of the Psalms).

Some scholars consider Daniel's use of "God of heaven" (Dan. 2:37) to be the final Old Testament development in the use of divine names. The absence of all divine names from the Book of Esther has long been a subject of theological discussion, the problem being posed by the fact that it is a conspicuous exception. Even the phrase "God of heaven" is found only in the Aramaic portions of Daniel-Ezra, and usually in a context relating to unbelievers; its correlation by some scholars with a descriptive phrase for God's sovereign and universal power found in Genesis (24:3-7) is questionable. In contexts in which the name YAHWEH is not employed, it is an apt description for general use.

In the post-Old Testament period, pronunciation of the divine Name was avoided through superstitious reverence, and the term *Heaven* became a substitute (cf. 1 Macc. 3:18-19, NEB, and elsewhere in the Apocrypha). But the inspired writings do not share any avoidance of the divine Name, since in the revealed Name the living God discloses his nature and individuality.

In the intertestamental period the name YAHWEH was no longer pronounced aloud in the synagogues, apparently to accommodate scribal superstition. The name was replaced orally (although not in writing) by ADONAI. Yet the Old Testament texts themselves not infrequently carry the conjunctive YAHWEH-ADONAI. When the medieval Masoretes later added vowel points to the consonantal text YHWH, they combined the Tetragrammaton with the vowel points of ADONAI. The curious end result was "Jehovah" (used by the American Standard Version). *The Jerusalem Bible* regularly uses YAHWEH. Recent studies emphasize the late emergence of the "ineffable Name" concept in Judaism, and support the notion that during the intertestamental and early Christian era Jews on occasion reversed their practice: if others held the name to be secret, they pronounced it; if others used it publicly, they declared it to be ineffable. The English translation of the Old Testament issued by the Jewish Publication Society of America in 1917, and especially adapted for use in Hebrew synagogues and schools, retained I AM for the name of God in Exodus 3:14. Except in Exodus 6:3, where YHWH was retained (with the footnote: "the ineffable name, read *Adonai*, which means, the Lord"), it elsewhere translated YAHWEH by LORD.

But the use of ADONAI for God carries over in the New Testament identification of Jesus Christ as LORD. The Septuagint commonly used the Greek word KURIOS (LORD) to render the Hebrew ADONAI and—as Vincent Taylor notes—"what is more important, it is the usual substitute for the personal name 'Yahweh'" (*The Names of Jesus*, p. 39). Taylor pointedly remarks: "The first Christians read the Old Testament with new eyes, and as soon as Jesus was confessed as 'the Lord,' many ancient passages which spoke of the Lord must have been applied to Him. Septuagint usage is not, therefore, a factor which can be ignored in stimulating the use of the title" (p. 51).

The Old Testament therefore exhibits two principle names of God, one of sovereign power and the other of redemptive presence: ELOHIM, the Creator and Ruler, and YAHWEH, the Covenantal Redeemer. Erich Sauer has pointed out that, while names of God occur about ten thousand times in the Old Testament, the name ELOHIM is found 2,570 and YAHWEH some 6,000 times (*The Dawn of World Redemption*, p. 187). ADONAI occurs 450 times, the next largest number. The double name YAHWEH-ELOHIM correlates the comprehensive work of God in creative power and redemptive grace, even as the New Testament depicts the LOGOS as the agent both in creation and in redemption.

16.
Jesus:
The Revelation
of the New Testament Name

SOME FORTY TIMES the New Testament focuses on *the name of God* (fifteen times in Old Testament quotations) and always in the Old Testament sense of "the revealed nature and character of the Savior God." The distinctive feature of New Testament usage is, as Raymond Abba says, "the way in which the name of Jesus is either substituted for, or placed alongside, the name of God. . . . Prophesying or speaking in the name of God becomes prophesying or speaking in the name of Jesus" ("Name," 3:506). In Ch. Biber's words, "The great novelty of the N.T. in the use of the supreme name is that *the name of Jesus Christ* comes to be subordinated, substituted, and joined to the name of God" ("Name," p. 280a). Miskotte more pointedly makes much the same comment: "From the beginning the church understood the Name of God and Jesus Christ to be one and the same. It has not merely experienced the 'infinite fascination' of combining by a process of thought the uniqueness of YHWH and the concrete 'once-for-all-ness' of Jesus; it knows no other name under heaven given among men by which they may be saved (Acts 4:12) except Christ" (*When the Gods Are Silent*, p. 77).

Recalling the sacred events of the first century, R. E. Brown remarks that if Jesus could be given the title LORD, "why could he not be called *theos*, which the Septuagint often used to translate *elohim?* The two Hebrew terms had become relatively interchangeable, and indeed YHWH was the more sacred term" (*Jesus, God and Man*, p. 29). In the early assertion of Jesus' absolute lordship Richard N. Longenecker already sees a rough equivalence to the title GOD, and correlates their definite ascription of this title by the apostles with the cosmic and philosophical claims they affirmed alongside the religious. Longenecker notes, moreover, that the explicit designation occurs more prominently in the Jewish-Christian literature than in writings distinctive of the church's Gentile mission (*The Christology of Early Jewish Christianity*, pp. 136–41; cf. pp. 44 f.).

Of the allusions to the divine name I AM (Isa. 43:10) in John 8:28 and 13:19, C. H. Dodd says that "the implication would seem to be that God has given his own Name to Christ," as is in fact stated in John 17:11. Associated in the Old Testament with God's glory (cf. Isa. 42:8), the Name appears in a series of Johannine assertions (12:23, 28; 17:5) in which "the eternal glory of God is given to Christ, and in the same act the Name of God is glorified" (*The Interpretation of the Fourth Gospel*, p. 95). According to John's Gospel Jesus Christ's mission in the world was to make the Name of God known (17:6), and this mission he fulfilled (17:26). In the high priestly prayer Jesus declared that as the obedient SON he had revealed the whole nature of God: "I have manifested thy name" (17:6, RSV).

In his high priestly prayer (John 17:6) Jesus refers to his disclosure of the Father's name. Dodd considers this a possible allusion to the *shem hammophorash* or disguised pronunciation of the Sacred Name in the interbiblical period, alongside God's quasi-identification with his people reflected in the Son's solidarity with the Father (ibid., pp. 94 ff.). With the unveiling of this name the New Testament acquiesces in the total loss of the Tetragrammaton. Whereas the Hebrews used the Tetragrammaton out of a sense of awe to emphasize the distance between God and man, their denial of Jesus as "the sent One" now implies the total forfeiture of the God of promise (cf. John 5:24–27). Israel's tragedy lies in its supposed devotion to YAHWEH in the Temple made with hands while repudiating Jesus Christ as a blasphemer, with a consequent loss of both the Temple and the enfleshed I AM (cf. John 2:19–21).

The schism between Judaism and Christianity rises from a conflict over divine sonship. Jewry understands itself in distinction from all mankind as the covenant-people of God specially accessible to repentance and spiritual renewal. Christianity points centrally to the incarnate Christ as the model of obedient divine sonship. "If the name of God is the symbol of His true nature," remarks Dodd on John 17:6, "then the revelation of the Name which Christ gives is that unity of Father and Son to which He bears witness" (ibid., p. 96). For Jews the Old Testament has its sequel in the Talmud; for Christianity, in the New Testament. Overshadowing this contrast is the interpretation of Scripture primarily as Law, dating from the exile, and the consequent emphasis on legalism at the expense of the divine Name and of prophetic fulfillment.

At the very outset, the New Testament locates in Old Testament prophecy the remarkable name of the promised Redeemer: GOD WITH US (Matt. 1:23). The words recall at once not only the Septuagint translation of EMMANUEL of Isaiah 7:14, but also YAHWEH's name revealed to Moses:

Present is what I am. The Gospels offer us, in a word, YAHWEH unchangeably faithful to his covenant engagement, the present I AM, the incarnate God.

The Gospels portray GOD WITH US for a limited season in the flesh: "Me ye have not always" (John 12:8, KJV). "Yet a little while am I with you" (John 7:33, KJV). "These things have I spoken . . . being yet present with you" (John 14:25, KJV). Yet only the spirit of antichrist can deny "that Jesus Christ is come in the flesh" (1 John 4:2, KJV). "Have I been so long with you?" (John 14:9, KJV). Emphasis on the presence-significance of Jesus' name not only occurs at the opening of Matthew's Gospel but also reappears later in Jesus' assurance of his ongoing presence in even the smallest gathering of believers assembling in his name (18:20). The three-year public ministry transforms claims for the Word become flesh into a global message, GOD WITH US incarnate and crucified and risen. The resurrection and exaltation effect the personal presence of the crucified Jesus in a more permanent way—CHRIST IN US.

Simon Peter's confession of Jesus' divine messiahship crowns the Nazarene's question: "Whom do men say that I the SON OF MAN AM?" (Matt. 16:13, KJV). That very claim upon Jesus' own lips provokes Jewish accusers to demand his death. "Then said they all, Art thou then THE SON OF GOD? And he said unto them, Ye say that I AM" (Luke 22:70, KJV).

None can miss the force of his claim: "Before Abraham was, I AM" (John 8:58, KJV; cf. 17:5, 24). The juxtaposition of the verbs *ginomai* (became, "Abraham came to be") and *eimi* (to be, "I am") contrasts the created with the unbegotten. A. J. MacLeod writes that "Jesus claims that He is the eternal 'I am'; His life partakes of the timeless quality of deity. The Jews realize the significance of His claim: absolute pre-existence means equality with God. This to them is blasphemy, so they take up stones to kill Him" ("The Gospel According to John," p. 883). His hearers claimed that Abraham was their father (8:39); he, the "sent one" (8:42), claims to be the manifested Covenant God of Abraham, the I AM veiled in flesh and now present in their midst. In the simplicity of the august name I AM, he claims the prerogatives of YAHWEH.

"I AM from above. . . . I AM he" (John 8:23-24, KJV)—that is the very heart of his teaching: "I that speak unto thee AM he" (John 4:26, KJV). "I AM the Bread of Life" (John 6:35, KJV)—the God-given manna without which man dies of spiritual famine. "I AM the Light of the world" (John 8:12, KJV; cf. 9:5; 12:35, 46), the divine pillar of fire supplying guidance and illumination to the Gentiles (Isa. 49:6) as well as to the Jews. "I AM the Resurrection and the Life" (John 11:25, KJV). "I AM the Way, the Truth, and the Life" (John 14:6, KJV; cf. 5:26; 17:2). "I AM the door of the sheep . . . I AM the Good Shepherd" (John 10:7, 11, KJV). "I AM the true vine" (John 15:1, KJV; cf. v. 5). Edwin Hoskyns notes that "the mysterious statement" I AM or *It is I* also is reminiscent of Exodus 3:14 in passages such as John 6:20, KJV, "It is I; be not afraid" (cf. 8:24, 58; 13:19; 18:5, 6) (*The Fourth Gospel*, p. 291). On John 8:24, "Except ye believe that I Aм he, ye shall die in your sins" (ASV), he comments (p. 334): "The absolute claim of Jesus is denoted by the majestic *I am:* majestic, and numinous, because of its Old Testament background (Exod. iii. 14; Deut. xxxii. 39; Isa. xliii. 10)."

These titles are irreducible elements of christology and remind us that the New Testament doctrine of God is centrally christological. They also emphasize that Jesus is related to his people not simply in terms of a future salvation, but as the bearer of a judgment from which they are already delivered (John 9:39; 12:31); as the present source of their new birth (John 3:3), of living water (7:38), and of abundant life (10:10). The Hebrew tense allows for I Aм either the past or the present or the future, or all three; the New Testament preempts all these options in its identification of Jesus Christ as the unveiled glory of God: "I am alpha and omega . . . which is, and which was, and which is to come, the Almighty" (Rev. 1:8, KJV). As Bishop Beveridge once noted, by the I Aм he "sets His hand, as it were, to a blank" that his people may append whatever is for their highest good: I Aм whatever is indispensable to life fit for time and eternity.

To the principal names and titles of JESUS CHRIST, Vincent Taylor devoted his 1951–52 Oxford lectures (*The Names of Jesus*), and introduced their published form with the comment that "the modern practice of beginning a study of the Person of Christ with the Names of Jesus is not without good reason. . . . The question, who Jesus is, is approached best by considering how men named Him, for it is by His names that He is revealed and known" (p. 1). The New Testament names and titles, Taylor declares, are "the signs and seals of the earliest Christology." By contrast, he notes, the "new names" for Jesus arising in modern times are generally lacking in depth. "We are left with such designations as 'the Man of Sorrows,' 'Our Blessed Lord,' 'Our Dear Lord,' 'the Great Galilean,' 'the Master,' 'the Elder Brother,' 'the Carpenter of Nazareth.' The list is not impressive. Indeed, it is as depressing as a group of raw, self-conscious recruits" (p. 174). "In the nineteenth century, and in certain circles, the title 'The Master' regained popularity, but generally as an understatement dependent on reverence of tone rather than precision of meaning" (p. 14).

In the context of the revelation of the divine Name, the title of Bruce Barton's *The Man Nobody Knows* is ironically appropriate. As Taylor remarks, "For the most part the new names are either pietistic or humanistic, laudatory or non-commital. Uninspired, they say too much or too little. The classic names are those of the New Testament, 'the Lord,' 'the Son,' 'the Word,' 'Jesus,' 'Jesus Christ,' 'our Lord Jesus Christ,' and they are the only names with a foreseeable future. This fact is one of the neglected arguments for the plenary inspiration of Holy Scripture, and a vindication of the claim that the examination of the names and titles is a necessary prelude to the study of the Person of Christ" (ibid., pp. 174 f.).

The name JESUS (from Jehoshua-Joshua) means "He whose salvation is YAHWEH" (or in brief, "God's Salvation"). The name Joshua is usually taken to mean simply "He will save," but it may be a combination of the usual *Jeho* with the verbal name *yeshua*, hence, "Jehovah will save." JESUS presumably is strictly *yeshua*, meaning "He will save," and shortened from Joshua. This is the New Testament interpretation (Matt. 1:21). From Qumran findings it seems likely that "God's Salvation" (or simply "Salvation") was a Jewish term for the expected MESSIAH. This sheds light on the reference to Jesus in the account of Simeon ("my eyes have seen your Salvation," Luke 2:30, NIV). Longenecker notes that this illumines Peter's proclamation "there is *the Salvation* in no one else" (Acts 4:12, RSV) and other passages (e.g., Luke 3:6; John 4:22) (*The Christology of Early Jewish Christianity*, pp. 102 f.). When the early Christians spoke the name JESUS, they expressed their awareness that the MESSIAH embodies Yahweh's promised salvation.

The New Testament use of exalted names and titles for Jesus of Nazareth has become a highly controversial issue because of Bultmann's claim that christology is based not in the life of Jesus but rather in the teaching of the early church. As Bultmann sees it, Jesus' followers applied such titles as MESSIAH, SON OF MAN, SON OF GOD and LORD with an eschatological intention, and with no objective precedent or basis in Jesus' own life and teaching. The christologized Jesus of the New Testament is therefore considered a product of the devout creative imagination of the Christian. But that pre-Pauline Hellenistic Christianity is the creative source of concepts deemed by critics as too advanced for native Palestinians, and that it originated many of the distinctive emphases of the New Testament, is an arbitrary notion. Longenecker does not question that Hellenistic Christians—both Jewish and Gentile—existed in the church before Paul's influential ministry. But he asks whether the notion that the major creative factor in the New Testament is to be traced to anonymous Hellenistic Christians rests upon an evasive reconstruction of early Christianity rooted "primarily in a priori assumptions" (ibid., p. 8, n. 15). Everett F. Harrison also defends the titles of Jesus against Bultmann's attempted dilution (*"Gemeindetheologie:* The Bane of Gospel Criticism").

That primitive Christianity recognized Jesus as the MESSIAH of Old Testament promise and hope is clear. The LXX uses *Christos* to translate the Hebrew *mashiah* ("anointed") of the promised SON OF DAVID through whom God was to deliver and rule His people (Luke 2:25–26). The earliest believers considered Jesus to be the promised MESSIAH, and the earliest Jewish Christians likewise proclaimed him to be so.

But the Old Testament does not often use this term of the Coming One. In Hebrew tradition, God's people are the kingdom over whom he reigns, and the invisible divine King expresses his earthly kingship not only through external intervention but also through anointed human agents, that is, through representatives whose divine appointment is symbolized by religious ritual. While this agent was usually a king, and David was the great ideal (cf. Song of Sol. 4:4 and Zech. 4:3; Ps. 110 presupposes a priest-king), priests and prophets are also sometimes designated as messiahs (cf. Ps. 105:15). Messiahship therefore covered a variety of offices, and its meaning is not as rigid as once thought; its functional designation is not exclusively that of a savior, but that of God's agent as well. Its Hebrew usage would not necessarily imply a redemptive role or a transcendent supernatural figure; it is not a term that Jews would have applied to express the concept of supernatural intervention or divine inbreaking. While it is not, therefore, the Old Testament Savior-term, it gains that significance for Christians through its connection with the suffering servant and its christological redemptive associations.

The term *Mashiah* was in Jesus' day a politically sensitive one, associated with expectations of deliverance through political insurrection. During his trial Jesus was in fact accused by Roman leaders of fitting this political mold. On certain important occasions in his ministry—as at Caesarea Philippi and before the Sanhedrin—he substituted for the term MESSIAH that others applied to him the preferred title of THE SON OF MAN. Bultmann has argued that Jesus' self-consciousness was nonmessianic. He supports this claim by appealing to what remains of the Gospels after he has first erased every passage to the contrary as either an Easter story projected back into the life of Jesus or as a legend (*The Theology of the New Testament*, 1:26 f.). Cullmann insists that the Gospel accounts require the notion of Jesus' messianic self-consciousness, but says that Jesus made no overt messianic claim and, in fact, consciously avoided the title (*The Christology of the New Testament*, pp. 117 ff.). Longenecker presses the point, however, that although Jesus dissociated himself from current expectations of a political messiah, he was crucified as a messianic pretender—a development more coherently compatible with passages in which Jesus at least implied he was the MESSIAH of Old Testament hope or accepted the title (e.g., John 4:26).

Ethelbert Stauffer considers the title MESSIAH as a predicate describing Jesus as specially authenticated since THE CHRIST was the first title Jesus accepted "as a valid and accurate description of his saving mission" (cf. Mark 8:29) (*New Testament Theology*, p. 112). Longenecker builds on David Flusser's observations on the use of *Mashiah* in the Dead Sea Scrolls ("Two Notes on the Midrash on 2 Sam. vii," p. 107), and says that "from the strictly theological point of view no man can be defined as messiah before he has accomplished the task of the anointed." He notes also that "only in Luke 24:26 and 24:46, accounts of the post-resurrection appearances, is Jesus presented as directly initiating the discussion regarding his messiahship and as relating the Old Testament to himself in explicit messianic terms. . . . Jesus was acknowledged Messiah in fact not just *after* his passion and resurrection but *because* of his passion and resurrection" (*The Christology of Early Jewish Christianity*, p. 74).

Taylor notes the contrast between the Gospels, which apply the title
to Jesus, and the Epistles, in which the title becomes a proper name (*The
Names of Jesus*, pp. 19 f.). This development followed from the frequent
association and juxtaposition of the title CHRIST with the name JESUS,
hence JESUS CHRIST. The Apostle Paul and the early Christian community
repeatedly used the name CHRIST until their larger outreach required a
different designation, since among the Gentiles the term MESSIAH lacked
meaning and adequacy to mirror Jesus' person. So numerous are the
references to CHRIST in one form or another, that more than one scholar
has remarked that this term, which in the Old Testament and the Gospels
bears such great developing theological importance, becomes in the Epistles "just another proper name" in a vast panoply of appropriate designations for Jesus of Nazareth. A striking development in the community of
believers lends new interest to the term, however. Recalling in the context
of the Aaronic benediction the words of Numbers 6:27 ("So shall they put
my name upon the children of Israel; and I will bless them," ASV), William
Phillips Hall notes that Christians themselves now bear the name of
CHRIST (*A Remarkable Biblical Discovery*, p. 108), and recalls the
early liturgy: "We thank thee that the Name of thy Christ is named (or
invoked) upon us, and so we are made one with thee" (J. S. Banks,
"Christian," 1:200). The disciples were "first called Christians at Antioch"
(Acts 11:26), a name that they still bear.

The name SON occurs not simply in the messianic title SON OF DAVID
(Matt. 1:1; 9:27; 12:23; 15:22; 20:30–31; 21:9, 15; Mark 10:47–48), but also
in the well-known forms, the SON OF MAN, which in the Gospels Jesus
alone uses of himself, and the SON OF GOD which both Jesus and the believing community employ. Here too, Bultmann contends that the only
authentic or original passages are third person SON OF MAN passages
which Jesus assertedly does not apply to himself but rather to a coming
apocalyptic figure with whom he would be somehow associated and who
would vindicate his ministry (*Theology of the New Testament*, 1:29 ff.).
The Palestinian church is then said to have applied the term SON OF MAN,
along with MESSIAH, in an apocalyptic christological sense, while the
Hellenistic church is said to have employed SON OF GOD, in a transfer of
the Greek sense of God-man and LORD to a further development of christological claims. Almost all recent critical expositions of the christological titles assume this disjunction between the claims made by Jesus of
Nazareth and those affirmed by the early Christians, and contend that the
presentation of Jesus as the divine SON is a projection of the Christian
community rather than a fact of Jesus' consciousness. Longenecker remarks that while such argumentation "is convincing on its own presuppositions, it runs rough shod over *prima facie* interpretations of the
evidence and bases itself upon hypothetical reconstructions in favour of
a more normal reading of the data. . . . We handle the evidence much
too loosely if we interpret the records as indicating the exact reverse of
what they purport" (*The Christology of Early Jewish Christianity*, p. 88).

SON OF MAN occurs 69 times in the Synoptics, 12 times in John, once each in Acts and Hebrews, and twice in Revelation. In other words all but four of the 85 New Testament uses occur in the Gospels, and there the title SON OF MAN is always spoken by Jesus and not by his disciples or the multitudes. Outside the Gospels, the title is used by Stephen (Acts 7:56) and occurs in Hebrews 2:6 (with reference to Ps. 8:4), and Revelation 1:13 and 14:14 (recalling Dan. 7:13). The reference in Hebrews is nontitular christologically. In Old Testament use the term bears three senses: (1) collectively, for mankind (e.g., Isa. 56:2; Jer. 49:18; Pss. 8:4; 80:17; etc.); (2) as a formula of address for the prophet Ezekiel (2:1 and almost a hundred other passages); (3) for the saints of God (Dan. 7:13–14, an eschatological passage interpreted in 7:15–18 in terms of a Hebrew martyr and hence, contrary to a widely held view, not of an individual).

Only later than Daniel, and beyond the Old Testament canonical writings in pre-Christian Jewish thought, do we first come upon the messianic concept of SON OF MAN as the eschatological agent of redemption with the connotation of irruptive divine power. Critical scholars have sought to find a precedent for the New Testament use of SON OF MAN in this apocalyptic literature, specifically in the noncanonical Book of Enoch which speaks of a righteous revealer (Book I, ch. 46), a preexistent transcendent figure whose Name carries salvation (ch. 48), and who is the coming glorified judge of the world.[1] They have pointed also to the pseudepigraphic work 4 Ezra which depicts an eschatological messianic deliverer of the creation (ch. 13). But this latter book was written about A.D. 80–100, and is therefore too late to be considered a source.

Bultmann contends that the Palestinian church applied the SON OF MAN concept of the Book of Enoch to Jesus. Many critics consider Enoch (note the reference in Jude 14, albeit to "Enoch, the seventh from Adam") to be the source of this name. Cullmann believes that the title SON OF MAN was aptly applied because of its use in Jewish apocalyptic literature for the "heavenly being, now hidden, who will appear only at the end of time on the clouds of heaven to judge and to establish 'the nation of the saints' " and because "the ideal Heavenly man" is "identified with the first man at the beginning of time" (*The Christology of the New Testament*, pp. 150 f.). But the Jewish apocalyptic usage appears in parts of Enoch that are not in the Dead Sea Scrolls and are now thought to be post-Christian. The title SON OF MAN is found in Enoch only in Book II, the Book of Similitudes. There is no evidence whatever for the pre-Christian nature of Book II of the Ethiopic Enoch. Although Qumran has yielded many copies of Enoch, none containing the Similitudes has yet been found, so that some scholars consider the Enochian Similitudes a reflection of early Jewish Christianity. It is therefore an argument from

---

1. Cf. "the SON OF MAN who is born into righteousness" (ch. 71, 1. 65). Yet it is Enoch himself, and not another, that is depicted as vindicated by God.

silence to hold that SON OF MAN is a messianic title borrowed by the
Christian community from Enoch. C. H. Dodd and others refuse to draw
this inference. The title may as readily be a christianization of the Dan-
ielic figure, a concentration by Jesus that summarizes in himself the
eschatological fortunes of Israel. Longenecker emphasizes that of the
three supposed sources adduced today in explaining the term SON OF MAN
(1 Enoch, 4 Ezra and Daniel 7) "only Daniel 7 is demonstrably pre-Christian" (*The Christology of Early Jewish Christianity*, pp. 84 f.).

On what basis must it be argued that not Jesus, but the early church,
identified Jesus as the SON OF MAN? Were that indeed the case, can we
then explain why, in the Gospels, the title never occurs other than on the
lips of Jesus, and why, in the Epistles, it is not used messianically of
Jesus (references in Acts 7:56; Rev. 1:13 and 14:14 are notable exceptions)? Where is the evidence, if the early church introduced the title as
part of its christology? It is far more coherent and convincing to assume,
as evangelical scholars do, that the Christ of faith and the Jesus of history, contrary to critical suppositions, are not to be contrasted and divorced. Jesus used the term SON OF MAN of his earthly ministry, of his
approaching passion and resurrection, and of his future eschatological
role, references that are found in all supposed literary sources of the
Gospels. The view most consistent with the historical data is that Jesus
employed the title SON OF MAN as a self-designation in the unprecedented
sense, that is, what was said of Israel he applied to himself, in terms of
the suffering SON OF MAN and eschatological deliverer.

Longenecker emphasizes that more important than the question whether
Daniel 7 requires an individual or a corporate meaning is the indisput-
able fact that it speaks of the glorification and vindication of the SON OF
MAN through suffering, so that the dual aspects of humiliation and glory
"are signalled by the expression SON OF MAN in the one passage in pre-
Christian Jewish literature which employs the term as a title" (ibid., pp.
87 f.). In the term, SON OF MAN, Jesus combined in himself as God's agent
the emphasis on supernatural intervention and divine unction. There is
no evidence that the title SON OF MAN was used in this full redemptive-
messianic sense in pre-Christian literature. Christian literature, however,
provides ample evidence that Jesus used it in this way and that his followers perpetuated the practice in fidelity to Jesus' own example. The
early church used SON OF MAN, not to fasten a christological title on Jesus,
for it never occurs in the Gospels on the lips of Jesus' followers, but
rather, as Robert Gulich asserts, to be faithful to Jesus' own way of designating his person and mission (lectures, August 1970).

On the basis of Daniel 7:13, T. W. Manson considers "the people of the
Holy One" a collective meaning of the SON OF MAN (*The Teaching of
Jesus*, pp. 227 ff.). Cullmann remarks that even if this view "is not generally acceptable, the double meaning of 'men' and 'the Son of Man' must
be reckoned with in Jesus' teachings, as T. Preiss points out ('The Mys-

tery of the Son of Man' in *Life in Christ*, 1954, pp. 43 ff.). . . . If this double meaning really goes back to Jesus, . . . the thought of a correspondence between Jesus and the little band of disciples would be at least already referred to; Jesus, the future Son of Man, is already present in the community" (*Salvation in History*, p. 201). The notion that the coming kingdom is anticipated in Jesus of Nazareth is thus extended to include the fellowship of Jesus and his disciples—in other words, the church. As Vincent Taylor comments, "It is the name chosen by Him, in conscious preference, we must suppose, to the more colorless 'Christos,' and the human and nationalistic 'Son of David.' It expresses the idea of lordship, of rule over the Messianic community, and its associations are supernatural" (*The Names of Jesus*, p. 35).

But the term SON OF MAN disappeared from primitive Christian use, Taylor suggests, because it was "not a generally accepted Messianic title" and because the corresponding Greek title was "meaningless to the Gentiles. . . . In later history it suffers depreciation in the theological use of the name to describe the Divine Christ in His human manifestation, the Son of God incarnate." Yet "during the last fifty years, its currency value has been increasingly restored; for . . . the conviction steadily grows that it contains in itself the secret of Jesus concerning His person and work" (ibid., p. 68).

While the incarnate Jesus spoke of himself as the SON OF MAN, the early Christians used the term LORD (KURIOS) to express their devotion to and worship of the risen and ascended Redeemer. The basic meaning of the term KURIOS in the extrabiblical world was that of authority, and in this sense it was applied to the head of the home, or master or guardian. Additionally it was used in polite address, much as *Herr* (Sir) in modern German speech. The fact that the Hellenistic world employed KURIOS with religious associations as well has led to spirited modern debate over whether this title was borrowed from the Greek mystery religions and applied to Jesus (William Bousset, *Kyrios Christos*, pp. 91 ff.), or whether the early church derived it from the Old Testament heritage and applied it in view of its own knowledge and experience of Jesus Christ (J. Gresham Machen, *The Origin of Paul's Religion;* W. D. Davies, *Paul and Rabbinic Judaism;* A. E. J. Rawlinson, *The New Testament Doctrine of Christ*). Adolf Deissmann holds that "it may be said with certainty that at the time when Christianity originated 'Lord' was a divine predicate intelligible to the whole Eastern world" (*Light from the Ancient East*, pp. 350). In the ancient Near East, the name of a deity was frequently conjoined with the title KURIOS, just as the Greeks designated Zeus as Lord of All, or the Romans designated their emperor as Dominus.

Vincent Taylor argues, however, that although its intelligibility to Gentile converts doubtless encouraged its frequent and widespread use, to explain the Christian ascription in terms of simple transfer of a popular Greek-cult name with additional Christian associations is "too naïve an explanation" (*The Names of Jesus*, p. 69). Taylor argues that the New Testament use of KURIOS is postresurrection (p. 43). But he emphasizes that this ascription of the title to Jesus was "aided by the Messianic use of the title in Psa. cx., and by the fact that in the Septuagint it is the name of God" (p. 69).

Greek-speaking Jews did in fact use KURIOS for the Hebrew YAHWEH and for ADONAI (and its Aramaic equivalent MAR), and the Septuagint uses KURIOS to translate not only ADONAI but the tetragram YHWH. But it is now widely held that the copies of the Septuagint, from which the view was deduced that KURIOS carries all the overtones of YAHWEH and in this sense was applied to Jesus by the early Christians, are really all Christian sources. Since the only demonstrated non-Christian copies of the Septuagint do not in fact use KURIOS for YHWH, but retain the tetragram, the equivalence of the two words is now held to reflect later Christian practice. Yet it must be granted that not only Philo and Josephus, but also apocryphal Old Testament books like Wisdom of Solomon use KURIOS for YAHWEH, an identification that was also made in Greek-speaking synagogues. Christians acquainted with Greek-speaking Jewry therefore would readily use the term KURIOS to include the connotation of God Almighty.

In the Synoptic Gospels KURIE often occurs as a form of address to Jesus. While on the lips of his disciples it can mean "master," the general public use may intend only "sir." The address form does not in any event carry the more technical post-Easter meaning of LORD.

In distinction from personal address, the Synoptic narratives do, however, carry references with the comprehensive post-Easter sense. To be sure, Mark's Gospel nowhere uses KURIOS in its technical meaning, and the sole use in Matthew 28:6 ("Come, see the place where the LORD lay," KJV) is a variant text. But Luke's Gospel includes the title in its technical meaning twelve times (cf. 11:39, KJV, "And the LORD said . . ."); Acts employs it more than a hundred times; Paul employs KURIOS more than two hundred times in a variety of forms (such kindred uses as "our LORD" and "in the LORD" occur in many instances), and it appears frequently in John's Gospel. In fact, as Taylor notes, "no other name of Jesus is used with anything like the same frequency" (ibid., p. 45).

From these facts it has been argued that the technical use of KURIOS was a Hellenistic takeover. Bultmann has revived Bousset's 1916 contention, abandoned in 1921, that the Hellenistic church borrowed the title from the imperial cult and applied it to Jesus; in other words, the lordship of Jesus of Nazareth is a creative invention of the Hellenistic church. This claim forces two questions upon us: does the New Testament church by its use of KURIOS intend what non-Christian usage implied by that title, and is it actually the case that the early Palestinian church did not employ the title KURIOS?

Evidence that the Palestinian church did address Jesus as Lord is supplied by the doxology of 1 Corinthians 16:22–24 where the otherwise

Greek text contains the Aramaic *Maranatha*.[2] Although one need not find in the Aramaic *Maran* at this early stage all the comprehensive significance of KURIOS, the fact that the usage is pre-Pauline and that the Palestinian Christians thus invoked the no longer visible Lord is highly significant. Additional evidence that the primitive church addressed Jesus as Lord is found in the Didache where the phrase *Marana-tha* appears in an early worship service ("Let grace come and let this world pass away. . . . Maranatha!" 10:6). It has been contended, however, that MAR in Aramaic is merely a form of polite address and never carries an absolute sense. But the preservation of *Maranatha* as an Aramaic formula by the Greek-speaking churches as a prayer, whether in a eucharistic or eschatological context, attests its earlier use as a christological ascription in the Aramaic-speaking church. Cullmann notes that the repeated citation of Psalm 110:1 in the canonical Jewish Christian materials attests "how vital was the present lordship of Christ in early Christian thought" (*Christology of the New Testament*, p. 223). Jesus' discussion of Psalm 110:1 indicates that he thought of himself as KURIOS (Matt. 22:45; Mark 12:37; Luke 20:44). After his resurrection and exaltation this verse gains great significance.

The early Christian confession in Philippians 2:6-11 speaks of Jesus being given, in consequence of his humiliation and exaltation, "a name . . . above every name" (KJV), that is, supreme honor and authority, so that "every tongue should confess that JESUS is KURIOS."[3] Already in Peter's sermon at Pentecost we find the declaration: "Let all Israel then accept as certain that God has made this JESUS, whom you crucified, both KURION and CHRISTON" (Acts 2:36). The Palestinian church may therefore be confidently represented as affirming that in the resurrection God exalted the crucified Jesus as LORD over all creation. Since Jesus was addressed as LORD, not only by the Hellenistic church, but also by the Jewish church, the basis for ascribing lordship was not a reflection of Greek or Roman religious motifs.

In our study of the term SON OF GOD we emphasize that Christians disowned the pagan notion of human rulers worshiping divine men or epiphanies of God (cf. Acts 25:26). Although KURIOS is specially used of the exalted LORD, it takes on special color in Paul's writings from the

---

2. The preservation of this Aramaic expression by Greek-speaking Christians reflects the earlier verbalized longing of the Palestinian Christians for the Lord's return. The King James Version divided the Aramaic phrase *Maran-atha*, and accordingly rendered it in the indicative "Our LORD has come" (in the incarnation). But the phrase is probably imperative (*Marana-tha*) and hence a prayer: "Our LORD, come!" The mood reappears in Revelation 22:20, where in the yearning of the Christian church the Greek KURIOS ("Even so, come LORD JESUS") corresponds to this early Aramaic watchword.

3. Ralph P. Martin initially insisted that this is basically an Aramaic hymn translated into Greek (*The Epistle of Paul to the Philippians*). But in a later reversal in his *Carmen Christi* he bows to Bultmann in agreeing that the hymn comes from the Hellenistic church.

theology of the passion. Paul often uses LORD for Jesus in the flesh (cf. 1 Cor. 7:10, which contrasts Jesus of Nazareth's spoken precept with Paul's apostolic command).

The Hellenistic church took over from the Palestinian church this representation of Jesus as KURIOS, and used it in the existential context of the Roman Caesars. But it did not create the concept of Jesus' lordship. The Christian confession that Jesus is LORD is, as Taylor writes, "the seed of Apostolic and post-Apostolic Christology, and today it is the basic conviction out of which emerges any serious apprehension of Christ's Person" (*The Names of Jesus*, p. 69). The sporadic New Testament use and avoidance for half a century of the term SAVIOR, despite its reflection of Old Testament motifs, until its frequent later appearance in the pastoral and catholic Epistles, may be due to the circumstance that "the use of the name in Greek religion, and above all in Caesar worship, restricted and delayed its currency in the primitive tradition" (ibid., p. 109). Stauffer notes that Pauline emphasis on Jesus' authority over "all the powers that affect our destiny" must surely have carried a sense of liberation to Hellenistic readers gripped by the notion of fate; the antithetic Pauline use of KURIOS confesses Jesus as LORD of the world to come over against all other lords (*New Testament Theology*, p. 116). Implicit in this recognition of lordship was the Christian acknowledgment of Jesus' essential divinity (Rawlinson, *The New Testament Doctrine of Christ*, p. 236).

It has been argued that since the title KURIOS is dated from the resurrection of the crucified Jesus, and since *Marana-tha* is a prayer, the term KURIOS carries functional and moral rather than metaphysical implications. It must be said that whatever cosmological elements were implicit in the early Jewish Christian attribution of KURIOS to Jesus, they were yet undeveloped, since the dominant interest is religiohistorical, and conveys no specific connotations concerning his relationship to the cosmic order. Not even Philippians 2, which begins by a statement of Jesus' divine nature from the first and affirms his transcendence over all, is expanded into the cosmological and philosophical perspectives latent in these affirmations, although it joins together his preexistent union with God and his postresurrection exaltation to lordship. But in the context of alien ideologies and philosophical pressures, as in Colossians, the implicit becomes increasingly explicit. Cullmann puts the point well: "The lordship of Christ must extend over every area of creation. If there were a single area excluded from his lordship, that lordship would not be complete and Christ would no longer be the *Kyrios*" (*Salvation in History*, p. 228). Indeed, consistently with Hebrew monotheism, Paul introduces the binitarian formula "one God, the Father . . . one Lord, Jesus Christ" (1 Cor. 8:5–6, RSV; cf. Eph. 4:5; 1 Tim. 2:5; Gal. 3:20), and, precisely where speculative metaphysical theories support a competitive cosmic understanding, he emphasizes to the Colossians the cosmic lordship of Jesus (Col. 1:15–20).

H. A. A. Kennedy notes that in modern times "the term 'Lord' has become one of the most lifeless words in the Christian vocabulary. To enter into its meaning and to give it practical effect would be to re-create, in great measure, the atmosphere of the Apostolic Age" (*St. Paul's Epistle to the Philippians*, p. 439). What that might mean is suggested by Longenecker's comments on the correlation of the Name (*to onoma*) with the title LORD. Assuredly "the name" is conjoined in the New Testament also with the SON, with CHRIST and with JESUS CHRIST. But the numerous associations of the name with KURIOS from Peter's references to the Old Testament in his Pentecost sermon (Acts 2:25, 34–35) and in other Acts addresses, to the Pauline Kenosis-passage reference to the "name . . . above every name" given to Jesus, attests the high Christian acclamation from this resurrection and exaltation. "What name is this that is above every name? Undoubtedly, it is the name by which God himself has been known; that is, in Greek, *kurios*. Or perhaps it would be truer to early Jewish Christian thought to say that since Jesus is the name of God, it is appropriate that the Old Testament title for God be his as well" (Longenecker, *Christology of Early Jewish Christianity*, p. 128). That Jesus has come in the Father's name is, in fact, a recurrent emphasis of John's Gospel (cf. 5:43; 10:25; 12:13).

The term SON OF GOD (and analogous names such as the SON, HIS SON, MY BELOVED SON, and ONLY BEGOTTEN SON) is used descriptively of Jesus' relation to God. The term had a wide use in the Old Testament (of angels, Job 1:6; 2:1; 38:7; of Israel, Exod. 4:22; Hos. 11:1; of the king, 2 Sam. 7:14). It was applied not to divine Being, but to individuals or groups occupying a specially close relationship to God.

In pagan religion the term is applied to Egyptian kings who were believed to be descendants of the god Re, and particularly to the Ptolemies, and also to the later Roman emperors. But the idea of divine men was notably foreign to Old Testament monotheism. Ralph E. Knudsen stresses that "it seems unwarranted to assume that the Hellenistic understanding of the designation 'son of God,' which can hardly be separated from pagan polytheism, is applicable to the use of the title in the New Testament" (*Theology of the New Testament*, p. 116).

First-century Judaism held side by side the concept of Israel as God's Son and that of the anointed king as God's Son. That the term SON OF GOD was also used as a messianic title in pre-Christian Judaism was evidenced by the Dead Sea Scrolls discovery of 4 Q Florilegium, which gives a messianic interpretation to 2 Samuel 7:14, "I will be for him a Father, and he shall be to Me a son" (Berkeley), although the coming Davidic messiah is joined to nationalistic expectations. Contrary to the notion that the title SON was nowhere used in the Old Testament of the MESSIAH (Gustav Dalman, *The Words of Jesus*, pp. 268 ff.) there is the possibility inherent in Psalm 2:7 ("The Lord hath said unto me, Thou art my son; this day have I begotten thee," KJV), which in Jesus' day was interpreted messianically, at least in some quarters (Mark 12:35–36; 14:61). In the intertestamental literature the passages often adduced from 4 Ezra and Wisdom of Solomon mistranslate *servant* (*pais*) as *son* (*huios*) of God; the reference in the Book of Enoch (ch. 105) that identifies the SON OF GOD as the MESSIAH is a late interpolation.

Bultmann and similarly-minded critics consider the New Testament christological messianic title SON OF GOD to be a devout borrowing of Greek mythological messianic conceptions that are reflected in the virgin birth, miracle, and resurrection accounts. According to Bultmann the early Christians used the name SON OF GOD to affirm "the divinity of Christ, his divine nature, by virtue of which he is differentiated from the human sphere" (*Theology of the New Testament*, 1:128 f.). Yet Bultmann objectionably correlates this ascription of "divine power" with an affirmation of "divine origin" and contends that the term SON OF GOD simultaneously "serves to differentiate Christ from the one true God and to indicate Christ's subordinate relation" (p. 129). His entire exposition of the names of Jesus shifts the initiative in their use to the faith of the early church, obscures the revelational aspects, and manipulates the texts to serve his prejudices. The LXX use of KURIOS as the usual translation of YAHWEH is assigned an influence subordinate to that of Hellenistic religious terminology (pp. 124 ff.).

The almost eighty occurrences of the term SON OF GOD are distributed widely throughout the New Testament, in contrast to the title SON OF MAN. In the Synoptic Gospels the term is almost invariably used to emphasize the unity of purpose and function of the FATHER and the SON; only Matthew 14:33 employs this title with a foreground emphasis on a metaphysical unity of power. The Synoptics therefore provide no basis for the notion that the early followers of Jesus employed the term to extend Greek metaphysical claims to Jesus. Throughout the New Testament the title SON OF GOD remains primarily a functional designation that emphasizes Jesus' obedience in the mission of divine revelation and redemption. The metaphysical claims are inherent in this emphasis on unity of mind, will, and purpose with that of the FATHER, but not as an extension of Greek speculative notions of divine substance. SON OF GOD clearly serves as a christological title in John's Gospel, in the Acts, and elsewhere in the New Testament, and amplifies the unique functional relation of Jesus to the Father.

The later creedal affirmations of the Christian church focused emphasis on the deity of the MESSIAH. In the expanding experience of the followers of Jesus, he was the SON OF GOD metaphysically because he was so functionally. While Jesus' awareness of his own nature gave insight into his mission, inferences from that mission gave to the disciples guidance into the nature of his person. Yet only because he was in fact and nature the SON OF GOD was he so functionally, as attested by the virgin birth and resurrection accounts, and his own teaching and work. The disciples' experience in Jesus of an absolutely unique relationship to God expressed itself in their use of the SON, a title favored by Jesus himself, but now stated in the more explicit form, the SON OF GOD. Although Jesus did not himself use this latter designation, it was pronounced at his birth in the angelic address to Mary (Luke 1:35) and at his baptism and transfiguration by the heavenly voice (Mark 1:11; 9:7).

There is no basis for the notion that the early followers of Jesus invented the term SON; they applied it to Jesus because he himself used it. Although the early Christians spoke of themselves as "sons of God," their application of the SON OF GOD to Jesus set him apart preeminently and uniquely. In this distinction they had unmistakable precedent in Jesus' teaching (Mark 13:32). In the title or name SON OF GOD, notes Taylor, we see an originally messianic title eclipsing and moving beyond its messianic sense ("These [things] are written that you may believe that Jesus is the CHRIST, the SON OF GOD," John 20:31, RSV) (*The Names of Jesus*, p. 70). Longenecker enumerates the passages in which the titles MESSIAH and SON OF GOD stand in juxtaposition, and notes that they are not intended as mere synonyms. But he rejects the notion of Dalman and Bousset that the title SON OF GOD held no messianic association in pre-Christian Judaism. From Jesus' use of FATHER for God, and from Jesus' divine sonship as the basic dictum of his ministry, Longenecker argues that "it is difficult to see why he could not have spoken of himself as 'the Son' and 'the Son of God' in the manner actually preserved in the Gospels" (*Christology of Early Jewish Christianity*, p. 96).

The notion of deity as father of mankind, of special tribes, families, or rulers, is a commonplace of the history of religion, and its implication is that of unconditional authority. But the scant fourteen passages in the Old Testament which introduce God as FATHER, as Joachim Jeremias asserts, show him not as ancestor or progenitor, but as Creator, standing in unparalleled relation to Israel as a covenant people, and manifesting undeserved mercy and forgiveness (*The Central Message of the New Testament*, pp. 9 f.). Yet no evidence exists that even in Palestinian Judaism of the first millenium was God addressed by any individual Jew as "my Father." "But Jesus did just this," and moreover used the Aramaic word ABBA—a term so familiar that, Jeremias contends, "the Jewish mind would have considered it irreverent and unthinkable" (pp. 17, 21). In this testimony of the Gospels, that in the use of ABBA as an address to God we have an authentic and original utterance of Jesus, Jeremias finds a refutation of the Bultmannian emphasis that the Gospels are mere confessions of faith disinterested in the historical Jesus.

Those passages in which the titles THE SON and THE FATHER appear in juxtaposition hold special importance for the Christian view. Jesus used the term FATHER in a unique way: in contrast with the Jewish reluctance to use the divine Name, Jesus spoke of God as FATHER, and, as already indicated, in the most intimate way possible (ABBA means daddy or papa). In the Synoptic Gospels Jesus refers four times to himself as SON. Mark 14:36 is the only passage in the Gospels that preserves ABBA, and in the context of this Gethsemane prayer Jesus speaks of the SON OF MAN be-

trayed into the hands of sinners (Mark 14:41). Matthew 11:27 and Luke
10:22 are the supposed Q-passage: "all things have been delivered unto
me of my FATHER: and no one knoweth the SON, save the FATHER; neither
doth any know the FATHER, save the SON, and he to whomsoever the SON
willeth to reveal him" (ASV). Mark 13:32 likewise contains the absolute
use of "the SON": "But of that day or that hour knoweth no one, not even
the angels in heaven, neither the SON, but the FATHER" (ASV). Mark 12:6
speaks of the BELOVED SON in a parable that turns prophetic. In the classic
saying about mutual knowledge (Matt. 11:27 and Luke 10:22), the terms
THE SON and THE FATHER appear three times. Because of its similarity to
Johannine sayings (John 3:35; 5:20; 10:15; 14:9), Dibelius and Bultmann
have questioned the genuineness of this passage, but this similarity actually confirms its authenticity. Reflecting the interpolation hypothesis,
Taylor insists that the passage should be taken as it stands. "The fact
that it stands alone in Q, and the claim that it transcends the utterances
of Old Testament piety, by no means rule out its originality. Again, Johannine sayings are frequently genuine logia expressed in a new idiom, not
creations ex nihilo. . . . Further, the Hellenistic tone of the saying is
greatly exaggerated" (The Names of Jesus, p. 64).

In further confirmation that the title SON OF GOD is grounded in the
thought and teaching of Jesus himself, we may note the final consciousness attested in many ways by references in different strata of the Gospel
records. Jesus' references to "my FATHER's house" (Luke 2:49), his assent
to the high priests' inquiry whether he was indeed "the CHRIST, the SON
OF THE BLESSED" (Mark 14:61, RSV), even the demoniac's acknowledgment
of him as the SON OF GOD (Mark 3:11; 5:11), are supportive.

The revelation of the name of JESUS leads on, therefore, to an examination of his person and teaching in the larger context of his life and work.
The terms FATHER, SON (and SPIRIT) emerge not simply as proper
names, but as personal names for irreducible distinctions within the one
God. The divine proper names, the personal names, and the essential (at-
tributive) names all press for consideration if we are indeed to utter
God's Name in the fullness of his manifested glory.[4]

---

4. Vincent Taylor also treats secondary names and titles of Jesus of Nazareth, such
as KING (Rev. 1:5; 17:14; 19:16; cf. 1 Tim. 6:15, where the reference is to God); the
HOLY ONE (Mark 1:24; Luke 1:35; John 6:69; Acts 3:14; cf. Ps. 16:10, where Christ is
in view, and 1 John 2:20, where it is uncertain whether Christ or the Father is intended); the RIGHTEOUS ONE (Acts 3:14; 7:52; 22:14); the JUDGE (Acts 10:42; 2 Tim. 4:8);
the LION OF THE TRIBE OF JUDAH; the ROOT AND OFFSPRING OF DAVID; the BRIDEGROOM; the
MEDIATOR (Heb. 8:6; 9:15; 12:24; 1 Tim. 2:5). In titles such as the HOLY ONE and the
RIGHTEOUS ONE, the doctrine of Christ is put on guard against modern sentimentality
and its reduction of his character to love. Here the proper names blend into the essential names or attributes. So, for example, Taylor comments that "to think of
Christ as 'the Judge' implies that His office and person transcend human standards
and dimensions" (ibid., p. 85). The specifically christological titles mark an attempt
to define the person of Christ in terms of the unique character of his personal relation to God and hence of essential divinity: the IMAGE OF GOD (2 Cor. 4:4; Col. 1:15;
cf. Heb. 1:3); the RESURRECTION and the LIFE (John 11:25); the WAY, the TRUTH and

Our study of the names of JESUS began with a reference to the manifested presence of YAHWEH. He who in the days of his flesh stressed the temporary character of his bodily presence as "GOD WITH US," at the same time emphasized that he must "go away" (John 14:2; 16:4–5, 28). Yet he would not "orphan" his disciples (John 14:18); he would return to them (14:28), not alone at the end of the age in his glory (Matt. 24:30), nor only at their death (John 14:3), nor even simply in his resurrection appearances (John 14:19; 16:16). He would both send the COMFORTER (John 14:16; 16:7) and himself come to indwell his followers personally in intimate spiritual presence (John 14:20, 23). "Abide in me, and I in you" (John 15:4, 5, RSV), he said. This remarkable relationship with the family of God throbs with the living power of his name: "At that day ye shall ask in my name" (John 16:26, KJV), "And whatsoever ye shall ask in my name, that will I do, that the FATHER may be glorified in the SON" (John 14:13, KJV).

The revelation of the Name, the manifested presence of YAHWEH, thus leads on through the proper names and the essential names to the Triune Name of God. "Thou camest forth from God" (John 16:30, KJV) is the disciples' verdict. "And the glory which thou gavest me I have given them," says Jesus in the priestly prayer, "that they may be one, even as we are one: I in them, and thou in me, that they may be made perfect in one" (John 17:22–23, KJV). The divine Name echoes throughout the priestly prayer in John 17 (KJV): "I have manifested thy name" (v. 6); "I kept them in thy name" (v. 12); "I have declared unto them thy name, and will declare it: that the love wherewith thou hast loved me may be in them, and I in them" (v. 26).

Only crucifixion and resurrection now stand between this threshold moment on the frontiers of death and the fulfilled promise to return to his own. With the divine Name on his lips, Jesus proceeds from the priestly prayer to the betrayal and arrest. "Whom seek ye? They answered him, Jesus of Nazareth. Jesus saith unto them, I AM. And Judas also, which betrayed him, stood with them. As soon then as he had said unto them, I AM, they went backward, and fell to the ground. Then asked he them again, Whom seek ye? And they said, Jesus of Nazareth. Jesus answered, I have told you that I AM. . ." (John 18:4–8, KJV). To the Hebrew Christian the revelation of the divine Name had immense significance; it was a fact of great importance, therefore, that although the MESSIAH's final triumph over Satan would not take place until the end of the age, his *Name* and invincible power had nonetheless been revealed.

---

the LIFE (John 14:6); the FIRSTBORN (Rom. 8:29; Col. 1:18; Heb. 1:6; Rev. 1:4–5; cf. Ps. 89:27); the POWER and WISDOM OF GOD (1 Cor. 1:24); ALPHA and OMEGA (Rev. 1:8; 21:6; 22:13; cf. 1:17–18, 2:8); the WORD (John 1:1–18; Col. 1:15–20; Heb. 1:1–3). In expositing the WORD in John's Prologue "the Logos stands over against God and is Himself divine, and this conception carries with it the view that within the riches of His Being there are personal distinctions" (p. 164).

All that Jesus had been while physically in the midst of his disciples he
would now continue to be. Through the SPIRIT he would manifest his
power and presence in those who are baptized in his name. Throughout
the preaching of the apostles the power of THE NAME OF JESUS comes
into view. As William M. Ramsay remarks, "For the earliest Christians,
'Jesus' was the new and powerful saving name" (*The Christ of the Earliest Christians*, p. 92). In the preaching of Peter, notes Ramsay (pp. 92 f.),
THE NAME appears in four associations: as the object of trust and devotion (Acts 3:16), as the source of healing (Acts 3:16; 4:19), as integral
to the formula of baptism (Acts 2:38), and as the ground of forgiveness
and salvation (Acts 4:12).

The New Testament exposition of the HOLY SPIRIT centers in the spiritual presence of Christ in the lives of believers. YAHWEH's law, once
written upon stone, is now being etched upon the hearts of his obedient
sons. Disclosed in the Old Testament as the power or presence of God,
the SPIRIT now permanently indwells believers (1 Cor. 6:19) and links
them directly to the exalted LORD in the present reality and assurance of
sonship (Rom. 8:15–17; Gal. 4:6). Not simply a principle, but a manifestation of the one invisible divine life, the SPIRIT is the indwelling divine
presence and power, and a distinct personal center and dynamic whereby
the glorified LORD reigns immediately over his subjects and rules their
lives.

"Jesus stands in a direct relationship to the early Christians comparable only to that of God," Ramsay emphasizes, and historical research
discovers no period when the early church did not recognize him in this
divine role (ibid., pp. 97 f.). In the words of the classic apostolic summary, it is at THE NAME OF JESUS that every knee shall bow (Phil. 2:9–10).
So the present age looks to the future age; all who trust CHRIST, and who
abide in him here and now (John 15:4–5), look to their heavenly abiding
with him (John 14:2–3). For the I AM is the one which "was and is and is
to come" (Rev. 4:8, RSV). The dead in CHRIST already are "present with
the LORD" (2 Cor. 5:8, KJV). But the I AM will also "come as a thief" (Rev.
16:15, KJV; cf. 2 Pet. 3:10), will "come quickly" (Rev. 22:7, 12, KJV), and
in that expectation both "the SPIRIT and the bride say, Come" (22:17,
KJV). The whole family of the redeemed will be gathered at last "in the
presence of the LAMB" (Rev. 14:10, KJV), whose name is declared in the
Revelation: "I AM ALPHA AND OMEGA" (Rev. 1:8, 11; 22:13, KJV).

The distinctive features of God the FATHER become known to the Chris-
tian community in and through the revelation of the incarnate SON OF
GOD. It is true, of course, that the Old Testament teaches the fatherhood
of God (Jer. 3:4; 31:9; Isa. 63:16; 64:8). But in Judaism, as Edmond
Jacob observes, the fatherhood of God is an expression of his lordship:
"Yahweh is called father not because he has certain qualities normally
connected with this title, but because he is the sole genuine creator of
His people and of the faithful who make up the people. . . . The Is-

raelites only rarely give to Yahweh the title father when they address him and . . . only rarely do they call themselves sons of Yahweh. It is rather God who designates himself as father by calling the Israelites his sons" (*Theology of the Old Testament*, p. 62). Significantly, therefore, "only Christianity has made the fatherhood of God the centre of religion" (p. 61). In the New Testament, the fatherhood of God expresses his love as well as his authority; the reality of redemptive sonship gains strength and warmth through the FATHER-SON relationship in the Godhead.

The loss of Jesus Christ as the SON OF GOD, therefore, can only require extensive reconstruction of the inherited view of God. Stauffer points out that in the New Testament "Jesus can be quite simply called 'God'. . . . In Rom. 9:5 [Paul] transfers a doxological formula which originally applied to God the Father to God the Son: 'who is over all, God blessed for ever, Amen.' The pastoral epistles abound in solemn formulae which are applied now to God and now to Christ. In the Johannine writings we find such *theos*-predicates as regular christological titles" (*New Testament Theology*, p. 114). Stauffer goes on to say that "the Apostles' Creed first attained its present form in the fourth or fifth century A.D., but its theological content is in the last resort derived from the New Testament" (p. 235). No one aware of the profound effect of the Christian revelation in its remarkable illumination of the nature of God can think for a moment that the warmth of the Christian view of God can be retained while the claim of Jesus Christ is rejected. More is at stake than the fact— serious as this is—that to dishonor the SON is to dishonor the FATHER also (John 5:23). To reject the SON requires revision of the biblical view of God. He who rejects Jesus as the One "whom the FATHER hath sent" must also delete "the sending God" from the sacred writings and beyond that, "the God of promise." That is why the alternative to biblical Christianity is not a quasibiblical theism that retains only some of God's names, but rather a speculative metaphysics which, if it retains God at all, renames him to suit its own fancy. "I am come in my FATHER's name, and ye receive me not: if another shall come in his own name, him ye will receive" (John 5:43, KJV). The warning is ever contemporary.

The New Testament contributes these remarkable features to our study of the names of God:

(1) The variety of Old Testament names is replaced by the simple term THEOS/GOD, not—in the Christian understanding—as merely a general term, but as one informed cognitively by the cumulative content of special divine revelation.

(2) The question of speaking aloud the Old Testament name YHWH is transcended; the meaning of the divine Name is now related to the self-manifestation of GOD in CHRIST.

(3) The fixed center of interest in the divine Name now becomes JESUS OF NAZARETH, the promised Deliverer, the incarnate and exalted LORD. More than a hundred names and titles are applied to him, all of which

blend into one in eternity (cf. "the LAMB is the LIGHT," Rev. 21:23, KJV), in illuminating the glory of the God of grace who shall be "all in all" (1 Cor. 15:24).

(4) In THE NAME OF JESUS the promised redemptive presence of God in the midst of human need finds supreme fulfillment—first in the I AM's historical work of redemption, then in the I AM's abiding presence through the HOLY SPIRIT (Matt. 28:20; 1 John 3:24; 4:13), and finally in the I AM's second advent (1 Cor. 15:23; Rev. 4:8).

(5) The Old Testament conception of God as FATHER is enriched by the revelation of JESUS CHRIST as the SON OF GOD, and by the Christian experience of sonship in the HOLY SPIRIT.

(6) By the realities of New Testament revelation the apostolic community is impelled to stress not simply God's proper names, but also the personal names that disclose the inner secret of the divine triune God in whom the God-man is now forever present and forever active in glorified human nature.

THESIS SEVEN:
God reveals himself not only universally
in the history of the cosmos and of the nations,
but also redemptively within this external history
in unique saving acts.

17.
Divine Revelation
in History

STIMULATED BY CONCERNS of ecology and conservation, recent interest in nature and cosmic processes as a created entrustment and an area of divine revelation has somewhat obscured the traditional emphasis on divine revelation in history. To the degree that this tendency challenges the claims of technocratic scientism to explain nature fully and reinstates cosmic realities as a sphere in which God discloses himself, it has genuine merit. But to the degree that it downgrades human history as a divine revelatory sphere this trend forfeits on the one hand what it gains on the other.

Twentieth-century theology unfortunately has questioned not only whether history is a main mode of divine revelation but, more astonishingly, whether the ancient Hebrews even professed to know and to confess Yahweh as the God of history. The Oriental nonbiblical religions characteristically assimilate God to nature. In the neo-pagan West the revival of faith in astrology reflects a similar connection of human destiny with cosmic processes rather than with once-for-all historical events. The recent reception of consciousness-expanding drugs to provide experiences considered as distinctively religious contrasts with an emphasis on external historical relationships as the realm where God is decisively at work.

To be sure, as in any colloquial language, the Old Testament does not rigidly distinguish "nature" and "history" as separate spheres of divine activity. It depicts Yahweh as everywhere advancing his moral purposes, whether in Israel's miraculous deliverance at the Red Sea or in its defeat of the Amalekites and other foes. In the very same hymns (e.g., Psalm 33) in which the Psalmist adores God for creating the universe by his

247

breath, he also praises him for bringing to naught the counsel of wicked nations.

While H. Wheeler Robinson emphasizes that the Old Testament "conception of the God who works in history is inseparably linked to His manifestation in natural phenomena," he insists that the Old Testament focuses on Yahweh specially as the divine moral will active in personal and social relationships. Contrasted with Babylonian astrology, Israel's conception of God is derived primarily not from natural phenomena but from the historical realm (*Inspiration and Revelation in the Old Testament*, pp. 1–4).

As the Creator's creation, man reflects his Maker in mind and conscience and is both a part of nature yet distinct from it. Because they are responsible personal beings, humans transcend biological processes and engage in sociocultural and historical activity. But Judeo-Christian religion repudiates the theory found both in ancient paganism and in modern Hegelian pantheism that culture and civilization directly reveal the Divine. Man was made not for the state nor for civilization but for God. To say that God discloses himself in history, even in universal history, need not mean that human history expressly mirrors the inner life of the Absolute. To say that human history or national history is an aspect of "divine history" objectionably assimilates deity to the historical process and man to the Divine much as does pantheism, which directly externalizes God in cosmic nature. Neither cosmic behavior nor human history is intrinsically divine. As Helmut Thielicke puts it, "civilization originates from God-given gifts of creation; indeed it is protected by the command, given at creation, to 'subdue the world'"; yet it is a broken human response to God's will, for man can devote himself as much to wrong ends as to fulfilling the divine purpose ("Civilization," p. 109a). By viewing concepts like process, event and evolution, that are drawn from historical experience as somehow paradigmatic of God, process theology mistakenly projects the Divine in the creaturely. Contemporary liberation and revolution theologies deplore deifying any history that is laden with human oppression and injustice. For them political revolution, not the once-for-all miraculous events in Jesus Christ's redemptive death and resurrection, is God's decisive speech and act.

Despite the continuing neo-Wellhausian revolt against biblical representations, current scholarship increasingly affirms the reliability of Old Testament historical perspectives. More and more it emphasizes that Moses was not the creator of Hebrew religion but appealed to the enslaved Hebrews on the basis rather of an earlier revelation by the "God of your fathers" (Exod. 3:6, 13, etc.). It was an earlier divine revelation that spurred Abraham from Ur to Haran on the way to Canaan (Gen. 11:31; 12:1–3). Abraham's God differed from the localized Mesopotamian and Canaanite deities who were confined to temples; Yahweh appeared and could be worshiped at Shechem (Gen. 12:6–7), Bethel (Gen. 12:8), Mamre (Gen. 18:1) and in other places. As Jacob M. Myers notes, "He was not primarily the God of a place, but the God of Abraham" the nomad who with his family anticipated Israel as a chosen people. "Abraham's God went with him and spoke to him wherever he went" ("The Way of the Fathers," p. 125). Yahweh was "readily available to the fathers wherever they happened to be" (p. 139). "The people of God conception" has its roots in patriarchal faith even before the Mosaic and prophetic eras (p. 140).

Even in patriarchal times, this interpersonal relationship involves much more than simply inner experience; it involves public decisions and deeds—the promise of a progeny and a land, the purchase of a burial place in the promised land for Sarah and other ancients in their time, and stipulated relationships with Canaanites and Egyptians. Yahweh is a personally present guide who makes promises and keeps them, who communicates and "covenants," who does what is right and just, and who notably discloses himself in external historical acts and vindicates his promises in the external world.

The continuity of patriarchal faith is clear; the God of Abraham becomes the God also of Isaac and Jacob. Yahweh who appears to Jacob is "the God of your father Abraham and of Isaac" (Gen. 28:13). If circumstances impel Jacob to leave his ancestral land, divine revelation enjoins him to return (Gen. 31:3), even as divine revelation spurs him to Bethel to construct a commemorative altar where God had earlier appeared to him (Gen. 35; cf. 28:19). As biblical religion unfolds, its sharp contrast with mystical-ecstatic religions becomes increasingly evident. Biblical religion neither denies the reality of history, nor is indifferent to it, but rather regards history as a focus for Yahweh's revelation and the realm where Yahweh actively operates as Redeemer and Judge.

The exodus as God's special deliverance of the Israelites from Egypt is indelibly stamped on Hebrew history. En route to the Promised Land, confession at the time of sacrifice regularly included the acknowledgment that "Yahweh Lord brought us out of Egypt with a mighty hand . . . and he brought us into this place and gave us this land" (Deut. 26:8-9, RSV). The memory of this historic event stimulated personal devotion and obedience: "I brought your fathers out of Egypt. . . . Now therefore fear Yahweh, and serve him in sincerity and in faithfulness" (Josh. 24:6, 14, RSV). When in danger of losing a vital awareness of God's purpose in the Hebrew nation, the second generation was reminded: "I led you up from Egypt, and brought you out of the house of bondage. . . . I am the Lord your God; you shall not pay reverence to the gods of the Amorites, in whose land you dwell" (Judg. 6:8, 10, RSV).

Years later, when Israel insisted on having a king like the other nations, Samuel reminded the people: "Now therefore stand still, that I may plead with you before Yahweh concerning all the saving deeds which he performed for you and for your fathers. . . . Yahweh sent Moses and Aaron, who brought forth your fathers out of Egypt, and made them dwell in this place. . . . If both you and the king who reigns over you will follow Yahweh your God, it will be well; but if you will not . . . then the hand of Yahweh will be against you and your king" (1 Sam. 12:7–8, 14–15, RSV). As the Psalmist sings, Yahweh "made known his ways unto Moses, his acts unto the children of Israel" (Ps. 103:7, KJV) and did "marvellous things . . . in the sight of their fathers . . . in the field of Zoan" (Ps. 78:12, KJV).

When exile seemed inevitable as a divine punishment for disobedience, the prophets repeated God's promise and their hope of ultimate restoration by recalling Yahweh's victory over Egypt. Amos declares: "Did I not bring up Israel from the land of Egypt. . . ? I will restore the fortunes of my people Israel, and they shall rebuild . . . cities and inhabit them" (Amos 9:7, 14, RSV). Hosea writes: "By a prophet Yahweh brought Israel up from Egypt, and by a prophet he was preserved. . . . I will heal their faithlessness. . . . They shall return and dwell beneath my shadow" (Hos. 12:13; 14:4, 7, RSV). Micah likewise proclaims: "As in the days when you came out of the land of Egypt I will show them marvelous things" (Mic. 7:15, RSV). And Isaiah states: "And there will be a highway from Assyria for the remnant which is left of his people, as there was for Israel when they came up from the land of Egypt" (Isa. 11:16, RSV). In distant Babylon Ezekiel recalled God's intervention in Egypt and anticipated divine restoration to the homeland: "I made myself known to them in bringing them out of the land of Egypt. . . . I will bring you out from the peoples and gather you out of the countries where you are scattered" (Ezek. 20:9, 34, RSV). Haggai, too, linked Israel's prospect for the future with God's past deliverance at the Exodus: "Take courage, all you people of the land, says the Lord; work, for I am with you, says the Lord of hosts, according to the promise that I made you when you came out of Egypt. . . . The latter splendor of this house shall be greater than the former" (Hag. 2:4–5, 9, RSV).

The Bible opens with the Creator God in action as the sovereign, purposive maker of the world and man. From then on his personal presence and purposive action pervade the cosmos and history ongoingly. The God of the Bible is the God of mighty deeds: the God of the exodus and founder of the nation Israel is the selfsame God of the incarnation and resurrection and the founder of the Christian church. The Bible clearly delineates the decisive issues in the human struggle as a course of events in which God is everywhere active either in mercy or in judgment. God in his providence not only chooses the Jewish nation as the social entity within which the Messiah is to appear, but also sovereignly destines the fortunes of all men and nations in relation to him. Just as Yahweh sets the Hebrew theocracy in the midst of the ancient world to witness to the blessings of serving the true and living God, so he charges the regenerate church ruled by the risen Lord to disperse among the modern nations to proclaim redemptive grace and promote justice and order. Christ's death and resurrection are decisively central to historical fortunes. The Creator who stands over the universe in its beginnings stands likewise over its future; Christ's return in apocalyptic vindication of righteousness will issue either in endless blessedness for the godly or in endless misery for the wicked.

The importance of the Protestant Reformation, says T. F. Torrance, lies partly in its reassertion, over against alien scholastic views of God as static Being, of "the biblical notion of the living God who freely and actively intervenes in history" (*Theology in Reconstruction*, p. 54). That the living God actively works in nature and history is an affirmation integral to Old and New Testament proclamation alike. Scripture reflects this divine activity so thoroughgoingly that Robert J. Blaikie ventures to identify as "the primary and essential presupposition of the Bible" the belief that "the true God is a God who really acts in our world and communicates personally with men" (*"Secular Christianity" and God Who Acts*, pp. 27 f.). "For those whose starting point is *biblical* . . . the basic presupposition is the reality, power and over-all authority of God as Agent, God who acts. This is the fundamental faith-affirmation of the biblical Christian: God is real and active" (p. 49).

While the Bible focuses specially on once-for-all divine redemptive revelation in Judeo-Christian history, it in no way denies but insists that God is universally disclosed in history. The Psalms echo and reecho the truth that God has a special purpose for Israel in the midst of history and that he, moreover, reveals himself in the history of every nation. The prophetic writings stress God's moral rule in and over universal history. Although specifically known to the Hebrews in his covenant revelation, Yahweh manifests himself to all peoples everywhere as Creator and Lord of the universe. Both Yahweh's judgments (Isa. 42:13–17; Jer. 25:12–14; Amos 1:3–2:3; Nahum 1–3; Zeph. 2:8–15), as well as his blessings, disclose him to all nations (Amos 9:7). By the preaching of his prophets he summons men everywhere to repentance (Jonah 3:4–8; 4:11). Jewish apocalyptic writing, notably the Book of Daniel, prominently sets forth world history in relation to Yahweh's moral will.

Many Old Testament passages portray the Yahweh who guides historical events as a warrior who overthrows and destroys nations (cf. Jer. 1:10; 12:17; 18:7). He destroys Israel's foes at the exodus (Deut. 8:20; 11:4). He demolishes Israel's corrupt pagan neighbor nations (e.g., Amman, Assyria, Babylon, Egypt; cf. Zeph. 2:5, 13; Jer. 49:38; 51:55; Ezek. 25:7, 16; 28:26; 30:13; Obad. 8). He stands invisibly but personally behind Israel's destruction of corrupt and idolatrous enemy nations (Deut. 7:24; 9:3; Num. 24:19; Esther 9:6, 12). Yahweh is implicitly portrayed as the author of the projected divine judgment and destruction of Israel's foes (Judg. 5:31; Pss. 2:12; 9:4; 10:16; 80:16; 83:17; Isa. 41:11; 60:12), of the Canaanites (Deut. 20:17), Egypt (Exod. 10:7), Moab (Num. 21:29–30; Jer. 48:9, 46) and the Philistines (Amos 1:8; Zech. 9:5) and Tyre (Ezek. 26:17). It is he who divinely wills the destruction of all that obdurately

oppose him by transgressing the Law (Lev. 23:30; Deut. 7:10) and op-
pressing the righteous (Ps. 143:12). His disdain for the liar is specially
indicated (Ps. 5:6; Prov. 19:9; 21:28).
Israel faces the same doom for disobedience (Lev. 26:38; Deut. 28:20,
22; Jer. 9:11) and for idolatry (Deut. 4:26; 8:19–20; 11:17; 30:18; Josh.
23:13, 16) as do others. Superintending the heathen onslaught against the
rebellious Hebrews (Josh. 7:7; 2 Kings 13:7; 24:2; Deut. 28:51; Lam. 2:9),
Yahweh will destroy disobedient Israel through invading nations (Jer.
15:7; 25:10; cf. Deut. 28:63). Israel will be expelled "from the land" and
will perish in exile (Jer. 27:10, 15; Obad. 15; cf. Isa. 27:13).

Yahweh is indeed reluctant to destroy Israel (Deut. 10:10; 2 Kings 8:19;
13:23). But his covenant with them seeks and stipulates a heart of faith
and personal trust in God, so that it is their rebellious reluctance ("but
you would not," Deut. 1:26; Isa. 30:15, rsv; cf. Matt. 23:37) that invites
judgment. Yahweh plays no favorites at the expense of spiritual and
moral criteria.

The Greek notion of revelation typically referred not to what is to be
but at best only to what always is, however empirically invisible that may
be. Only polytheistic Homeric religion assumed that this or that god will
act, punish or reward in accordance with a man's deeds. Old Testament
revelation, by contrast, refers to despoiled beginnings and to the glorious
future, and to Yahweh's decisive redemptive acts at a given historical
moment. The Psalmist gives assurance that Yahweh who revealed himself
in past history and reveals himself in present history will reveal himself also in events that lie ahead. Isaiah rebuked the folly of trust in
political wisdom and foresight (20:5–6; 29:14–15; 30:11–12; 31:1–2) which
cannot foretell a future which is God's creative work. "Among the writings of all peoples," Martin Buber notes, Scripture is "the only record of
concrete action between God and the generations of men, touching in
narrative form upon the origin of this action and in promissory form
upon its goal." Buber remarks that "in the vast edifice of Plato's thought,
in the vast edifice of Kant's thought" there was for such concrete divine
action "not only no place but absolutely no room" (*Kampf um Israel*,
1933, pp. 181 f., quoted by Helmut Gollwitzer, *The Existence of God as
Confessed by Faith*, p. 161).

The prophets speak both of a final age of salvation (Amos 9:11–15;
Hos. 2:16–20; Mic. 4:1–4) and of a coming day of terror (Amos 5:15–
20). Yahweh will overtake a wicked humanity; his periodic judgments
in history anticipate the place of final destruction of the spiritual under-
world (Job 26:6; Prov. 15:11; 27:20; Ps. 88:11; Job 28:22; cf. Rev. 9:11).
In a critical time Yahweh in dire judgment will blind the mind of impenitent humanity to truth (Jer. 7:28), knowledge of the Law (Jer. 18:18,
Ezek. 7:26), righteousness (Mic. 7:2), wisdom and good counsel (Isa.
29:14; Jer. 18:18; Ezek. 7:26), and courage (Jer. 4:9). He will destroy the
heathen in a decisive and climactic end-time. The divine overruling of

history commends faith in God's agency and intervention as the only efficacious principle of redemption (Gal. 3:23).

The more wicked the trend of world affairs, the more the prophet focuses on Yahweh's future exercise of world dominion as King of the nations (Pss. 46, 47, 96–99). God has made himself anticipatively and universally known even to those unreached by special scriptural revelation (Rom. 1:19–21). The Creator's revelation throughout the universe enlists nature, man and history. By deferring to partial aspects of what the Law demands (Rom. 2:14–16) the Gentiles disclose the Law still written on their hearts (Rom. 1:32; Gal. 3:15). Throughout his writings, the apostle Paul affirms the universal reality of an extra-Christian, extra-Hebrew, extrabiblical knowledge of God. Not only Romans 3:29–30, but also Acts 14:15–17 and 17:22–27 declare that the self-witness of God abides in the world and in the human heart. But because human recalcitrance frustrates this revelation, the revelation itself ongoingly indicts and condemns mankind. Additional knowledge of God given in special Judeo-Christian revelation confirms the fact of God's righteousness and divine wrath and proclaims eternal life reserved only for believers of the gospel.

While "salvation is of the Jews" (John 4:22, KJV), the Old Testament looks forward to sharing redemptive revelation with the Gentiles (Isa. 42:6; 49:6). All nations will one day participate in Yahweh's redemptive revelation (Isa. 2:2–4; Mic. 4:1–3). Albrecht Oepke remarks that in fulfilling the revelation of the Old Testament, New Testament revelation is "on the frontier between national restriction and full universalism" ("Apokaluptō," 3:589). God has not left himself without worldwide witness, but it is the Hebrews who are the locus of his special redemptive revelation. For all that, the historical revelation consummated in Jesus of Nazareth is directed and available to all mankind universally (Mark 13:10; 14:9; Luke 2:32; Acts 1:8; 2:39).

In a world where others interpreted all that happens as cyclical process, the Hebrews with their awareness of God's active revelation in external human affairs instituted the very idea of history. Long before later historians and philosophers viewed human events as a comprehensive whole, the Old Testament sees them in relation to the transcendent God who works out his sovereign moral purpose in history. The great prophets of antiquity grasp the unity of history not through political interconnections or mechanical causation but through the steadfast purpose of Yahweh; it is his creative activity that constitutes the very possibility of human history; it is his moral and redemptive revelation that unveils history's inner meaning and shapes the destinies of men and nations. G. Ernest Wright notes that other Near Eastern religions thought that man is "embedded in society" and society in turn embedded "in the rhythm and balance of nature which was the realm of the gods" —so that the aim of human existence was "to fit into the rhythm and integration of the cosmic society of nature" (*God Who Acts*, p. 20). Israel, however, sought to live in history in accordance with Yahweh's transcendent purpose and will, and saw universal history as "a meaningful process *en route* to a goal" (p. 40). The inspired prophets understood the history of their times in relation to Yahweh's relentless devotion to the truth and right that he affirms, his relentless hostility to evil and untruth, and his sovereign grace to a penitent people.

Yahweh is declared to be decisively active even in events that seem most flagrantly to deny him, and even in the clash of wills that we tend to deplore as simply the outcome of perverse human motives. Yahweh vindicates his holy purpose even amid human actions that defiantly repudiate him and his concerns. All historical events are subject to his overruling omnipotence and inescapably serve his intended ends; even the untoward actions of wicked men are made sovereignly instrumental to God's purposes of redemptive grace and triumphant righteousness. Mankind's self-assertive and rebellious will in no case diminishes the course of events under Yahweh's sovereign control; even the most insolent actions of unregenerate humanity promote a divine overarching purpose. As Harold Knight observes, "the actions of the king of Assyria, viewed from the angle of man and his space-time world, may be characterized as determined by lust and ambition, and . . . the prophet puts before us the overweening thoughts which surge up in the conqueror's heart (Isa. 10:7–11). But the characteristic note . . . which stamps (this passage) as springing from the inspired insight of the prophet . . . is that this piece of psychological analysis is given a supernatural setting and pictured in strictest relation to the thought of God. Just when the will of the human agent, in its pride and egotism, is seen in sharpest conflict with all that we mean by the divine, and would therefore seem to be most stubbornly self-determined in rebellion against God, it is represented as the instrument for the fulfilment of a divine purpose. The savage conquests of the Assyrian, though proceeding from brutal lust, are yet the means by which Yahwe makes manifest to Israel the divine condemnation of its sin" (*The Hebrew Prophetic Consciousness*, pp. 165 f.).

Even the Babylonian exile, which seemed to "give the lie" to the covenants and the promises and which to a "nationalistic theology" could only indicate Yahweh's tragic defeat by pagan powers, is declared by Jeremiah to be Yahweh's act. Nebuchadnezzar, in fact, is depicted as Yahweh's servant (Jer. 25:9). To resist the Babylonian armies storming Jerusalem's gates is to resist the very will of God (21:5). Yahweh rewards the king of Babylon with Egypt for his service to Yahweh in punishing Tyre (Ezek. 29:18–19). The words of Amos ring out the theme: "Shall evil befall a city, and the Lord hath not done it?" (3:6, ASV).

The return from exile was no inevitable historical turn of fortunes. Rather, Cyrus the heathen conqueror is depicted as God's elect and anointed instrument for restoring the Hebrews to their land (Isa. 44:24–28; 45:1–3).

It was in this dual context of human wickedness and divine providence that the early Christians comprehended the supreme significance of the crucifixion of Jesus Christ: "This Jesus, delivered up according to the definite plan and foreknowledge of God, you crucified and killed by the hands of lawless men" (Acts 2:23, RSV).

It is noteworthy that Polybius found the incentive for his *Universal History* in the Roman conquest that brought into purview "one world" ruled by military might. In recent times the Nazi vision of power and the communist struggle for world revolution and domination have followed a similar course. "Can anyone be so indifferent or idle as not to care to know," asks Polybius, "by what means, and under what kind of polity, almost all the inhabited world was conquered, and brought under the single domination of the Romans and that too within a period of not quite fifty-three years?" (*Universal History*, I.1). Alert to the God of creation and universal history, the Hebrew prophet Isaiah had spoken centuries earlier, in the context of messianic redemption, of the coming day when all government would be upon the Messiah's shoulder and universal peace would prevail (Isa. 9:6–7). Just as the *pax Romana* has crumbled, and the *pax Brittanica*, so the *pax Americana* is now crumbling, as must any man-made peace built upon human unregeneracy (John 14:27). But the messianic eschatological climax of all history is biblically assured. The pretentious modern views of universal history, based on conjectural theories such as evolutionary utopianism, political aggrandizement or cultural relativism, dismiss the worship of the Hebrews as an outgrown perspective or the retarded viewpoint of a prescientific people. The inspired prophets insist, however, that the unity and disunity of human history turn on God's purpose and man's response to it, that Yahweh ultimately bends hostility to his will and amidst the confusing admixture of good and evil works out his gracious redemptive purpose.

Because God made peace and achieved spiritual reconciliation through "the blood of the cross" (Col. 1:20), to surrender his activity in history would forfeit the Christian faith. The distinctive nature of the Christian revelation of God rests upon the historical life of Jesus of Nazareth who definitively manifests in word and deed the nature and will of the living God of prophetic promise, and who reveals the ultimate reality with which all men must finally reckon. Jesus' resurrection is for the New Testament, as H. M. Kuitert emphasizes, "an event of the same order, in the same historical sense, as the crucifixion (1 Cor. 15:4). . . . Against any temptation to lift Christianity out of history, we must stubbornly hold that historical events form the hardcore of the biblical witness. They are historical events in the full sense; they belong to past time" (*The Reality of Faith*, pp. 163 f.). As Kenneth Cragg reminds us, "The incarnation itself means a *sitz im leben*—a context of geography and land-scape, of circumstance and generation. Military occupation and 'the second mile'; absentee landlords and rapacious publicans; 'letters of Greek and Latin and Hebrew'; bread and wine; sheep astray and patches on old clothes; 'secrets' of 'initiates'; synagogues of dispersion; ships of Adramyttium—all these, and endless else, are the *mise en scène* of the Gospels and the Acts" ("The Convertibility of Man," p. 130).

For the New Testament as for the Old, faith in the living God cannot be divorced from historical actualities. The Hebrew canon that records the history of the acts of Yahweh calls into question every rival under-standing of ancient history; that record is carried forward by the New Testament. Both Testaments affirm the ongoing significance of the re-demptive acts of God and their revealed meaning for man in all ages. The Old Testament, and the New Testament no less so, are at the same time a primary resource of redemptive faith and a historical sourcebook. That sourcebook speaks of history as a moral arena in which the God of creation and redemption and final judgment is even now rewarding righteousness and judging evil in anticipation of an irreversible end-time.

18.
The Leveling of Biblical History

THE SCANDINAVIAN SCHOLAR Bertil Albrektson challenges the view that ancient Israelitish religion was unique in its appeal to divine activity and revelation in history. Other Mesopotamian religions, he contends, contain ready testimony to a divine activity in history (*History and the Gods*). Albrektson compares passages in ancient non-Israelite religious writings with Old Testament representations and concludes that other Near Eastern religions parallel the Hebrew view of divine self-revelation through history.

The Mesopotamian gods (Shamash, for example), Albrektson contends, were not mere nature gods but were viewed as interfering in historical events. Their devotees attributed the outcome of human affairs to an exercise of divine will. Albrektson adduces parallels in the Mesopotamian texts for the Hebrew emphasis on a "word of the Lord" as an active power in human affairs. The Moabites, Sumerians, Babylonians, Assyrians and Hittites—no claims are made concerning the ancient Egyptians who in many ways were distinct from other Near Eastern civilizations —viewed their gods, Albrektson emphasizes, as willfully active in history much as the Hebrews depict Yahweh's intervention.

There is in fact considerable evidence that the religious thought of the ancient Near East widely acknowledged ad hoc divine intervention in history. Famine, destruction or calamity is frequently ascribed to an offended deity.

Albrektson's failure to adduce relevant data from Egyptian religion, however, renders somewhat excessive his claim that divine intervention in historical processes was "the common Near Eastern view" (ibid., p. 112). Moreover, Albrektson's identification with biblical representations of religious phenomena outside Egypt requires careful scrutiny. His

257

claims gain undeserved force from an insistence that the Old Testament exhibits almost no comprehensive goal or purpose in history because only Israel sporadically and not all nations equally are related in Hebrew Scripture to God's historical intervention.

Albretkson is of course right in contending that the Old Testament pays comparatively little attention to universal history. The Bible does not at its outset present us with a comprehensive philosophy of history or of nature, or of man for that matter, nor is such a philosophy systematically adduced in orderly stages.

But to argue from this, as Albrektson does, to the incidental significance of revelational history in the Old Testament overlooks important factors. For one thing, as W. G. Lambert contends, much of the Old Testament, as well as the New Testament, does in fact represent Yahweh as actively at work in history toward the realization of a future goal ("History and the Gods: A Review Article," p. 173). Across the centuries theologians and Christian philosophers not arbitrarily prejudiced about the nature, sources or sequence of the biblical writings have readily exhibited the main turning points of a distinctive scriptural view of history.

To be sure, Karl R. Popper argues that even the Christian insistence "that God reveals himself in history" has hardly any support in the New Testament, and he resists as "pure idolatry and superstition . . . from the Christian point of view itself" the emphasis that "history has meaning" and that its meaning is "the purpose of God" (*The Open Society and Its Enemies*, p. 454). But this verdict circumvents both the Old and the New Testament teaching. That God accomplishes his sovereign purposes in history is affirmed by the Pentateuch and by the Gospels, by the prophets and by the apostles. The Old Testament writers refer repeatedly to God's activity in history, the Gospels speak of God's providential and redemptive involvement in the world. Hence it would be more correct to say that from the Christian standpoint any denial that God is sovereignly active in history reflects a basic departure from the classic texts. The God of the Old and New Testaments exerts moral judgment in and upon human affairs and is purposively and actively at work in history.

Gordon H. Clark emphasizes that Christian theory has both a conception of universal history and a particularistic center of gravity. "That the Christian theory of history is universal in scope is a necessary implication of its basic theism. If God is the creator of the universe and exercises omniscient providential control, the theory must embrace all nations in some way or other, no matter how little we know of them" (*Historiography—Secular and Religious*, p. 241). He adds: "From Abraham to Christ all important events occurred either within the Jewish nation or in relation to it. . . . Since the time of Christ the geographical or national center of gravity has been replaced by a spiritual center, the Church" (p. 242). That Yahweh's dealings in the Old Testament center in redemptive relationships with Israel, therefore, hardly sustains the complaint that Yahweh acts provincially in respect to human history; the Judeo-Christian revelation embraces a history of all mankind.

While Sumerian and Babylonian religion viewed social norms as divinely originated and sanctioned, Israel by contrast, as Lambert emphasizes, considered its standards of righteousness to be rooted in Yahweh's own holy nature and will ("History and the Gods," p. 174). The supposed deity of the ruler as an incarnation of divinity gave wide currency in the ancient religious world to the view that social standards have divine status. But whereas the Sumerian king-list begins with a description of how the kingship was let down from heaven, the God of the Bible is reluctant to give the Hebrews a king. Lambert abandons the view, once shared with Albrektson, that the "eternal destinies" in Babylonian religion are divine decrees with historical application. In Akkadian religion, he emphasizes, the destinies presume not an unfolding plan in history but a status quo; social patterns like birth and marriage rites are simply viewed as belonging to the divinely given order of things.

Lambert further rejects, as lacking in convincing textual support and therefore conjectural, the notion that Hebrew apocalyptic was derived from the Babylonian notion of the destinies (ibid., p. 175). Babylonian texts do indeed contain some predictions, but such decreeing of the future falls within no comprehensive plan of history and is often highly general in nature and capable of multiple fulfillment. R. D. Biggs contends that astrologically connected prophecies look forward not to a particularly specified king but to whatever king may be ruling at the time of the designated omen (*Iraq* 29 [1967]: 117 f.). Where detailed predictions of historical events do appear, uncertainties over the dating of the Babylonian fragments, Lambert says, leave their purpose too unclear for precise conclusions about any connection between the Babylonian and the Hebrew genres; moreover, the predictions do not in any event "lead up to a grand climax of history, or indeed to any climax at all" ("History and the Gods: A Review Article," p. 177).

For all Albrektson's generalizations about religious parallelism, he nonetheless concedes that "the idea of divine acts in history" in ancient Israel and in ancient Mesopotamia "may well have occupied a rather different place in the different patterns of belief" (*History and the Gods*, p. 115). But within the basic premise that "historical events as a *medium* of revelation is a general Near Eastern conception" and the insistence that Israel's view of history was not unique, Albrektson's observation is more confusing than clarifying. This is all the more the case when he asserts "with some confidence . . . that the idea of historical events as divine manifestations has marked the Israelite cult in a way that lacks real parallels among Israel's neighbors" (pp. 114 f.). Bernhard Anderson stresses the fundamental role that historical remembrance holds in the ancient Israelite cult in contrast to the sporadic evidence of incidental historical interest in the Mesopotamian religions (*Understanding the Old*

Testament, pp. 1 ff., 163 ff.). Von Rad speaks of Israel's "stubborn need to push forward to the perception of far-reaching historical continuities" attested in the Old Testament historical books (*Weisheit in Israel*, pp. 366 ff.). But the fundamental difference between Hebrew and Near Eastern religions generally lay not simply in contrary patterns of belief, or in the central role of remembrance of past traditions or deep internal Hebrew longings for a spiritually significant future, but in the transcendent revelation of Yahweh whose self-vindication in the history of Israel undermined the validity of alternative belief-patterns, traditions and longings.

Before the "history of religions" investigations of a century ago, special revelation was more readily regarded as a uniquely Israelite-Jewish phenomenon, since the distinctive prophetic character of the Old Testament revelation was not widely challenged. But many who engaged in controversy over the rise and development of religion viewed Hebrew religion on very different assumptions as but one expression of the universal quest for religious reality. Babylonian creation narratives, especially the Gilgamish epic, and Egyptian Wisdom writings were said to "confirm" a deep and wide tradition of literature reflecting a common religious impulse to which Hebrew religion must be assimilated. Even the Hebrew temple had roots in an older Canaanite-Phoenician tradition of temple-building; presumably, therefore, the Hebrew conception of Yahweh was not without similar links.

Intensive Old Testament studies shaped an inevitable reaction against this reductionist tendency. Without denying all continuities with the culture and world of the past, Walther Eichrodt and other scholars emphasized the irreducible uniqueness of Israelite religion. The dissimilarity of Israel's religion from that of ancient contemporaries was clarified by unprejudiced study of the larger Near Eastern milieu in contrast with the Hebrew cult. But it was equally evident from the severe penalties the Hebrew Scriptures impose for confusing the two types. While the Old Testament itself witnesses to Israel's adoption of Canaanitish practices and rites, it deplores this syncretism as religious harlotry. Albright described Solomon's temple as "the height of syncretism" but this neither left in doubt the superiority of Yahweh nor issued in a mixture of religions (*Archaeology and the Religion of Israel*, pp. 142–55).

In his monumental 1933 work *Theologie des alten Testaments* (*Theology of the Old Testament*) Walther Eichrodt singles out the concept of the covenant as the basic category that provides the overall pattern of Scripture. The covenant-hypothesis gained emphasis through the renewal of interest in biblical theology. It also attracted special attention during the kerygmatic shift of concentration from historical events or "the mighty acts of God" to the internal interpersonal perception of divine revelation. Scholars who minimized the relationship of Yahweh to external historical processes searched the canonical literature in support of the hypothesis that redemptive events reflect the faith-perspective of the worshiping community.

Since George E. Mendenhall's analysis of "Covenant Forms in Israelite Tradition," and his *Law and Covenant in Israel and the Ancient Near East* (1955), the covenant motif has increasingly served as a framework for understanding the Old Testament. Theodorus C. Vriezen emphasizes that the Old Testament's use of the covenant symbol to express God's relationship to man shows that the special relationship between Yahweh and Israel is not a natural relationship but has, in contrast with other ancient Oriental religions, a historical basis (*An Outline of Old Testament Theology*, p. 140).

Mendenhall emphasizes that the covenant tradition was no late invention projected upon Hebrew history, but that covenantal pacts were a common feature of the ancient world even in pre-Mosaic times. He sees in the Old Testament covenant materials a reflection of the Hittite treaty form. John Bright follows Mendenhall in viewing the theory as rather firmly established.

Form critics, historians and archaeologists are divided over numerous aspects of the treaty-covenant theory, notably disagreeing not only with each other but among themselves. American biblical scholarship largely concedes that "the religious foundations of the twelve-tribes federation stemmed from Moses and the Sinai covenant" as Mendenhall affirms ("The Monarchy," p. 188). Not all treaty ingredients are present in the biblical accounts prior to the Book of Deuteronomy, which critics date no earlier than the end of the eighth century B.C. In earlier portrayals of Yahweh's covenant, apparent parallels are found only for some ingredients of the Hittite treaty form. Even so, there are evident difficulties in holding that a treaty form in existence between 1450 and 1200 B.C. should have been adopted as a format to depict Yahweh's relation to his people in the eighth century or later.

Scholars disagree over whether Exodus 19–24 and Joshua 24 provide evidence of the treaty-covenant hypothesis. Mendenhall considers it "quite likely" that the oldest designation of the Decalogue as "the Ten Words" rests upon a covenant tradition, since covenants were considered and called "words" of the suzerain. He speculates that "theological usage of the 'word' of God may therefore be very closely bound up in its very origin with the covenant" ("Covenant," 1:716a). But the first explicit occurrence of covenant terminology appears in Genesis 6:18 in the prediluvian Noahic context. Genesis also refers to an even earlier Edenic testamentary promise (cf. L. Alonso-Shökel, "Motivos sapienciales y de alianza en Gn 2–3," pp. 295 ff., and Meredith Kline, "Law Covenant," p. 9), immediately after Adam's fall (3:15), and prior to that of God's disclosure of verbal commandments and statutes during Adam's still unfallen state (2:16). Many hesitate to view the Ten Commandments as treaty stipulations since these stipulations are entirely given in "thou

shalt/thou shalt not" apodictic form. Even should the apodictic form of
the Decalogue prove not wholly original, that would hardly attest the
nonoriginality of its basic principles of unqualified allegiance to the one
sovereign King Yahweh to be mirrored in a particular quality of life that
includes love to strangers as well as love for neighbors "as yourself"
and moral obligations not simply to the privileged but also to widows,
orphans and indentured slaves.

To what extent if any the Old Testament covenant materials deliberately reflect the ancient suzerainty treaty forms is therefore widely de-
bated, in part because of the partial nature of archaeological finds, in
part because one price of redaction theory is that it leaves its opponents
unsure about the history, and in part because the data can be organized
according to differing presuppositions. More important than the origin
of forms and the employment of common vocabulary in any event is
semantic usage and theological nuance.

The absence of a full-blown treaty form in the Old Testament is,
moreover, not the only respect in which the covenant form and treaty
forms notably differ. The arrogant tone of some ancient Egyptian treaties
sets them apart from the biblical covenant. Besides that, the supposed
Old Testament dependence on standard literary forms does not, insofar
as we know them, involve a simple duplication. The presumed parallels
exhibit an independent use reflecting, in Edward F. Campbell, Jr.'s words,
"radical transformation of the borrowed forms and, of course, content"
("Moses and the Foundations of Israel," p. 150). The special characteristics of Israel's own commitment stand in the forefront. Mendenhall's
assumption of an analogy between the Old Testament covenant and
other ancient Near Eastern treaty pacts runs dead-end, as he himself
acknowledges, into the contrary fact of a conditionless covenant that
imposes no obligations on Abraham (cf. Vriezen's criticism of Mendenhall's view in *The Religion of Ancient Israel*, pp. 145 f.). In his latest work
(*Old Testament Covenant: A Survey of Current Opinions*, 1972), Dennis J.
McCarthy provides a comprehensive survey of the development and criticism of covenant theory. He himself, in his earlier work *Treaty and
Covenant* (1963), shares the more cautious approach of German scholars
like Noth and von Rad and the latter's student Klaus Baltzer (*The
Covenant Formulary*).

More recently scholars holding neo-Wellhausian positions have thrust
aside the hypothesis of an early emergence of the Old Testament covenant based on treaty similarities. Dependence of the Old Testament
covenant theology upon ancient Near Eastern treaty forms is dismissed
as inconclusive and improbable. Those who emphasized the internal
perspectival rather than external historical basis of the covenant concept
unwittingly prepared the way for a relapse to post-Wellhausian commitments which move the covenant treaty theme once again to the outer
margin of interest. But the search for historical continuities at the expense of transcendent revelation in aiming to vindicate an early role for

the Hebrew covenant also served a theory that, seeking a nonsupernaturalistic explanation, emphasized later rather than earlier dependence on the Near Eastern milieu. Lothar Perlitt returns almost the whole distance to Wellhausian notions by viewing covenant theology in Deuteronomy as a development in the seventh century B.C. (*Bundestheologie im Alten Testament*).

In a retreat from theological interest in the Old Testament, Georg Fohrer and his follower Ernst Kutsch not only reject the recent covenant theological constructions but also espouse a hermeneutical shift that considers contemporary theological concerns (meaning for me) not the central significance of the scriptural texts. Fohrer regards international political realities as ultimately no less important than Mosaic Yahwehism for the establishment of the Hebrew monarchy (*History of Israelite Religion*). He rules out the totally new in the religious development of the Hebrews, not excepting the category of covenant. Fohrer follows an existentialist methodology but his results (cf. *Theologische Grundstrukturen des Alten Testaments*) are a variety of Old Testament theology colored by personal idealism. He rejects revelation in the sense of truths divinely given in the word of the Old Testament text or given in the recorded witness of inspired prophets, or given in divine acts in history. The rejection of historical revelation serves Fohrer's synthetic approach which from the outset assimilates wisdom literature and psalms to existential idealism. While the Old Testament prophets are said to have personal experiences of revelation, the cultural and sociopolitical value judgments that Fohrer promulgates seem underivable from these experiences. His theological method in fact lacks a basis for considering the revelation experiences of the prophets as normative, or for translating those experiences into valid truth and principles of action. Not unlike Johannes Hempel (*Gott und Mensch im Alten Testament*) he holds that revelation comes as an inner experience gained in trust in God's rule over all reality and in pursuit of a community of faith that this confidence supports.

The "God who acts" theology initially reasserted transcendent divine intervention in the form of biblical redemptive events, and in correlation with this affirmed a distinction of Hebrew religion from that of the environing religious milieu. But James Barr notes that when more recent writers picked up this theme they minimized and even ignored any miraculous divine intervention, emphasizing instead a providential ordering of circumstances, or even simply a religious faith that views history in terms of acts of God—a faith expressed in the covenant pattern. The covenant form was held to be derived from the Hittite treaties, and the covenant content from the religious imagination of the Hebrews, since historically real saving events were now considered mythical representations of an inner spiritual reality (*The Bible in the Modern World*, p. 83). That the redemptive historical-act form was simply an Israelite way of thinking is then reinforced by the insistence that representations of a worldwide flood or of Noah's ark or of Jonah and the leviathan are really legendary accounts and not to be considered factual. What therefore began as an emphasis on divine saving acts ends in the reduction of biblical religion to a literary rather than historical representation.

What centrality one ascribes to the covenant in Hebrew religion matters little, nor does whether one attributes the covenant concept to an early or to a late sociopolitical context, if its underlying theological stance and content are not derived from transcendent revelational considerations. The basic idea of the covenant, Yahweh's divinely initiated fellowship with the chosen people, occurs in fact in Old Testament contexts unrelated to the covenant theme, and this circumstance prompts some interpreters to regard the covenant alone as too restrictive a theme through which to comprehend all the realities of the Old Testament literature. Yet the importance of the covenant in the Hebrew history of salvation (the Noahic covenant, the Abrahamic covenant, the Sinai covenant, the Shechem covenant, the Davidic covenant, the New covenant) raises it to unquestionable significance. Yahweh's covenant with his chosen ones reaches to the earliest era of Old Testament history, antedating the conquest of Canaan, and extending back not only into the seminomadic but into the primitive nomadic life of patriarchal Israel. Through the covenant with the patriarchs, renewed with Moses and David in behalf of the Hebrew peoples, Yahweh ongoingly published his saving purpose and his holy ordinances.

The term *diathēkē* occurs 270 times in the Septuagint for the Hebrew *b'rith* as expressive of its essential meaning. The etymology of the Hebrew original is elusive; perhaps the most likely theory links the term to the Akkadian *bâru* for "to bind" or "bond." Whether the stipulated relationships are between man and man or between God and man, the Old Testament concept always includes the conviction that God personally participates in the covenant. Even if the so-called secular covenant (e.g., 1 Sam. 18:3; 20:8; 23:18) involves basic legal commitments, it does not differ from the theological covenant in respect to Yahweh's transcendent participation, which does not at all have the character of a legal contract although it may be legal in structure. Yahweh stands watch over the sworn duties between fellow participants in covenant. Violation is considered a sinful disregard of the divine will evocative of Yahweh's wrath (Amos 1:9). This intrahuman legal compact was sealed by oath and sacrifice (Gen. 31:54), integrating all Israel's social life as a community of Yahweh. The theological covenant lifts the Old Testament revelation securely above any reduction of Hebrew religion to a transactional works-legalism, since it emphasizes the initiative of God and the indispensability of faith as the context of spiritual obedience.

Mendenhall rightly notes that the covenant cannot really be equated with a modern political "constitution" which binds people to each other and to a common political structure, since the covenant binds the Hebrews to a common divine Sovereign who stipulates a particular religious ethic and law. He notes governing convictions that underlie the covenant commitment and distinguish it from ancient political perspectives, even as Saul learned to his discredit: that Yahweh and not some earthly sovereign defines what is licit and illicit in warfare, that no human ruler can automatically assume that a war he commands has divine sanction, and that when acting on divine authority no political figure can claim personal prestige in victory.

Against the explanation of Hebrew religion by surrounding Near Eastern culture, Jakob Jocz argues effectively that even patriarchal Hebrew society cannot be regarded as culturally primitive; that the Hexateuch, or first six books of the Bible, already discloses all typical features of the prophetic outlook; and that the covenantal document (the Ten Words), Sinai-covenant and the exile, testify to "the utter difference between ancient Israel and the Canaanites in respect to religion" (*The Covenant*, p. 11).

The Hebrew relapse to the old Bronze Age paganism, with its trust in political force and military power rather than in Yahweh, shaped the society and state against whose deterioration the great prophets inveighed. It may be too much to claim, as Mendenhall does, that "the cultic/political system of Jerusalem during the monarchy had nothing to do with the Yahwist revolution and was actually completely incompatible with it" and that "during Solomon's regime the Jerusalem state became a very typical Syro-Hittite political system" (ibid., p. 166). But the displeasure of the preexilic prophets can hardly be overstated. With the prospect and fact of exile, the center of hope shifts to the Suffering Servant (Isa. 52:13–53:12), God's obedient and innocent servant, who for the sake of others bears pain in consequence of their failings, and is condemned to death as a criminal for a crime he did not commit, but in his devotion to life and kingly authority claims and receives a redeemed humanity.

One can assuredly parallel bits and pieces of Old Testament religion here and there in the ancient Semitic world. Even in this respect we must be on guard against confusing etymological similarity with theological identity, since conceptual use and intention rather than linguistic form are decisive for meaning. The differences are often more striking than the similarities—the absence of pure monotheism amid the emphasis on the uniqueness of certain divinities, the mechanistic rather than personalistic conceptions of predestination and destiny, the absence of absolute creation in so-called creation accounts, and so on. One does not elsewhere really find prophecy in the Old Testament sense of God who foretells what will happen and who keeps his Word. More striking still is the total structure of Hebrew religion. If one sets Old Testament religion as a comprehensive whole (monotheism, creation, revelation, election-love and the exodus, sin and redemption, law as an obligation to God, promise and fulfillment, redemptive history and universal judg-

ment) alongside other views, one cannot escape the impression of incomparable uniqueness. Above all stands the one living God of the Old
Testament, the God in whose nature righteousness and love are equally
ultimate, the transcendent Creator who prohibits images, the Lord who
vindicates his purposes in history.

To refer one or more of these features to gods X, Y, Z, Q and so on
would have been intellectually less difficult. Belief in the one true God
was the great Hebrew distinctive, a belief the Hebrews referred to God's
own self-disclosure. As David Noel Freedman notes, "in evaluating the
competitive claims of Yahweh and other gods and goddesses, the biblical
writers invariably appeal to the data of history, to the mighty deeds
wrought in the presence of a cloud of witnesses—sympathetic, hostile,
and indifferent—for these deeds constituted testimony to the world"
("The Biblical Idea of History," p. 37). "From the beginning it was recognized that Yahweh was the Lord of history, horizontally as well as
vertically, and that all the nations and the whole of their experience
belonged to his scheme of things" (p. 39).

Eric Voegelin reminds us that "in pragmatic history the event was too
unimportant to be registered in the Egyptian records" (*Israel and Revelation*, p. 112). "What emerged from the alembic of the Desert was not
a people like the Egyptians or Babylonians, the Canaanites or Philistines,
the Hittites or Arameans, but a new genus of society, set off from the
civilizations of the age by the divine choice. It was a people that moved
on the historical scene while living toward a goal beyond history" (p.
113). Israel's history marks "a break in the pattern of civilizational
courses" (p. 116), says Voegelin. "Israel does not owe its importance to
numbers" (p. 119). "Here was a people that began its existence in history
with a radical leap in being; and only after the people had been constituted by that initial experience did it acquire, in the course of centuries,
a mundane body of organization to sustain itself in existence. This
sequence, reversing the ordinary course of social evolution, is unique in
history. It is so unbelievable that positivist historians, as for instance
Eduard Meyer, do not believe it at all" (p. 315), because a society is supposed to start from primitive myths and advance gradually to the spirituality of transcendent religion rather than "start where a respectable
society has difficulties even ending" (p. 316).

19.
Faith, Tradition and History

IN JUDAISM'S ONGOING HISTORY divine revelation came to mean many things; the term acquired so wide a circumference that exact definition became unsure. In his *summa theologicae* of Judaism, Maimonides would not even comment on Mount Sinai and the giving of the Law, and emphasized mainly prophetic intuition. Spinoza in the seventeenth century dismissed the unique historical events and nature miracles of the Old Testament as having originated in prophetic misinterpretation and therefore devoid of philosophical significance. Today, while twentieth-century theologians frequently stress the redemptive faith of the Hebrew Old Testament, they minimize the historical factuality of the miraculous events that so prominently mark the ancient Jewish literature.

In his monumental two-volume work which first appeared in German in 1957 (*Old Testament Theology*), Gerhard von Rad, the most influential Old Testament theologian of our time, proposes a prestigious reconciliation of history and faith. Von Rad recognizes that Israel's confessional account of her experiences in terms of revelation and faith differs vastly from the view of Israel's history held by modern historians who interpret the past without reference to supernatural realities. As von Rad sees it, both approaches are needed: the theologian must faithfully reflect Israel's faith-perspective, and the secular historian must interpret the past without the hypothesis of God.

"For us," von Rad writes, "the sources' simple picture, which the pioneers of literary analysis took as the starting-point of their investigations, has now to be seen as an end-stage, in which a long process of interpretation of Israel's early history came finally to rest. Here everything is shaped by faith; even the association of the events into a grand

267

path of salvation is not merely historical record, but is in itself already an acknowledgment of the leadership of God. This history of the traditions before they reach their final form in the written sources comprises an incalculably diversified chapter of Israel's theology. In general, even the simplest fusion of two originally independent units of tradition was in itself already a process of theological interpretation" (1:4 f.).

This leaves the question of the historical factuality and of cognitive validity so much in mid-air that later writers influenced by von Rad's emphasis on faith-traditions, and by Martin Noth's theory (*History of Israel*) of the gradual formation of Hebrew tradition-cycles, move in both more positive and more negative directions. Franz Hesse, who dismisses interest in Israel's confessional or kerygmatic account of her history, contends that Christian theology should concern itself with Israel's history in the same way that the modern historian depicts it. He distinguishes the events as Israel interpreted them from how they must appear to others. For Friedrich Baumgärtel neither the secular nor the sacred account of Israel's faith has Christian relevance, since Israel's faith is assertedly not built on historical fact, and Christianity must look to its own concerns.

Declaring for historical revelation, the Pannenberg school encourages reconciliation between faith and history by insisting that they imply each other in both the Old and New Testaments. According to Rolf Rendtorff ("The Concept of Revelation in Ancient Israel") all of Israel's history has inherent theological relevance; for him the interpretation of the Old Testament events is not arbitrarily imposed but belongs to the history no less than the events themselves. Rendtorff resists any approach in terms of events held in isolation; God's act in the history of Israel he equates with the dynamic totality of Israel's historical career, a totality that includes the confessional interpretation known as "tradition history." The historical episodes and their kerygmatic interests so interpenetrate each other that later aspects of the history actualize the past in a new and profounder way. The act of God is not to be limited simply to isolated historical events as seen by critical historical research or to the confessional account of the meaning of history but includes also the transmission of the redemptive happenings and their meaning.

Christopher R. North reflects the tensions posed for recent Old Testament studies by the counterclaims of faith and history. "It is not too much to say," he remarks, "that the whole edifice of Jewish religion and morality" rests upon the assurance that Yahweh rescued the Hebrews from Egyptian bondage in the crossing of the Red Sea and that he is with them throughout their history ("History," 2:608a). It is significant that North here makes Hebrew religion rest upon internal "assurance" more clearly than upon external revelational events. "A nation's life and character," he notes, "can be even more powerfully influenced by what it believes to have been its history than it is by events long past [and] only 'remembered' as they are embodied in national tradition."

North observes that conservative scholars resist correlating a sound theistic faith with a biblical history that is not "academic-scientific"; critics, on the other hand, do not regard faith as incompatible with theologically interpreted history. Critics, concedes North, "differ among themselves" about "just how much" of the Old Testament historical writing is to be considered objective history, or rather, to be considered salvation history. But then, instead of identifying as indispensable to a viable biblical faith a modicum of salvation history that is also authentic history, North observes that as long as critics are "reasonably conservative" in treating history and share the Christian faith in salvation history "as almost all of them do," differences between fundamentalists and critics may be "less acute than they often are believed to be" (p. 608a).

We are less interested in fundamentalist-nonfundamentalist controversy than in precisely identifying divine redemptive history that is more than simply divine redemptive tradition. Presumably to elaborate a "reasonably conservative" criticism, North tells us that the Old Testament "prophets and historical writers were not concerned with pure history," but they give us "an interpretation of history viewed, as it were, sub specie aeternitatis" as "in the sagas of the Pentateuch and in the prophetical writings" (ibid., p. 608b). Early Genesis "stories of the Creation and the Flood . . . were almost certainly ultimately derived from Babylonian mythology" (p. 609a). North then adds the traditional biblical interpretation: "The world had its origin in the creative will of God," man was made in the divine image, and human disobedience had "disastrous consequences, culminating in the Flood, from which only Noah and his family were preserved." "It is probable," he adds, "that Jacob and Joseph were originally gods" whereas "Noah is the Utnahpishtim of Babylonian mythology" (p. 611b). In context, North provides a confusing explanatory note on how salvation history, mythology and history are to be correlated. Later he tells us that "it is probable that the Genesis saga was prefixed, so to speak, to an Israelite *Heilsgeschichte* whose primary impulse was the Exodus, and that some of it was originally of pagan Semitic milieu." As North sees it, the Yahwist redactor "adapted" both Israelite and Canaanite folk traditions "with consummate skill to the Israelite *Heilsgeschichte.*"

At both the beginning and end of his essay North raises the problem of theological validity posed by these faith-tradition and history-tradition tensions. "Can Christians today subscribe with undivided conscience," he asks, to the conception of biblical history "as a series of happenings according to the 'definite plan and foreknowledge of God' (Acts 2:23)?" (ibid., p. 607b). Is the biblical interpretation of history "one to which an intelligent man can subscribe with an undivided conscience?" (p. 611b).

North answers: "If we approach the question from the standpoint of Christian faith . . . our conclusion may be that the biblical interpretation of history is, at least in broad outline, right. . . . The *Geschichte* which produced the Bible is, take it by and large, only explicable in terms of the biblical *Heilsgeschichte*. In short, biblical history *is* salvation history" (ibid., pp. 611b, 612a). So ambiguous and so qualified is this conclusion that North's view pointedly illustrates the dilemma of scholars who evade scientific-historical questions concerning the biblical redemptive acts while they rely instead on theological interpretation to compensate for the supposed factuality of these acts. By refusing to insist that biblical redemptive history is the very same history that scientific historians investigate, such biblical critics unnecessarily bequeath Old Testament historical concerns to neo-Wellhausian anti-supernaturalism.

Like North and others, Daniel Jenkins agrees that "perhaps the most important element in the Old Testament understanding of history" is its "rich conception of tradition as an active power in the fulfilment of the destiny of the people" (*Tradition, Freedom and the Spirit*, p. 37). Jenkins says that "there is no certainty" that God's promise to Moses came precisely as Exodus 3:15 states (p. 36), although the major reforms in Israel "drew their inspiration and their authority from reinterpretation of the past." Yet primeval history was rewritten to reflect "a remarkable development in the religious imagination of Israel. . . . The ascription of these interpretations, which are obviously the work of later writers," says Jenkins, "has frequently proved a puzzle to modern readers, but an understanding of the Hebrew attitude to tradition makes it intelligible" (p. 39). "Thus what happened to the Patriarchs, and, in particular, what happened to Moses and the children of Israel in the Exodus, happened in a very definite way to all generations of Israelites and was a relevant factor in their experience" (p. 41). To thus contemporize revelational events not only shifts the revelational locus from the past to the present, but also clouds the primacy and factuality of underlying, once-for-all historical acts. To emphasize the simultaneity of past history with the ongoing stream of community consciousness, instead of focusing on objective redemptive acts in past history, elevates living tradition to the central reality, and gives religious tradition an undeserved "revelatory significance" (p. 43).

Evidence that many biblical critics remain dissatisfied with recent modern attempts to achieve a faith-history synthesis based on critical assumptions is not hard to find, yet projected reconstructions seldom challenge these assumptions in depth. Frank M. Cross's *Canaanite Myth and Hebrew Epic* ventures a "preliminary" investigation in quest of a "new synthesis" of the history of Hebrew religion premised on the "perennial and unrelaxed tension" between myth and history as characteristic of the Hebrew outlook. Canaanite mythic motives are said to impinge upon such formative events as the exodus, the covenant and the conquest "to point to their cosmic or transcendent meaning" (pp. 87, 143 f.). Cross gives significant scope to the contributions of David and

Solomon, whereas the role of Moses and of Joshua, dwarfed in fragmentary tradition, is obscure.

Existentially oriented biblical scholars are disposed to put visible or invisible quotes around "the Sinai-event" in what Lou Silberman calls "a sort of phenomenological suspension or legerdemainish movement from *Geschichte to Historie*." The emphasis on faith-factors in interpretation tends to devalue the importance of external history, eclipse objective historical elements, and shift discussion of divine disclosure to internal considerations. Silberman himself reflects this changed understanding of biblical revelation when he asserts that the Sinai-event "turns out on inspection to be less central than is often taken for granted" ("Revelation in Judaism"). It would be highly interesting to learn when and under what circumstances Silberman "inspected" the Sinai-event. He reinterprets Sinai on the thesis that "the revelation is not bound up with external events" and that "the biblical tradition is not tied to a literal affirmation of Sinai's public account." What clearly underlies his exposition is a bias against historical revelation common to those who regard revelation as a sporadic internal experience.

This movement away from an emphasis on external historical revelation was anticipated in Judaism by medieval mystics who stressed an immediate revelatory relationship between man and God. Gershom Scholem notes, however, that while many earlier Jewish mystics emphasized a direct revelatory contact between the individual and God, they had "no thought of denying Revelation as a fact of history." The public revelation of Sinai they viewed as the original act of divine disclosure to the Hebrews "whose true meaning has yet to unfold itself" (*Major Trends in Jewish Mysticism*, p. 9). Such divorcing of historical revelation from rational revelation, that is, from the divine communication of the meaning of revelatory acts to chosen prophets, prepares the way for universal mystical disclosure, an immediate revelation given to all men. Whatever may have been the intention of earlier Jewish mystics, this view runs counter to the traditional emphasis that Jewish religion involves a definitive revelatory history.

As twentieth-century kerygmatic theologians internalized revelational disclosure, some scholars who were reluctant to forego the Bible's insistence upon history as a revelational locus ventured to redefine history. Erling Hammershaimb of Denmark insists that the Greek confinement of history to external events probed by historical research need not be binding for the Hebrew view. Hammershaimb broadens the term's meaning to include phenomenal activities that affect human life; narratives that refer to such phenomenal or spiritual influences he then considers historical narratives (address on "Cult and History in the Old Testament"). The Hebrew cult's correlation of confidence in Yahweh's deliverance of his chosen people with specially important historical events Hammershaimb contrasts with the Canaanite confidence in repetitive

nature-cycles. But the line here between myth and history vacillates uncertainly, since he does not resolve the question whether Yahweh truly
intervenes in historical outcomes. More than other communities of faith,
Israel may indeed have accepted the view that events express the will
of their gods, and therefore history plays a larger role in the Israelitish
cult. But the question still remains whether this understanding of history
as a revelation of Yahweh's will has any credible basis.

Growing knowledge of the pre-Israelite history of Palestine and of
the ancient Near East increasingly calls into question Wellhausen's
skeptical assault on the role of Moses and on the religious history of
the premonarchic period. Today there is widening criticism of both
Noth's theory that the Old Testament rests on the gradual formation of
Hebrew tradition-cycles and von Rad's emphasis on faith-tradition that
leaves the actual historical elements much in doubt. The efforts of critical scholars who deny that the Mosaic era involves a sequence of events
including the Hebrew exodus from Egyptian oppression, the wilderness
wanderings, the Sinai experience, and the conquest and settlement of
Palestine are less and less convincing. The many projected alternatives
are often highly speculative and signal a sorry accumulation of untenable hypotheses. The end result of tradition-history, which has in recent years become the fashionable methodology in biblical study, is often
as atomistic as that of the older literary criticism; it produces a series
of discrete traditions vouchsafed by the insight of modern authorities
as to who transmitted (*überlieferte*) each separate tradition and why.
Yet it was not simply a random collection of traditions but the whole
that the community of faith found sufficiently helpful and was constrained to canonize. All too often it is the critical biblical scholar who
is least able to show how the Bible is spiritually significant for the
church as a corpus of literature.

Against critics who support a late evolutionary emergence of ethical
monotheism in the eighth century B.C. and espouse a post-Mosaic origin
of the divine name Yahweh, Martin Buber insists that "tradition criticism" carries back at least to Moses' time the prophetic confidence in
Yahweh. Buber contends that higher criticism has established at most
only that the biblical tradition contains a number of fundamental literary
types, but not that the Old Testament is a composite of parts, chapters
and sentences drawn from a plurality of documents. Even indisputably
recognized sources and dates would ascertain only literary layers, not
layers of religious development, since a primitive religious element could
be found in a late literary form, and vice versa. Hence he proposes by
"tradition criticism" rather than by "source criticism" to resolve the
question whether the biblical history of Israel's faith stays near the
actual historical events. Here the basic question becomes: what primitive unity is presupposed from earlier times in each significant crisis of
faith? (*The Prophetic Faith*, pp. 4 ff.).

Buber begins with the Song of Deborah, almost universally regarded as genuine. Its repeated conjunction of Yahweh and Israel, he insists, involves "the presupposition . . . that Israel is not simply an ethnological unity, but a religio-active one" and that "the faith and the relationship to God of the faithful" therein expressed "cannot have come into being at the time of the composition of the Song itself" (ibid., pp. 10, 13). This indispensable background Buber finds in Joshua's assembly at Shechem (Josh. 24:1–28), where Joshua demands that the people choose between Yahweh and other gods. The Israelites, swearing not to forsake Yahweh "for he is our God" (24:18), put away foreign deities for "Jehovah, the God of Israel" (24:23, ASV).

This historical life-decision links Yahweh and Israel in a manner that presupposes a still earlier history and relationship, for it involves renewal of a covenant which had been unfaithfully preserved, rather than initiation of a sacramental covenant (vs. Micha Joseph Bin Gorian, *Sinai und Garazim*, p. 405; Ernst Sellin, *Geschichte des israelitisch-juedischen Volkes*, 1:84 f.; Martin Noth, *Das System der zwoelf Staemme Israels*, pp. 66 f.). This conviction of Yahweh's compact with Israel finds its prior background in the covenant "which Yahweh has made with you" in Exodus 24.

Yet Buber notes that there the "first appearance of the credal formula YHVH God of Israel" (Exod. 24:10) occurs in a narrative passage, whereas "its actual origin . . . of necessity . . . must be a divine saying handed down, a word of YHVH Himself" (*The Prophetic Faith*, p. 20). Hence Exodus 20 provides a primitive form of the Decalogue whose contents in no way exclude their assignment to the time of Moses (so also Ludwig Koehler, *Der Dekalog*, p. 184, vs. the attribution of formation of the Decalogue to the disciples of Isaiah by Mowinckel, *Le décalogue*, p. 160, and "Zur Geschichte der Dekaloge," 1937, or to the later exilic and postexilic period by Hoelscher, *Geschichte der israelitischen und juedischen Religion*, p. 129). At the origin of the creedal formula stands the divine Word of Yahweh which prefaces the Ten Commandments: "I am Yahweh thy God, who brought thee out of the land of Egypt, out of the house of bondage" (Exod. 20:2, ASV). From this it is clear that the link between Yahweh and Israel antedates the beginning of the covenant between God and the Hebrew people.

Consequently there arises what Buber calls "the most important question in the history of Israel's faith" (*The Prophetic Faith*, p. 23), that is, whether this unique relation has its beginning in the exodus from Egypt. And the history of the Decalogue indeed presupposes the earlier events of the Book of Exodus. In Exodus 3, in the dialogue of the burning bush, Buber notes Yahweh's double reference to "my people," so that "YHVH here declares with utmost emphasis (such repetition is the Biblical way of expressing emphasis), that Israel already now is His people, although He, YHVH, does not yet—before revealing Himself to the people—designate Himself as their God, but as God of the people's fathers" (p. 27). Hence it is not only on Sinai, but at the Red Sea, that Yahweh is Israel's

God, and the Old Testament prophets fully recognize this background of their faith (Hos. 11:1; 12:10).

Thus Buber finds a unitary center of religious experience reaching back across a millennium of Old Testament history at least to the time of the exodus and therefore refuses to confine the reality of Yahweh to a post-Mosaic prophetic awareness of God. The principles by which Buber shows the prophetic faith to be that of Mosaic times can be extended backward in time to show indissoluble links to the patriarchal era. John Bright not only champions Mosaic monotheism (*Early Israel in Recent History Writing*) but, like W. F. Albright, vindicates facets of patriarchal history as well. Albright insists that "only the most extreme criticism can see any appreciable difference between the God of Moses in J E and the God of Jeremiah, or between the God of Elijah and the God of Deutero-Isaiah. . . . A balanced organismic position may consistently hold that the religion of Moses and of Elijah, of David and of the Psalmists was the same in all essentials" (*History, Archaeology and Christian Humanism*, p. 154).

According to Bright there was not enough time for separate and diverse traditions to be welded into a single narrative. If we ignore Moses as the divine "word-bearer" who stands at the center of God's mighty redemptive acts and in that sense is founder of Israel's faith we would have to "posit another person of the same name" (*A History of Israel*, p. 124). For Edward F. Campbell, Jr., Moses represents and articulates a monolatrous faith that stresses the transcendence of Yahweh and opposes magic, divination and necromancy. Moses, he thinks, introduced "the comprehensive model of covenant, which attaches ethical content and motivation to the high transcendence of Israel's God" and "provided the means for social cohesiveness" ("Moses and the Foundations of Israel," pp. 145 f.). On some datings, Campbell notes, there is now "less than a quarter-century between Moses' death and the earliest Hebrew epic poetry about the deliverance from Egypt and the covenant-giving at Sinai" (p. 154).

Few New Testament scholars have emphasized more than John Knox that only faith can recognize the revelatory and salvatory character of biblical events. Knox upholds a dynamic view of history, in which the creative knower is fully as important as what is externally given. Biblical history must be understood not within a philosophy of history that embraces all historical reality but within the faith of the church. Even the actual "event of Christ" has as a revelational event no fixed being or duration. Knox does not question that Jesus is a particular historical person and makes more room for the historical than does Bultmann. But to know that Jesus is Christ requires a faith-commitment, a faith-response evoked by the church as a community of faith. But "the historical Event to which all distinctively Christian faith returns is not an event antedating the Church, or in any sense or degree prior to it" (*The Church and the Reality of Christ*, p. 20). Since the existence of Jesus

Christ is an aspect of the one Event in and by which the church lives, the church cannot deny Jesus' existence. While not irrational, this faith-commitment is deeper than individual rational consent: "Accepting the Cross does not mean understanding it; it means almost the contrary—recognizing a dimension and a potency in human life which defy our comprehension and our little systems, whether of law or truth" (Knox, *The Death of Christ*, p. 168).

Such representations elicit warnings from W. Norman Pittenger (he too readily exempts Knox from them) that such emphases dwarf the central importance of the "actual historical career of Jesus" and un-critically elevate church tradition which may follow a false no less than true course ("Some Implications, Philosophical and Theological, in John Knox's Writing," an essay included in the Zeitschrift for Knox, pp. 14 ff.). "The career of Jesus of Nazareth simply as a human career, was," Knox says, "a relatively unimportant incident in Jewish history. The event of Jesus Christ the Lord was historically the important thing; and this event happened only in the life of the Church. . . . In a word, except for its connection with the Church, the event of Jesus of Nazareth was hardly an event at all" (*The Early Church and the Coming Great Church*, pp. 46 f.).

In a later work, *The Church and the Reality of Christ* (pp. 55 ff.), Knox curiously assures us that the church witnesses more fully to her Lord than anything that written records can say about him. One cannot escape the impression that the christology of the church is for Knox a product of the church, that is, a Christian way of understanding whatever the "factual" data may have been. Not only is history not self-interpreting, as is indeed the case, but for Knox it carries no objective or intrinsic meaning, and the church as a community of faith transcendently gives the meaning. Knox does not view the acts of God as objectively histori-cal; faith is what supplies the transcendent references. Nowhere does he speak significantly of the being of God or of revelational history as objectively transcendent realities and as being distinct from the faith-per-spectives of the Christian community. While this stance disallows him any universally valid cognitive claims, he as a universalist would none-theless exclude no one from the salvation that only Christians can know.

Champions of secular theology often elaborate their plea for Chris-tian social involvement in the modern historical arena within a theo-logical context that excludes the objective reality of God and tran-scendent divine agency in the external world. As Blaikie notes, secular Christianity dispenses with the divine Agent of biblical theology and retains, at best, only an emphasis on divine acts (*"Secular Christianity" and God Who Acts*, p. 62). Theories now frequently grouped under the rubric of secular Christianity reject the transcendent Creator who is personally active in nature and history and admit no external activity of God distinguishable from natural processes and human events. While they cling to remnants of biblical theology, such theories forfeit the

foundational biblical world view that sets all reality within the framework of the supernatural, living, acting God. Reliance on scientific empiricism as the decisive test of reality and truth requires that one finally
speak only of events stripped of all personal divine reference.

Ronald Gregor Smith, whose *The New Man* (1956) in some ways anticipates Harvey Cox's *The Secular City* (1965), combines secular theology
with an existential stance. While Smith equates God's act with "what
happens to us in the relation of faith" (*Secular Christianity*, p. 119), he
does not convincingly answer criticism that in these circumstances "the
concept of God's being" is not strictly "deducible from his act." To existentially exclude the objectivity of God necessarily dissolves all rational
basis for belief in divine agency, a point that David Jenkins makes in
critiquing Paul Tillich's view of reconciliation.

Of Tillich's exhortation to faith merely "that one is 'accepted'"—and
of his notable use of passive verbs that in no way mention a divine Agent
because of his refusal to objectify God—Jenkins remarks: "If there cannot be said to be an agent, it is extremely difficult to see what meaning
can be given to the notion of 'being accepted'" (*Guide to the Debate
about God*, p. 93). Jenkins rightly insists that the term "acts of God"
cannot logically be retained "unless the transcendent God exists both
transcendentally and in an object-like manner (i.e., He is 'there' to be
the agent)" (pp. 93 f.). While Tillich spoke of historical revelation, he
did so in his own way. He requires us to distinguish clearly between
objective revelation in historical events (whether in contrast to or in con-
cert with revelation in nature, in inspired utterance, and other external
media) and revelation considered to be internal but depicted as historical
because it is received at a particular moment in history as all communication to man must be. Tillich writes: "Historical revelation is not revelation in history but through history. Since man is essentially historical,
every revelation, even if it is mediated through a rock or a tree, occurs
in history. But history itself is revelatory only if a special event or a
series of events is experienced ecstatically as miracle" (*Systematic
Theology*, 1:120). Much as Tillich insists that "the unique event Jesus the
Christ . . . is given to experience and not derived from it" (1:46), his
existential orientation provided no objective basis for any transcendent
ontological claim or implication.

In view of the contemporary loss of awareness of a divine presence
and activity in the external cosmic order and in human events, Arnold E.
Loen focuses the debate over secularization squarely on the issue of acts
of God (*Secularization*, p. 8). Paul van Buren's "God-is-dead" theology
asserts that "men today can no longer give credence" to the New Testament conception of divine action "as an intervention in this world by
heavenly, transcendent powers"—"language about 'God who acts' must
be interpreted in some other way" (*The Secular Meaning of the Gospel*,
pp. 5, 100). Because empirical validation is lacking, all supernatural realities and all reference to a transcendent Actor and to divine purposeful

activity in historical and cosmic events must be dismissed. To speak of an "act of God," van Buren contends, is simply to express our private commitment to a particular perspective. Thomas J. J. Altizer makes the death of "the God who is sovereign Creator and transcendent Lord" necessary to radical Christianity and to the "contemporary Christian atheism" that he espouses (*The Gospel of Christian Atheism*, pp. 31 ff., 89 f.). Although John Macquarrie correlates the two in the title of his book *God and Secularity*, he properly insists on the ontological reality of God and distinguishes secularity as a this-worldly scientific outlook. He does not, however, disown secularity as a way of regarding reality that is incompatible with scriptural revelation, and maintains that Christians must view God and the world as in polar tension. But no world view can do justice to reality unless it leaves room for personal agency, both divine and human; to emphasize the indispensable role of such personal agency requires unhesitating rejection of the "secular presupposition."

The incentive for a swing to this-worldly political theology stemmed in part, no doubt, from reaction to Barth's other-worldly dialectic of revelation that Bonhoeffer deplored in *Letters and Papers from Prison*. As Regin Prenter emphasizes, revelational "actualism" runs through Barth's writings all the way from his *Epistle to the Romans* to his *Church Dogmatics*. By this Barth means that "God is in the world of man only in each specific act of revelation," so that there is no *"being* of the revealed or the revealer in the world"* (Prenter, "Dietrich Bonhoeffer and Karl Barth's Positivism of Revelation," p. 106). In Barth's view divine revelation has "no extension in time but occurs afresh each time." "After the act of revelation there is . . . no reality of revelation in the temporal realm . . . only the memory of the act of revelation" (p. 106). Denied any extension in time, the reality of revelation is bound ongoingly to momentary acts of God's disclosure. Barth remarks on Romans 3:28: "The 'instant' is and remains unique, different and something foreign over and against all 'periods' before or after, it does not continue into the 'after' nor find its roots in the 'before', it stands in no temporal, logical context, it is always and everywhere the utterly new, always what God—who alone is immortal—is, has and does. *'Credo quia absurdum'*." Prenter comments that in Barth's view "God's word cannot have an extension in time, a history as such. It can only touch the world of sinful man in the form of a *futurum aeternum*, which breaks into man's existence each time anew, in the act of God's self-revelation" (p. 109). While Barth does not deny the temporal reality of revelation, "God's revelation has no extension in time, no worldly history, it is never . . . a possession. It is never 'being', but always an expected or remembered 'act' " (p. 112).

The implications of Barth's view for the content of the Bible are staggering. While the Old Testament looks ahead to the New, and both Testaments await the eschatological future, the prophets and the apostles nonetheless claimed to have conveyed truths which are objectively given and authoritative and for which men need no longer wait. The implications of Barth's view for revelation in history and nature are no less astonishing. As Bonhoeffer pointed out, an unrelatedness of divine revelation to the world means confrontation only in terms of negation. Prenter argues that Bonhoeffer too much ignores Barth's emphasis on the relevance of revelation to man's secular life and his insistence that God is a partner in the covenant with his people (ibid., p. 123). Bonhoeffer's point is, however, that to concentrate on God as nonobjective Subject dwarfs his role as the Creator and Lord who confronts mankind in the time-sphere (*Act and Being*, pp. 90 f., 138 f.). God's being for man, and concern for the world, then exists only to the extent that man has faith in him. Barth came later to emphasize God's eternal decree and his inner trinitarian revelation. Nonetheless those who shared Bonhoeffer's interest in God's *being* for us and for the world, as a reality that precedes personal faith-response, demanded a theology directed to *this world*.

In time, dialectical-existential theology with its nonobjectifying faith-claims erupted into controversy over the reality or nonreality of God. An emerging vanguard of theologians emphasized that whether God is for real or not, this world is certainly for real, and that injustice, oppression, pollution and other social problems not extraneous to God in his revelation call for urgent revolutionary change. Here the recorrelation of God and history works itself free of both once-for-all supernatural redemptive acts in the Judeo-Christian past and supernatural inspired interpretation. It focuses instead on radical social change in the present for spearheading an ongoing divine demand for radical change.

The emphasis on supposedly divine action divorced from both biblical once-for-all miracles and a scripturally disclosed meaning is being exploited today by the theology of revolution. This current movement transmutes an appeal to the God of action into theological justification for Marxist-type economic social change. When and as it claims biblical legitimacy, it differs from the recent existentializing of faith-concerns in at least three ways. First, it insists that divine action involves transforming external history and demands the forced alternation of unjust social structures. Second, it champions a literal divine deliverance of the Hebrews from Egyptian oppression under the leadership of Moses since it considers the exodus a paradigmatic sanction and imperative for revolutionary sociopolitical action. Third, it assumes the validity of eschatological representations of God's vindication of righteousness and final containment of evil, and in present history promotes an anticipation of this ultimate triumph. By losing the larger redemptive understanding, if not the historical factuality, of the biblical redemptive acts, neo-Christian theology moves toward contemporary revolutionary violence that forces social structural change (instant millennium?) by the church; meanwhile it eclipses the supernatural God who in accord with his new covenant seeks not only the renewal of vagrant society but the regeneration of rebellious mankind in personal conformity to Jesus Christ, the risen exemplar of a new humanity. Instead of being driven by the prophet Moses to the fulfilling exodus to be found in Jesus Christ (Luke 9:31), this neo-Christian perspective blurs interest in the redemptive resurrection of the Crucified One and finds instead in the story of Moses and the exodus a model for socioeconomic revolution.

God's historical revelation does, to be sure, carry inescapable political implications. One need only recall the Exodus account set in the context of Egyptian oppression, or the politically relevant emphases of Amos, Hosea and Isaiah. The Old Testament often speaks theistically in political terminology. Gerhard von Rad remarks, and rightly, that the ancient Hebrews were specially aware of God's sovereignty in political history. The political model of God as King and Lord in relation to man is prominent in Hebrew thought; Yahweh's sovereign triumphant holy will takes kingdom form and even the covenant has certain outward political treaty resemblances. Any appeal to the Bible, however, that exaggerates and elevates political metaphors to redemptive primacy tends to misinterpret and manipulate these into ideological motifs. Political imagery in the Bible does not exhaust nor fully delineate God's historical disclosure; even the Old Testament contains a variety of models. In expounding Yahweh's revelation, the Bible is concerned with far more than the relation of political man to his Creator. The attempts of both Israel and Judah to orient life to a political pattern rather than to the transcendent kingdom of God led to collapse and exile. Eventual restoration is beyond the reach of the generation of exile; the history of redemption turns aside from the creative prospect of the Mosaic era for a time. The future is a matter of Yahweh's judgment and grace and glory, and its radiant prospect reappears in Jesus of Nazareth the Messiah of promise.

With an eye on structural changes in the social order, revolutionary theology molds "the active God" of the Bible to forced and violent change of the status quo. Jitsuo Morikawa, combining the demand for radical social change with an emphasis on evangelism, asks in a booklet, *Pastors for a Servant People*, whether economic revolution devoid of specific religious orientation falls completely outside divine redemptive activity. Or, as he thinks, does it reflect God's "working in the midst of world revolutions, judging and redeeming as the Lord of the world?" (p. 11). That the living God is truly active in secular affairs is evident from the scriptural designation of Cyrus as the Lord's "anointed" to accomplish certain divine purposes (Isa. 45:1-7; cf. Ezra 1:1). But to assimilate this principle to a universal salvation history equated with sociopolitical structural changes, and usually moreover in terms of some debatable modern ideology, is quite another matter, especially when revolutionary violence is accommodated as the transforming dynamic.

If God is "where the (revolutionary) action is" and acts in revolution per se, then no transcendent criterion remains to distinguish one revolution from another as demonic or divine. German Christianity once tended to identify God's act and voice in history with Hitler's seizure of power in 1933. Ancient Mesopotamian kings similarly represented major political and military policies as products of a divine Word or Command, and hence identified their gods as the moving force in history. We find here, however, no true parallel to the biblical motif of divine promise and fulfillment. From the outset, authentic Christianity nourished deep interest in the predicament of mankind for whom Christ died, and every effort by Christians to seal themselves off from society at large has eventually been disowned as a grievous mistake. An even more serious error, however, is that of dwarfing the biblical God of covenant and redemptive intervention in history. This arises by neglecting the central biblical realities and the larger righteousness demanded by Yahweh in a mixture of both desirable and undesirable social changes and perhaps even terror tactics that leave rebellious man's inner nature untouched by the dynamic of divine redemption. Here nature and history are manipulated by modern mythologies of human destiny. Biblical tradition is reinterpreted to provide a religious aura for this-worldly aspirations, and the living God's historical redemptive activity, consummated in him of whom Moses spoke (John 5:46), is completely secularized.

20.
Revelation and History:
Barth, Bultmann and Cullmann

THEOLOGIANS AND PHILOSOPHERS have taken highly divergent positions in the revelation-and-history debate. These range, on the one hand, from the claim that all history directly unveils God's inner experience to the contradictory assertion, on the other, that no historical event whatever has or can have any revelational value.

Various premises underlie the denial that history in any way reveals God's nature or ways. Some scholars consider the past without value because they assume either that anything historical is insignificant or that anything temporal is relative, or that the present has evolutionary superiority, or that only the supertemporal and eternal has divine import or, more radically, that no God whatever exists to reveal himself in history.

Existentialists maintain that God's reality is communicated in internal confrontation only. Some dialectical theologians correlate divine disclosure with an external superhistory that can allegedly be distinguished from the historical events investigated by scientific historians. Technocratic scientism has served notice of eviction from the world of experience not only upon supernatural events but also upon such claims of inner transcendent divine confrontation. We can speak only with tongue in cheek of earthquakes and tornadoes as "acts of God." All talk of God's Word and God's Act—whether in the Pauline or Barthian or Bultmannian sense—must go, so it is said. Tested by the methodology of empirical science, the very idea of God allegedly reduces to meaninglessness and unintelligibility. This antimetaphysical note issues especially from recent empirical philosophy of the so-called analytic or logical positivist type. In *Language, Truth and Logic*, A. J. Ayer argues, as did Ludwig Wittgenstein, Rudolf Carnap and Herbert Feigl, that human language provides information only about sense objects; it is fraudulent, he suggests, to claim knowledge of a divine being who transcends sense-experience.

That all history has divine revelatory significance has also been affirmed on diverse assumptions. Hegel, the pantheistic idealist, regarded both human activities and the world process as direct externalizations of the Absolute. Philosophical theism has generally viewed historical events as a mirror of universal divine providence and purpose. According to Judeo-Christian theology, God is present and active in all historical events either in grace or in judgment; moreover, within the history of the cosmos and of nations God reveals himself further in special redemptive acts attested in Scripture.

The Christian emphasis on the temporal incarnation of the Logos and on God redemptively at work in history countered the ancient Greek idealistic notion that events are but a shadow world and eternal forms or ideas ultimately real. This radical dichotomy required, as Thomas F. Torrance notes, discarding the biblical view "of the Eternal entering the world of space and time, as unreal, or at best as a 'mythological' way of expressing certain timeless truths" (*Theological Science*, p. 17). This supposed Christian "mythology" the Gnostics ventured to transform into a speculative *gnosis* wherein Christian symbols had merely cosmological significance. But a later idealist like Fichte could say—and in profound contempt of redemptive history—"it is the metaphysical element alone and not the historical that saves us." Torrance mentions Tillich and Bultmann as among contemporary thinkers who use thought-forms of their own to repeat the ancient effort "to 'demythologize' the Christian Gospel by subjecting the crudities of faith to scientific treatment and so producing a Christian understanding acceptable to the world of culture and science" (p. 18). In the interest of the living God who speaks and acts neoorthodox theologians rightly deplored medieval scholastic and modern notions of a "static divinity," but in speaking of God only in inner revelational commerce and communion with man they surrender God's divine disclosure in historical events.

Contemporary scholarship tends to eclipse the theme of divine revelation in history because of the epistemological principles that currently govern historical science. By circumventing the resurrection of Jesus of Nazareth and the anticipatory redemptive acts integral to Christian theism, the restrictive presuppositions of modern history pose a crisis for the theology of revelation.

For the most part, modern historicism espouses critical concepts of reason and of science that reflect the influence of Hume and Kant. To be sure, Kant tried to rescue mathematics and physics from Humean skepticism and aimed to preserve the possibility of religious faith; many post-Kantian thinkers adjust his epistemology in an effort to make it serviceable to Christian belief. But Kantian Criticism no less than Humean skepticism connected both historical and natural science with an epistemological theory that excluded a theology of historical and cosmic revelation. Kant's theory not only deprived mankind of any cognitive knowledge of supernatural reality, but also held that it was the human mind alone that contributed whatever order and coherence is found in sense percepts and historical events. As a result, any arguments for God that invoked the design of nature or the providential ordering of history are contravened, since the inner mind of man becomes the architect of order in the external world. On Kantian presuppositions, nature and history are always known as a uniformly closed system of causes and effects, being so ordered by the knowing mind, with the result that miracles in nature and once-for-all events in history were automatically excluded. As Kant conceived it, human thought presents cosmic and historical processes in all-inclusive causal continuity and unbroken regularity. In brief, Kant's theory not only eliminates from history any proof or evidence for divine being and action, but also any intelligible need for it.

For more than a century after Kant projected his system, critical interpretation presupposed the uncompromised causal continuity of nature and history. Whether pantheistic or naturalistic, the prevailing philosophy of both history and philosophy of nature assumed the unbroken continuity of events. The reality or nonreality of God therefore makes no difference whatever in respect to the possibility of miracles and unique historical events. The nature of the cosmos and history—whether in view of external causal relationships or of the innate conditions of human knowing—rules out the miraculous a priori. Such segregation of theistic belief from historical revelation found ardent support in the radical liberalism of Harvard Old Testament scholar Robert H. Pfeiffer. He regarded as "a snare and a delusion" the attempt to correlate theology and history, and ventured the remarkable verdict: "Not only scholars, but even the humble untutored believers of all faiths, intuitively know that facts and faith do not mix" ("Facts and Faith in Biblical History," pp. 13 f.).

The early twentieth century witnessed declining confidence, however, that the scientifically represented "laws of nature" are indeed truly objective readings of the external world. Repeated revisions of scientific formulas, and finally the acceptance of revision as something ongoing, nurtured the conviction that scientific explanations indicate only what is useful for purposes of prediction and control, and not what objectively and necessarily "is" the case. While they broke with the concept of causality, champions of technocratic science nonetheless retained the ideal of exhibiting nature in terms of predictable mathematical continuities; their nuclear and missile experiments made increasingly undesirable and even abhorrent the possibility of any "act of God" that might miscarry the hopes of their expensive and life-jeopardizing ventures. The notion that historical events are causally determined also began to crumble, inasmuch as human volition influences and complicates historical happenings.

But declining certainty over objective natural uniformity and historical continuity produced no revival of faith in biblical miracles nor in divine once-for-all redemptive acts. In fact, on the one hand the radically secular view gained ground that nature is inherently haphazard, history intrinsically unpredictable, and all events unique. Scientific creativity, it was emphasized, imposes on nature whatever patterns are pragmatically most serviceable to man; it is the interpreter who selectively and creatively molds the meaning of history. On the other hand, uncritical acceptance of empirical positivism that excludes all spiritual forces from the outer world of nature and history heightened interest in existential-dialectical thinking in which divine action is redefined as internal divine-human confrontation.

Indebted to theories about man's creative contribution to knowing and knowledge, dialectical-existential theology made internal personal response the locus of divine disclosure, and deprived the revelation of the living God of any external manifestation in nature, history and even human reason universally. Existentialism deliberately rejected the subject-object interpretation of the knowledge-situation and insisted instead that the knower in his act of reception contributes decisively to both the content and the form of knowledge. Human decision becomes creatively formative in interpreting historical events, whose meaning is therefore not universally valid and objectively accessible to all men but gains significance for individuals only through subjective inner decision. The existential historian has no interest in recovering the past as a collection of objectively given fact and meaning; instead, he absorbs information with a view to the future.

Those who tried to correlate such an approach with an insistence on the reality of God were bound to locate the supposed special or revelational meaning of history not in external considerations but in man's internal response. Divine revelation was now held to be given not in outer historical events, but rather in the inner historicity of the self, that is, in the subject's personal response to those events. Such an encounter is not valid revelation, however, because it is based not on objective disclosure but on experience.

In previous centuries even heretics like Celsus (in the third century) recognized that Christianity claims to be a historical religion and conceded that the God of the Bible is concerned with the concrete realities of history, and shapes memorable events in the history of humanity. But in recent times theologians like Bultmann have insisted that historical redemptive events are inessential to Christianity. The revelation of God in historical redemptive acts, upon which orthodox Christian theism has insisted, they transmute into transcendental eschatology that makes all centuries simultaneous, and every man and woman the recipient of special revelation.

Bultmann's commitment to Heidegger's ontology and to a causally determined cosmos ruled out any active divine role in nature and history, a view completely at odds with the biblical emphasis that God acts in a real way in the external world. Bultmann sounds impressively orthodox in his criticism of those who cannot find meaning in history. But his own theology finds that meaning in such radically personal and individual terms that he too is found to exclude any objective meaning, whether in universal or in biblical history. His volume devoted to the question of meaning in history closes with these words: "Man who complains: 'I cannot see meaning in history, and therefore my life, interwoven in history, is meaningless,' is to be admonished: do not look around yourself into universal history, you must look into your own personal history. Always in your present lies the meaning in history, and . . . only in your responsible decisions" (*History and Eschatology*, p. 155). In other words, Bultmann tries to relocate divine disclosure in the historicity of the individual.

If the kerygma or apostolic proclamation is at the center of the Christian faith but excludes the resurrection of Jesus Christ as an objective historical event in deference to positivistic views of science or history, then the Easter kerygma must be explained as a historical development either on the basis of Jesus' attitude or self-understanding, or of the disciples' self-understanding, or of contemporary Christian self-understanding. According to Bultmann, the Gospels are not historical accounts but simply forms used to present a message that propels us to existential decision. Jesus remains the content of the kerygma as an eschatological occurrence; he is God's saving act experienced in existential response. Nothing historically factual is relevant except that he lived and was crucified, and even this historical requirement flows not by any logical necessity from an existential stance but issues rather from Bultmann's desire to avoid the total collapse of what is historical into simply a Redeemer-myth.

The post-Bultmannians wrestle with the fact that in the Gospels history and kerygma interpenetrate each other, but they remain eager to exempt the content of faith from answerability to historical investigation. By moving beyond the historical, Gerhard Ebeling arrives at encounter with God in Jesus, and a faith that renders biographical interest superfluous (*Word and Faith*, pp. 288 ff.). Herbert Braun breaks completely with objective-external history, and finds in Jesus only a symbol of our own self-understanding ("Der Sinn der neutestamentlichen Christologie," *Gesammelte Studien zum Neuen Testament und seiner Umwelt*, pp. 243–82). Van A. Harvey (*The Historian and the Believer*) rejects specifically the faith-stance of those kerygmatic theologians who confidently insist that the essence of New Testament Christianity is unimpaired by the acceptance of positivistic historical criticism.

Basic to Heinrich Ott's detachment of faith from objective factuality is his definition of faith as "a relation of confrontation with the one God" (*Theology and Preaching*, p. 37). But why should the fact that in matters of faith the Christian deals with one indivisible God argue persuasively against the historical reality and coherent plurality of the "saving facts" stated in the Apostles' Creed and in various Christian catechisms? While Ott does not insist that the "saving facts" did not "happen," he does insist that "creation, incarnation, crucifixion and resurrection, ascension and second coming move on quite another plane of 'happening' and belong to a quite different dimension of divine history" and that "we gain access to the integrating historical moments . . . solely through faith" (pp. 37-38). These emphases he links with the post-Bultmannian notion that faith is far more than a matter of self-understanding—it is an encounter with God *extra nos*, indeed, with Jesus Christ himself as a personal relationship contained necessarily in self-understanding (pp. 45, 47). Neither option carries us, however, to the indispensability and centrality of external redemptive history on which Christian theism insists.

A certain attractiveness may surround views like those of Bultmann and the post-Bultmannians, who make the Christian faith independent of the historical events described only in the Gospels, and that of Hegel, for whom those events illustrate a more fundamental spiritual principle or general truth. However much existential theology was a protest against Hegelian idealism, it, like Hegelianism, was dedicated to rescuing Christianity from bondage to a particular history. Both systems accordingly eliminated the very historical redemptive revelation that earmarks biblical religion. Influential contemporary theologians tried to escape the historical problems attaching to Christianity by resorting to an almost agnostic view of Jesus' historical existence, and then reducing the Gospels to creative faith-projections of the believing community. Donald MacKinnon calls this effort a maneuver "doomed in the end to evacuate Christian faith of any serious intellectual content" (*Borderlands of Theology*, p. 30). He remarks further: "The mistake of supposing that one can translate propositions concerning actual historical transactions into propositions relating to the spiritual lives and religious activities of individuals and of groups is a radical one; perhaps a crowning illustration of the entrenched habits of the idealist of supposing that the inner life of the subject is alone truly significant, and that when we deal with its supposed, evident realities, we are on firm ground from which the onslaught of critical reflection, whether historical or philosophical, cannot dislodge us. . . . But . . . we have in fact committed ourselves to an anthropocentrism in theology that could be criticized as a most dangerous species of mythological illusion . . . and this, let us not forget, on the threshold of the new 'Copernican revolutions' of the space-age" (p. 88).

The dialectical and existential intent to combine christology with historical skepticism unwittingly negated the crucial center of Christian faith, namely, Jesus of Nazareth. Kierkegaard had said that it "would be more than enough" were the words of witnesses to inform us "that in such and such a year God appeared among us in the humble figure of a servant, that He lived and taught in our community, and finally died" (*Philosophical Fragments*, pp. 51 ff., 87). In this approach, events decisively important to the Gospel writers are blurred into a thin, dispensable verbal tradition. If divine disclosure occurs only internally, then no necessity remains for external objective events as carriers of revelation. Bultmann was able to define the resurrection of Christ in terms of the believer's existential rise to new being on the condition of responsive trust in a transcendent Word that internally confronts us. The miracle of the historical resurrection of the crucified Jesus he twisted into mythological code-language for this inner experience.

Because the gospel centers in a redemption accomplished in the past and once for all in Jesus Christ, Barth recognized such existential attacks on the miraculous biblical events as an unbelieving assault on the central citadels of Christianity. Despite this insight, Barth made concessions to the modern critical theory of history and thus frustrated his own best efforts to vindicate the past redemptive acts and miracles of the Bible. In contrast with his earlier dilution of the resurrection into "the pure presence of God," Barth in his later writings spoke insistently both of Jesus' resurrection as external and of a coming future resurrection. But since he retained the basic thesis that divine revelation is given to man only in responsive trust, and is never objectively disclosed in historical events or in natural phenomena, his efforts to vindicate the externality of revelation were less than successful, for he assigned revelation to the stratosphere of superhistory rather than to the realm of universal history investigated by historical research. The early Barth posited revelation in *Urgeschichte* (prehistory); he later abandoned this for a different correlation with present history that distinguishes between *Geschichte* and *Historie*, but that is no less subject to many of the earlier criticisms.

Somewhat unclearly, Bonhoeffer charges Barth with "the positivism of revelation" (*Letters and Papers from Prison*, pp. 91 f., 95, 106 ff.). Seeking to clarify this criticism, Regin Prenter directs it against Barth's view that the supernatural and miracles like the virgin birth are realities out of all relatedness to the world to be accepted "take it or leave it" by a law of faith ("Dietrich Bonhoeffer and Karl Barth's Positivism of Revelation," p. 97). On this approach, says Prenter, "all the truths of revelation confront the whole worldly life of man without meaning" (p. 98).

"The so-called historico-critical method of handling Holy Scripture ceases to be theologically possible," says Barth, "the moment it conceives its task to work out from the testimonies of Holy Scripture (which does ascribe to revelation throughout the character of miracle) . . . a reality that lacks this character" (*Church Dogmatics*, I/2, p. 64). Here he is on firm ground; ordinary methods of historical research, as Barth says elsewhere, can neither "assert nor deny that there and there God has acted on man" (I/1, p. 375), that is, can adjudicate with certainty the occurrence or nonoccurrence of a revelational event.

But Barth also accepts Martin Kähler's notion that "we possess no sources of a life of Jesus which an historian could accept as reliable" (ibid., I/2, p. 64). He insists that revelation is real only in inner response and is impossible to the neutral or scientific observer. He maintains, in addition, that divine revelation was not conveyed in the historical aspects of the life, ministry and resurrection of Jesus of Nazareth. Barth writes: "For the non-neutral . . . historically there could be established not merely little but nothing, that is to say, a thing that invariably was . . . quite without importance for the event of revelation" (I/1, pp. 373 f.). Here one recalls the similar comment of Eduard Schweizer: "Even if we had the best sound film of a Jerusalem newsreel of the year 30 A.D. (or whatever it was), it would not help us much, since it could not show what really happened on that day. Only Easter, the revelation of the Spirit, shows what really happened" ("The Relation of Scripture, Church Tradition and Modern Interpretation," pp. 45 f.).

In a detailed analysis of Barth's representations of *Geschichte* and *Historie*, Gordon Clark criticizes Barth's notion that *Historie* (the sphere of historical research) involves a "neutral" investigator. Clark criticizes even more Barth's ambiguous assertion that the Bible is disinterested in the historical certainty of revelational-events (*Historiography—Secular and Religious*, p. 292). Barth believes, and rightly, that historical investigation cannot absolutely—but only with relative exactitude if at all—determine the history of ancient biblical times (also of ancient non-biblical times, we would add). But he errs seriously in saying that Christians have no historical interest in the documents of revelation in the sense of events "possible in that time and civilization," and that acceptance of a biblical *Geschichte* in its theological and revelational aspect is "quite independent of the historical judgment upon its temporal form" (*Church Dogmatics*, I/1, p. 373).

Barth's concept of history, Richard R. Niebuhr protests, requires him "to extrude the resurrection event from the sequence that anchors it in the New Testament" (*Resurrection and Historical Reason*, p. 48). Nor can Brunner, by depicting it as superhistorical, says Niebuhr, give the resurrection a footing in history (p. 27). Barth seems to be saying nothing less than that even if historical research were to disprove its occurrence we may accept an asserted biblical event as divine action and revelation. Here the basic issue is not whether the methodology of historical research can in truth absolutely prove or disprove a past event-claim, but whether Christian faith remains credible if the resurrection of Jesus from the dead and other biblical miracles did not actually occur. The apostle Paul's position is diametrically opposed to this; to forfeit Jesus' resurrection from the grave on the third day would, says Paul, vitiate Christian faith (1 Cor. 15:1-8).

In challenging Barth's view, John Marsh emphasizes that "no distinction between fact and interpretation in history, between history and meta-history, between what the Germans call '*Geschichte*' and '*Urgeschichte*,' is satisfactory to the Christian philosopher and theologian. Indeed, any such distinction must prove in the end unchristian, for it makes inevitable a distinction between the sphere where ordinary historical events happen and that in which the divine activity takes place. And that, in the end, is to make the incarnation impossible" (*The Fulness of Time*, p. 13). Christian revelation is nullified unless the crucifixion and resurrection of Jesus Christ belong to the same history that includes the death of Julius Caesar and of Adolf Hitler. The Christian must either believe that the great redemptive events belong to the realm of history or forfeit his faith. As Dewey Beegle writes: "Faith is not being blindfolded, spun around a number of times, and challenged to leap. . . . Without criteria of differentiation, faith in the Golden Tablets of Joseph Smith is just as valid as trust in the New Testament accounts about Jesus Christ. Fortunately, the primitive church knew the difference between the extraordinary appearances of the risen Jesus and ordinary visions stemming from experiences with the earthly Jesus" (*Scripture, Tradition, and Infallibility*, pp. 62 f.).

To avoid Bultmann's mythologizing the resurrection of Christ into an inner spiritual experience, Barth insists—as do evangelical scholars—on the external occurrence of miracles like the resurrection and the virgin birth, even if historical research cannot finally demonstrate that such events have occurred. But Barth elaborates this insistence in a way that evangelical theology must repudiate: he surrenders the revelational-miraculous in the sense of historical factuality (*Historie*) and shifts it instead to the realm of superhistory (*Geschichte*). In short, redemptive events for Barth occur, not internally as says Bultmann, but externally; contrary to evangelical theology, however, Barth places them, not in objective temporal history (the data historians investigate), but in a "historical" sphere of a different kind (*Geschichte*) that is accessible to believers only. No one will be surprised, therefore, that for all of his warning against hurried dismissal of Gospel accounts of the empty tomb, and his reminder that historical investigation cannot "verify" either the empty tomb or the postresurrection appearances, Barth apparently cannot bring himself to say also that God's raising Jesus from the tomb was a historical (belonging to *Historie*) actuality.

In contrast to Barth's dialectical reconstruction and Bultmann's existential restatement of Christian revelation, the salvation-history (*Heilsgeschichte*) school meritoriously identifies the central redemptive events of the theology of revelation as historical happenings. It does not distort the biblical sequence of horizontally related redemptive acts into an inner, divine self-revelation supposedly communicated to man in person-to-person confrontation and response on the sporadic perpendicular-punctiliar basis of transcendental eschatology. Moreover, it revives a biblically oriented emphasis on God's creation as the beginning of history, on the events of the Gospels as the midpoint of history and on eschatological themes in relation to a final future. Against those who lose the scriptural emphasis on Old Testament promise and New Testament fulfillment in subjectivity, Oscar Cullmann insists that the revelational events of the Bible must be correlated with external sequential history.

Through the linear pattern of history which stretches from the creation of mankind at one end to a final consummation at the other, runs a thread of salvific events, namely, the once-for-all incarnation, crucifixion and resurrection of the Logos of God in Palestine on specific calendar dates.

Putting aside for the moment other questions such as how these saving acts acquire redemptive importance and to what extent, if any, they convey ontological information about God's own nature, we must note as one weakness of the *Heilsgeschichte* approach its failure to clarify the connection between redemptive acts and universal history. In important respects the salvation-history theologians progress beyond Barth's and Bultmann's imaginative transference of divine disclosure to the metahistorical realm; for all that, they wrest from critical historical science little more than the right to coexistence. Implicit in their emphasis that God is revealed in sacred history is an unorthodox and somewhat deistic retirement or retreat of God from history as a totality. Their espousal of saving events does not adequately put historicism on the defensive. Any tendency to relate God to only one strand or segment of historical acts seriously burdens the problem of defending the revelatory significance even of salvation history.

It is questionable, moreover, whether this right to the coexistence of sacred events alongside secular history is consistently sustained and successfully prosecuted. Cullmann, for one, has no intention of distinguishing the time-line of redemptive revelation from mythology in every respect. He contends that even "in opposition to primitive Christianity . . . the placing of history and myth together upon one common line of development *in time* belongs to the essential core of the Primitive Christian conception of salvation. The demonstration that a myth is not 'historical' does not imply that the happening whose account it preserves is not 'temporal'" (*Christ and Time*, pp. 94 f.). For Cullmann, creation in the past and eschatology in the future are nonhistorical myth but are nonetheless to be viewed as temporal event rather than nontemporal. The reason for insisting on temporality is clear; the analogy between Christ and Adam, who, says Cullmann, "was not an historical personality" (p. 100), would otherwise land us back in Bultmann's notion of a merely existential Christ. While Cullmann professes to allow "the earliest formulas of faith" (p. 192) to stipulate what is indispensably historical in the Christian outlook, he ignores New Testament passages that correlate the historical actuality of the first and second Adams (Rom. 5:14–17; 1 Cor. 15:22).

Nor does Cullman elucidate how the mythological becomes temporal. As Gordon Clark remarks, Bultmann's demythologizing is replaced by Cullmann's "enmythologizing" (*Historiography—Secular and Religious*, p. 344). Cullmann's claim that prophecy or theological interpretation transcends the contrast between myth and history suggests, as Clark notes, that the redemptive significance of certain events, and indeed their asserted once-for-allness, is due basically to the interpretation that is imposed upon them. Cullmann leaves little doubt of his position when he says, "that this Jesus is the Son of God remains concealed from the historian as such" (*Christ and Time*, p. 98). Although he insists on the historical character of the Gospel events, Cullmann nonetheless imperils their historical redemptive significance by failing to challenge an anti-supernatural historicism and scientism. Instead he treats the creation account and future eschatology as nonhistorical temporality, places the central Gospel miracles on the same linear line with them, and while he insists on the calendar significance of the Gospel events he locates their supernatural status solely in theological explanation. As Clark points out, the idea of a midpoint in time between a not historical Adam and a non-historical future is nonsense (*Historiography—Secular and Religious*, p. 345).

Robert J. Blaikie indicates that Cullmann also leans toward the positivist misunderstanding of history by tending to speak of divine *events* rather than *acts*, thus preferring a term more appropriate to impersonal connections than to personal agency. While the Bible distinguishes a "fixed order" activity (cf. Jer. 31:35–36), or what we now call "natural events," it does so, Blaikie stresses, within the activity of God; actions must always be viewed as primary and events as derivative (*"Secular Christianity" and God Who Acts*, p. 148). To correlate history with events rather than acts, he thinks, reflects a dualistic perspective in which the comprehensive concept of events is adjusted to make room for "a special sort of event called 'actions' " (p. 149).

If Cullmann does indeed view all historical events as inherently purposeless, and regards interpretation alone as bestowing faith-significance upon "saving events," then he has in no way escaped the existentialist theology he disowns. Cullmann speaks of general history as a connected causal series (*Salvation in History*, p. 78). He insists that salvation history involves "a sequence of events taking place within history" and is not "a history alongside history . . . ; it unfolds in history, and in this sense belongs to it" (p. 153), and asserts that "the divine selection of a few events out of the whole of history" connects them in a special way as salvation-history (p. 109). Yet he writes also not simply of inspired interpretation but of "progressive divine revelation in events." Blaikie faults Cullmann's failure to say outright that saving events are acts whose cause lies in God as their agent rather than given events interpretatively connected through divine decision and revelation: "One receives the strong impression that . . . Cullmann has . . . ceded all 'objective' general history to impersonal causality, retaining only 'the act of revelation' as the sphere of God's action" (*"Secular Christianity" and God Who Acts*, p. 153). If this is so, then Cullmann does not differ decisively from Bultmann, despite his announced intention to emphasize that a divinely identified history and not a punctiliar internal activity of God is the sphere of divine disclosure. In any event, any failure to insist upon God's activity in universal history spells a costly compromise with a mechanical-positivist view of nature and history.

In the foreword and throughout *Salvation in History*, Cullmann uses "saving act" and "saving event" interchangeably, and writes of salvation history, moreover, as "a sequence of events brought about by God." Such phrasing implies, at least on the surface, that he uses the terms *acts* and *events* interchangeably. The crucial question, however, is whether events become divine merely through the interpolation of a special purpose or personal intention, or whether, in contrast to other events in the external world, as divine events they stand in distinctive causal relationships. Blaikie suggests that Cullmann not only adopts a terminology but also espouses a perspective that is alien to Scripture: "The Bible does *not* speak of bare impersonal, naturally caused 'events' to some of which, by 'revelation' superimposed, God gives a special divine meaning or quality, as Cullmann seems to suggest" (*"Secular Christianity" and God Who Acts*, p. 150).

Blaikie emphasizes that in this age, evangelical Christians cannot avoid wrestling with the linguistic and logical problems connected with concepts such as "event" and "action" (ibid., p. 151). Evangelical writers frequently use the terms *acts* and *events* interchangeably. They do not apply the latter only to impersonal happenings but to personal acts as well, much as in everyday language we speak of a "blessed event." Systematic and biblical theologians who directly oppose positivist-oriented theories of history and nature often have been too imprecise in their designation of what are divine or human events. In present-day thought-contexts they may need to refine their concepts and terminology to best serve the evangelical cause. Blaikie reminds us that dualistic views that stress interpretative kerygma often assimilate historical external events to positivistic theory; as a consequence, the external observable world comes to manifest no purpose or personal activity but only mechanical regularity.

Their attempted reinstatement of biblical history notwithstanding, *Heilsgeschichte* theologians have failed to counterattack modern critical theories of historical science; they have, instead, perpetuated the prominence and popularity of arbitrary views that attempt to discredit the salvation acts of Scripture as antiquarian sentiment. Jürgen Moltmann remarks that "the theology of sacred history was never itself able to bring about a critical change in the epistemological principles of historical science, and consequently always appears in the age of critical historical research to be an anachronistic means of glossing over the crisis in which the theology of revelation finds itself in the modern age" (*Theology of Hope*, p. 73). In order to confront seriously the revelation-and-history problem and not simply gloss over it, the controlling premises of the modern critical-historical concept influenced by Kantian motifs must be directly challenged and countered. This counterattack against "unhistoric historicism," as Moltmann labels it, is presently underway on a growing scale. It is not enough simply to heed Cullmann's and Paul Althaus's warnings that the fate of Christianity is tied to certain past events whose factuality must be strenuously insisted upon. As Wolfhart Pannenberg emphasizes, too nebulous or casual a correlation of revelation and history per se leaves in doubt both the unity of redemptive and universal history and the accessibility of revelational history for critical historical investigation ("Heilsgeschehen und Geschichte," pp. 259 ff.). Indispensable to the theology of historical revelation are the unmasking of arbitrarily imposed positivist prejudices and a different understanding of the reality of all history.

21.
Revelation and History:
Moltmann and Pannenberg

JÜRGEN MOLTMANN AND WOLFHART PANNENBERG restore history as the locus of divine disclosure and link their exposition of historical revelation with countercriticism of the prejudicial modern theory of historical science. For both men, redemptive history centers in the resurrection of the crucified Jesus; it is the decisive past event that anticipates the final climax of all history. Pannenberg, moreover, connects the revelatory purpose of God's redemptive events with all history as revelational. Moltmann and Pannenberg thus try to remove from salvation history the apparent oddity of a special cluster of events in which God appears to be exclusively active.

The theology of revelation, Moltmann emphasizes, does not depict the resurrection of Jesus as an exception in an otherwise unbroken causal continuum. To do so would defer to an untenably prejudiced contextual theory of nature and history. The resurrection of the crucified Jesus occurs not as a gap in cosmic or historical continuities but in consummation of God's promise in a universe that is everywhere and always open to divine promise and fulfillment. Contrary to the existentialist reduction of promise and fulfillment to the internal antithesis of inauthentic and authentic being, and contrary to the dialectical consignment of revelatory history to transcendental eschatology, the historical Christ-event, says Moltmann, fulfills the Old Testament's historical testimony to God's promise. Universal history is related to the eschatological future provisionally anticipated in the Word of promise and proleptically depicted in the resurrection of Jesus who is the first-fruits of a general resurrection and the coming King. Moltmann does not consider revelation a predicate of history, as though history were a progressive disclosure of the divine; emphasizing that history is open to the future of God, he views history,

294

rather, as the "predicate" of eschatological revelation (*Theology of Hope*, pp. 75–76).

One difficulty of Moltmann's exposition is that while he concentrates proleptic historical fulfillment of the Word of promise completely in the resurrection of Jesus, at the same time he readily yields much of biblical miracle elsewhere to myth and legend. Despite the supportive biblical evidence that Moltmann invokes for the miracle of the empty tomb, one is therefore hard pressed to preserve the resurrection claim against those who contend that legend and myth are specially prominent in the resurrection narratives. For Moltmann states no firm criterion for distinguishing assuredly historical from supposedly mythical and legendary elements in Scripture. When he tells us, for example, that "even where the historic tradition passes over into legendary tradition, the peculiarly Israelite tradition is still dominated by the hopes and expectations kindled by Yahweh's promises" (ibid., p. 108), we must then ask, even more seriously than Moltmann, whether the resurrection stories perhaps represent this supposed legendary tradition at its acme; whether the projected literary or legendary tradition and not historic fact is the basis of Hebrew faith; whether a legendary past deeply grounded in human desire may not likewise anticipate a legendary future similarly postulated; the question, in brief, becomes whether myth more than history shapes the promise. Moltmann complains that von Rad's portrayal of Old Testament theology in terms of divine facts of history susceptible of manifold interpretation leaves one unsure whether the faith in saving events is shaped by history open to critical examination, or only by divine promise which reads the historical scene in a special way (p. 110, n. 1). This very complaint can be turned also against Moltmann's exposition.

Another difficulty derives from Moltmann's attempt to preserve the proleptic significance of the resurrection of Jesus alone in a context that relativizes all other history in advance of the eschatological future. But if the resurrection of Jesus has a special significance, why must all other biblical acts be deprived of a related significance? If on the other hand the future of God is open, as Moltmann insists, why is the resurrection assuredly decisive for it?

By forfeiting rational revelation, Moltmann leaves us no secure basis for confidently interpreting the Nazarene's survival of death as either a resurrection to absolute life or the paradigm of a future universal resurrection of mankind. The category of *logos*, and hence the idea of eschatology, Moltmann contends, is Greek and therefore alien to Judeo-Christian revelation. But no revival of emphasis on biblical promise and fulfillment can long serve Christian theism, or for that matter any alternative option, if it is divorced from logical considerations. Moltmann is right in rejecting Bultmann's reduction of the meaning of history to internal personal decision and the eschatological moment, and right in rejecting the communist deflection and distortion of the Judeo-Christian hope for the future in view of God's promise and fulfillment in history.

But by forfeiting the rational and intelligible content of biblical revelation, Moltmann vulnerably exposes both the reality of promise and fulfillment and the authentic meaning of the related events to subjective mythologizing whose only link to the Bible is through a preferential retention of selected portions of Scripture.

In the Bible, God's intelligible revelation both in deed and word provides the basis for the Christian hope. In Moltmann's view, promise and fulfillment are introduced as categories that relativize rational revelation. They seem, despite Moltmann's strictures against eschatology, to impose upon the Bible a speculatively oriented eschatology that gains theological power only from what it selectively borrows from the biblical view. If revelation communicates no new knowledge of religious truth, and divine disclosure in Word as well as Act is historically conditioned (ibid., p. 74), then it is not as easy as Moltmann thinks to center the content of divine revelation in a divine word of promise that intimates future directions and shapes a decisive proleptic event in history.

Wolfhart Pannenberg holds that contemporary expositions of "the self-revelation of God" obscure the *indirect* nature of the revelation of the God of the Bible. The Judeo-Christian God, he emphasizes, mediates his disclosure only through historical deeds, so that our knowledge of God is not face-to-face. "Event" rather than "Word," he says, discloses God; divine revelation is "seen," not "heard."

Pannenberg's rejection of Word-theology should be viewed first and foremost as a revolt against kerygmatic misconceptions, although it has further implications as well for orthodox biblical theism. Existentialist Word-theology dissolves history into the "historicity" of individual existence. At the expense of objective, external actuality in the biblical past it dilutes history into the events of subjective here-and-now personal experience. This is the case whether authentic personal existence is viewed in terms of self-understanding, as does Bultmann, or in terms of language, as do Ernst Fuchs and Gerhard Ebeling. Pannenberg repudiates Bultmann's existential notion (in *Gospel of John: A Commentary*, p. 432) that "only in the Word was Jesus the revealer, and only in the Word will he be that." Faith in Christ's resurrection is concerned, he says, not simply with proclamation but with historical occurrence and objective truth. Pannenberg objects to a Word-theology which represents God, as does Fuchs, in terms of inner "speaking" alone, an approach that suppresses the objective truth and objective fact of revelation. Over against this, Pannenberg champions a deed-revelation centered in the resurrection of Jesus Christ. Pannenberg therefore views *revelation as history* per se as an alternative not only to *revelation in history*, but also to *revelation in word*, or the divine disclosure of the meaning of revelational events. For him the objective historical revelation communicates the whole reality of revelation.

Pannenberg deplores Troeltsch's emphasis (in "Über historische und dogmatische Methode in der Theologie," p. 732) that the "all-prevailing power of analogy" allows the historian to acknowledge only that with which he is previously familiar, so that human experience becomes the measure of historical probability. The admission of very pronounced deviations in history does not render historical knowledge impossible. "If analogies are applied with a recognition of the limit of their validity, they will surely not function as a criterion for the factuality of what a tradition declares has happened, as Troeltsch . . . has decreed. Just because a reported event breaks with the analogy of what is otherwise customary or usually reported is no reason, in itself, for disputing its occurrence" ("Heilsgeschehen und Geschichte," pp. 266 f.). Although reports of the wholly novel require us rigidly to press for tests distinguishing imagination from responsible attestation, no basis exists for automatically depicting a report of what has never happened elsewhere as merely imaginative.

One must not, Pannenberg emphasizes, use the term *history* in different senses of salvation history and universal history, as does Cullmann who distinguishes them (*Salvation in History*, pp. 150 ff.) in terms of analogy (cf. *Theology as History*, Robinson and Cobb, eds., p. 247, n. 46). "It belongs to the full meaning of the Incarnation that God's saving deed took place within the universal relationships of mankind's history and not in a ghetto of *Heilsgeschichte* or in an *Urgeschichte* the dimensions of which 'cut across' ordinary history" (*Grundfragen systematischer Theologie*, pp. 4 f.). The most comprehensive horizon of divine revelation is the history of God's relations with man and with his whole creation whose future in Christ is now manifest though hidden from the world.

Against the notion that revelation occurs in superhistory or primal history or subjectivity, and that it cannot be historically verified, Pannenberg considers *Heilsgeschichte* historically examinable in principle and not beyond or above "ordinary" history (cf. C. E. Braaten, *History and Hermeneutics*, regarding the way in which Pannenberg and Rendtorff go beyond von Rad). The events are themselves the revelation of God. Determination of the historicity of resurrection appearances belongs not to the scientist working with natural laws but rather to the historian (*Jesus —God and Man*, pp. 96 ff.). The historian should even assume "the burden of proof" that God has revealed himself in Jesus of Nazareth.

Pannenberg emphasizes that the revelation in history has a universal character, and is there for all to see. The events are not "brute facts"; the positivist's "bare facts" are always an abstraction that reflect his special interests. Knowledge of revelation is grasped by reason like any other knowledge of history; the events carry their own intrinsic and inherent meaning. The meaning is not veiled to the eye of natural man; he needs only his "normal powers of apprehension," not a special work of the Holy Spirit, to recognize revelation. Nonrecognition is man's fault, and not the Spirit's.

Over against Pannenberg, Paul Althaus insists that the knowledge of historical revelation rests on historical faith (*fides historica*) and that this as a rational historical knowledge is not identical with saving faith (*fides salvifica*); the former, namely historical faith, he says, concerns the historical side of revelation, whereas the latter (saving faith) concerns the revelatory side of history ("Offenbarung als Geschichte und Glaube," pp. 321 ff.).

This approach, Pannenberg replies, sacrifices the unity of revelation, of history (saving and secular) and of knowledge (faith-knowledge and historical knowledge) in deference to neo-Kantian prejudices. It preserves the towering influence of Kant, who considers the limits of reason to be such that man cannot *know* the object of religious faith, namely, God. Hence, on the neo-Kantian premise that the meaning or value of facts is not universally valid but is of the nature of faith, a separation of faith and knowledge is assumed. Pannenberg accordingly opposes Barth's and Bultmann's claims for an authoritarian revelation that is exempt from questions of "critical rationality." Knowledge, not faith, he says, is man's response to divine revelation. Similarly, he opposes Althaus's claim that knowledge of God's revelation comes only with faith, and Alan Richardson's view that faith is the correlative of divine revelation. Pannenberg maintains that faith is based on the knowledge of God's revelation in history. Faith is not a necessary condition or concurrent element for finding God's revelation in the history of Israel or of Jesus Christ. Revelation is not ambiguous and obscure but conveys clear and essential information about the grounds of faith as a trust directed to the future.

Alan Richardson shares Pannenberg's emphasis that revelation occurs in "ordinary, secular history . . . not some eschatological realm of sacred history in which the secular historian's tools cannot be used" (*History Sacred and Profane*, p. 195, cf. p. 259). He agrees, moreover, that "theological statements are historical, not metaphysical, in character" and that their verification "involves us in the interpretation of the historian *qua* historian" (p. 294). But, Richardson emphasizes, the historian qua historian cannot pronounce the final verdict on the truth of Christianity because, although revelation is historical, its meaning is given "by the faith and insight of the prophets and the apostles of the Bible" (*Christian Apologetics*, p. 92). For the moment we postpone comment on two issues, namely, whether on the basis of historical revelation Christianity vouchsafes not metaphysical but only historical revelation, and whether the meaning supplied by the biblical writers is adequately explained in terms of their personal faith and insight. But at this point it is essential to emphasize, against Richardson, that although sinful man does not discern the meaning of God's revelational events unaided but must depend upon scriptural disclosure to perceive the meaning of history properly, he has no basis for denying that the events themselves carry a divinely invested objective meaning which man by a proper use of his normal powers could recognize and comprehend.

Pannenberg avoids Hegel's notion that revelation is a predicate of history, as if world history is the direct externalization of God, a premise that underlay the Protestant modernist view of scientific-historical-political developments as a progressive manifestation of the kingdom of God. Pannenberg agrees with Hegel that one must view history from the perspective of its end in order to understand history as a whole and to see truth as a totality, and stresses the openness of history to an unfinished future. He criticizes Hegel, however, for identifying the absolute end of history with his own philosophy of idealism, and insists that the end has occurred proleptically in the resurrection of Jesus of Nazareth as first-fruits. Hegel held also that the whole of reality, understood as history, alone can supply the perspective for grasping the whole, and that only the totality of the Absolute's historical revelation can supply the definitive revelation. Consequently no particular one event is God's self-revelation; the truth is the whole, and Christ is but one stage in the larger process and is superseded by the whole. Pannenberg argues, however, that the Christ-event not only *foresees* the end (as do the apocalyptic writings) but also anticipates and discloses it proleptically: the resurrection is the anticipation of the end. While historically particular, the Christ-event manifests the universal absolutely; and since this revelation anticipates the end of history "there will be no further self-disclosure of God going beyond it." Contrary to the Hegelian thesis that all history is the logical evolutionary unfolding of the Idea, Pannenberg presupposes an apocalyptic reading of history which grasps God's universal plan anticipatively disclosed in the resurrection of Jesus the crucified. Hence he preserves alongside the decisive importance of the resurrected Jesus an emphasis on the objective factuality of historical revelation and the occurrence of salvation events within the totality of this larger revelatory history.

"The universal revelation of the deity of God is not yet realized in the history of Israel," Pannenberg writes, "but first in the fate of Jesus of Nazareth, insofar as the end of all events is anticipated in his fate. . . . The Christ-event does not reveal the deity of the God of Israel as an isolated event, but rather insofar as it is a part of the history of God with Israel" ("Dogmatic Theses on the Doctrine of Revelation," pp. 139, 145). He insists, therefore, on the connection between revelation in Israel's history and Jesus of Nazareth. "In the formulation of the non-Jewish conceptions of revelation in the Gentile Christian church, the universality of the eschatological self-vindication of God in the fate of Jesus comes to actual expression" (p. 149). While this is somewhat obscure, Pannenberg does emphasize that the eschatological character of the Christ-event implies world-proclamation of the gospel and that God is now finally revealed as the one true God not only of Israel but of all mankind.

In wholly emptying the reality of divine revelation into history, Pannenberg deliberately overleaps the ideas and words of the Bible. He contends that traditional evangelical Christianity submerges the distinctive problems of the present in a primitive world view. Instead of a repristination of biblical truths, he proposes an exhibition of universal history long and broad enough to span the biblical past and the contemporary scene as parts of one historical process and plateau. Christian theology as a theology of history comprehends biblical history, church history and world history related to the revelation of the one God, the Creator and Redeemer. While insisting that universal history reveals God, he does not expound what this implies for the history of nations. But if universal history reveals God at work, and this disclosure is in fact wholly lucid to man independent of a Bible, then why does Pannenberg not choose Chinese or Greek or Korean rather than Hebrew history to expose the revelation to be found there?

Not only does Pannenberg insist on the indivisible wholeness of history as a sphere of divine revelation, but he does so in connection with the assertion of the indivisible wholeness of reality. Like Moltmann, he explicitly disowns the transcendent "supernatural"; any contrast between the supernatural and the natural, Pannenberg holds, implies an objectionable split in the qualitative spatial and temporal oneness of reality. Rejection of the supernatural assures that divine acts and human acts occur in the very same field of activity. Revelation, says Pannenberg, does not enter history from outside or above, as a superhistorical entity: "The total reality as history is God's world which he creates and through which he reveals himself." "If all reality . . . is marked by historicality, then the divinity of God can only be thought of in relation to the whole of reality understood as history" ("Response to the Discussion," p. 242). One is tempted to add that if all reality is marked by historicalness, God too must be a historical event.

Blaikie thinks that Pannenberg achieves this undivided unity of nature and history through an idealist philosophical regard for events and acts "as 'ideas' of thinking Subjects" (*"Secular Christianity" and God Who Acts*, p. 160), and that his contrast of part and whole, within an underlying one-level view of reality and history, is essentially idealistic in perspective. In order to avoid transferring divine revelation to "superhistory" one does not need to historicize God. It may assuredly be true that one cannot empirically tell what is possible in history or nature until the whole is complete. But if the biblical revelation is understood on its own premises, there is no basis for claiming, as Pannenberg does, that assertions about God can be made only "in view of the *whole* of reality and not of certain special experiences" and that "the words of the prophets . . . have the character of revelation . . . at most as the anticipation of the whole of reality . . . ," and that even the history of Jesus is final revelation "precisely in the form of mere anticipation" (quoted by Blaikie, ibid., pp. 158 ff.; cf. Pannenberg, *Jesus—God and Man*, pp. 127 ff.). Pannenberg's own theory forces him to the notion that "only the *eschaton* will ultimately disclose what really happened in Jesus' resurrection from the dead. Until then we must speak favorably in . . . metaphorical and symbolic form about Jesus' resurrection and the significance inherent in it" (*Jesus—God and Man*, p. 397). "When we speak today of God's revelation in Jesus . . . our statements always contain a proleptic element" (p. 108). An idealistic philosophy seems implicit in Pannenberg's notions, therefore, namely, that all reality is of one kind, that all history is *eo ipso* revelatory of God, and that only in view of the whole toward which the process moves can final claims be made.

Like Cullmann, Pannenberg frequently interchanges the terms *event* and *act*. Blaikie thinks, however, that his preferential use of the latter elevates *acts* to the role of a key-word in Pannenberg's vocabulary, and that Pannenberg considers the concept of divine action as fundamental (*"Secular Christianity" and God Who Acts*, p. 155). But exceptions in which Pannenberg speaks with equal force about "event" nullify this verdict. While Pannenberg reads Cullmann as if *event* and *act* are used interchangeably, he objects to Cullmann's handling of "the events . . . reported by the Biblical writings as decisive acts of God" because Cullmann's approach makes saving events appear to differ from others "not only in their historical peculiarity, but also qualitatively" in a metaphysical sense ("Response to the Discussion," pp. 247 f.). We must not forget, however, that Pannenberg insists not only that all history is divine revelation, but also that no history and no reality is supernatural. That God is everywhere active and revealed in history is indeed, Cullmann notwithstanding, a necessary emphasis. On the basis of Scripture, God's action in history cannot be viewed merely as a periodic insertion from above; failure to acknowledge God's activity in universal history reflects in some measure a compromise with mechanical-positivist concepts of nature and history. But Pannenberg's rejection of the supernatural is quite another matter and deprives us, in principle, not only of supernatural miracle but also of supernaturally revealed truth.

In *Revelation as History*, Pannenberg argues for God's "indirect self-revelation as a reflex of his activity in history" ("Introduction," p. 13). For Pannenberg and his associates this distinction does not contrast the directness or indirectness in the act of communication, but the direct or indirect coincidence of the content of the communication with its intention: direct revelation has God himself as its content, indirect revelation has God only mediately as its content. The facts of history in their first intention mean something other than a revelation of God but, as deeds of God, says Pannenberg, they indirectly reveal God himself.

Pannenberg insists, moreover, that the indirectness of divine disclosure implies that divine self-revelation is complete not at the beginning "but at the end of revealing history" ("Dogmatic Theses," p. 131), somewhat as Moltmann holds that revelation is the promise of truth and that God's self-disclosure is future prospect (*Theology of Hope*, p. 46). Only "the eschaton," the end of history, will reveal Yahweh as the one unique God of mankind. Pannenberg further declares about the Scriptures that "the self-revelation of God in the biblical witnesses is not of a direct type in the sense of a theophany, but is indirect and brought about by means of the historical acts of God" ("Dogmatic Theses," p. 125). This places him at the same time on the side of and against the Bible and historic Christian theism. For while he rightly emphasizes the indispensability of historical divine revelation for the Judeo-Christian religion, he disengages Scripture from ontological revelation of the essential nature of God, ignores the preliminary role of theophany in the Bible, and virtually eclipses the self-revelation of God in Jesus Christ. While declaring the resurrection to be the incontrovertible revelation of Jesus' sovereign claim to be the Son of God, Pannenberg denies that Jesus' teaching and deeds disclose his divinity. He rightly opposes God's direct self-revelation as promulgated by kerygmatic Word-theology, but he dismisses the very passages that support an orthodox Word-theology (Heb. 1:2; John 1:1-3; Col. 1:25-27) as being Gnostic in mood and not normative but tangential to the New Testament. Pannenberg contends that by their relation to the Jesus-tradition these emphases became altered from original Gnostic ideas so that the revelation of God in Christ is perceived "only indirectly" (ibid, p. 130). In the biblical view, by contrast, God's revelation is given not indirectly but directly, and, although it is not immediate revelation, it is mediated always through the Logos, and is given in diverse modes.

Pannenberg acknowledges Barth's influence when he asserts that divine self-revelation comes only when God reveals himself as he is, namely, as the triune God; he disagrees, however, with Barth's contention that no genuine knowledge of God exists outside the kerygma and asserts, instead, that as a presupposition of the Christ-proclamation to the world, a "provisional" knowledge is necessary, a faith in God that is a precondition of faith in Christ (*Grundzüge der Christologie*, p. 13, cf. n. 2). Hence an indirect historical knowledge of God is said to be universally vouchsafed to mankind.

If revelation is a developing historical process, rather than an endless process, one must assuredly wait for the end before one can speak assuredly, if one will assuredly be there to speak. Otherwise, revelational process would seem to be a basis for skepticism or agnosticism rather than for even a minimal *gnōsis*. The revelational knowledge that we have, Moltmann and Pannenberg contend, is not universally valid truth. While Moltmann emphasizes the promise character of revelation, Pannenberg stresses its proleptic and doxological character. Pannenberg contends, however, that in adoration theological language sacrifices human conceptualization and inescapably embraces "contradictory conceptions" (*Jesus—God and Man*, pp. 184 f.). In other words, although creedal statements are historically and logically inappropriate, one can affirm the virgin birth in worship without sacrificing truthfulness (p. 150).

If there is intelligible transcendent revelation at some point before the end—as evangelical orthodoxy insists in regard to inspired Scripture—then one can confidently affirm a great deal about God and his ways. According to the biblical view of revelation, the coming end-time disclosure does not negate the permanent validity of what prophets and apostles were given to know "in part" (1 Cor. 13:12, RSV).

If we say that God's historical manifestation of his power—as in the deliverance of Israel from Egypt, for example, or the apocalyptic expectation of eschatological salvation or the resurrection of Jesus from the dead —supplies the key to understanding God's self-revelation, can we say this assuredly simply on the basis of historical deeds and without dependence on the reliability of a divinely inspired scriptural interpretation? Pannenberg says: "I limit the concept of *revelation* to the *self-confirmation* of Yahweh through his deeds, which were to prove his divinity to Israel and—according to Israelite expectation—also to the nations" ("Response to the Discussion," p. 234, n. 12). Yet he says even of the biblical data concerning Jesus' resurrection: "The appearances reported in the Gospels, which are not mentioned by Paul, have such a strong legendary character that one can scarcely find a historical kernel of their own in them" (*Jesus—God and Man*, p. 89). In other words, Pannenberg adduces no consistent principle by which to select and use scriptural data to support his limiting view of revelation; his radical criticism of the biblical testimony, including rejection of the virgin birth of Jesus, leaves no secure basis for regarding the resurrection as historical. As G. G. O'Collins puts it, it is misleading for Pannenberg to claim that "according to the testimony of the Bible" God's self-revelation has taken place "indirectly through God's deeds in history"; Pannenberg ought instead to say that the only aspects of biblical testimony to revelation that he as a "modern theologian" finds convincing are those which attest "an indirect self-revelation through God's actions" ("The Theology of Revelation in Some Recent Discussion," pp. 82 f.).

Pannenberg detaches the category of revelation from the divine Word, and assumes that the external historical events with which he fully identifies divine revelation are self-explanatory. In this maneuver he blurs the unity of event and interpretation, a unity that even salvation-history theologians like Cullmann maintain, however inadequately. Because of his prior denial of supernatural cognitive disclosure, Pannenberg is compelled to shift the entire focus of divine revelation to history alone. No doubt the cryptic notions of sporadic noncognitive existential revelation promoted by the kerygmatic theologians supplied some of the impetus for neglecting divine self-revelation in deference to historical revelation. But Pannenberg nonetheless dismisses as mythological any and every emphasis on a revealed Word of God: "In any case, the task of theology is not accomplished in the long run by mythologizing talk about the Word of God (which was originally a mythological expression, anyway), nor by confronting the hearer, threatened by the *asserted* authority of this divine Word, with the naked demand for obedience" (*Basic Questions in Theology*, p. 147). It would be interesting to get from Pannenberg the historical proof that validates his dogmatic verdict that the Word of God was originally a mythological conception; the decisive consideration is far less likely to be found in the remote origins of man than in the conjectural armory of some nineteenth-century theologian.

Does Christian faith rest only upon a content of revelation derived from reason's knowledge of history and vouchsafed by historians? Is there some further indispensable source of noetic content over and above the historical possibility or probability of biblical events? Does faith affirm a basis and content that if not over and above and independent of history, exists alongside historical reasoning? "It is an occupational idiosyncracy of professional biblical scholars," says Alan Richardson, "to imagine that Christian faith rests upon their ability or inability to solve the historical problems that are raised by it. It does not. It rests upon the testimony of a people" (*History Sacred and Profane*, pp. 46 f.). Does that adequately state the Christian alternative?

To say that divine revelation is not given in the form of Word-revelation so contradicts the biblical witness as to be well-nigh incredible. The Old Testament prophets affirm "thus saith the Lord" some twelve hundred times not only to sanction the source of their teaching, but frequently also to expressly contradict pagan ideas of pagan gods. According to Pannenberg even the word of prophecy proclaimed by prophets is not direct self-revelation of God; only fulfillment of the promises, he says, only actual realization of the prophetic word reveals Yahweh: "The word is related to revelation as prophecy, direction and report." Hence he denies that God reveals himself personally in his Word; divine revelation for him is only historically indirect. The apocalyptic writings, laws, commands, even Jesus' preaching, have no revelatory character. Pannenberg argues that God's Word has in the New Testament a kerygmatic function, and is not properly revelation. Since he holds revelation to be a truth conveyed by what God does, the whole biblical narrative is but a witness to it. As O'Collins puts it, "for Pannenberg the proclamation does not constitute nor add anything to revelation; it merely passes on information about the eschatological happening which in itself is the self-revelation of God to all men and which provides the impulse for this kerygma" ("The Theology of Revelation in Some Recent Discussion," p. 76). The event needs no "inspired interpretation" to supplement it and identify it as revelation; like earlier events in which God revealed himself, the Christ-event is self-evident.

Pannenberg thus in principle makes dogmatics totally dependent on historiography. If divine revelation comes *as* history, then not only our knowledge of the past but also the whole content and basis of the Christian faith depend upon and can be discerned only by historical research. As proposed not only by Pannenberg but by R. R. Niebuhr as well, this sole dependence on historical reason forfeits all certainty for Christianity. As Braaten puts it: "The critique of historical reason . . . seems calculated to secure for theology a high degree of objective probability, but at the high cost of complete subjective uncertainty" (*History and Hermeneutics*, pp. 46 f.) and in the final analysis faith rests upon the shifting tides of historical consensus. "There seems to be something pseudo," he adds, "about a faith that hangs on the changing opinion of historical authorities, giving assent to their problematical assurances" (p. 47). More than this, there is something peculiar about a historical investigation of the Bible that can so readily overlook the Scripture's insistent attestations that God's deeds prominently include the revelation of his Word to chosen spokesmen.

Pannenberg tries to overcome the alliance of modern historicism with Kantian motifs in two ways, by affirming that all history together with Christ's lordship over that history is the revelation of God, and by emphasizing, contrary to Moltmann, that divine revelation in history can in principle be historically verified. Moltmann labels as "particularly difficult" Pannenberg's thesis that Jesus' resurrection is "the historically demonstrable prolepsis, the anticipation and forestalling of the end of universal history, so that in it the totality of reality as history can be contemplated in a provisional way" (*Theology of Hope*, p. 82). Moltmann feels that this requires altering the concept of what is historical both to allow God's raising of the dead and to see in this raising the prophesied end of history in a general resurrection of the dead, and that it narrows this expectation to a universal duplication of Jesus' resurrection at the expense of the world-transforming hope centered in Jesus himself as the coming King. Moltmann adds: "Certain as it is that the Easter appearances of Jesus were experienced and proclaimed in the apocalyptic categories of the expectation of the general resurrection of the dead and as a beginning of the end of all history, it is nevertheless equally certain that the raising of Jesus was not merely conceived solely as the first instance of the final resurrection of the dead, but as the source of the risen life of all believers. It is not merely said that Jesus is the first to arise and that believers will attain *like him* to resurrection, but it is proclaimed that he is himself the resurrection and the life and that consequently believers find their future *in* him and not merely *like* him" (pp. 82–83).

But Moltmann's own exposition of the eschatological future is remarkably thin, alongside biblical specifics, when it comes to expounding the direction and content of God's eschatological manifestation. As much as the New Testament concentrates on the unveiling of the risen Lord in power and glory, it speaks more precisely of a final judgment and separation of righteous and wicked mankind. Moltmann puts the kingdom of God in the current social scene and not beyond it (there is for him no supernatural but only what lies ahead). The activation of the Christian hope for peace and righteousness on earth must not overleap the eschatological horizon of human obedience and disobedience, nor the content of the kingdom left so indefinite that both pacifist and revolutionary strategies may claim to unveil it.

Moltmann complains that Pannenberg does not boldly "construct . . . theological concepts" to terminate the "negative alliance with the spirit of the modern age," but seems only to circumvent its "methodical, practical and speculative atheism" (ibid., p. 83). Yet Moltmann himself, who

in confronting negative critical historiography calls for a theology to
vindicate the resurrection of the crucified Jesus, at the same time disowns
universally valid revelational truth and emphasizes instead a resurrection
theology—or more precisely an eschatology of the resurrection—in terms
of "the future of the crucified Lord" (p. 84). When Moltmann affirms that
the risen Lord's revelation becomes "historic" in the sense that "it stands
as a sort of *primum movens* at the head of the process of history" (p. 88)
he leaves unclear just how the event of Jesus' resurrection relates to the
causal power of God in distinction from all other events.

To be sure, Moltmann insists that "Christian theology will . . . not be
able to come to terms with, but will have to free itself from, the cos-
mologico-mechanistic way of thinking such as is found in the positivistic
sciences." And he contends that theology can accomplish this "only by
breaking up this kind of thinking and these relationships and striving to
set them in the eschatological movement of history" (ibid., p. 93). But
this is assertion and not closely reasoned elaboration of a counterview of
history. To say, as Moltmann does, that "every view [of] the world as a
self-contained cosmos, or history as a universal whole that contains and
manifests the divine truth, is broken down into the eschatological key
of 'not yet' " (p. 92) stops far short of indicating what the implications
of a future climax of history are for the world of causal relationships. The
concept of "historically flowing conditions" (p. 50) is much too general
and obscure to be philosophically serviceable. Moltmann rejects resurrection as superhistory and as inner historicity; he correlates it with world
history through the eschatological future and, in the name of history open
everywhere to the free, purposive activity of God, challenges the positivist world history construct. For all that, does he nonetheless concede
world history as it now is and must be known to a causally deterministic
view? While he considers the positivist-causal view to be prejudicial if it
presumes to be totalitarian, and while he insists that room be left for the
promise and fulfillment of God in history, he nevertheless surrenders
much of biblical history to myth and legend and even where he does not,
declares salvation history to be beyond historical investigation. Blaikie's
verdict is therefore not without some basis: "Instead of fleeing like the
others . . . to a supra-historical plane or a subjective-existentialist level
of history, which may be imagined as *parallel* to their basically positivist
world-history, Moltmann takes refuge in the unborn and still unreal future, *after* the deterministic history of the scientific historians has run
its course" (*"Secular Christianity" and God Who Acts*, p. 130).

Moltmann's devaluation of reason in deference to promise precludes
his exposition of a covering rationale. This is what he says: "the faith
which lives in terms of promise could prove to be the *primum movens*
which enabled Israel, or at least specific circles in the empirical Israel,
to master the situations of the land settlement and later . . . of world
history. The whole force of promise, and of faith in terms of promise,
is essentially to keep men on the move in a tense *inadaequatio rei et in-*

tellectus as long as the *promissio* which governs the *intellectus* has not yet found its answer in reality" (*Theology of Hope*, p. 102). Not even this generous sprinkling of Latin can obscure the tenuousness of a position which so vulnerably imperils the historical dimension and truth status of "faith in the future," the more so because Moltmann concedes that the expectations kindled by Yahweh's promises remain potent "even where the historic tradition passes over into legendary tradition" (p. 108). As long as the future alone is invoked as an alternative to a logically coherent statement of possibilities, no reason can be given for preferring one interpretative option to another, or none to any and all. By forfeiting reason as inadequate for understanding history, Moltmann deprives himself of the only instrument by which one can elaborate an intellectually compelling alternative to negative critical historiography. Moltmann may question whether any "other picture of history and the designations derived from it are really adequate to the understanding of history in a historic sense and can stand theological and philosophical comparison with Israel's experience of history, conditioned as it was by faith in the promise and determined by hope" (p. 110). But the manner in which he expounds his theology of revelation hardly offers a compelling "reason" for his hope.

Just as Pannenberg, Moltmann and others assailed kerygmatic theology's obscure and unsatisfactory references to biblical historical concerns and its evasion of historical revelation, so recent criticism has risen against correlating revelation exclusively with history. Braaten specially challenges the reactionary insistence that divine disclosure is exclusively historical and that all the media of revelation therefore reduce to the field of history. Reflecting on this recent preoccupation, he writes: "The coupling of revelation with history is an omnipresent feature of modern theology. It is almost unthinkable that revelation could be mediated except through something called historical events or historical existence" (*History and Hermeneutics*, p. 18). An example on the American scene is Carl Michalson, for whom history is the absolute datum of theology and who rigorously sets Christian understanding wholly within "the logic of history" (*The Rationality of Faith*, pp. 18 f.). Knowledge of God, he contends, is derived solely from history. Michalson virtually equates the term *God* with special facets of history; instead of referring the term to "some transcendent reality" he relates every aspect of God's being to the historical (p. 146). More and more scholars are emphasizing that to insist on "revelation through history" as the only channel of divine disclosure does violence to the biblical texts and to Judeo-Christian theology; not all the biblical evidence for revelation, they emphasize, can be subsumed under the category of history.

Over against those who think that all our knowledge about God and his purposes can be extrapolated from historical revelation, Frederick Herzog insists that history by itself "is unable to give meaning to the word 'God'" (*Understanding God*, p. 59). History is ambiguous and not self-explicating. "The present situation in Protestant theology demands," he says, "that the relationship between history and God be thought through once more" in the interest of human understanding of God (p. 57). Against Pannenberg, who denies that the teaching and deeds of Jesus disclose his divine being, but who contends that the resurrection incontrovertibly reveals his sovereign claim, Herzog replies that "the meaning of the resurrection is not something that everyone can read off the bare events of history, if only he uses the right method. History as such does not speak directly of God, in a resurrection as little as in a cross" (p. 62). Of scholars who rest the understanding of God exclusively on the death of Christ, Herzog asks why man should be confronted with God in the history of one man—more particularly in that of a man on a cross (p. 61). "If God was involved in the cross, it certainly was incognito" (p. 62). "Does the life preceding the cross lift God's *incognito?* Are there factors in the life that interpret the cross?" (p. 62)

Herzog consequently stresses the need for an interpretation of history: "History does not tell us why a particular historical event should point beyond itself to God. It is not at all a matter of course that Jesus should be understood as the revelation of the very heart of reality, or as God speaking, or as the illumination of the word 'God'. . . . The merely 'historical' approach to Jesus Christ does not give us an answer" (ibid., p. 50). The cross and the resurrection became intelligible, says Herzog, because of the Scripture teaching interpreted by Jesus. "Only after the risen one himself had interpreted the Scriptures . . . and had given them a sign in the breaking of bread were their eyes opened. Thus in the resurrection the meaning of the suffering was interpreted. Without a grasp of the unity of the cross and resurrection interpreted by the reality to which they point the resurrection remains mute. Historical interpretation and historical fact are fused in the biblical texts. . . . But the interpretation that makes God meaningful in the resurrection transcends the merely historical interpretation" (p. 63).

While Herzog does not adduce Scripture as an objective revelational principle, nor present a Christian philosophy of history that vindicates miraculous redemptive event, he nonetheless clearly recognizes that the meaning of the life and work of Christ is not an inference from redemptive acts but depends upon the scriptural interpretation of those acts. He disavows any desire to belittle the historical-causal method, or any other, that deals with historical phenomena. He does, however, oppose absolutizing any one model of history as properly interpretative of all reality. By appealing to the particle and wave theories of atomic structure, he implies that what is logically contradictory can be correct (ibid., pp. 155 f., n. 55). This approach is obviously no secure foundation for biblical faith, nor does it satisfactorily answer the question of where one locates the meaning of history.

Recent protest against relegating revelation to the field of history alone does not, however, consist simply of an indictment for neglecting other modes of revelation, and stress on the need for considering other modes of revelation, including that of biblical interpretation. A basic complaint is that the Judeo-Christian view of revelation does not champion historical revelation as its central and primary emphasis. As James Barr puts it: "Substantial areas of the Old Testament . . . do not support and do not fit in with the idea that revelation through history is the fundamental motif of Old Testament thought" ("Revelation through History in the Old Testament and in Modern Theology," pp. 193 ff.). Barr might have said more. However strikingly important historical revelation is even in the New Testament, such revelation in history does not exhaust the apostolic conception, nor is it the basic motif of the New Testament. According to historic Christianity, God is universally revealed in history, but this premise does not exhaust the totality of divine revelation, nor does it eclipse God's transcendent supernatural relationship to history, nor minimize Scripture's disclosure of the normative meaning of once-for-all redemptive acts.

In summary, we may welcome the following emphases in recent historical-revelation theology:

1. God's revelation is given in external, objective history.

2. All historical divine revelation, universal and particular, takes place in the same historical matrix.

3. Redemptive historical revelation does not occur as a gap in causal uniformity (or whatever uniformity there may be) inasmuch as all history is open to God's will and promise.

4. Historical revelation—universal and particular—looks to an eschatological climax that involves a final judgment and the universal kingship of Christ.

5. Revelation is a quality of all historical events (Pannenberg).

6. Revelation is to be grasped by reason, that is, normal powers of human apprehension; this requires no special work of the Spirit (Pannenberg).

7. Salvation history including Christ's resurrection is in principle historically investigatable (Pannenberg versus Moltmann).

8. Divine historical revelation, including Christ's resurrection, is not demonstrably verifiable by historical research (Moltmann versus Pannenberg).

Evangelical Christianity must, however, reject many correlative emphases, namely:

1. That the indivisible wholeness of reality excludes the supernatural and is totally historical.

2. That except for Jesus' resurrection, most of the biblical miraculous is myth and legend.

3. That only selected and preferred elements of scriptural teaching are to be retained.

4. That divine revelation is indirect and excludes ontological knowledge of God, and that theological statements are nonmetaphysical in intention.

5. That divine self-revelation is restricted to the eschatological future.

6. That revelation is not conceptual-verbal.

7. That the burden of proof that God specially reveals himself in Jesus rests upon the historian (Pannenberg).

8. That historical revelation, including Jesus' resurrection, cannot be historically investigated (Moltmann versus Pannenberg).

9. That historical revelation is self-interpreting (Pannenberg: it conveys clear and necessary information about the grounds of faith as a trust directed to the future).

10. That all certainty for Christianity must be forfeited since theology allegedly depends wholly on historiography (Pannenberg).

Evangelical theology, rather, affirms:

1. That the Christian certainties are not suspended on the probabilities of historical investigation.

2. That other media of revelation exist besides historical revelation.

3. That all media of divine disclosure stand in necessary connection with God's ongoing self-revelation.

4. That the historical revelation stands in indissoluble unity with inspired prophetic-apostolic interpretation.

5. That the biblical revelation is epistemically foundational in enabling man in sin to perceive revelational meaning undistorted by his volitional rebellion.

6. That God's revelation is mediated always through the Logos and never unmediated; it is nonetheless direct rather than indirect, its content being objectively given and cognitively valid information about God and his purposes.

22.
Revelation and History
in Evangelical Perspective

EVANGELICAL CHRISTIANITY INSISTS that certain specific historical acts are integral and indispensable to Judeo-Christian revelation. Biblical Christianity claims to be true not only in its many statements about man's inner life and about the nature of God, but also in a panoply of statements concerning redemptive historical acts. Evangelical Christians maintain that the object of biblical faith can be historically investigated, at least to some extent. Their apologists, J. Gresham Machen among them, have emphasized, and rightly, that orthodox theism has nothing in common with a faith that sacrifices either sound historical method or intellectual honesty.

For that reason evangelical theism sharply disputes the misguided notion of ancient Gnosticism and recent existentialism that historical considerations are irrelevant to genuine religious faith. It rejects the dialectical projection of two kinds of history, two kinds of truth and rival criteria for identifying truth. Evangelical Christians repudiate the thesis shared by Barth, Brunner and Bultmann that divine revelation is never historically given and is therefore in no way historically investigable. The dialectical-existential notion that disproof of the empty tomb would not at all affect the case for the resurrection of Jesus of Nazareth runs counter, evangelicals insist, to both New Testament teaching and logic. Instead evangelical theists maintain that divine revelation is given in identifiable historical acts; moreover, a negative verdict concerning redemption history, if justified, would annul the credibility of Judeo-Christian religion.

Evangelical theism did not accept the relevance of historical method reluctantly or only after great heartsearching. It has always espoused its appropriateness in approaching and evaluating the Bible. The present

311

generation has all but forgotten that modern historical consciousness
and the stimulus to historical criticism sprang from Christian concerns.
Long before the modern era, and more than a millennium before Hegel,
Augustine insisted on the importance of history as an arena in which
God works out his purposes, and was profoundly interested in the biblical past. The seventeenth-century rationalists and eighteenth-century
Enlightenment were antihistorical. From the very outset biblical religion
distinguished itself from false religion by emphasizing among other
things Yahweh's historical revelation. Christianity claims to be a historical religion not simply in the sense that all world religions are historical,
that is, phenomena of human history; it asserts more than this, namely,
that the living God decisively grounds divine revelation in specific external events attested in the Judeo-Christian Scriptures. Critical speculation over similarities and differences between the religion of the Bible
and other ancient Near Eastern faiths heightened modern interest in the
biblical past and in its religious environment. Growing attention to world
religions in turn stimulated intensive global study of revelation-and-
history concerns.

   Not only does the God of the Bible reveal himself in history, but the
very idea of history takes its rise from biblical religion. While no word
in the Hebrew language can be translated by the modern term *history*,
the term is nonetheless appropriate and necessary in expounding Israel's
existence. The Hebrew authors incorporate and expound the idea of
history even if they do not sophisticate it into a technical vocabulary.
In fact, the idea has its origin in the history of the Hebrews, even if
the modern conception at times includes features outside the range of
Israelite understanding, or excludes dimensions integral to the biblical
view. Later Israelites looked back to Moses and the exodus, and the
Hebrew people insisted on the details of 1 and 2 Kings and 1 and 2
Chronicles as integral to a proper understanding of their past.

   The ancient world perceived human events in relation to cosmic or
astral processes which it often divinized, or it viewed these events in the
context of repetitive cycles or as significant only within a given culture
or civilization, if indeed it regarded what happens in time as significant
at all. Contemporary extensions of such theories may be seen in current
notions of dialectical materialism, cultural relativity, and astrological influence upon human affairs. In contrast to the Greeks to whom the idea
of history was fundamentally foreign, and who sought nothing of per-
petual and abiding significance in history, the Hebrew prophets knew
that history is the realm in which God decisively acts and works out his
purposes. The Bible throughout insists that God the Creator holds mankind eternally accountable for every thought, word and deed, and that
each successive generation moves toward a final future in which the
God not only of creation but also of redemption and judgment will consummate human history in the light of his divine offer of salvation.
Human events are therefore no chaotic jumble to which man must cre-

atively impart some shrewd order and plan but stand inescapably in relationship to the purpose, and promise and plan of God. That plan is not reducible to self-repeating structures; it embraces, rather, a constant, abiding order and God's progressive once-for-all redemptive revelation within a history climaxed in Jesus Christ in fulfillment of divinely given prophetic promises.

The Bible accordingly sponsors its own historiography, or writing of history, by a distinctive exhibition of particular events and affirmation of their meaning, and by emphasizing the nature of the comprehensive course and climax of human affairs. The Bible instructs us therefore in the difference between adequate and inadequate and arbitrary approaches to history. It sees all history in terms of the governing purpose of God.

It serves neither Christianity, historiography nor truth in general to try to preserve isolated aspects of apostolic belief in a context of the historicist view of history which is essentially positivist in its notion of repeated regularities similar to the laws of physics. It is usually religious theorists eager to escape the orthodox theological commitments of evangelical Christianity who espouse such mediating views. Some scholars, for example, who balk at Jesus' virgin birth and resurrection will defend certain of his miracles, especially the healings, on the ground of our advanced modern insights into physical and mental illness. But the risks of this evacuation route are much higher than such escapees suspect. Anyone who would retain a sound interest in the Christian revelation will not presume to vindicate even an iota of it by submitting its claims to contemporary empirical arbitration of what could or could not have taken place in the past, or of what has exhaustive relevance for the future.

No evangelical philosopher has more notably challenged the modern historiographical exclusion of the supernatural as a significant explanatory referent than has Gordon H. Clark. Clark emphasizes a thesis that distinguishes Christianity from all other religions, namely, that God who is independent of the world is personally active in history (*A Christian View of Men and Things*, pp. 37–93). Clark bases a Christian philosophy of history on three principles: (1) God controls history (Dan. 2:21; Acts 17:26), and works out his purposes even in particular events (Gen. 50:20; Exod. 12:36; 1 Sam. 16:12; 2 Sam. 24:1; Isa. 10:5–6); (2) God will bring history to its climax and end in the second advent of Christ (2 Thess. 1:8); (3) God personally acts in history.

To those who contend that the revelational acts of the Bible should be bracketed as myth, saga or *Geschichte* because they are unverifiable by the scientific method of historiography, Clark replies not by defending the absolute empirical verifiability of these acts but by insisting that "no event [whatever] is subject to absolute verification" (*Historiography: Secular and Religious*, p. 368). Clark rejects the view of Ernst Hengstenberg in a previous generation and of John W. Montgomery in ours that the biblical revelation and history can be historically verified. He insists that limitations of the historical method preclude absolute historical verification of nonbiblical and biblical past events, and that "probability-verification" is not truly verification. The empirical evidence for all past events is only partial and circumstantial. To assume that scriptural history is subject to special objections not applicable to history in general, and therefore to categorize biblical events differently from other past events is arbitrary, he says. Brunner is not to be disputed—for example, when he writes: "The question whether Jesus never existed will always hover upon the margin of history as a possibility. . . . The bare fact of the existence of Christ as an historical person is not assured" (*The Mediator*, pp. 186 f.)—if what Brunner here has in view is absolute demonstration by historical research. What is to be challenged, however, is any implication that by contrast the existence of secular historical personages is assuredly certain, or that Christian faith can skeptically dispense with the gospel data, or that our only source of reliable information about Christ's existence is historical investigation.

Over against neoorthodox readiness to devalue the Scriptures as historical sources, Clark insists on the historical reliability of the Gospel accounts about Jesus of Nazareth. To deny historical certainty does not at all require the enthronement of historical skepticism. Clark does not dispute but rather defends the historical aspects of Judeo-Christian revelation.

Clark observes that many modern theologians apply a skepticism to the biblical accounts that they abandon everywhere else. A. N. Sherwin-White similarly considers it "astonishing" that the study of the Gospels in our century has made Jesus of Nazareth unknowable despite the possession of "no less promising material" than that used to "write a history" of Christ's likewise well-documented contemporary, Tiberius Caesar (*Roman Society and Roman Law in the New Testament*, p. 187). It is impossible to apply less stringent criteria to secular history than to the biblical writings unless one is prejudiced against the historical representations of the Bible. The norms that existential and dialectical theologians apply to scriptural history differ from those they apply to secular history, and indeed from the norms that reputable secular historians apply to historical events of any kind. If the norms that many kerygmatic theologians apply to the biblical narratives were applied to secular history, much of what is now accepted as secular history would on a priori grounds become suspect.

Martin Kähler abetted this confusion by needlessly conceding that, as regards the New Testament, "it is impossible to attain that degree of certainty which can, to some extent at least, be achieved in other areas of antiquity" (*The So-Called Historical Jesus*, p. 100). His contrast reflects an underlying bias against the historical reliability of the Gospels: "We do indeed possess historical accounts, but certainly not of the kind which can be demonstrated to have the value of historical documents in the strict sense of the term. . . . We possess no historical documents concerning Jesus' public ministry" (pp. 125 f.). Much as Kähler may emphasize that the Gospels are not strict biographies of the life of the Nazarene, the essentials of Jesus' conception of himself are no different from those reported by the New Testament writers, nor are the writers' references to historical matters to be devalued. While it is doubtless "an illusion," as Walter Künneth emphasizes, "to think that in the Gospels we can get behind Easter and reconstruct a life of Jesus as such, untouched by the knowledge of Easter" (*The Theology of the Resurrection*, p. 148)—even as we can now scarcely reconstruct a life of Hitler without seeing him through the later devastation of Europe—the result is hardly disconcerting when one possesses manuscripts written by those most intimately familiar with what took place.

By emphasizing the limits of empirical investigation, Clark in no way intends to suggest that what occurs externally is inconsequential; historical revelation is an indispensable Christian affirmation. By no means may Christians disparage historical investigation or dispense with credible witnesses to the biblical events or with tests of their testimony. The fact that historical evidence does not convey logical or apodictic certainty (of which mathematics is a species), and at best yields only probability, does not reduce it to worthlessness; all legal and ordinary judgments are rendered on the basis of just such evidence. To turn from historical considerations to subjective certitude and to say on this basis alone that Christian realities are given only internally and are therefore historically uninvestigatable makes religious belief completely subjective, and also forfeits the fact that the living God has revealed himself in ordinary "secular" history.

Whether or not the historical method can of itself "prove" that a particular miracle occurred is not the same question as whether miracles occur. The issue is whether in view of his methodology the historian must always explain the past in nonmiraculous terms. Shall we accept historical evidence for miracles or rule them a priori impossible on mechanistic or naturalistic grounds? The objection against miracles is hardly ever directed against one particular miracle (except by some candidates for ordination) but is part of a general view of nature.

Important though it is, historical research has serious limitations. When applied to the Bible the historical method may indeed be impotent to assess the significance of the miraculous. In investigating the articles of the Apostles' Creed, for example, historical criteria are much more serviceable to the confession that Jesus "suffered under Pontius Pilate" than that "he descended into hell" or that he is the Father's "only Son, our Lord." The impossibility of establishing theological doctrines by historical method is not here disputed. No amount of historical inquiry can prove that Jesus is the Christ, or that the Hebrews rightly believed that Yahweh rescued them from Egypt. "It is hard to overemphasize the impossibility of obtaining *historical* evidence for the view that certain events are 'the mighty acts of God'," writes John Marsh (*The Fulness of Time*, p. 7).

One need only add that it is likewise impossible to find *historical* evidence that some or all events are not acts of God. Historical observation can neither demonstratively prove nor disprove the operative providence of God in history. Nor can it demonstratively certify that Jesus did or did not rise from the dead. Nor, for that matter, can the historical method indubitably establish that Jesus was crucified by Roman soldiers, or even that Caesar crossed the Rubicon on some past momentous day, however "probable" it may be that he crossed the Rubicon routinely, if indeed he crossed it at all. Historical research is equally limited in investigating both biblical and secular claims about the past. Whether conducted by Cornelius Van Til or by Arnold Toynbee, historical investigation provides only provisional and not certain knowledge of the past. Should the historian arrive at certainty it is not because of absolutely compelling empirical considerations. Unlike the axioms of geometry and the truths of logic, historical actualities are never self-evident nor can they be indubitably proved.

Does this mean that mental reservation must under all circumstances overhang life's decisions and commitments, especially in the supremely important matter of spiritual destiny? Are we to emphasize that historical research does not get beyond historical probability at best, or historical improbability at worst even when it deals with the nonmiraculous? To what extent is faith dependent upon projecting some probability grounded in historical evidence? Certainly no leap between "historical probability" and faith's certainty has the character of historical evidence, for certainty turns on factors not derived from historical investigation. It is true that varying degrees of intellectual assent to the factuality of some historical event can be raised to personal certainty on the basis of naked faith. But is such certainty any different from the certainty that some people have on the basis of personal experience that vinegar cures warts or that grapefruit juice relieves migraine? Are moral considerations just as relevant as historical data? Would the inner serenity of knowing one has "played it safe" compensate for overcoming the inner anxiety and struggle of agnosticism? After commenting that we cannot obtain historical evidence that certain events are indeed God's mighty acts, Marsh remarks, rightly or wrongly, that "the 'evidence' for Christian faith seems to be very largely subjective" (ibid., p. 7).

To what extent if at all does faith depend on possibilities inherent in the evidence? Probability does indeed provide a great deal of guidance amid one's daily decisions; it is far better to have some empirical probabilities in life than none at all. But is probability an adequate support for the Christian certainties? What in any event does probability signify in respect to historical happenings? Clark doubts that the word means anything when historical considerations are at stake. When one casts dice the probability of shooting "seven" is 6 in 36 or 1 in 6. But what is the probability that Caesar crossed the Rubicon? Is it 1/365 or 364/365? How does one count? How are we to define historical probability? Clark emphasizes that historical inferences are not inductive in the sense of collecting cases and then extrapolating. There is only one case of each historical event. Is probability then tied not to events but rather to the number of times the historians have succeeded or failed in properly identifying or explaining them? Would a 60 percent probability supply confident projection of a leap over 40 percent uncertainty? Does not any degree of probability imply also a proportionate degree of doubt? Can Christian faith rest on an 89 percent probability that Jesus of Nazareth was God incarnate and a 76 percent probability that he died for the sins of men?

The results of historical investigation are by nature less than absolutely conclusive; what finally determines whether one believes or disbelieves what the Gospels narrate or what any historical documentary affirms about the past is therefore not a conclusive negative or positive word of historical criticism. The underlying principles of interpretation are not actually derived from external data. The interpreter of history invariably assesses the flow of human affairs through a cohesive framework of meaning that he brings along to the observation of events rather than derives from them; the Christian brings one principle of interpretation, the non-Christian brings a variety of others. Claiming to use only objective historical techniques, liberal, humanist and secular theologians have compressed the New Testament data to support only the humanity of Jesus. For all that, Paul van Buren insists also that Jesus' exemplification of agape is permanently valid; humanists have ongoingly championed as well Jesus' supposed advocacy of democratic values, and modernists have contended that Jesus' unreserved trust in the Father best demonstrates how the discordant self can find inner tranquillity. No impartial reader would identify the central message of the New Testament in these terms, however, nor profess to derive such conclusions from empirical observation. Bultmann's notion that the historical method discerns very little about the "real Jesus," except that he lived and died, he claimed to base on form-critical analysis of the Gospels. But the "real Jesus" of Bultmann differs markedly from the "real Jesus" of G. C. Berkouwer or F. F. Bruce. The historical data can be approached on very different premises. If Jesus was who and what he and the apostles claimed he was and is—the premise is at least a hypothetical possibility—then certain ways and works attributed to him are not at all incredible.

Clark is especially critical of the premise, espoused by Barth, Brunner, Bultmann, Cullmann and others, that history can be written with scientific objectivity devoid of presuppositions and interpretation. The difference between Marx's interpretation of history as a reflex of dialectical materialism, and Cullman's appeal to prophetic interpretation, Clark emphasizes, lies in their explicit and differing presuppositions, and not in a total avoidance of them. That the historian is one who gathers data from the past but frustrates this objective if he approaches the past under the influence of any interpretative principle whatever, is a popular but naïve notion. The writing of history rests inescapably on philosophical or theological premises. According to some nineteenth-century historians, Hittites never existed in patriarchal times and the kings mentioned in Genesis 14 were not historical; Moses could not have written the Pentateuch because the Hebrews did not know how to write until the period of the Judges; Isaiah invented the figure named Sargon in chapter 20, and the crucified Jesus did not rise from the tomb. Such conclusions were presumably based on scholarly investigation of the past; they were in fact, however, not at all acquired from examination of the past but were implicit in philosophical premises brought to the investigation of history. The claims of some scholars that Jesus of Nazareth never lived, or that his death occurred other than by crucifixion, or that the Hittites were an invention of ancient religionists, were in no sense an achievement of historical research but were the by-product rather of some specific interpretative principle or philosophy of history.

Writing of Thomas Altizer's representations of Jesus of Nazareth in the context of death-of-God theology, John W. Montgomery remarks that "what we get here is a Jesus who fits with remarkable precision the theological presuppositions Professor Altizer brings to the investigation to begin with" (*The Suicide of Christian Theology*, p. 162). Montgomery brings his own very different presuppositions to the biblical data. Reviewing the traditions about a universal flood and citing explorations of Mount Ararat in search of remnants of Noah's Ark, Montgomery assures us that the undiscovered Ark is there and that its discovery at this time in history could be a divine reminder that we are now already in the eschatological end-time ("As it was in Noah's day, so will it be when the Son of Man comes," Matt. 24:37, JB) (*The Quest for Noah's Ark*, 1972). Philosopher W. T. Jones tells us unqualifiedly—surely without historical attestation—that "Paul first made the historical Jesus into a Saviour God and then built up a mythical setting for this god out of the Jewish legends and stories that he and Jesus, as Jews, knew in common" (*The Medieval Mind*, p. 41).

Blaikie gives two pointed illustrations of how historians of different perspectives divergently assess the importance of particular events for understanding human affairs. As we know, the New Testament record of the apostolic witness to the resurrection of the crucified Jesus has decisively shaped the history of the West, and through the Christian missionary movement greatly altered the life of multitudes of people. But the *Cambridge Modern History*, which devotes one of its fourteen volumes to the French Revolution and another to Napoleon, notes Blaikie, has but a single index reference to "missionary" matters, and that to Missionary Hill, a Civil War battlesite east of Chattanooga. Yet, as John Foster remarks, modern Christian missions did "as much to change the world as the French Revolution and to have far more permanent effects than Napoleon" (Blaikie quotes these words in *"Secular Christianity" and God Who Acts,* p. 144, from a film-strip series on "The Spread of Christianity"). Lesslie Newbigin observes that at a time when about 85 percent of all schoolchildren in Africa were in mission schools, the massive report of the 1962 UNESCO Conference on Education in Africa "contrives to provide a survey of the total situation without conveying the impression that such a thing as a mission school exists" (*Honest Religion for Secular Man,* p. 103).

"Such omissions are not due to any lack of documentary evidence," Blaikie comments, "but to a selection made, without intention of bias, by historians or reporters whose presuppositions and attitudes predispose them to see certain things as important and true, and to dismiss as insignificant or even fail to notice other things" (*"Secular Christianity" and God Who Acts,* p. 144). According to Moltmann it was Christianity's sense of worldwide mission that first popularized the concept of universal or world history; what's more, modern views of history are unable to renounce this governing idea even though Christian realities may no longer seem to stand at the center of history (*Theology of Hope,* p. 262). He adds that while modern philosophy of history has broken with the Christian revelation of the future, it has "the character of a philosophic, enlightened millenarianism [and] . . . further, the character of eschatological spirit mysticism" (p. 264).

One could continue indefinitely to illustrate how interpreters of the past reflect their underlying assumptions by what they select to serve as evidence. Far more than recent generations we today understand why Plato warned against those who think historians merely catalogue human events (*Meno* 97AB) and why Aristotle associated historians with artists and poets rather than with rational philosophers (*Poetics,* 1451B). Gordon Clark notes Harry Elmer Barnes's complaint (in *A History of Historical Writing,* p. 122) that the theological orientation of Protestant Reformation writers precluded any pursuit of "historical studies for the mere love of acquiring information." But Barnes's approach, he comments, would leave unsure just *what* information is significant and *why.* The differences between Barnes and the Reformers in assessing the Reformation, Clark adds, are not due to anything that a twentieth-century humanist like Barnes has gathered from the past.

Empirical historiography can show no pervasive unity in history; whatever unity it does espouse, if any, is necessarily simplistic and vulnerable to ongoing revision. The appeal made by even some Christian scholars to empirical and historical considerations as being primary and decisive for faith results in pitting probabilities against counterprobabilities; more than that, it leaves Christian beliefs uncertainly suspended on empirical ambiguity. While "the historical character of the biblical witness establishes the legitimacy of historical-critical research," says H. M. Kuitert, "this does not mean that historical research provides the basis for Christian faith" (*The Reality of Faith,* p. 164). To be sure, "faith stands or falls with the real eventfulness of this history" (p. 165). But orthodoxy would err no less than positivism if it held that only scientific research—however contradictory the findings were—can rule on the truth or untruth of the Christian faith. Evangelical Christianity in no way presumes to regard historical investigation, now or in the past, as the sufficient method of knowing the truth of revelation.

While archaeological discoveries have to some extent significantly reversed nineteenth-century historical criticism, not even they supply any firm basis for Christian faith. The special value of archaeological and linguistic research is the light it sheds on certain doubtful terms and on the social and literary milieu of various biblical times. The distinguished archaeologist Nelson Glueck, commenting on the Bible's amazing accuracy, declared that "no archaeological discovery has ever controverted a single properly understood Biblical statement." For all that, archaeology neither confirms the history that remains unconfirmed, nor first establishes its factuality when it has confirmed that history; in no case can archaeology confirm transcendent aspects of the biblical revelation, nor attain demonstrative certainty about the findings it reports.

Without some norm of importance, some pattern of meaning, events are chaotic. History requires a meaning-scheme. This interpretative principle, moreover, is never an empirical inference from events but always a premise of faith. It is no academic secret that historians disagree considerably over precisely what historical methodology involves. Positivist historians try to wrest a principle from the details of history by which then to explain what happens universally, but no such universal principle—and hence no principle at all—can be extrapolated from isolated particulars. The Christian, on the other hand, derives his philosophy of history not by examining isolated events or from internal impressions, but from the Bible, that is, from divinely inspired writers who convey God's revealed purpose in human affairs. Contrary to William Temple's insistence in *Nature, Man and God* that "the main field of revelation must be in the history of men," Clark emphasizes that human history gives us no knowledge of God unless we can discern its direction and goal and thus establish the significance of great events. Apart from the Bible would we even know which events are great? (Egyptian analysts ignored the exodus and Roman historians virtually ignored Jesus Christ.) What secular historiography cannot do, inspired Scripture can do and does: it declares the direction and goal of history and identifies the great events and their redemptive meaning.

Divine revelation is the epistemic source and Scripture the methodological principle of the Christian interpretation of history. For Pannenberg revelation is the predicate of history, and for Moltmann history is the predicate of eschatology; for Clark historical revelation and Scripture are in some respects predicates of each other. To be sure, not all revelation is Scripture; the apostle Paul speaks, for example, of things revealed to him that he did not write down. Moreover, if all historical events are revelation, they are not all Scripture, if by this one means this or that particular historical event. Yet justification by faith, or any other scripturally revealed truth, is historical revelation, in the sense that it was divinely revealed at a certain place and time. But simply by reading the Bible conscientiously anyone can learn the meaning it attaches to crucial historical events; neither the study of archaeology nor of Ugaritic nor of world religions nor of the Vienna School of logical positivism is necessary for knowing the Christian philosophy of history. Alongside descriptive statements about men and nations, the Bible gives a theoretical or theological explanation of the events in its purview, and affirms that all men and nations are alike subject to one and the same sovereignty. Scripture combines testimony to historical acts with divine revelation concerning the meaning of those acts. The biblical context sets historical acts and their meaning in an intelligibly consistent framework that includes prior knowledge about the nature, purpose and promises of God.

How then are revelational truth and faith dependent on, yet distinguished from, external acts which historical investigation pursues within certain unavoidable limits? Surely Christian faith is not independent of nor does it cancel specific historical salvific events; without factual redemptive history evangelical faith would be null and void, and in fact, impossible. If a negative historical judgment were possible, it would invalidate the faith in Christ's incarnation and resurrection. Christianity, if true, requires historical reality in its claims about the incarnation, atonement and resurrection of Jesus Christ, and indeed about God's revelation in earlier biblical history. Orthodox Christianity does not postulate "superhistorical" revelation (myth, saga, *Geschichte*) to compensate for supposedly subhistorical narratives. But neither does it promote historical improbabilities together with divine revelation. In no sense does it combine revelation and historical skepticism.

The evangelical Christian has no reason or basis for conceding that the Gospels are demonstrably unreliable. Instead he challenges and contests the gratuitous surrender of biblical reliability in historical matters and the ready sacrifice of biblical representations to alien critical theories. For the biblical writers *what* happened is no less important than the *who* and *why;* they are concerned for historical precision in reporting salvific acts and redemptive realities. The inspired writers promulgate specific historical facts; Luke even remarks that he had engaged in careful historical research (1:1–4). The evangelists never promote faith in a person at the expense of historical factuality, for they themselves came to know Jesus of Nazareth not independently of historical realities but in and through his historical revelation.

Yet evangelicals also insist, as we have seen, that historical investigation and methodology are not sources of faith; the source of faith is God. Historical study cannot demonstrate either secular or biblical history to be certainly factual. By itself historical research alone never absolutely certifies an event. At most, historical evidence is always congruous with revelational truth; whether historical method can attest an event to be "highly probably" factual is another matter. Nothing in historical investigation absolutely negates Christian faith or absolutely justifies an alternative faith. Even someone who espouses premises wholly contrary to Christianity cannot demonstrate historical impossibility; he can only affirm historical improbability. In any event, not only the "highest probability," but in some instances—for reasons that we shall see—even the barest possibility (against the tide of a prejudiced historiography, for example) is compatible with an evangelical regard for historical actualities as a ground of belief rather than of unbelief. As Montgomery rightly emphasizes, even a relativistic age cannot rule out a priori the possibility of the miraculous; intellectual integrity always demands an examination of the evidence (*History and Christianity*, 1971). Yet without examining history as a whole, no one can tell what is possible in history; obviously the whole of history and its meaning are not accessible for such examination.

Do we then exercise faith only because we cannot assuredly know that Christ did not rise from the dead? Far from it. If that were the case, our faith would rest not on fact but on superstition. Yet not even "historical probability" can be derived by examining objective data divorced from the "understanding" of "historical truth" that the historian subjectively brings to objective events. *Possibility* and *probability* are not something on whose content scholars universally agree irrespective of their governing assumptions, any more than are concepts of God and the good. The terms need to be defined, and then methods must be adduced for recognizing them in particular instances. What Van A. Harvey considers historically probable and possible differs greatly from what Kenneth Scott Latourette considers historically probable and possible. The difference between the Christian and the non-Christian, the evangelical and the nonevangelical, therefore, lies not in different external data, but in differing presuppositions about what is and is not possible in the realm of history. Whether to dignify as true the idealist, positivist, existentialist, communist or Christian view of history depends finally on which approach offers the most consistent account of the evidence. The non-Christian historian tends to decide what was possible in the historical past and what is possible in the historical future on the basis of certain current metaphysical conceptions of reality, conceptions that run quite counter to Christian theism. The present-day interpreter is predisposed to disbelieve miracles such as the resurrection of Jesus Christ from the dead and to assume the nonreliability of the Bible.

Aware of this secular readiness to judge the possibility of God, revelation and miracle by the norms of nonrevelational theorizing, Barth says something very significant in his massive *Church Dogmatics* about speculative notions of possibility. Divine actuality, he stresses, takes precedence over such speculation. To this Clark comments that "past and future actualities are not to be denied on the ground of a limited and irrelevant concept of possibility. Specifically, if the Virgin Birth actually occurred in the past, and if Christ is actually to return in the future, these events cannot be judged impossible on grounds restricted to the present" (*Karl Barth's Theological Method*, p. 81). Over against the biblical prophets who saw history as conditioned by God's truth and promise and action, modern theologians increasingly speak of a historically conditioned theology. The Christian interpreter sees the hand of God in all history and nature and therefore has no reason to face any of it with premises based on restrictive inquiry.

Some readers may feel that we have overstated the uncertainties of history, and that recent events are in any case far less open to debate than are happenings in the distant past. Contemporary American history confutes this notion, however. Ongoing demands to reopen the assassination investigations of President John F. Kennedy, of his brother, Robert, and of Martin Luther King, Jr., stem from the limitations of circumstantial evidence. Despite painstaking official probes and unprecedented mass-media coverage of "the facts," no one is sure why the Kennedys and King were murdered. No one is sure where the ultimate incentive came from; doubts persist, moreover, that the real culprits have been punished. Although the nation's highest criminal and judicial agencies are assured that circumstantial evidence has properly assigned culpability for these crimes, even some outstanding government leaders are unconvinced of the verdicts. And despite investigations by the police, the Federal Bureau of Investigation and the Warren Commission into the 1963 assassination of President Kennedy, eighty-seven U.S. Congressmen have urged a resolution for reinvestigation. Did Lee Harvey Oswald slay the president; if so, was he acting alone; if not, was he leagued with Marxists? Some have argued that Kennedy was the victim of a CIA-Mafia conspiracy; Lyndon Johnson suspected a Castro connection in his predecessor's assassination; others think that the CIA suppressed relevant information. Questions persist also over James Earl Ray's sole responsibility for the assassination of King. What actually "occurred" not only ranges contemporary reporters on different and even opposite sides, but also involves contradictory interpretations.

In all human history no historical writings have appeared so contemporaneously with the events they relate as in our time. It is obvious that the proximity of historical reports to the date of the events themselves does not establish certainty; in many matters even the probabilities are in doubt. Some critics have contended that the New Testament accounts of Christ's resurrection are at a disadvantage because they must be dated, at the earliest, fifteen years or more after the crucifixion; as historical writings go such timing is in fact notably close to the recorded events. Some modern critics have said that more time must elapse before Americans can gain trustworthy perspective on recent political assassinations and the Watergate era.

According to some modern historians the New Testament is historically untrustworthy because this literature is written from the standpoint of faith and little evidence about the life of Jesus can be found outside the Bible. But because the Gospel accounts came from intimately associated sources are they therefore unreliably biased and distorted? Would such early writings be more reliable had they come from Pontius Pilate or from the Sanhedrin, or from onlookers who simply watched from the sidelines? Is that how trustworthy history is written in our own time? Would a book about the Watergate era in America be more trustworthy if written by George McGovern or the Democratic National Committee than by those who were personally involved and who came to change their ways?

To further illustrate the governing influence of philosophical assumptions in interpreting historical data, let us consider Van A. Harvey's book *The Historian and the Believer*, which aligns modern historical method against miraculous supernaturalism. Past events, says Harvey, must be "analogous" to events in the historian's present experience if they are to survive historical scrutiny. Nothing can be known in history except what is analogous to ordinary human experience.

We need not be detoured into the ambiguities of the term *experience;* it is obvious that unless in some broad sense we have experience of it we cannot know anything either in the present or in the past. Nor is this the place to reopen discussion of what experience means in empirical methodology, and more especially in historical over against scientific investigation. Instead, the issue here centers on biblical miracle and contemporary analogy. When the modern positivistic historian demands that nothing be admitted in past history for which analogies cannot be adduced in the present, is this really, as Harvey would have us believe, a requirement of evidential morality or the morality of historical understanding? Or is Harvey, rather, integrating the insistent biblical avowal of once-for-all redemptive acts into a view of history that prejudicially excludes in advance the very possibility of any miraculous divine manifestation in history?

While the notion of historical "analogy" is somewhat looser than that of repetition, and somewhat modifies Troeltsch's notion of uniformity, it comes in the last analysis as routinely to rule out miracles. Its requirement is rigid enough to disallow the resurrection of Jesus Christ, an occurrence affirmed by traditional evangelical theists and recent neo-Protestants like Moltmann and Pannenberg. Although many scholars who personally disbelieve the bodily resurrection of Jesus Christ would, like G. W. H. Lampe (in *The Resurrection*, pp. 17, 58), hesitate to say that an intelligent Christian must disavow it, Harvey declares that the morality of historical consciousness rules out accepting it as historical fact.

Harvey adduces five considerations that assertedly attest the incompatibility of miracles with modern historical methodology: (1) the "negative function of scientific laws" makes modern belief in the supernatural world "impossible" (*The Historian and the Believer*, pp. 74 f.); (2) the absolute uniqueness of miracles precludes knowing what would count for or against their actual occurrence since we cannot rationally assess what lies outside our experience (p. 228); (3) comparative religions study evidences that miracles are often fictitiously attributed to founders of religions (p. 88); (4) miracle reports come from mythologically minded persons insensitive to scientific laws (p. 10); (5) even if it were theoretically established that "Jesus was probably alive on the third day" after crucifixion, the morality of historical knowledge requires the historian to affirm this probability only tentatively and not passionately as would a believer.

Harvey avers that where natural events are concerned (e.g., a supposed bodily resurrection), scientific laws have the negative function of telling the historian "what could have happened" in the past (ibid., pp. 74 f.). Harvey does not go so far as to say that miracles are metaphysically or logically "impossible" (pp. 85, 229) but simply that modern historical methodology cannot validate them. Belief in miracles is "no longer practically *possible*," he says, because "it is *impossible* to escape from the categories and presuppositions of the intellectual culture of which one is a part. . . . *Possibility and actuality are relative* to our own time" (pp. 114 f., italics mine).

Actually the true reason that historical method cannot validate miracles is quite different. The fact is that the historical method is inherently incapable of coping with transcendent supernatural concerns, and unable to demonstratively validate any past event. Harvey's emphasis is that historical method must be welded to the cultural prejudices of one's own age, and he assumes that these contemporary prejudices are valid. He accordingly weds historical possibility and actuality not to God but to contemporary positivistic philosophy. Surely it is not the scientist's task and even less so the historian's to formulate fixed laws of behavior that preestablish the limits of possibility, that stipulate in advance, for example, that man cannot fly in space, or walk on the moon, or that Christ cannot walk on water or that God cannot act in history.

Committed to historical positivism, Harvey invokes the limits of historical method however it suits his interpretative needs. He asks: "If modern historians are unable to decipher the mystery of Abraham Lincoln even though they possess volumes of authentic sayings, intimate letters, and the accounts of eyewitnesses, are we to believe that we can encounter the real Jesus of Nazareth on the basis of a handful of sayings preserved in no chronological order by a community that was especially anxious to prove that he was the Messiah?" (ibid., p. 193). With the alternatives presented so prejudicially, it is no surprise that, despite Harvey's emphasis on the limits of historical method, he invokes it to invalidate conclusively the incarnation and resurrection of Jesus Christ. Although his statement that "the issue in the case of Christian belief is the degree to which the apostolic witness with respect to facts is to be trusted" (p. 222) is surely correct, his a priori disbelief in miracles prejudges the claim to be eyewitnesses by those who died as martyrs in their commitment to the Jesus they authoritatively interpreted.

Every assumption Harvey makes that is not empirically demonstrable collides with his bold decree that "faith has no function in the justification of historical arguments respecting fact" (ibid., p. 112), and that "faith has no clear relation to any particular set of historical beliefs at all" (p. 280), including these selfsame empirically undemonstrable dogmas. It is true that to invoke faith alone to justify historical claims might bring "the machinery of rational assessment . . . to a shuddering halt" (p. 112), but reason is also swiftly brought to a standstill by excluding all a prioris, something with which Harvey is himself secretly and excessively armed. When he insists, for example, that "no remote historical event . . . can . . . be the basis for a religious confidence about the present" (p. 282) but at the same time claims that present events provide a basis for disbelieving the historical resurrection of Jesus of Nazareth, we are forced to conclude that Harvey's view excludes miracles per se.

Those who criticize the biblical miracles because of the lack of analogy in present experience assume that present-day empirical science is normative for what may or may not have taken place in the past or may occur in the future. The objection here is not simply to the covert acceptance of a metaphysical theory that stipulates in advance of empirical investigation what is possible and impossible as cosmic or historical event; the objection is to the notion, rather, that despite the inherent demand of empirical science to continually revise its conclusions, contemporary scientific knowledge is made the test of any and all possibilities. This assumption not only requires a theory of "progress" that positions the contemporary historian or scientist at the sluice gates of decisive knowledge but, as Clark somewhere comments, must also assume that "progress" has now stopped—in brief, as some philosophical scientists actually believe, that the basic principles are now unalterable and that only minor refinements remain as extension in details and applications. The positivistic assumption that scientific method will not change, and that the third stage of Comte's evolutionary philosophy is final, is a stellar example. This approach brims with conceit, for it makes empiricist dogmas of the past distinctively contemporary and on this basis permanently normative, but labels scholars who do not subscribe to such prejudices as antiquarians.

The demand for an "analogy" in contemporary experience as the minimal price for accepting any past event as historical mirrors the same prejudice. The modern historian, in effect, claims the right not only to establish the credibility of past witnesses but also to declare them genuine on the basis of conformity to a contemporary philosophy of history. In Harvey's words, "the historian *confers* authority upon a witness"; "he is no longer a seeker of knowledge but a mediator of past belief" (ibid., p. 42). When the biblical past is filtered through Harvey's presuppositions "the conclusion one is driven to," he tells us, is that "the content of faith can as well be mediated through a historically false story of a certain kind as through a true one, through a myth as well as through history" (p. 280). We may be sure that Harvey was least of all surprised by this "conclusion"; it is the hidden premise with which he sets out in evaluating the data.

The insistence on contemporary analogy so gives the primacy to present-day experience that it precludes any incomparably unique event anywhere in past history and arbitrarily excludes even the possibility of once-for-all events in the future. If miracles occur anywhere and at any time, they must occur also at a command performance attended by the twentieth-century historian.

This requirement of analogies in present history as the price of historical credibility in other times runs counter not only to the biblical miraculous but also to exceptional nonmiraculous events. Another historian, Polybius, wrote in his day of "an event for which the past has no precedent"; are we to disallow it now as historically inadmissible because no present-day analogy can be adduced? Writing of military conquest which in less than fifty-three years brought "almost the whole inhabited world . . . under the single dominion of the Romans," Polybius asked whether anyone "can be so completely absorbed in other subjects of contemplation or study as to think any of them superior in importance to an accurate understanding of an event for which the past offers no precedent?" (*Universal History*, I, 1). When contemporary events held to be unparalleled in history fall into the past, are future generations to disown them for lack of analogy? Here one thinks of the regathering of Jewry to Palestine, and beyond that of the brutal Nazi destruction of six million Jews. While human history was known to be replete with suffering and injustice, the Nazi genocide of European Jews in a pogrom of "annihilation for annihilation's sake," Emil L. Fackenheim says, defies any comparison: "The Nazi holocaust has no precedent in ancient Jewish history—or medieval or modern. . . . Nor . . . will one find a precedent outside Jewish history" (*God's Presence in History*, pp. 69 f.). This is somewhat an overstatement; Stalin massacred six million Ukranians and Mao twenty million Chinese.

When dealing with miracles, Harvey tells us, we are concerned with absolutely unique events for which there can be no criteria (*The Historian and the Believer*, p. 277). But, replies Ronald J. Sider, our ability to "conceive and conceptualize reported miraculous events" shows that they are not absolutely unique ("The Historian, the Miraculous, and Post-Newtonian Man," p. 314). This rejoinder is less than persuasive, however, since we can also conceive of and conceptualize God who is incomparably unique. Sider's remark demonstrates only that miracles are intelligible (otherwise not even Harvey could write meaningfully against them). Yet the fact is that anyone recognizes an empty tomb when he sees one, and knows what birth by a virgin implies. "The biblical miracles, moreover, have reputedly occurred within the range of experience of some human beings in other generations," and they no less than we would contend that miracles cannot be explained either in terms of empirical scientific inquiry or of human experience generally.

Harvey emphasizes that since dead men tend to stay dead the conclusion follows that Jesus of Nazareth almost certainly was not alive three days after crucifixion. Christianity holds, however, that the absence of present-day resurrections settles nothing unless one illicitly universalizes contemporary observations; all humans are destined to a future resurrection of which Christ's past resurrection is an anticipatory paradigm. This displaces Harvey's requirement of an analogy between present and past events by an analogy between past and future events. The notion of analogy in respect to historical events is itself obscure and requires close examination, since human acts do not reduce readily to scientific samplings of cases of the same phenomenon. Are we to speak of the raising of Lazarus and the translation of Elisha as analogous? For that matter, are the murder of Caesar and the assassination of John F. Kennedy *historically* "analogous"?

Sider proceeds, commendably, to emphasize that miracles involve both familiar and unfamiliar aspects, the unfamiliar frequently being inexplicable by current scientific knowledge and methodology (ibid., p. 314). If an alleged miracle is to be disputed, he stresses, it should be not on the ground of "absolute uniqueness" but on that of adequate or inadequate historical sources and evidence (p. 315). The criteria for dealing with once-for-all events, and no less with once-for-all allegations that there are no criteria for dealing with them, are the laws of logic and of sufficient evidence.

The refusal of a historian to concede the possibility of miracle "practically," no less than logically and metaphysically, reflects not the stance of an objective and disinterested investigator, as Harvey contends, but rather a covert commitment to practical atheism. Sider stresses that for the historian qua historian to rule out miracles in advance includes "a significant metaphysical presupposition in one's historical methodology." Instead of deciding the historicity of alleged miracles "on the basis of evidence," such an approach automatically excludes them on the basis of a philosophical assumption about the way all events must occur (ibid., pp. 312 f.). But the historian can sponsor no advance "metaphysical veto" against the report of any particular miracle (p. 317). While professing in theory to be metaphysically agnostic, the positivist historian, in supposed deference to the morality of historical consciousness, turns out in practice to be covertly a metaphysical gnostic devoted to an antimiraculous philosophy. Merold Westphal puts it this way: "If God exists, miracles are not merely logically possible, but really and genuinely possible every moment. The only condition hindering the actualizing of this possibility lies in the divine will" (Review of *The Historian and the Believer*, p. 280).

Westphal, moreover, stresses the limits of empirical inquiry: "To say that scientific knowledge has rendered belief in miracles intellectually irresponsible is to affirm that scientific knowledge provides us with knowledge of limits within which the divine will always operates. . . . Since the question of morality has been introduced, one may perhaps be permitted to inquire about the intellectual integrity of such an affirmation" (ibid.). On the same point Sider comments that the historian qua historian "could never prove that an unusual event was inexplicable in terms of natural causes much less that it was due to direct divine activity" ("The Historian, the Miraculous, and Post-Newtonian Man," p. 317).

Harvey's correlation of all miracle stories with the myths and legends commonly associated with the founders of religions simply prejudges the data according to the assumptions of a biased *Religionsgeschichte*. To say that miracle-reports reflect a naïve prescientific mentality that lacks comprehension of "natural law" does injustice to a disciple who in the context of a miracle wrote that "never since the world began has it been heard that any one opened the eyes of a man born blind" (John 9:32, RSV) and to apostles who emphasized the once-for-allness of the redemptive acts of Jesus Christ. It is no doubt true that careful historical investigation casts deep doubt over many of the miracle-stories associated with venerated religious leaders. But, asks Sider, is the historian on that account "warranted in rejecting any particular report of miracle without examining the evidence for that particular alleged miracle?" (ibid., p. 316). Surely one cannot on the basis of current scientific "laws" rule out any particular event in the past or future; counterinstances make for "progress" in science. In any case, contemporary science makes no legitimate claim to depict objectively the course of nature, let alone the flow of historical events.

The historian's inability to identify an unusual event as actually a miracle does not, Sider emphasizes, preclude his ruling on its historical factuality. The Christian does not demand belief at the expense of historical judgment. Harvey asks, and implies a negative answer, "Can one and the same man hold the same judgment tentatively as a historian but believe it passionately as a Christian?" (*The Historian and the Believer*, p. 18). Sider would reply affirmatively, and for a noteworthy reason. Appealing to William James's essay, "The Will to Believe," Sider indicates that the consequences of believing or disbelieving the resurrection of Jesus are so momentous that to avoid the risk of losing truth and salvation justifies the risk of believing falsehood "in moving from a probable historical judgment . . . to a passionate religious affirmation ('I firmly believe that Jesus rose from the dead and therefore can also trust him as my Saviour')" ("The Historian, the Miraculous, and Post-Newtonian Man," pp. 318 f.). Such a "leap of faith" does not decide the historical question, Sider emphasizes, and is legitimate "only if the historian *qua* historian has concluded in view of the evidence that Jesus probably was alive on the third day" (p. 319). But since historical method can never lead to certainty, would not historical events then be compatible with an assortment of leaps of faith? On what basis, then, are licit and illicit leaps to be distinguished?

Montgomery contends, on the other hand, that Christ's historical resurrection validates his claims to deity; personal faith in Christ therefore becomes intellectually imperative. Contrary to Harvey, Montgomery believes that history reveals God's redemptive actions, and that to deny the biblical miraculous means not only shunning the historical data but also violating the historical method. Montgomery is right about divine revelation in historical acts, supremely in the resurrection of the crucified Jesus, but he expects more from historical method than it can yield. The historical redemptive acts are no more self-interpreting than are other historical acts, and their factuality cannot be defended apart from their divinely given meaning. Lloyd G. Patterson laments the tendency to pursue the meaning of history in "empirical or existential descriptions of human happenings" and, while he does not himself set a pattern, holds that modern Christians must engage in "discussion of the nature of *historia*" like the church fathers did (*God and History in Early Christian Thought*, p. 163). To speak of biblical thought as locating God's action wholly "in 'history'," says Patterson, obscures "the relation of the Gospel to modern historiography" (p. 4).

Empirical probability can indeed be combined with inner certainty when the meaning of specific happenings is transcendently vouchsafed, that is, when that meaning is objectively given by divine revelation. While historical investigation cannot show with certainty that Jesus Christ rose from the tomb, divine revelation, that is, inspired Scripture, does tell us that he was crucified and rose historically in the context of divine promise and fulfillment (1 Cor. 15:3–4).

Jesus himself indicated that as an isolated act or oddity in history the resurrection in and of itself would not persuade those who refuse to hear the Old Testament witness to the promised Messiah (Luke 16:31). On the Emmaus Way he reminded even the disciples who were confounded by reports of the resurrection (Luke 24:22–24) of the witness of the prophets (Luke 24:25–27). Christian faith requires not simply the redemptive historical act but its meaning or significance as well; historical research alone is impotent either to guarantee any past event or to adduce its meaning or theological import.

On the other hand, the theological meaning of a historical act indispensably requires the act if we speak of such an act's significance. Revelation is the act plus its communicated meaning; both historical act and its interpretation belong to the totality of revelation. There would be no biblical meaning of the incarnation, crucifixion and resurrection of Christ apart from these historical redemptive acts. There is no Christian doctrine of the atonement without the historic death of Christ. The evangelical believer affirms the truth of revelation, a revelation of God that interprets crucial redemptive acts, and he finds in Scripture a reliable and authoritative record of God's truth and ways. He knows the logic that illumines the meaning of biblical and secular history in relation to the comprehensive purpose of God. Historical investigation, on the contrary, is unable absolutely to demonstrate or demolish the biblical or any other event-claims; certainty is derived from other than empirical considerations.

The Bible sets miraculous redemptive history and the secular world history in which it occurs in the context of two governing facts, namely, God's creation of the world and his final consummation and judgment of human affairs. The Bible speaks not simply of the exodus from Egypt and of the resurrection of Christ, critically central as are these redemptive acts for the Old and New Testaments. Its emphasis falls rather on the relationship between the God of creation and the exodus, between the God of resurrection and the coming judgment. Not only does the validity of the meaning of biblical history depend upon the sovereign God of creation, redemption and judgment; the permanence of that meaning also depends upon the God who providentially governs the past, present and future. The overarching context of universal history within which we study history must enable us to comprehend not only the present, but the totality including the past and the future as seen in terms of its anticipatively given content and goal.

"The creation of the world itself," observes Giovanni Miegge, "is, from the point of view of the Old Testament, an event not in the cosmological but in the historical order. It is the first chapter, the solemn introduction to the history of the covenant of God with men, and with Israel on their behalf" (*Gospel and Myth in the Thought of Bultmann*, p. 103). The Old Testament uses the term *ma'aseh*—usually translated "work"—of both God's "works" of creation and his "deeds" of history: in the former he creates what is other than himself, in the latter he distinguishes himself in the creation from that creation. As Miskotte says, "His revelation could never be distinguished from the facticity of the world if it coincided with the universe or were mingled with the totality of history" (*When the Gods Are Silent*, p. 194). "Israel thought of the creation as being the first act of holy history" (p. 199). The Bible opens not with the time of Jacob, the ancestor of the twelve tribes, nor with the life of Abraham, nor even with the generation of Noah. It begins with cosmogonic concerns, and places the genealogies of the patriarchs within this context of the Creator's purposive beginnings.

Before the twentieth century and its saturation with evolutionary naturalism, God's creation of the world and man was the point at which Christian theology unhesitatingly began its emphasis on divine revelation in history. Nowhere does the Bible dismiss creation merely as an existential presupposition and remove it from the historical realm. The

Old Testament opens with the theologically interpreted biography of the created cosmos much as the New Testament opens with the theologically interpreted narrative of the incarnate Christ. Over against the notion of the eternity of the world espoused by Aristotle, Plotinus and later speculative thinkers, the fact of divine creation—a once-for-all event—prepares the way for a distinctive philosophy of history. As Clark notes, "this is an event which happened just once and forms the temporal basis of all those unique events of history to which Christianity attaches so much significance. The concept of creation therefore produces a world view in which humanity plays the central role while nature is the stage setting, as opposed to Greek and all other naturalism in which man is a minor detail" (*A Christian View of Men and Things*, p. 85).

Hence the acts of God are in principle related to a future open to his divine promise, purpose and presence; creation is the first sign and pledge of those acts. It is Yahweh, the creator of man and the world, who charts the meaning of existence in his covenant with Israel and in ultimately bringing in the kingdom of God. While God's special covenant with Israel appears within the larger context of the Noahic covenant with all mankind, their unifying factor is Yahweh who works out his purposes in the created order and in the new community. Eric Voegelin remarks: "The drama of divine creation moves through . . . the creation of the world, the rescue from Egypt, and the conquest of Canaan. Each of the three acts wrests meaning from the meaningless: the world emerges from Nothing, Israel from the Sheol of Egypt, and the promised land from the desert. The acts thus interpret one another as works of divine creation and as historical stages in which a realm of meaning grows. In history God continues his work of creation, and the creation of the world is the first event in history" (*Israel and Revelation*, p. 135).

What we see is God, who by his word calls the world into being and calls Israel for channeling his ongoing purpose throughout world history. The very concept of a history of mankind presupposes a constancy of human nature that excludes disruption and dissolution of the unity of humanity into different species. The Old Testament expansion of this meaning is not an achievement of historiography, whether by editorial redactors or by sacred writers to whom the Old Testament records may be ascribed, nor is it achieved by a fusion of literary sources; the source of this concept of history is first and foremost in God's active disclosure. Martin Buber has noted how the term *ruach* used of the creation agrees with the *ruach* that animated the Judges, how God's ordering of the world typifies the building of the Tent of Divine Presence, how the Creator's Sabbath-rest points to the Sabbath-commandment of the Law—all suggest the unity of God's creation and covenant. The day of creation in which the world is good as the work of God's hands (Gen. 1) looks ahead to a coming Day of the Lord (Pss. 8, 104).

For the naturalist the final end of all history is death. The only wakening of the dead he knows is an immortality of influence, dependent upon the historian's bestowal of fame or infamy, and doomed to fade with each passing generation into a dim irrecoverable past. Remarkable about the Christian view of history, by contrast, is its assessment of human fortunes not in terms of an irretrievable past and generations of the dead, but in the framework of divine redemption and the life and judgment to come.

Except for fears of nuclear destruction that would return the earth once again to a desolation and a waste, contemporary references to a possible curtain call for human history occur usually in terms of some dire natural calamity. In an editorial in *Science* (170, Oct. 9, 1970), S. Fred Singer answers the question "Will the World Come to a Horrible End?" with a caution against crying "wolf" needlessly or too often. Mankind, he says, has almost learned to live with doomsday predictions of famine, war and pestilence. While some faint possibility exists for an end to earth-life by the impact of a large asteroid, or by the radiation effect of a supernova or solar superflare, it is ecology that now most insistently sounds the survival alarm. Singer pleads for "the voice of reason" lest scientific credibility be sacrificed because of exaggerated claims and extravagant statements. Any reference to a divine consummation of history in moral judgment is wholly out of view; to the modern scientific mind that possibility is apparently unthinkable. Nor is it possible, by empirically weighing human fortunes, to ascertain man's final future judgment. In its reaction to extreme concentration on the Lord's return which considers interest in man's earthly future a mark of distraction from spiritual priorities, the secular view, equally extreme, regards deference to the will and purpose of God in earthly affairs as an obstacle to human progress and worldly felicity that scientific planning can presumably achieve.

Modern philosophy of history actually retained the concept of *logos*, of a divine rationale and final goal of history, for an extended period. But in doing so it subordinated Christ the incarnate Logos of God to merely the Greek *logos*, a rational principle immanent in man and nature. By adding to this Greek idea certain features borrowed from the Bible, it tried to find permanent significance for history; it retained the sense of enduring historical mission fostered by Christianity, and correlated it with secular messianism and utopianism. This perspective dominated much of modern philosophy well into the twentieth century. If it is now fading from Anglo-Saxon historiography and philosophy—and is translated by communism into an alternative naturalistic version—it is still nonetheless indirectly inspiring contemporary politics in its waning vision of one world and universal peace and brotherhood. In this way a concept of world history has come about in which the end of history is related to the whole of history, but in which the revelation of God no longer is given a decisive role, and in which man's creative reason displaces the transcendent Logos as the source of the structures and substance of the real world. The commitment to evolution so overshadows even this view of the immanent *logos*, however, that developmental process is no longer considered the fundamental Idea or Reason or Mind. Mind itself is considered an evolutionary emergent, and all concepts and truths are regarded as elastic culture-bound products of history. Given this contemporary approach to life and history, any attempt to escape relativism and pessimism is futile; not only nature and history but also man himself becomes an enigma, simply a chance emergent in a cosmos born of an explosion and moving like all other animals toward death as his final end.

Only the Bible brackets all the experiences of this life and world within the moral judgment of God. Even if one views history as revelational but strips divine disclosure of its normative meaning specially vouchsafed to inspired prophets and apostles, it becomes difficult to avoid Reinhold Niebuhr's observation that "the processes of historical justice are . . . not exact enough to warrant . . . simple confidence in the moral character of history" (*Faith and History*, p. 129). History as we discern it does not exhaust God's plan. Not even the Bible provides a fully detailed account of God's purposive activity in history. But biblical revelation leaves no doubt that God's righteousness requires more than the inescapable physical death and inevitable historical replacement of barbarous tyrants and all ungodly mortals. God executes judgment not simply within history but climactically and finally at the end of history. The inspired writers tell us authoritatively not only what God is saying and doing now in nature and in history, but also give us intimations of what he will say and do when he consummates all things.

Volume III will complete the exposition of the Fifteen Theses on divine revelation.

Bibliography

Abbott, Walter M., ed. *The Documents of Vatican Two*. New York: Association Press, 1966.

Albrektson, Bertil. *History and the Gods: An Essay on the Idea of Historical Events as Divine Manifestations in the Ancient Near East and in Israel*. Lund: C. W. K. Gleerup, 1967.

Albright, William F. *Archaeology and the Religion of Israel*. 4th ed. Baltimore: Johns Hopkins Press, 1956.

————. *From the Stone Age to Christianity*. 2d ed. Baltimore: Johns Hopkins Press, 1957.

————. *History, Archaeology and Christian Humanism*. New York: McGraw-Hill, 1964.

Alford, Henry. *The Greek Testament*. 2 vols. Chicago: Moody Press, 1958.

Allis, Oswald T. *The Five Books of Moses*. Philadelphia: Presbyterian and Reformed Pub. Co., 1943.

Alonso-Shökel, L. "Motivos sapienciales y de alianza en Gn 2–3." *Biblica* 43 (1962): 295.

Alt, Albrecht. "Der Gott der Väter." *Kleine Schriften* 1 (1959): 24.

————. *Essays of Old Testament History and Religion*. Oxford: Basil Blackwell, 1966.

Althaus, Paul. "Offenbarung als Geschichte und Glaube: Bermerkungen zu Wolfhart Pannenbergs Begriff der Offenbarung." *Theologische Literaturzeitung* 87 (1962): 321.

Altizer, Thomas J. J. *The Gospel of Christian Atheism*. London: Collins, 1967.

Anderson, Bernhard. "Man's Dominion over Nature." Address to the American Theological Society, 14 April 1972, New York, New York.

————. *Understanding the Old Testament*. Englewood Cliffs, NJ: Prentice-Hall, 1957.

————, and Harrelson, Walter, eds. *Israel's Prophetic Heritage*. New York: Harper & Row, 1962.

335

Archer, Gleason L., Jr. *A Survey of Old Testament Introduction.* Chicago: Moody Press, 1964.

Ayer, Alfred J. *Language, Truth and Logic.* London: Victor Gollancz, 1936. 2d rev. ed. New York: Dover Publishers, 1946.

Ayers, Robert H. "Religious Discourse and Myth." In *Religious Language and Knowledge,* edited by Robert H. Ayers and William T. Blackstone.

———, and Blackstone, William T., eds. *Religious Language and Knowledge.* Athens: University of Georgia Press, 1972.

Baltzer, Klaus. *The Covenant Formulary.* Philadelphia: Fortress Press, 1971.

Banks, J. S. "Christian." In *Dictionary of the Apostolic Church,* edited by James Hastings.

Barnes, Harry Elmer. *A History of Historical Writing.* Oklahoma City: University of Oklahoma Press, 1937.

Barr, James. *The Bible in the Modern World.* London: SCM Press, 1973.

———. "God." In *Dictionary of the Bible,* 1963 rev. ed., edited by James Hastings.

———. "Revelation through History in the Old Testament and in Modern Theology." *Interpretation* 17: 193.

Barrett, C. K. *The Gospel According to John.* London: S.P.C.K., 1955.

Barth, Karl. *Church Dogmatics.* Edited by G. W. Bromiley and Thomas F. Torrance. Edinburgh: T. and T. Clark, 1936–69. Naperville, IL: Alec R. Allenson, 1969.

———. *Epistle to the Romans.* Translated by E. C. Hoskyns. New York: Oxford University Press, 1933.

———. *Evangelical Theology: An Introduction.* New York: Holt, Rinehart and Winston, 1963.

———. *The Knowledge of God and the Service of God, According to the Teaching of the Reformation, Recalling the Scottish Confession of 1560.* Translated by J. M. L. Haire and Ian Henderson. New York: Charles Scribner's Sons, 1939.

———. "No!" In *Natural Theology,* by Emil Brunner and Karl Barth.

———. "Rudolf Bultmann—An Attempt to Understand Him." In *Kerygma and Myth,* vol. 2, edited by Hans W. Bartsch.

———. *Theology and Church.* Translated by Louise P. Smith. Naperville, IL: Alec R. Allenson, 1962.

Bartsch, Hans W., ed. *Kerygma and Myth: A Theological Debate,* vol. 1. London: S.P.C.K., 1953. New York: Harper & Bros., Harper Torchbooks, 1961.

———, ed. *Kerygma and Myth: A Theological Debate,* vol. 2. London: S.P.C.K., 1962.

Bavinck, Herman. *The Doctrine of God.* Grand Rapids: Wm. B. Eerdmans, 1951.

Beare, Francis W. "Introduction and Exegesis: The Epistle to the Colossians." In *The Interpreter's Bible,* vol. 11, edited by George A. Buttrick, et al.

Beegle, Dewey. *Scripture, Tradition, and Infallibility.* Grand Rapids: Wm. B. Eerdmans, 1973.

Benson, Herbert. *The Relaxation Response.* New York: William Morrow, 1975.

Bentzen, Aage. *Messias-Moses redivivus-Menschensohn.* Zurich: Zwingli-Verlag, 1948. *King and Messiah.* Translated by Aage Bentzen. London: Lutterworth Press, 1955.

Berkelbach, S. F. H. *Handboek Voor de Prediking.* Vol. 1, 1948.

Berkhof, Louis. *Systematic Theology.* Grand Rapids: Wm. B. Eerdmans, 1946.

Berkouwer, Gerrit C. "General and Special Revelation." In *Revelation and the Bible*, edited by Carl F. H. Henry.

——. *The Triumph of Grace in the Theology of Karl Barth*. Grand Rapids: Wm. B. Eerdmans, 1956.

Bertram, Georg. "Thauma." In *Theological Dictionary of the New Testament*, edited by Gerhard Kittel and Gerhard Friedrich.

Biber, Ch. "Name." In *A Companion to the Bible*, edited by Jean-Jacques von Allmen.

Biggs, R. D. "Babylonian Prophecy." *Iraq* 29 (1967: 117–32.

Bin Gorian, Micha Joseph. *Sinai und Garazim*. Berlin: Morgenland-Verlag, 1925.

Blaikie, Robert J. *"Secular Christianity" and God Who Acts*. Grand Rapids: Wm. B. Eerdmans, 1970.

Blamires, Harry. *The Christian Mind*. New York: Seabury Press, 1963. London: S.P.C.K., 1966.

Blank, Sheldon H. *Jeremiah: Man and Prophet*. Cincinnati: Hebrew Union College Press, 1961.

Blanshard, Brand. *The Nature of Thought*. 2 vols. New York: Humanities Press, 1964.

Bonhoeffer, Dietrich. *Act and Being*. New York: Harper & Row, 1962.

——. *Letters and Papers from Prison*. New York: The Macmillan Co., 1962.

Bousset, William. *Kyrios Christos*. 3d ed., Göttingen: Vandenhoeck & Ruprecht, 1926. Translated by John E. Steely. Nashville: Abingdon Press, 1970.

Braaten, Carl E. *History and Hermeneutics*. New Directions in Theology Today, vol. 2. Philadelphia: Westminster Press, 1966. London: Lutterworth Press, 1968.

Braun, Herbert. *Gesammelte Studien zum Neuen Testament und seiner Umwelt*. Tübingen: J. C. B. Mohr, 1962.

Bright, John. *Early Israel in Recent History Writing*. London: SCM Press; Naperville, IL: Alec R. Allenson, 1956.

——. *A History of Israel*. 2d ed. Philadelphia: Westminster Press, 1972.

——, ed. *Jeremiah*. Anchor Bible Series, vol. 21. Garden City, NY: Doubleday and Co., 1965.

Brown, R. E. *Jesus, God and Man*. Milwaukee: Bruce Pub. Co., 1967.

Brunner, Emil. *The Christian Doctrine of God*. Philadelphia: Westminster Press, 1950.

——. *The Mediator*. Philadelphia: Westminster Press, 1947.

——. "Nature and Grace." In *Natural Theology*, by Emil Brunner and Karl Barth.

——. *Revelation and Reason*. Philadelphia: Westminster Press, 1946.

——, and Barth, Karl. *Natural Theology*. Translated by Peter Frankel. London: Centenary Press, 1946.

Buber, Martin. *Kingship of God*. Translated by Richard Schedmann. London: George Allen and Unwin; New York: Harper & Row, 1967.

——. *Moses: The Revelation and the Covenants*. New York: Crown Publishers, 1948.

——. *The Prophetic Faith*. New York: The Macmillan Co., 1949.

Bultmann, Rudolf. *Glauben und Verstehen*. Vol. 1. Tübingen: J. C. B. Mohr, 1933.

——. "Bultmann Replies to his Critics." In *Kerygma and Myth*, edited by Hans W. Bartsch.

———. *Gospel of John: A Commentary.* Philadelphia: Westminster Press, 1971.

———. *History and Eschatology: The Presence of Eternity.* Gifford Lectures. New York: Harper & Bros., 1957.

———. *Primitive Christianity in Its Contemporary Setting.* Translated by Reginald Fuller. New York: Meridian Books, 1956.

———. *The Theology of the New Testament.* London: SCM Press, 1952.

Buttrick, George A., ed. *The Interpreter's Dictionary of the Bible.* 4 vols. New York and Nashville: Abingdon Press, 1962.

———, et al, eds. *The Interpreter's Bible.* 12 vols. New York and Nashville: Abingdon Press, 1955.

Cadman, W. H. *The Open Heaven: The Revelation in the Johannine Sayings of Jesus.* Edited by G. B. Caird. Oxford: Basil Blackwell; New York: Herder and Herder, 1969.

Calvin, John. *Epistle to the Romans and Thessalonians.* New Testament Commentaries. 6 vols., vol. 3. Edited by David W. and Thomas F. Torrance. Translated by R. Mackenzie. Grand Rapids: Wm. B. Eerdmans, 1961.

———. *First Epistle to the Corinthians.* New Testament Commentaries. 6 vols., vol. 4. Edited by David W. and Thomas F. Torrance. Translated by John W. Fraser. Grand Rapids: Wm. B. Eerdmans, 1960.

———. *Institutes of the Christian Religion.* 2 vols. Translated by Henry Beveridge. Grand Rapids: Wm. B. Eerdmans, 1953.

Campbell, Edward F., Jr. "Moses and the Foundations of Israel." *Interpretation* 24 (April 1975).

Carnell, Edward John. *A Philosophy of the Christian Religion.* Grand Rapids: Wm. B. Eerdmans, 1952.

Cassuto, Umberto. *The Documentary Hypothesis.* Translated by Israel Abrahams. Jerusalem: Magnes Press, The Hebrew University, 1941.

Clark, Gordon H. "Apologetics." In *Contemporary Evangelical Thought,* edited by Carl F. H. Henry.

———. "The Axiom of Revelation." In *The Philosophy of Gordon H. Clark,* edited by Ronald H. Nash.

———. "The Bible as Truth." *Bibliotheca Sacra,* April 1957.

———. *A Christian View of Men and Things.* Grand Rapids: Wm. B. Eerdmans, 1952.

———. *Historiography: Secular and Religious.* Nutley, NJ: Craig Press, 1971.

———. *Karl Barth's Theological Method.* Nutley, NJ: Presbyterian and Reformed Pub. Co., 1963.

Clarke, Samuel. *A Demonstration of the Being and Attributes of God.* London: John and Paul Knapton, 1738.

Cobb, John B., Jr., and Robinson, James M. *Theology of History.* New York: Harper & Row, 1967.

Conybeare, F. C. "Christian Demonology." *Jewish Quarterly Review* 8 (1896): 576–608; 9 (1896): 59–114; 11 (1897): 444–70; 12 (1897): 581–603.

Cotter, James P., ed. *The Word in the Third World.* Washington: Corpus Books, 1968.

Coulson, C. A. *Science and Christian Belief.* London: Fontana, 1958.

Cox, Harvey. *The Secular City.* New York: The Macmillan Co., 1966.

Cragg, Kenneth. "The Convertibility of Man." In *The Word in the Third World,* edited by James P. Cotter.

Cross, Frank M. *Canaanite Myth and Hebrew Epic: Essays in the History of the Religion of Israel.* Cambridge: Harvard University Press, 1973.

Cullmann, Oscar. *Christ and Time.* Philadelphia: Westminster Press, 1950.
———. *The Christology of the New Testament.* London: SCM Press; Philadelphia: Westminster Press, 1959.
———. *Salvation in History.* New York: Harper & Row, 1967.
Dalman, Gustav. *The Words of Jesus.* Edinburgh: T. & T. Clark, 1902.
Davidson, A. B. *The Theology of the Old Testament.* Edinburgh: T. & T. Clark, 1925.
Davidson, Francis, et al, eds. *The New Bible Commentary.* Grand Rapids: Wm. B. Eerdmans, 1953.
Davies, W. D. *Paul and Rabbinic Judaism.* London: S.P.C.K., 1948. 2d ed. New York: Seabury Press, 1955.
Deissmann, Adolf. *Light from the Ancient East.* New York: Harper & Bros., 1927. London: Hodder and Stoughton, 1929. Reprint edition. Grand Rapids: Baker Book House.
Delitzsch, Franz. *A New Commentary on Genesis.* Edinburgh: T. &. T. Clark, 1899.
Dodd, C. H. *The Interpretation of the Fourth Gospel.* Cambridge: Cambridge University Press, 1953.
Donnelly, John. *Logical Analysis and Contemporary Theism.* New York: Fordham University Press, 1972.
Douglas, James D., ed. *The New Bible Dictionary.* Grand Rapids: Wm. B. Eerdmans, 1962.
———, ed. *The New International Dictionary of the Christian Church.* Grand Rapids: Zondervan, 1974.
Dowey, Edward A., Jr. *The Knowledge of God in Calvin's Theology.* New York: Columbia University Press, 1952.
Dubarle, A. M. "La signification du nom de Iahweh." *Revue des sciences philosophiques et theologiques* (1951).
Ebeling, Gerhard. *Word and Faith.* Philadelphia: Fortress Press, 1963.
Edwards, Paul. "The Cosmological Argument." In *Philosophy of Religion,* edited by William L. Rowe and William J. Wainwright.
———. "Some Notes on Anthropomorphic Theology." In *Religious Experience and Truth,* edited by Sidney Hook.
Edwards, Rem B. *Reason and Religion: An Introduction to the Philosophy of Religion.* New York: Harcourt Brace Jovanovich, 1972.
Eichrodt, Walther. "In the Beginning." In *Israel's Prophetic Heritage,* edited by Bernhard Anderson and Walter Harrelson.
———. *Theologie des alten Testaments.* Leipzig: J. C. Heinricks, 1933. *Theology of the Old Testament.* 2 vols. Translated by John Baker. Philadelphia: Westminster Press, 1961.
Eissfeldt, Otto. "El and Yahweh." *Journal of Semitic Studies* 1 (January 1956).
Emmet, Dorothy M. *The Nature of Metaphysical Thinking.* New York: St. Martin's Press, 1945.
Engnell, Ivan. *Gamla Testamentet, En traditionshistorisk inledning.* Stockholm: Svenska Kyrkans diakonistyrelses bokförlag, 1945.
———. *Studies in Divine Kingship in the Ancient Near East.* Uppsala: Lamquist & Wiksells boktr., 1943. 2d ed. Naperville, IL: Alec R. Allenson, 1967.
Fackenheim, Emil L. *God's Presence in History.* New York: Harper & Row, 1972.
Farmer, W. R., et al, eds. *Christian History and Interpretation.* Cambridge: University Press, 1967.

Flusser, David. "Two Notes on the Midrash on 2 Sam. vii." *Israel Exploration Journal* 9 (1959).

Foerster, Werner. "Klēros." In *Theological Dictionary of the New Testament*, edited by Gerhard Kittel and Gerhard Friedrich.

Fohrer, Georg. *History of Israelite Religion.* Translated by David E. Green. Nashville: Abingdon Press, 1972.

———. *Theologische Grundstrukturen des Alten Testaments.* New York: Walter De Gruyter, 1972.

Freedman, David Noel. "The Biblical Idea of History." *Interpretation* 21 (January 1967).

———. "The Name of the God of Moses." *Journal of Biblical Literature* 79 (1960): 151–56.

Garvie, A. E. *The Ritschlian Theology.* Edinburgh: T. & T. Clark, 1902.

Geisler, Norman. *Philosophy of Religion.* Grand Rapids: Zondervan, 1974.

Gilkey, Langdon. "A Christian Natural Theology." *Theology Today* 22 (1966): 530.

———. *Naming the Whirlwind: The Renewal of God Language.* Indianapolis: Bobbs-Merrill, 1969.

Goitein, S. D. "YHWH The Passionate." *Vetus Testamentum* 6 (1956): 1.

Gollwitzer, Helmut. *The Existence of God as Confessed by Faith.* London: SCM Press; Philadelphia: Westminster Press, 1965.

Gordon, Cyrus H. "Higher Critics and Forbidden Fruit." *Christianity Today*, 23 November 1959, p. 3.

Gray, G. B. "Name." In *Dictionary of the Bible*, edited by James Hastings.

Green, William Henry. *Higher Criticism of the Pentateuch.* New York: Charles Scribner's Sons, 1896.

———. *The Unity of the Book of Genesis.* New York: Charles Scribner's Sons, 1895.

Guinness, Os. *The Dust of Death.* Downers Grove, IL: Inter-Varsity Press, 1973.

Gulich, Robert. 1970. Lectures at Pastor's Conference, August 1970, at Bethel Theological Seminary, St. Paul, Minnesota.

Gurr, John E. *The Principle of Sufficient Reason in Some Scholastic Systems, 1750–1900.* Milwaukee: Marquette University Press, 1959.

Hackett, Stuart C. *The Resurrection of Theism.* Chicago: Moody Press, 1957.

Hahn, Hebert F. *Old Testament in Modern Research.* Philadelphia: Muehlenberg Press, 1954.

Hall, William Phillips. *A Remarkable Biblical Discovery, or "The Name" of God According to the Scriptures.* New York: American Tract Society, 1929.

Hamilton, Floyd E. "Lots." In *The Zondervan Pictorial Encyclopedia of the Bible*, edited by Merrill C. Tenney.

Hammershaimb, Erling. 1969. "Cult and History in the Old Testament." Address to the Cambridge Theological Society, England. 27 February 1969.

Harrelson, Walter. *Interpreting the Old Testament.* New York: Holt, Rinehart and Winston, 1964.

Harrison, Everett F. "*Gemeinde-theologie:* The Bane of Gospel Criticism." In *Jesus of Nazareth: Savior and Lord*, edited by Carl F. H. Henry.

Hartshorne, Charles. "Can There Be Proofs for the Existence of God?" In *Religious Language and Knowledge*, edited by Robert H. Ayers and William T. Blackstone.

Harvey, Van Austin. *The Historian and the Believer.* New York: The Macmillan Co., 1969.

Hastings, James, ed. *Dictionary of the Apostolic Church.* New York: Charles Scribner's Sons, 1916–22.

———, ed. *Dictionary of the Bible.* Rev. ed. New York: Charles Scribner's Sons, 1927, 1963.

Hazelton, Roger. 1972. Address to the American Theological Society. 11 April 1972.

———. *Knowing the Living God.* Valley Forge, PA: Judson Press, 1969.

Headlam, A. C. *Christian Theology: The Doctrine of God.* Oxford: Clarendon Press, 1934.

Hebert, A. G. *The Authority of the Old Testament.* London: Faber and Faber, 1947. Naperville, IL: Alec R. Allenson, 1957.

Heinisch, Paul. *Theology of the Old Testament.* Collegeville, Minneapolis: Liturgical Press, 1950.

Hempel, Johannes. *Gott und Mensch im Alten Testament.* Stuttgart: W. Kohlhammer, 1936.

Hendry, George S. "Eclipse of Creation." *Theology Today* 28 (1972): 420.

Henry, Carl F. H. "Apologetics." In *Contemporary Evangelical Thought,* edited by Carl F. H. Henry.

———, ed. *Baker's Dictionary of Christian Ethics.* Grand Rapids: Baker Book House, 1973.

———, ed. *Contemporary Evangelical Thought.* New York: Harper & Bros., 1957.

———, ed. *Jesus of Nazareth: Savior and Lord.* Grand Rapids: Wm. B. Eerdmans, 1966.

———, ed. *Revelation and the Bible.* Grand Rapids: Baker Book House, 1958.

Hepburn, Ronald. *Christianity and Paradox: Critical Studies in Twentieth Century Theology.* London: Watts, 1958: New York: Humanities Press, 1968.

Herrmann, Wilhelm. *Der Begriff der Offenbarung.* 1887.

———. *The Communion of the Christian with God.* Edited by Robert T. Voelkel. Philadelphia: Fortress Press, 1971.

———. *Gesammelte Aufsätze.* Tübingen: J. C. B. Mohr, 1923.

———. *Gottes Offenbarung an uns.* 1908.

Herzog, Frederick. *Understanding God: The Key Issue in Present-Day Protestant Thought.* New York: Charles Scribner's Sons, 1966.

Heschel, Abraham J. *Prophets.* New York: Harper & Row, 1962.

Hick, John H. "A Critique of the 'Second Argument.'" In *The Many-Faced Argument,* edited by John H. Hick and Arthur C. McGill.

———. "God as Necessary Being." *Journal of Philosophy* 87 (1960).

———, ed. *The Existence of God.* New York: The Macmillan Co., 1964.

———, and McGill, Arthur C., eds. *The Many-Faced Argument: Recent Studies in the Ontological Argument for the Existence of God.* New York: The Macmillan Co., 1967.

Hoelscher, Gustav. *Geschichte der israelitischen und juedischen Religion.* Giessen: A. Göpelmann, 1922.

Hook, Sidney, ed. *Religious Experience and Truth: Proceedings.* New York University Institute of Philosophy, 4th Symposium, 1960. New York: New York University Press, 1961.

Hordern, William. *Speaking of God: The Nature and Purpose of Theological Language.* New York: The Macmillan Co., 1964. London: Epworth Press, 1965.

Hoskyns, Edwin C., and Davey, F. Noel. *The Fourth Gospel.* London: Faber and Faber, 1947. 2d rev. ed. Naperville, IL: Alec R. Allenson, 1956.

Hume, David. *Dialogues Concerning Natural Religion.* Edited by Norman Kemp Smith. Indianapolis: Bobbs-Merrill, Liberal Arts Press, 1962.

Jacob, Edmond. *Theology of the Old Testament.* London: Hodder and Stoughton; New York: Harper & Row, 1958.

Jenkins, Daniel T. *Tradition, Freedom and the Spirit.* Philadelphia: Westminster Press, 1951.

Jenkins, David E. *Guide to the Debate about God.* London: Lutterworth Press; Philadelphia: Westminster Press, 1966.

Jeremias, Joachim. *The Central Message of the New Testament.* New York: Charles Scribner's Sons, 1965.

Jocz, Jacob. *The Covenant: A Theology of Human Destiny.* Grand Rapids: Wm. B. Eerdmans, 1968.

Johnson, Aubrey R. *The Vitality of the Individual in the Thought of Ancient Israel.* Cardiff: University of Wales, 1949. Mystic, CT: Lawrence Verry, 1964.

Jones, W. T. *The Medieval Mind. A History of Western Philosophy,* vol. 2. New York: Harcourt, Brace & World, 1969.

Kähler, Martin. *The So-Called Historical Jesus.* Translated by Carl E. Braaten. Philadelphia: Fortress Press, 1964.

Kaufman, Gordon. *Systematic Theology: A Historicist Perspective.* New York: Charles Scribner's Sons, 1968.

Keil, Carl F., and Delitzsch, Franz. *The Pentateuch.* Biblical Commentary of the Old Testament, vol. 1. Edinburgh: T. and T. Clark, 1875. Commentaries on the Old Testament, vols. 1–3. Grand Rapids: Wm. B. Eerdmans, 1949.

Kennedy, Henry A. A. *St. Paul's Epistle to the Philippians. The Expositor's Greek Testament.* 5 vols., vol. 3. Edited by W. Robertson Nicoll. Grand Rapids: Wm. B. Eerdmans, 1952.

Key, Andrew F. "The Giving of Proper Names in the Old Testament." *Journal of Biblical Literature.* 83 (1964): 55–59.

Kidner, Derek. *Genesis: An Introduction and Commentary.* London: Tyndale Press, 1967. Downers Grove, IL: Inter-Varsity Press, 1968.

Kierkegaard, Sören. *Philosophical Fragments.* Princeton, NJ: Princeton University Press, 1936.

Kittel, Gerhard, and Friedrich, Gerhard, eds. *Theological Dictionary of the New Testament.* 9 vols. Grand Rapids: Wm. B. Eerdmans, 1964–73.

Kline, Meredith. "Law Covenant." *Westminster Theological Journal* 27 (1964).

Knight, Harold. *The Hebrew Prophetic Consciousness.* London: Lutterworth Press, 1947.

Knox, John. *The Church and the Reality of Christ.* New York: Harper & Row, 1962.

———. *The Death of Christ.* Nashville: Abingdon Press, 1958.

———. *The Early Church and the Coming Great Church.* New York: Abingdon Press, 1955.

Knudsen, Ralph E. *Theology of the New Testament.* Valley Forge, PA: Judson Press, 1964.

Koehler, Ludwig. *Der Dekalog.* Theologische Rundschau, vol. 1.

———. *Old Testament Theology.* Philadelphia: Westminster Press, 1957.

———, and Baumgartner, Walter. *Lexicon in Veteris Testimenti Libros: Hebrew-Aramaic Lexicon.* Grand Rapids: Wm. B. Eerdmans, 1951–53.

Kuitert, H. M. *The Reality of Faith.* Grand Rapids: Wm. B. Eerdmans, 1968.

Künneth, Walter. *The Theology of the Resurrection*. St. Louis: Concordia Publishing House, 1965.

Kurtz, J. H. *History of the Old Covenant*, vol. 2. Philadelphia: Lindsey and Blakiston, 1859.

Labuschagne, C. J. *The Incomparability of Yahweh in the Old Testament*. Leiden: E. J. Brill, 1966.

Lambert, Gustav. "Que signifie le nom divin YHWH?" *Nouevelle revue theologique* (1952): 897.

Lambert, W. G. "History and the Gods: A Review Article." *Orientalia* W. 5. 39 (1970).

Lampe, Geoffrey W. H., and MacKinnon, Donald M. *The Resurrection*. London: Mowbray, 1966. Philadelphia: Westminster Press, 1967.

Lang, Andrew. *The Making of Religion*. London: Longmans, Green and Co.; New York: AMS Press, 1898.

Leach, Edmund. *A Runaway World?* New York: Oxford University Press; London: BBC, 1968.

Lods, Adolphe. *Israel*. New York: Alfred A. Knopf, 1932.

Loen, Arnold E. *Secularization: Science Without God*. London: SCM Press; Philadelphia: Westminster Press, 1967.

Longenecker, Richard N. *The Christology of Early Jewish Christianity*. London: SCM Press; Naperville, IL: Alec R. Allenson, 1970.

McCarthy, Dennis J. *Old Testament Covenant: A Survey of Current Opinions*. Richmond: John Knox Press, 1972.

———. *Treaty and Covenant*. Rome: Pontifical Biblical Institute, 1963.

McDonald, H. D. "Revelation." In *The New International Dictionary of the Christian Church*, edited by James D. Douglas.

Macgregor, G. H. C. "Introduction and Exegesis: The Acts of the Apostles." In *The Interpreter's Bible*, vol. 9, edited by George A. Buttrick, et al.

Machen, J. Gresham. *The Origin of Paul's Religion*. New York: The Macmillan Co., 1921.

Mack, Edward. "Names of God." In *International Standard Bible Encyclopedia*, edited by James Orr.

MacKinnon, Donald M. *Borderlands of Theology and Other Essays*. Edited by G. W. Roberts and D. E. Smucker. Philadelphia: J. B. Lippincott Co., 1969.

Mackintosh, H. R. *The Christian Apprehension of God*. New York: Harper & Bros., 1929.

———. *The Problem of Religious Knowledge*. London: Nisbet and Co., 1949.

MacLeod, A. J. "The Gospel According to John." In *The New Bible Commentary*, edited by Francis Davidson, et al.

Macmurray, John. *The Boundaries of Science*. London: Faber and Faber, 1939.

McNeile, Alan H. *Westminster Commentary: Exodus*. London: Methuen & Co., 1908.

Macquarrie, John. *God and Secularity*. New Directions in Theology Today, vol. 3. Philadelphia: Westminster Press, 1967.

Malik, Charles H. *The Wonder of Being*. Waco, TX: Word Books, Publisher, 1974.

Manley, G. T. "The God of Abraham." *Tyndale House Bulletin* (1963).

Manson, Thomas W. *The Teaching of Jesus*. New York: Cambridge University Press, 1935.

Marin, Peter. "The New Narcissism." *Harper's*, October 1975.

Marsh, John. *The Fulness of Time*. New York: Harper & Bros., 1952.

Martin, Ralph P. *Carmen Christi: Philippians 2:5-11.* New York: Cambridge University Press, 1967.

————. *The Epistle of Paul to the Philippians: An Introduction and Commentary.* Grand Rapids: Wm. B. Eerdmans, 1957.

Marty, Martin E., and Peerman, Dean G., eds. *New Theology No. 1.* New York: The Macmillan Co., 1964.

Mendelsohn, Isaac. "Lots." In *The Interpreter's Dictionary of the Bible,* edited by George A. Buttrick.

Mendenhall, George E. "Covenant." In *The Interpreter's Dictionary of the Bible,* edited by George A. Buttrick.

————. "Covenant Forms in Israelite Tradition." *Biblical Archaeologist* 17 (1954): 50-76.

————. *Law and Covenant in Israel and the Ancient Near East.* Pittsburgh: Biblical Colloquiam, 1955.

————. "The Monarchy." *Interpretation* 24 (April 1975).

Michalson, Carl. *The Rationality of Faith.* New York: Charles Scribner's Sons, 1963.

Michaud, H. "Name." In *A Companion to the Bible,* edited by Jean-Jacques von Allmen.

Miegge, Giovanni. *Gospel and Myth in the Thought of Rudolf Bultmann,* Translated by Stephen Neill. London: Lutterworth Press; Richmond: John Knox Press, 1960.

Miller, E. L. *God and Reason: A Historical Approach to Philosophical Theology.* New York: The Macmillan Co., 1972.

Miskotte, Kornelis H. *When the Gods Are Silent.* London: Collins, 1967. New York: Harper & Row, 1968.

Moltmann, Jürgen. *Theology of Hope.* New York: Harper & Row, 1967.

Monod, Victor. *Dieu dans l'univers.* Paris: Libraire Fischbacker, 1933.

Montgomery, John W. *History and Christianity.* Downers Grove, IL: Inter-Varsity Press, 1971.

————. *The Quest for Noah's Ark.* Minneapolis: Bethany Fellowship, 1972.

————. *The Suicide of Christian Theology.* Minneapolis: Bethany Fellowship, 1970.

Morikawa, Jitsuo. *Pastors for a Servant People.*

Morris, Leon. *The Biblical Doctrine of Judgment.* Grand Rapids: Wm. B. Eerdmans, 1960.

————. *The Gospel According to John.* Grand Rapids: Wm. B. Eerdmans, 1971.

Motyer, J. A. *The Revelation of the Divine Name.* London: Tyndale Press, 1959.

Mowinckel, Sigmund. *Le décalogue.* Paris: F. Alcan, 1927.

————. "Zur Geschichte der Dekaloge." In *Zeitschrift für alttestamentliche Wissenschaft.* [Neue Folge, vol. 14, Nos. 3 & 4, 1937.]

————. *The Two Sources of the Predeuteronomic Primeval History (JE) in Gen. i-xi.* Oslo: I. Kommisjon bros. J. Dybwady.

————. In *Zeitschrift für Altertumswissen-schaft.* 1930.

Murray, J. A. H., et al, eds. *Oxford English Dictionary.* 13 vols. New York and London: Oxford University Press.

Murtoneau, A. *A Philological and Literary Treatise on the Old Testament Divine Names.* Helsinki: 1952.

Myers, Jacob M. "The Way of The Fathers." *Interpretation* 29 (April 1975): 125.

Nash, Ronald H., ed. *The Philosophy of Gordon H. Clark.* Philadelphia: Presbyterian and Reformed Pub. Co., 1968.

Newbigin, Lesslie. *Honest Religion for Secular Man.* London: SCM Press; Philadelphia: Westminster Press, 1966.

Niebuhr, Reinhold. *Faith and History.* New York: Charles Scribner's Sons, 1949.

————. *The Nature and Destiny of Man.* 2 vols. Vol. 1. *Human Nature.* New York: Charles Scribner's Sons, 1943.

Niebuhr, Richard R. *Resurrection and Historical Reason: A Study in Theological Method.* New York: Charles Scribner's Sons, 1957.

Nielson, Kai. "Religion and Commitment." In *Religious Language and Knowledge,* edited by Robert H. Ayers and William T. Blackstone.

North, Christopher R. "History." In *The Interpreter's Dictionary of the Bible,* vol. 2, edited by George A. Buttrick.

————. "Pentateuchal Criticism." In *The Old Testament and Modern Study,* edited by Harold H. Rowley.

Noth, Martin. *History of Israel.* New York: Harper & Bros., 1958.

————. *Das System der zwoelf Staemme Israels.* Stuttgart: W. Kohlhammer, 1930.

Nyberg, H. S. *Irans forntida religioner.* Stockholm: Svenska Kyrkans diakonstyrelses bokförlag, 1937.

Obermann, Julian. "The Divine Name YHWH in the Light of Recent Discoveries." *Journal of Biblical Literature* 68 (1949): 301.

O'Collins, G. G. "The Theology of Revelation in Some Recent Discussion." Ph.D. dissertation, Cambridge University, 1968.

Oehler, Gustave F. *Theology of the Old Testament.* Edinburgh: T. and T. Clark, 1883. Grand Rapids: Zondervan, 1950.

Oepke, Albrecht. "Apokaluptō" In *Theological Dictionary of the New Testament,* edited by Gerhard Kittel and Gerhard Friedrich.

Oesterley, William O. E., and Robinson, Theodore H. *Hebrew Religion.* 2d ed. New York: Seabury Press, 1937. London: SPCK, 1952.

Orr, James. *The Christian View of God and the World.* 8th ed. Edinburgh: Andrew Elliot, 1907. Reprint edition. Grand Rapids: Wm. B. Eerdmans.

————, ed. *International Standard Bible Encyclopedia.* 5 vols. Rev. ed. Grand Rapids: Wm. B. Eerdmans, 1930.

Ott, Heinrich. *Theology and Preaching.* Philadelphia: Westminster Press, 1965.

Pannenberg, Wolfhart. *Basic Questions in Theology.* Vol. 1. Translated by George H. Kehm. Philadelphia: Fortress Press, 1970.

————. "Dogmatic Theses on the Doctrine of Revelation." In *Revelation as History,* edited by Wolfhart Pannenberg.

————. *Grundfragen systematischer Theologie.* Göttingen: Vandenhoeck & Ruprecht, 1967.

————. *Grundzüge der Christologie.*

————. "Heilsgeschehen und Geschichte." *Kerygma und Dogma* 5 (1959): 259.

————. *Jesus—God and Man.* Translated by Lewis T. Wilkins and Duane A. Priebe. Philadelphia: Fortress Press, 1968.

————. "Response to the Discussion." In *Theology as History,* edited by James M. Robinson and John B. Cobb, Jr.

————, ed. *Revelation as History.* Translated by David Granskou. New York: The Macmillan Co., 1968.

Parker, T. H. L. *Calvin's Doctrine of the Knowledge of God.* Grand Rapids: Wm. B. Eerdmans, 1959.

Patterson, Lloyd G. *God and History in Early Christian Thought.* New York: Seabury Press, 1967.

Payne, J. Barton. *The Theology of the Older Testament.* Grand Rapids: Zondervan, 1962.

Perlitt, Lothar. *Bundestheologie im Alten Testament.* Neukirchen-Vluyn: Neukirchener Verlag, 1968.

Pettazzoni, Raffaele. *Essays on the History of Religions.* Translated by H. J. Rose. Atlantic Highlands, NJ: Humanities Press, 1954.

———. *Formazione e sviluppo del monoteismo nella storia della religione.* 3 vols. Rome: 1922.

Pfeiffer, Charles F. *Old Testament History.* Grand Rapids: Baker Book House, 1973.

Pfeiffer, Robert H. "Facts and Faith in Biblical History." *Journal of Biblical Literature* 70 (March 1951): 13.

———. *Introduction to the Old Testament.* New York: Harper & Bros., 1948.

Pinnock, Clark. *Biblical Revelation.* Chicago: Moody Press, 1971.

Pittenger, W. Norman. "Some Implications, Philosophical and Theological in John Knox's Writing." In *Christian History and Interpretation,* edited by W. R. Farmer, C. F. D. Moule and R. R. Niebuhr.

Plantinga, Alvin. *God and Other Minds: A Study of the Rational Justification of the Belief in God.* Ithaca, NY: Cornell University Press, 1967.

Polanyi, Michael. *Personal Knowledge: Towards a Post-Critical Philosophy.* Chicago: University of Chicago Press, 1958. London: Routledge and Kegan Paul, 1959.

Popper, Karl R. *The Open Society and Its Enemies.* 4th rev. ed. 2 vols. Princeton: Princeton University Press, 1963.

Prenter, Regin. "Dietrich Bonhoeffer and Karl Barth's Positivism of Revelation." In *World Come of Age,* edited by Ronald Gregor Smith.

Ramm, Bernard. *Types of Apologetic Systems.* Wheaton, IL: Van Kampen Press, 1953.

Ramsay, William M. *The Christ of the Earliest Christians.* Richmond: John Knox Press, 1959.

Ramsey, Ian T. *Religious Language: An Empirical Placing of Theological Phrases.* New York: The Macmillan Co., 1957.

Rawlinson, Alfred E. J. *The New Testament Doctrine of Christ.* Toronto: Longmans, Green, 1926.

Rees, T. "God." In *International Standard Bible Encyclopedia,* edited by James Orr.

Reichenbach, Bruce. *The Cosmological Argument.* Springfield, IL: Charles C. Thomas, 1972.

Rendtorff, Rolf. "The Concept of Revelation in Ancient Israel." In *Revelation as History,* edited by Wolfhart Pannenberg.

Rengstorf, Karl Heinrich. "Sēmeion." In *Theological Dictionary of the New Testament,* vol. 7, edited by Gerhard Kittel and Gerhard Friedrich.

———. "Teras." In *Theological Dictionary of the New Testament,* vol. 8, edited by Gerhard Kittel and Gerhard Friedrich.

Richardson, Alan. *Christian Apologetics.* London: SCM Press; New York: Harper & Bros., 1947.

———. *History Sacred and Profane*. London: Faber and Faber; Philadelphia, Westminster Press, 1964.

———. *An Introduction to the Theology of the New Testament*. New York: Harper & Bros., 1959. London: SCM Press, 1961.

Ringgren, Helmer. *Word and Wisdom: Studies in the Hypostatization of Divine Qualities and Functions in the Ancient Near East*. Lund: H. Ohlssons boktr., 1947.

Robinson, H. Wheeler. *Inspiration and Revelation in the Old Testament*. New York: Oxford University Press, 1946.

Robinson, James M., and Cobb, John B., Jr., eds. *Theology as History*. New Frontiers in Theology, vol. 3. New York: Harper & Row, 1967.

Rosin, Helmut. *The Lord Is God: The Translation of the Divine Names and the Missionary Calling of the Church*. Amsterdam: Nederlandsch Bijbelgenootschap, 1956.

Rowe, William L. "Two Criticisms of the Cosmological Argument." In *Logical Analysis and Contemporary Theism*, edited by John Donnelly.

———, and Wainwright, William J., eds. *Philosophy of Religion: Selected Readings*. New York: Harcourt Brace Jovanovich, 1973.

Rowley, Harold H. *The Biblical Doctrine of Election*. London: Lutterworth Press, 1950.

———. *The Growth of the Old Testament*. London: Hutchinson and Co., 1950. New York: Hutchinson, Hillary, 1961.

———, ed. *The Old Testament and Modern Study*. Oxford: Clarendon Press, 1951. New York: Oxford University Press, 1952.

Sabatier, Auguste. *Outlines of a Philosophy of Religion Based on Psychology and History*. London: Hodder & Stoughton; Folcroft, PA: Folcroft, 1906.

Sasse, Hermann. *Flucht vor dem Dogma: Bemerkungen zu Bultmanns Entmythologisierung des Neuen Testaments*. Bleckmar: Verlag Lutherische Blätter, 1965.

Sauer, Erich. *The Dawn of World Redemption*. London: Paternoster Press; Grand Rapids: Wm. B. Eerdmans, 1951.

Scharff, Ned. Report in *Washington Star*, 18 January 1976, sec. C, p. 15.

Schilling, S. Paul. *God Incognito*. Nashville: Abingdon Press, 1974.

Schmidt, Werner H. *Die Schöpfungsgeschichte der Priestschrift*. Neukirchen-Vluyn: Neukirchener Verlag, 1967.

Schmidt, Wilhelm. *The Origin and Growth of Religion*. New York: Dial Press, 1935.

Scholem, Gershom. *Major Trends in Jewish Mysticism*. New York: Schocken Books, 1945.

Schweizer, Edward. "The Relation of Scripture, Church Tradition and Modern Interpretation." In *New Theology No. 1*, edited by Martin E. Marty and Dean G. Peerman.

Scofield, C. I., ed. *Scofield Reference Bible*. New York: Oxford University Press, 1917.

Sellin, Ernst. *Geschichte des israelitisch-juedischen Volkes*. Leipzig: Quelle & Meyer, 1924.

Sherwin-White, Adrian N. *Roman Society and Roman Law in the New Testament*. London and New York: Oxford University Press, 1963.

Sider, Ronald J. "The Historian, the Miraculous, and Post-Newtonian Man." *Scottish Journal of Theology* 25: 1972.

Silberman, Lou H. "Revelation in Judaism." Paper read to the American Theological Society, 14 April 1973.

Silver, Abba Hillel. *Moses and the Original Torah.* New York: The Macmillan Co., 1961.

———. *Where Judaism Differed.* New York: The Macmillan Co., 1956.

Singer, S. Fred. "Will the World Come to a Horrible End?" *Science* 170 (1970).

Skinner, John. *The Divine Names in Genesis.* London: Hodder and Stoughton, 1914.

Smart, James D. *The Divided Mind of Modern Theology: Karl Barth and Rudolf Bultmann.* Philadelphia: Westminster Press, 1967.

Smith, Morton. "Common Theology." *Journal of Biblical Literature* 71 (1952): 136.

Smith, Ronald Gregor. *The New Man: Studies in Christian Anthropology.* Philadelphia: Westminster Press, 1969.

———. *Secular Christianity.* London: Collins; New York: Harper & Row, 1966.

———, ed. *World Come of Age.* London: Collins. 1957.

Söderblom, Nathan. *Dieu Vivant dans l'histoire.* Paris: Libraire Fischbacker, 1937. Boston: Beacon Press, 1962.

Speiser, E. A., ed. *Genesis.* Anchor Bible Series. Garden City, NY: Doubleday and Co., 1964.

Stauffer, Ethelbert. *New Testament Theology.* New York: The Macmillan Co., 1955.

Strong, A. H. *Systematic Theology.* Vol. 1. Philadelphia: Griffith & Rowland Press, 1901.

Taylor, Richard. *Metaphysics.* Englewood Cliffs, NJ: Prentice-Hall, 1963.

Taylor, Vincent. *The Names of Jesus.* London: Macmillan and Co.; New York: St. Martin's Press, 1953.

Temple, William. *Nature, Man and God: Gifford Lectures, 1932–34.* New York: St. Martin's Press, 1934.

———. *Readings in Saint John's Gospel.* New York: St. Martin's Press, 1968.

Tenney, Merrill C. *The Zondervan Pictorial Encyclopedia of the Bible.* Grand Rapids: Zondervan, 1975.

Thielicke, Helmut. "Civilization." In *Baker's Dictionary of Christian Ethics,* edited by Carl F. H. Henry.

Thiessen, H. C. *Lectures in Systematic Theology.* Grand Rapids: Wm. B. Eerdmans, 1963.

Tillich, Paul. *The Shaking of the Foundations.* New York: Charles Scribner's Sons, 1949.

———. *Systematic Theology.* 3 vols. Chicago: University of Chicago Press, 1951–63.

Torrance, Thomas F. *Theological Science.* London and New York: Oxford University Press, 1969.

———. *Theology in Reconstruction.* London: SCM Press, 1965. Grand Rapids: Wm. B. Eerdmans, 1966.

Troeltsch, Ernst. *Gesammelte Schriften.* 4 vols., vol. 2. Tübingen: J. C. B. Mohr, 1912–25.

Unger, Merrill F. *Introductory Guide to the Old Testament.* Grand Rapids: Wm. B. Eerdmans, 1949.

Van Buren, Paul M. *The Secular Meaning of the Gospel.* New York: The Macmillan Co., 1963.

Van Der Leeuw, Gerardus. *Sacred and Profane Beauty*. New York: Holt, Rinehart & Winston, 1963.

Vanderlip, George. *Paul and Romans*. Valley Forge, PA: Judson Press, 1967.

Voegelin, Eric. *The New Science of Politics*. Chicago: University of Chicago Press, 1952.

———. *Order and History*, 4 vols. Vol. 1, *Israel and Revelation*. Baton Rouge, LA: Louisiana State University Press, 1956.

Von Allmen, Jean-Jacques, ed. *A Companion to the Bible*. New York: Oxford University Press, 1958.

Von Rad, Gerhard. *Genesis*. Old Testament Library. Philadelphia: Westminster Press, 1961.

———. *Old Testament Theology*. 2 vols. Edinburgh: Oliver and Boyd, 1962, 1965. New York: Harper & Row.

———. "Some Aspects of the Old Testament World-View." In *The Problem of the Hexateuch and Other Essays*, edited by Gerhard Von Rad.

———. *Weisheit in Israel*. Neukirchen-Vluyn: Neukirchener Verlag, 1970. *Wisdom in Israel*. Translated by James D. Martin. Nashville: Abingdon Press, 1973.

———, ed. *The Problem of the Hexateuch and Other Essays*. London: Oliver & Boyd; New York: McGraw-Hill, 1966.

Vos, Geerhardus. *Biblical Theology: Old and New Testaments*. Grand Rapids: Wm. B. Eerdmans, 1948.

Vriezen, Theodorus C. *An Outline of Old Testament Theology*. Oxford: Basil Blackwell, 1966. Newton Centre, MA: Charles T. Branford, 1969.

———. *The Religion of Ancient Israel*. Philadelphia: Westminster Press, 1967.

Ward, A. W., et al, eds. *Cambridge Modern History*. 13 vols. New York: Cambridge University Press, 1970.

Warfield, B. B. *The Inspiration and Authority of the Bible*. Philadelphia: Presbyterian and Reformed Pub. Co., 1948.

Westermann, Claus. *Genesis*. Neukirchen-Vluyn: Neukirchener Verlag, 1974.

Westphal, Merold. Review of *The Historian and the Believer* by Van Austin Harvey. *Religious Studies* 11 (1967): 280.

White, Lynn, Jr. "The Historical Roots of our Ecological Crisis." *Science* 155 (1967): 1203. Reprinted in Barrett de Bell, ed., *The Environmental Handbook*. New York: Ballantine Books, 1970.

Widengren, George. *Hochgottglaube im alten Iran*. Uppsala: A.-b. Lundequistska bokhandeln, 1938.

———. *Religions värld*. Stockholm: Svenska Kyrkans diakonestyrelses, 1945.

Wiles, M. F. *The Spiritual Gospel: The Interpretation of the Fourth Gospel in the Early Church*. London and New York: Cambridge University Press, 1960.

Williams, Daniel Day. *The Spirit and the Forms of Love*. New York: Harper & Row, 1968.

Wilson, Robert Dick. "Critical Note on Exodus vi. 3." *Princeton Theological Review* 22 (January 1924): 108–19.

———. "The Names of God in the Psalms." *Princeton Theological Review* 25 (January 1927): 1–39.

Wiseman, Donald J. "Creation." In *The New Bible Dictionary*, edited by James D. Douglas.

Wright, G. Ernest. *God Who Acts.* London: SCM Press, 1952. Naperville, IL: Alec R. Allenson, 1958.

———. *The Old Testament against Its Environment.* Studies in Biblical Theology, vol. 2. Chicago: Henry Regnery, 1951.

Young, Edward J. *An Introduction to The Old Testament.* Grand Rapids: Wm. B. Eerdmans, 1949.

Zahrnt, Heinz. *The Question of God.* New York: Harcourt Brace Jovanovich, 1970.

Zwemer, S. W. *The Origin of Religion.* Nashville: Cokesbury, 1935.

Person Index

Scripture Index

Old Testament

New Testament

Subject Index

nations, 250, 253 ff., 258 f.,
266
naturalism, 7, 61, 65, 78,
95 ff., 98 f., 110, 137, 169,
180, 211, 263, 267, 270,
283, 315, 331 ff.
natural law, 92, 283, 297,
325, 329
natural theology, 24, 55, 73,
83, 86, 88 f., 94, 102 f.,
104–15, 115–18, 119,
122 f., 128, 130, 135, 176
nature, 24 f., 38, 51, 53, 56,
62, 66, 71 ff., 76, 78, 83,
86 f., 89, 91–103, 130 f.,
140, 163 f., 194 f., 247 f.,
315, 329, 334
Nazis, 255, 327
Near Eastern religions,
92 f., 139 ff., 152 ff., 173,
257, 260, 265, 272, 312
necessary being, 108 ff.,
111 ff.
neglect, 38, 41, 45
neighbor, 64 f., 99, 125, 135,
262
neoorthodoxy, 53, 60 f., 80,
83
Neo-Protestant theology, 7,
82 f., 88, 91, 96, 157 ff.,
161 f., 166
New Covenant, 278
new man, 35, 66
New York Times, 31
New Testament, 15 f., 21 f.,
27 f., 34, 41, 45, 74 ff., 81,
88, 90, 92, 101, 129, 155,
179 f., 226 f., 233, 245,
253, 256, 258, 268, 274,
277, 288, 307, 311, 317 f.,
323 f., 332
nihilism, 96
norms, 25, 36, 50, 52, 65 f.,
79, 100, 263, 279, 297, 303,
314, 320, 322, 326, 334

oath, 205, 264
obedience, 31, 35 f., 44 f., 64,
71, 85, 129, 134, 164, 222,
227, 240, 249, 252, 264 f.,
303, 305
Old Testament, 13 ff., 21 f.,
25, 27, 33 f., 74 ff., 81, 88,
90, 92 f., 101, 129, 138 ff.,
151, 153 ff., 170, 174,
179 f., 181 ff., 187 ff.,
197 f., 207, 229, 233, 235,

238 f., 241, 244 f., 248,
253, 256, 258, 261, 265 ff.,
268, 270, 272, 277, 294 f.,
304, 309, 330 ff.
omniscience, 52
ontological argument, 116
ontology, 174, 277, 283, 290,
298, 302, 309
oppression, 278
oracles, 80
order, 283, 313, 326
Oriental religions, 247, 261
orphan, 262

pacifism, 305
paganism, 29, 50, 68, 69 f.,
81, 88, 94, 98, 156, 170 ff.,
173 f., 183 ff., 187 f.,
190 f., 200, 214, 222 f.,
239, 247 f., 265, 304
Palestine, 81
Palestinian church, 227, 233,
237 f.
pantheism, 9, 47, 50 f., 53,
56, 94, 98, 124, 149, 155,
171, 181, 248, 282 f.
parables, 41, 55, 101
paradox, 12, 55, 60, 91, 122,
128, 277
parallelism, 183
paraphrases of Bible, 14
paronomasia, 174
patriarchs, 76, 192 ff., 196 ff.,
200 ff., 204 ff., 207 f.,
219 ff., 248 f., 264 f., 270,
274, 331
peace, 22, 31, 142, 255, 316,
333
Pentecost, 20, 33, 40, 82, 239
perfection, 106 ff.
persecution, 26, 35
personal, 62, 96 ff., 100,
164 f., 169, 248, 277, 291 f.
perspective, 56, 61, 67, 107,
261 f., 267, 317 ff.
pessimism, 334
pestilence, 333
Pharisees, 44, 186
Pharaoh, 139 ff., 148, 153,
191, 206
phenomenology, 118, 161,
219, 271
Philistines, 251
philology, 193 f.
philosophy, 10 ff., 19, 23 f.,
42, 60 f., 65 f., 70, 76,
77 f., 83, 91, 95, 99, 102,

104 ff., 107, 118 f., 121,
137, 154, 160 f., 163,
167 ff., 176, 188, 214, 238,
306, 319, 333
philosophy of history,
258 ff., 274, 283, 300, 308,
313 ff., 317 ff., 320 ff.,
326 ff., 333
philosophy of nature, 95 ff.,
283, 313, 315
philosophy of religion, 23 f.,
156, 167 ff., 172, 176, 218,
226
Phoenician inscriptions, 218
poetry, 183, 191, 200, 211
pogrom, 81, 327
point of contact, 128
politics, 36 f., 231, 248, 252 f.,
255, 263 ff., 277 ff., 333
polytheism, 9, 28, 69, 153,
169, 171, 178, 181 ff.,
184 ff., 187 f., 190 f., 194,
196, 239, 252
population, 65, 138
poverty, 65
power, 15, 22, 35, 37
pragmatism, 284
praise, 90, 140, 153 f.
prayer, 81 f., 154, 177, 204,
222, 227, 236, 238, 243
prediction, 106 f.
prehensions, 103
presence, 60 f., 214, 219 ff.,
222 f., 227 ff., 243 ff., 332
presuppositions (see interpretation; perspective),
317 ff., 322 ff., 326 ff.
pride, 58
priest, 231, 243
process, 106 ff., 248, 253, 275,
299, 302, 312 ff.
process theology, 61, 94, 99,
107, 122 f., 128, 149 f.,
218, 248
proclamation, 22 f., 25, 36,
64, 67, 143 f., 146 f., 162
projection, 66, 72, 78, 209
proofs, 20, 23, 86, 104 ff.,
113 ff., 122 f., 297, 310,
315
propaganda, 67, 96
property, 137
prophecy, 9, 20, 48, 49 f., 81
prophetic promise, 11, 13,
22, 26 f., 31, 33 f., 38, 74,
76, 206 ff., 222–27, 245,
249 f., 252, 259, 263, 265,